D0621091

# HOW TO INVEST IN HEDGE FUNDS

# HOW TO INVEST IN HEDGE FUNDS

## An Investment Professional's Guide

Matthew Ridley

**KOGAN
PAGE**

London & Sterling, VA

*Dedicated, with thanks, to David Ridley*

**Publisher's note**

Every possible effort has been made to ensure that the information contained in this book is accurate at the time of going to press, and the publishers and author cannot accept responsibility for any errors or omissions, however caused. No responsibility for loss or damage occasioned to any person acting, or refraining from action, as a result of the material in this publication can be accepted by the editor, the publisher or the author.

First published in Great Britain and the United States in 2004 by Kogan Page Limited

120 Pentonville Road
London N1 9JN
United Kingdom
www.kogan-page.co.uk

22883 Quicksilver Drive
Sterling VA 20166–2012
USA

© Matthew Ridley, 2004

The right of Matthew Ridley to be identified as the author of this work has been asserted by him in accordance with the Copyright, Designs and Patents Act 1988.

ISBN 0 7494 4084 8

**British Library Cataloguing-in-Publication Data**

A CIP record for this book is available from the British Library.

**Library of Congress Cataloging-in-Publication Data**

Ridley, Matthew
   How to invest in hedge funds : an investment professional's guide / Matthew Ridley.
      p. cm.
   ISBN 0-7494-4084-8
   1. Hedge funds. I. Title.
HG4530.R53 2004
332.64'5--dc22
                                     2004002560

Typeset by Saxon Graphics Ltd, Derby
Printed and bound in Great Britain by Biddles Ltd, King's Lynn, Norfolk

# Contents

# List of figures

# List of tables

# Foreword

The fund management business of Consulta commenced in 1978 and shortly thereafter we were persuaded by one of our brokers to invest in call options on shares of an international oil company whose prospects were deemed attractive. Needless to say, like the vast majority of calls purchased, these options were not exercised and expired worthless. This caused me to spend a few hours analysing in greater detail the merits of the transaction. In particular it set me wondering from whom the purchase had been made, and I endeavoured to calculate the vendor's annualized rate of return under various assumptions.

That occasion represented the one and only time we purchased share options, but it heralded a period when we became active sellers of both covered call and put options. Thus began our firm's enthusiasm for generating incremental returns from equity and bond holdings, which in turn led to the conviction that our clients would be well served in both good and bad times from holding assets with varying correlations to the principal markets.

We recognized there was a clear distinction between market risk and manager risk, and we began to invest in a range of alternative investments including hedge funds, in the early 1990s. Hedge funds now represent an important allocation in client portfolios wherever fiscally possible, and this emphasis enabled our clients to participate in the equity bubble of the late 1990s and avoid the downdraught of the 2000 bear market.

Consulta's initial investments in hedge funds were in traditional long–short equity funds, but today these investments cover a wide range of alternatives including merger arbitrage, asset backed lending, relative value trading and distressed securities amongst others.

There is a growing consensus emerging in the hedge fund community that investors should not pay high fees for market beta. Exposure to the markets can be purchased at a low cost from mainstream asset managers, or through index products. Investors should only pay fees to secure alpha. In practice, it seems that only a small minority of fund managers are capable of generating alpha, and it is our task to identify these individuals. When it can be isolated, this alpha proves to be non-correlated to other asset classes. This is what makes the hedge fund area so interesting. Hedge funds take investors into a totally different world.

Perhaps as a consequence of the recent bear market there has been growing investor disillusionment with traditional long-only market risk investments, and therefore Matthew Ridley's analysis of hedge funds is most timely. His book outlines the history of hedge funds and describes in great detail the numerous strategies which constitute this important asset class. For existing and potential investors in hedge funds and students of finance this comprehensive book is essential reading, and we at Consulta are delighted to be associated with its publication.

*Gary Brass*
*Managing Director*
*Consulta Limited*
*December 2003*

# Acknowledgements

I would like to thank a number of people for their kind help with the production of this book. First of all, I must thank the partners of Consulta Limited for their generous support and for their enthusiasm. I am indebted to Emily Steel and to Kogan Page for commissioning the work, as well as to Jon Finch who inspired me to propose it in the first place. Luke Ridley and Farley Thomas both helped early on by reading sections of the book, for which I am most grateful. Thanks are also owed to Alastair Smith and Ruth Berry of Aspect Capital Ltd, and to David McCarthy of Martello Investment Management LLC, who kindly went out of their way to provide me with additional information about CTAs. Mark Law's assistance with the graphics was invaluable.

I am particularly appreciative of those individuals who kindly agreed to read specific chapters and to provide their expert advice on how they might be improved. They have been very generous in offering their time and effort. Their input has been invaluable and their help enormously appreciated:

Harry Lloyd Owen of Consulta Limited, for reading almost the entire book and making a large number of excellent suggestions;
Chris Jones of IO Investors, for reading the chapter on statistical arbitrage and providing useful comments;
Sarah Allen of Liberty Ermitage UK Ltd for checking the chapter on convertible arbitrage and providing some excellent advice;
Philip Schaeffer and Philip Acinapuro of Scott's Cove Capital Management LLC, for reading the chapter on distressed securities, commenting and providing valuable additional information;
Molly Bell for providing a legal perspective on the distressed securities chapter;

Beth Travers, Christian Jones and Paul Ullman of Highland Financial Holdings, LLC for carefully reading and improving the chapter on mortgage backed securities;

Jim Sheehan of Brencourt Advisors LLC for his helpful advice on, and enhancement of, the merger arbitrage chapter;

Tom O'Malley and Mark Schmidt of PilotRock Capital LLC, for reading the equity long–short chapter and suggesting alterations and additions;

Chris Danielian of Precept Asset Management LLC, for his thorough examination of the fixed income arbitrage chapter and his enrichment of it.

On a more personal note, I would like to express my gratitude to my family and friends for showing such interest and understanding at all times. In particular, I would like to thank Molly Bell for all of her patience and her encouragement.

*Matthew Ridley*

# Introduction

## FROM PARIAH TO PANACEA

Ten years ago, hedge funds were despised by the investment community. The overwhelming majority of investment professionals had little concept of what hedge funds were and showed little interest in finding out. A 20-year equity bull market was in progress, fuelled by falling interest rates and the expansion of valuation multiples. Bonds did not seem to be doing too badly either. There was little incentive to consider the questionable activities of these obscure and dangerous investment vehicles. Hedge funds remained the preserve of anonymous boutique investment companies, while the financial world at large remained remarkably ignorant of their workings. In 2000 the bull market started to stutter, and subsequently attitudes towards hedge funds seemed to change. Their steady performance during the downturn attracted attention. Cynicism, antipathy and ignorance gave way to overwhelming enthusiasm. Many investors who once treated hedge funds with disdain began to embrace them as a new panacea.

The fashion for hedge funds may pass in time but hedge funds are unlikely to fade back into obscurity. A well-kept secret has escaped and hedge funds have left a permanent mark on the world of asset management. Hedge funds have provided investors with an important reminder of the attractions of absolute return targets and have challenged entrenched beliefs about relative returns.

# THE PURPOSE OF THIS BOOK

The aim of this book is to equip professional investors to make informed hedge fund allocation decisions. Although the essence of hedge fund strategies is usually simple, the detail involved in executing them can be complicated. Unfortunately the detail is as important as the essence, since investors are often caught out by the technical aspects of hedge fund strategies. Therefore a good understanding of the workings of hedge funds is required in order to take investment decisions with confidence.

The book can be divided into two halves. The first half introduces readers to hedge funds, outlines the arguments for and against their use, and offers guidelines for analysing and investing in them. However these are general discussions. The hedge fund universe spans a wide range of specialized strategies and it is hard to discuss 'hedge funds' in general without knowledge of how specific strategies work. Each chapter in the second half of the book is dedicated to examining separate hedge fund strategies, the opportunities they offer and the problems associated with each.

I hope you will conclude that hedge funds are worthy neither of contempt nor of over-enthusiasm. They are not 'good' or 'bad' but they are certainly 'different', and this is their most attractive attribute. Furthermore, the relative merits and demerits of hedge fund strategies vary depending upon the circumstances of each investor and are liable to change over time. Although the attractions of many hedge fund strategies seem self-evident today, there is little value in making observations that are only valid from one perspective at one moment in time. The real value lies in dishing up the right questions. This book aims to equip its readers to make their own judgements, drawing to their attention the key issues that they should consider before investing. Establishing an understanding of hedge funds is the key to extracting the most benefit from them. This book is therefore intended to be an accessible guide for investment professionals, written from the perspective of an industry practitioner. I hope you will find it useful.

# 1

# Introducing hedge funds

His had been an intellectual decision founded on his conviction that if a little knowledge was a dangerous thing, a lot was lethal.

Tom Sharpe

## COMMON MISCONCEPTIONS

A commonly held view of hedge funds suggests that they are risky, speculative, leveraged investment vehicles. This image has been supported by the financial media, which until very recently was poorly informed on the subject. Hedge fund managers are partly to blame for the misconceptions. The hedge fund world used to be so secretive that only occasional, dramatic developments would catch the attention of journalists. Their stories invariably focused on the aggressive activities of an unrepresentative collection of funds, such as LTCM or George Soros's Quantum Fund.

Such perceptions are based on a fundamental misunderstanding of hedge funds. The hedge fund universe encompasses a broad range of strategies spanning the entire risk–reward spectrum, rather as mutual funds encompass a range from money market products to technology funds. While some hedge funds are indeed aggressive, the vast majority of hedge funds target a risk profile that is lower than one would associate with traditional long-only equity investments. Those that employ leverage usually do so within the context of a carefully hedged portfolio that greatly mitigates the associated risks. Where derivatives are used they tend to be hedging tools or a cost-efficient means of establishing exposure. Few hedge funds use them for adopting additional risk.

# IN SEARCH OF A DEFINITION FOR HEDGE FUNDS

Unfortunately, a concise, all-encompassing definition for the term 'hedge fund' would conflict with the various definitions that apply to specific hedge fund strategies and would therefore prove inaccurate. In practice the term 'hedge fund' gets applied to a broad range of investment approaches, and we must be prepared to use it quite loosely.

Strictly speaking a 'hedge fund' ought to be required to 'hedge'. By this measure, any fund with the capability to sell short in order to protect its portfolio would qualify as a 'hedge fund'. This would restrict the use of the term to various long–short and arbitrage strategies. This definition is inadequate because a number of strategies that fall under the hedge fund heading do not use shorting for risk reduction.[1] Some use shorts as directional investment positions, possibly adding to risk rather than reducing it. Other alternative investment funds come under the hedge fund umbrella but do not use shorting at all. Instead one might retreat into generalizations about hedge funds simply being 'alternative investments'. However, this would confuse them with other alternatives such as private equity and property. So rather than present a neat but controversial definition for hedge funds, here is a list of features commonly associated with them. Most of these characteristics apply to most hedge funds:

- **Alternative:** hedge funds adopt investment approaches that provide a clear alternative to mainstream styles of investment. 'Alternative' refers both to the methods used and to the pattern of returns that result from them.

- **Absolute return:** hedge funds seek to generate absolute returns, rather than returns relative to a benchmark index.

- **Capital preservation:** likewise, most hedge funds specifically aim to defend investors' capital and employ a range of techniques designed to limit the potential for losses.[2]

- **Hedged:** most hedge funds employ short selling, either to hedge specific long positions or to reduce the overall volatility of a long portfolio.

---

1. Including global macro, CTAs, distressed securities investing and dedicated short sellers.
2. The capital preservation objective is not quite the same as the absolute return objective. A few of the more aggressive hedge funds target absolute returns, irrespective of any benchmark, but are comparatively tolerant of losses that may occur as a result of their strategy.

- **Proprietary trading:** many hedge fund strategies were originally the preserve of the proprietary trading desks of investment banks. They have subsequently been made available to outside investors in a fund format.

- **Unconstrained:** hedge funds tend to have few investment restrictions. They enjoy the freedom to employ a wide variety of investment tools, including leverage and derivatives.

- **Specialist:** hedge fund managers tend to be specialists within narrow areas of expertise. Their ability to master specific complexities is the source of their added value.

- **Incentivized:** hedge fund managers are rewarded for success, receiving a performance fee if they generate absolute returns.

- **Outlook:** at the risk of sounding pretentious, hedge fund managers share a certain outlook. Hedge fund managers are entrepreneurial and inventive. They seek to maintain an edge over other market participants by employing newer and more sophisticated investment techniques. Theirs is a frontier spirit.

# THE BASICS OF SELLING SHORT

Almost all hedge funds make extensive use of short selling, and perhaps this is the best single means of distinguishing hedge funds from conventional investment funds. While all investment professionals are familiar with the principles of short selling, few sell short themselves. Because shorting is so fundamental to hedge funds it is worth briefly reviewing the mechanics and the implications of this activity.

Selling short requires hedge fund managers to sell an asset they do not own in the expectation of being able to buy it back again at a lower price, realizing a profit. Assume that some managers believe that XYZ Co is about to suffer from a surprise fall in profits and that the share price will fall from its current level of $100 over the ensuing period. The managers borrow one share from a long-term holder of XYZ Co shares, possibly an index or pension fund. The managers pay the lender a small fee for this privilege (known as the 'cost of borrow') and are obliged to return the share at some stage. The managers then sell the borrowed XYZ Co share into the open market at the prevailing price of $100 and as a result receive $100 in cash. At this point the managers owe the lender one XYZ Co share but have $100 in cash earning interest in the bank. The interest earned is referred to as the 'short rebate'.

If the scenario unfolds as anticipated, a fall in XYZ Co profits drives its share price down to $70. The managers then buy back one XYZ Co share in the open market, using part of the $100 they have in the bank. They return the share to the lender and still have $30 left over. This is their profit. In addition, they pocket the interest they earned on the $100 while it sat in their account, less the small cost incurred from borrowing the share from the lender.

On the other hand, the managers may be proven wrong. Perhaps a surprise rise in XYZ Co profits drives the share price up to $130. The managers then buy the share back in the open market using all of the $100 they received from its sale, plus a further $30 from their own resources. They return the share to the lender and suffer a $30 loss (offset very slightly by the short rebate, net of the cost of borrow).

XYZ Co may pay a dividend while the managers are short of the share. If this happens then the original owner that has lent the XYZ share does not receive the dividend. The managers have to compensate the lender by paying an equivalent cash sum. This represents a drain on the managers' cash flow, since they have sold the share and do not receive the dividend either.[3] Likewise, managers who sell bonds short are required to compensate lenders for any missed coupon payments. The managers' standstill rate of return from maintaining a short position, their 'carry', can be summarized as follows:

Carry = interest on cash received – cost of borrow – dividends/coupons paid

The interest received from selling a liquid equity short, net of the cost of borrow, is likely to be around 80 per cent of LIBOR. One can see that in most environments managers who sell equities short often enjoy positive carry because the interest rate received usually exceeds the dividend yield paid. However, shorting bonds almost always results in negative carry, since the interest received is likely to be exceeded by the coupons paid. Higher short-term interest rates and lower equity/bond yields improve the standstill rate of return from shorting.

Short sales can be used for four main purposes:

---

3. Dividends do not necessarily represent a cost because a share price is likely to fall commensurately once a share goes ex-dividend, resulting in a mark-to-market profit on a short position that offsets the dividend paid.

- Shorts may be used as a **hedge**, reducing the risk of holding long positions. In order for hedges to be effective, securities sold short must embody similar risks to the securities bought long.

- A short may be used to profit from an anticipated fall in a specific security's price, without any regard for movements in other securities. This is referred to as an **outright short**.

- A manager may also seek to benefit from a change in one security's price relative to that of another. This is a **relative value trade** and it is established by being short of a more expensive security and long of a cheaper one. The prices of these two securities can rise and fall in tandem, and the profits on the one position will be offset by the losses on the other. However if the price of the long position rises further than that of the short, a net profit will arise. Likewise, if the price of the short position falls further than that of the long position then again the manager will make a net profit.

- Last, shorting may be used to **support leverage**. The cash managers receive from short sales does not have to be kept in the bank. Most of it may be used to purchase additional long positions. A little cash has to be held back for margin but one can envisage how very large long exposures can be funded using cash taken in from very large short sales. This arrangement would not involve any financial gearing.[4]

A variety of tools exist that permit managers to mimic the economics of selling securities short. These include contracts for differences (CFDs), futures, options, forward currency agreements, repos, asset swaps and credit default swaps.

## THE COMPLEXITIES OF SELLING SHORT

It is tempting to think of going short as the opposite of going long and to leave it at that. This would be a great mistake. Star mutual fund managers often fall into this trap when they first transfer to running long–short funds. In reality, going short is much more difficult than

---

4. The effect is similar to financial gearing because the short rebate is sacrificed, an opportunity cost comparable with the cost of borrowing. However the difficulties associated with persuading a bank to lend money are circumvented.

going long, not least for practical reasons. There also seem to be psychological implications to selling short that can affect even the most experienced hedge fund managers.

- Once an equity has been purchased the maximum potential loss is 100 per cent of capital, since its price can fall by no more than 100 per cent. Once an equity has been shorted the maximum potential loss exceeds 100 per cent because the price can rise by more than 100 per cent. Theoretically, the potential price rise, and the manager's potential loss, is infinite.

- If a long position loses money then its size as a percentage of a portfolio is reduced. Therefore the impact of subsequent losses is less than that of earlier losses. However, as a short position loses money the size of the exposure grows and the impact of subsequent losses increases. Short positions that go wrong grow against the manager.

- The inverse is also true. As short positions move into profit they make an ever-decreasing contribution to portfolio performance.

- Over the long term, equity markets (and therefore equities) have shown a tendency to rise. Therefore managers who buy securities indiscriminately may profit from doing so. By the same token, indiscriminate shorting is a 'losing trade' over the long term. Managers are thus required to be more discerning when shorting equities than when buying them. In order to be profitable, short positions must be either:
  - selective;
  - carefully timed; or
  - carefully combined with appropriate long positions.

- There is a risk that the lenders of a security will demand it back at an inopportune moment (when the price is plummeting and they themselves wish to sell it). This 'risk of recall' is very low with liquid securities since prime brokers can usually arrange alternative sources of borrow without even informing a hedge fund manager. However the risk is more meaningful with smaller, less liquid issues.

- Corporate executives take offence when hedge funds short their securities. Short positions must therefore be kept a secret, otherwise managers may find their access to information is blocked. There is even a risk that company executives may start to militate against them in an attempt to trigger a 'short squeeze' (see below).

- When a large number of managers short the same security they create a 'crowded short'. A rise in this security's price may induce a number of them to cover their shorts by buying the security back. This is likely to push the security's price still higher, triggering a self-feeding frenzy of short covering (a 'short squeeze'). This is a terrifying situation for a manager since the security's price movements become divorced from its fundamentals. It is a panic event. Because many investors wish to short the same vulnerable securities, crowded shorts are a relatively common problem.[5]

- Securities can be sold short as hedges against long positions if they embody similar risks. If long and short positions are mismatched the hedging may not work. Yet there must be some mismatch between them or else movements in the two would cancel each other out perfectly. The art of using shorts as hedges is managing the extent and nature of this mismatch and being prepared for changes in relationships that occur over time.

---

### Classifying hedge funds

Hedge funds can be classified in a variety of ways. However, hedge fund strategies can be divided up into five broad categories: relative value, long–short, event driven, directional and specialists. These categories are often overlapping and some hedge fund strategies fall into more than one of them. A number of the more popular strategies are examined in detail in dedicated chapters later in the book, but here are some brief definitions:

**Equity long–short:** long positions in equities whose prices are expected to rise combined with short positions in those expected to fall. The portfolio of short positions reduces the market exposure arising from the portfolio of long positions.

**Merger arbitrage:** long positions in the equities of companies subject to announced takeover bids, purchased at a discount to the cash price offered by the bidding company. In stock-for-stock deals, the arbitrageur hedges by shorting shares of the bidding company. Also known as 'risk arbitrage' because the arbitrageur assumes the risk that the deal will fail to complete as planned.

**Convertible arbitrage:** the purchase of a convertible bond protected by an appropriately sized short position in the issuer's equity and sometimes a credit hedge as well. Returns may be extracted either by establishing a

---

5. Apart from the danger of a short squeeze, crowded shorts may also cause a rise in the cost of borrowing a security.

positive carry position or by trading the undervalued call option embedded within the convertible.

**Statistical arbitrage:** long and short positions in equities that have similar characteristics, assembled upon the basis of one or more quantitative models. Designed to eliminate directional exposure to most types of risk, concentrating instead on statistical pricing discrepancies.

**Fixed income arbitrage:** long and short positions in closely related fixed income securities, aiming to profit from pricing anomalies.

**Distressed securities:** investments in securities of stressed and bankrupt companies made at discounts to intrinsic value. Distressed securities specialists understand the restructuring process, how to predict a security's end value and the length of time until this value is released.

**Capital structure arbitrage:** a long and a short position in two securities in different parts of the capital structure of the same company. Designed to take advantage of price inconsistencies between the two.

**Other event driven:** the term 'event driven' is used to describe those strategies that rely on corporate events in order to drive their strategies. Merger arbitrage and distressed securities investing are the most commonly cited event driven strategies. However, corporate events such as spins-off and rights issues also provide event driven opportunities.

**Hedged mortgage backed securities (MBS arbitrage):** the purchase of mortgage backed securities, hedged with interest rate instruments and other mortgage backed securities with a view to isolating the excess returns offered by MBS instruments.

**CTAs (commodity trading advisors):** directional trading using leveraged directional positions in futures contracts, on either a discretionary or a systematic basis. The futures contracts may relate to any asset class. Usually driven by technical analysis or quantitative models. Also known as 'managed futures'.

**Global macro:** directional positions taken in any asset class in any region on the basis of top-down fundamental views.

**Volatility arbitrage:** the purchase and sale of closely related options in an attempt to profit from premium that has been incorrectly priced by the market.

**Depositary receipt and closed-end fund arbitrage:** depositary receipt arbitrage consists of long or short positions in locally listed equities offset with corresponding positions in American Depositary Receipts (ADRs) or Global Depositary Receipts (GDRs) in the expectation that a discount (or premium) will erode. Closed-end fund arbitrage is similar. It involves long or short positions in closed-end funds, hedged with offsetting exposure to index futures or relevant baskets of stocks.

**Commodity arbitrage:** long and short positions in closely related commodities and commodity derivatives, aiming to profit from pricing anomalies.

**'Reg D':** privately issued securities (subject to US 'Regulation D' rules), hedged with short positions in the listed equity of the same company, until such a time that the privately issued securities can be publicly traded.

**Asset backed lending strategies:** incorporates a variety of forms of lending, all of which are conducted on the basis of strong collateralization rather than credit work.

**Mutual fund timing:** the use of mutual funds as a cost efficient means of trading in and out of markets, normally on the basis of trading signals generated by a systematic model. The strategy has come under serious threat because some mutual fund timers have been caught gaining unfair advantages over other mutual fund investors.

**Funds of hedge funds:** portfolios consisting of other hedge funds, rather than securities. Some funds of hedge funds target specific levels of risk and return, while others are dedicated to specific types of hedge fund strategy.

# 'ARBITRAGE GREY'

Arbitrage is a grey area. A perfect arbitrage is the ability to generate a profit by simultaneously purchasing and selling the same security at two different prices. Such opportunities are extremely rare, other than for market makers. The term 'arbitrage' is generally used more loosely, referring to relative value trades between securities that are so similar they are almost fungible. An example opportunity is a price discrepancy between a government bond future and the cheapest-to-deliver bond off which the future is priced.

However, some people use the term more loosely still. They incorporate relative value trades between any two related instruments where fundamental reasons, confirmed by experience, suggest their values should be linked. At this point the definition of arbitrage becomes open to interpretation: how closely should the two securities be linked for a trade to qualify as arbitrage? Because of this ambiguity investors must take care to understand exactly what hedge fund managers mean when they use the term, as it may refer to relative value trades between securities that are only vaguely related. One might illustrate the shades of 'arbitrage grey' as follows, lighter to darker:

- a trade between a depositary receipt and the locally listed equivalent with which it is fungible;

- a basis trade between a government bond future and its cheapest to deliver;

- merger arbitrage between a takeover candidate and the company bidding for it;

- convertible bond arbitrage between a convertible and its underlying equity;

- capital structure arbitrage between stressed securities within the same capital structure;

- mortgage backed securities (MBS) arbitrage between MBS, US Treasuries and MBS derivatives;

- credit 'arbitrage' between the bonds of two similar companies;

- statistical arbitrage between the equities of similar companies.

# ATTRIBUTES OF A TYPICAL HEDGE FUND

Below is a profile of a 'typical' hedge fund. These generalizations provide a guide of what to expect in most instances.

### Fund structure
Hedge funds are usually created in one of two formats. The first is a 'domestic' vehicle for US investors, usually structured as a US limited partnership (referred to as the 'onshore fund' or the 'LP').[6] The second is an offshore vehicle for non-US investors, usually structured as a limited company in an offshore jurisdiction (referred to as the 'offshore fund'). Popular domiciles for the offshore funds include Bermuda, the Cayman Islands, Curacao, the British Virgin Islands, Jersey and Guernsey. In order to broaden the range of potential investors an offshore fund sometimes obtains a listing in Dublin or Luxembourg.

### Ownership of the investment management company
Usually the fund managers own all or most of the investment management company. Early seed investors are sometimes granted a minority stake. Those hedge funds run by large fund management houses usually maintain full ownership of their hedge fund management subsidiaries (but not always).

### Assets under management
Assets under management are usually capped, lest excessive growth reduce the managers' manoeuvrability and detract from performance. However, competition to attract investors is often fierce, which also tends to limit the size of the average fund. In December 2001 only 17.5 per cent of hedge funds were said to have had assets in excess of US $100 million.[7]

### Profile of the investor base
It once seemed that hedge funds were the exclusive preserve of high net worth individuals and wealthy families. These still represent a

---

6.  The US LP may only be permitted to accommodate a limited number of investors.
7.  Putnam Lovell / Van Hedge Fund Advisors. A mere 3.0 per cent were said to have assets in excess of US $500 million. Many hedge fund managers run more than one fund (both onshore and offshore, plus different mandates) but most operations are nevertheless modest in size.

significant proportion of the hedge fund investor base. However Swiss private banks, US university endowments and funds of hedge funds became major investors during the 1990s. More recently there has been increasing interest from pension funds and other institutional investors, who formerly felt uncomfortable with the active management style of hedge funds. More retail investors have also been gaining access, often through expensive structured and funds of funds products. Retail investors do not usually have direct access to hedge funds because of high minimum investment levels and punitive rates of taxation.[8]

## Location of manager
The majority of hedge fund managers are located in the United States, the birthplace of the hedge fund industry. New York City and its surrounding commuter towns are the most popular locations but managers are also found in San Francisco, Los Angeles, Boston, Minneapolis, Chicago, Florida and elsewhere. Almost all European-based hedge funds are to be found in London and most Asian hedge funds are located in Hong Kong. However Singapore is also a popular Asian centre as the local authorities have made a particular effort to encourage hedge funds to locate there. Strictly speaking the manager of an offshore hedge fund is usually located in the offshore centre where the fund is domiciled, with 'investment advice' being relayed by an 'investment advisor' located in one of the better known financial centres. However this 'investment advisor' is usually referred to as the hedge fund manager.

## Regulation
Hedge fund investment vehicles, US limited partnerships and offshore funds, are only subject to light regulation. At the present time US-based hedge fund managers are not required to be regulated by the SEC for their activities. Those that have volunteered for regulation seem to have been paid little attention by the US authorities in the past.[9] However, hedge fund managers located outside the United

---

8.  Few regulatory regimes bar private investors from hedge funds, provided they have received proper advice. A prohibitively high rate of taxation is more often the limiting factor. This book does not address the regulatory and taxation implications of investing in hedge funds. These areas are immensely complex, vary enormously from jurisdiction to jurisdiction and are subject to constant change. Any investor, professional or private, considering investments in hedge funds should seek proper advice about their situation.

9.  With increasing numbers of retail investors gaining exposure to hedge funds in the United States, this looks set to change.

States (notably in the UK, Hong Kong and Singapore) are usually heavily regulated. This does not restrict their investment activities but does ensure their probity.

### Prime broker
A 'prime broker' is a hedge fund's principal dealing counterparty, usually being entirely responsible for sourcing and providing securities on loan for hedge funds to sell short (for which the prime brokers take a fee). Most of the large global investment banks compete to provide prime brokerage services, with Morgan Stanley and Goldman Sachs vying for top spot in providing to equity-based hedge funds.[10]

### Sponsor
Although the arrangement is becoming less common, many hedge funds used to have a 'sponsor'. This is a fund management organization which provides seed capital for a new hedge fund and markets the fund to its investor base under its own brand name. The hedge fund management firm remains independent of the sponsoring company and is hired to run the fund.

### Fees
Hedge funds usually charge management fees of 1–1.5 per cent a year. In addition they charge a performance (or 'incentive') fee of 20 per cent of profits. Later in the chapter these fees are discussed further.

### Minimum investment
The standard minimum investment for a hedge fund is US $1 million. Occasionally minimums are as low as US $100,000 or as high as US $5 million.

### Applications and redemptions
Traditionally, hedge funds provide monthly access for applications to their funds. In order to maintain portfolio stability redeeming tends to be more restricted. Investors are often subject to an initial lock-up period, usually one year, during which they are unable to withdraw their capital. Alternatively, they may be penalized with a redemption

---

10. Deutsche Bank and Bear Stearns have also been market leaders. Salomon Smith Barney has been a major provider for fixed income hedge funds.

fee for leaving after a brief period of investment.[11] Thereafter they are usually required to provide one or more months' notice before redeeming. Redemptions may not be permitted at every month-end, some funds only permitting investors to exit quarterly, or even annually. There is likely to be a limit of 10 per cent of a fund's net assets that may be redeemed at any one redemption date.

### Custody
Most hedge funds rely on their prime brokers for custody services.

### Administration
An offshore fund is usually obliged to have its administration performed where it is domiciled, usually by a small local firm. This provides the offshore centre with a greater measure of control and generates employment opportunities for the local population. The growth of the hedge fund industry has been far more rapid than the growth of qualified employees working in offshore centres, leading to administration problems in recent years. For convenience, US limited partnerships are sometimes administered offshore but usually they are administered by a firm in the United States.

### Transparency
The level of transparency afforded to investors is usually limited. Hedge fund managers are keen to hide their ideas from other market participants, for fear of being either manipulated or copied. Equity long–short managers are particularly keen to hide their positions from the executives of those companies they have sold short, lest their access to information be restricted as a result. Most funds provide investors with regular newsletters and allocation breakdowns and are generally very open in face-to-face meetings or telephone conversations. Only a limited number of hedge funds provide full transparency but the number is increasing.

### Life cycle
Although some hedge funds achieve longevity, the typical life cycle is quite short. Even successful hedge funds rarely last longer than 10 years. This is because investors place money with hedge funds princi-

---

11. This redemption penalty is usually payable to the fund, as compensation to the other shareholders for disrupting the portfolio. Sometimes it is payable to the investment manager, however.

pally because of their faith in individual fund managers. The managers 'are' the funds. Unfortunately these managers have a habit of quitting after a few years. Sometimes they quit because they have earned such large performance fees they choose to retire to the beach. On other occasions a period of poor performance leaves them with little prospect of earning performance fees for the foreseeable future. The economics cease to be attractive for them.[12]

# EVOLUTION OF THE HEDGE FUND INDUSTRY

The origins of the hedge fund industry are traditionally traced back to A W Jones, who seems to have established the first equity long–short fund. A W Jones was a sociologist and an editor of *Fortune* magazine. He recognized that while he had an ability to select outperforming stocks his ability to predict the direction of the overall market was comparatively poor. Jones combined long positions in undervalued equities with short positions in overvalued equities, generating returns from both rising and falling prices in a variety of market conditions. He used leverage to enhance his returns but did so in the knowledge that his short positions helped to mitigate the additional risks that leverage created. In 1952 he launched a public fund which enjoyed remarkable success over two decades. Today, equity long–short funds tend to be run by stock pickers who have graduated from traditional long-only fund management backgrounds. Most still operate on a similar basis to that which Jones established.

Equity long–short funds are only a minority of the hedge fund universe, which also encompasses directional trading, global macro and various forms of arbitrage. Since short selling is an investment technique that long predates A W Jones, it seems likely that many of these strategies would have developed in his absence. It seems fairer to attribute the emergence of these strategies to the proprietary activities of investment banks. Indeed, the majority of hedge funds replicate the activities of investment bank prop desks, and their managers first developed their skills as proprietary traders. Perhaps, therefore, the hedge fund industry has two separate origins. It has certainly had two separate lines of development.

---

12. Even if managers are prepared to take a long-term view the situation is de-motivating for their team of analysts, who are likely to depart in search of an employer who can afford to pay them a bonus.

A limited number of hedge funds conducted business discreetly for several decades before the industry experienced a small explosion in the 1990s. With events of 1987 fresh in their minds, an increasing number of private investors began to seek an alternative means of participating in capital markets. With the equity bull market of the 1990s in progress, they sought a way of participating in the upside, yet they were wary of valuation levels that seemed unnaturally high and wanted some protection. For many of these investors hedge funds seemed to provide a good compromise. Hedge funds began to grow in number and in size.

This growth was not without its setbacks. When the Federal Reserve suddenly raised interest rates in 1994 the bond market went into reverse and a number of arbitrage funds suffered losses. However it was Russia's default in 1998 that triggered the most serious crisis of the decade. Various hedge fund managers suffered terrible losses in Russian bonds, losses that created a knock-on effect as they liquidated other types of position. This triggered a broader crisis, when the infamous LTCM unwound enormous exposures in an effort to cover its losses. Because LTCM was involved in a wide variety of trading strategies its liquidation had a devastating impact on the portfolios of various other hedge funds, many of which followed suit by liquidating their own positions. Even hedge funds operating in seemingly unrelated areas suffered, experiencing redemptions from their investors who were facing losses in other parts of their hedge fund portfolios. At the same time most investment banks reined in the trading activities of their proprietary desks, some of them shutting down their prop desks altogether. This self-feeding panic resulted in a classic liquidity crisis that forced a number of hedge funds out of business and irreparably tarnished the reputation of various others.

The 1998 crisis was a severe setback for hedge funds and it seemed to reinforce the perceptions that investors had about them, namely that they were highly risky vehicles that were best avoided. The equity bull market resumed quite quickly afterwards, allowing mainstream investors to resume their long-only investment activities in the firm belief that the shortcomings of hedge funds had been clearly established. In fact, 1998 acted as a catalyst for change in the world of hedge funds, change which provided the basis for further growth.

● First, the liquidity crisis tested the risk controls of hedge funds, controls that often proved lacking. The worst offenders were punished by investors who deserted them entirely. Other funds learnt valuable lessons, as a result of which they became more risk conscious and tightened their investment parameters. The industry matured as a result of the experience, investors were afforded greater transparency and hedge fund managers moderated their activities.

- Second, although a number of hedge funds failed during the crisis and hedge funds suffered as a group, the overall losses were not too severe. Investors in a diversified portfolio of hedge funds experienced smaller losses than one would associate with a severe bear market in equities, or a major reversal in the bond markets. Frustration amongst hedge fund investors was more attributable to the swift resumption of the bull market in conventional assets and the failure of hedge funds to participate. However, most hedge fund investors suspected that this bull market would be ending soon, and in their eyes the market's temporary setback in 1998 reinforced their desire for the protection that hedge funds afforded.

- Third, many arbitrage funds enjoyed strong returns in the ensuing period as the spreads that they traded narrowed once again to normal levels. This demonstrated a valuable principle to sceptical investors, illustrating that liquidity crises can force arbitrage spreads out but the losses incurred are usually followed by outsized returns.

- Fourth, many arbitrageurs working on the prop desks of investment banks subsequently found their activities being restricted by senior management. Some found themselves out of a job altogether. It seemed that the senior managers had little understanding of the activities of their prop desks and had unwittingly permitted considerable risk-taking.[13] Once the 1998 crisis brought these risks to their attention many senior executives decided to concentrate on increasing their investment banking fee revenues instead. As a consequence, a large number of arbitrageurs and traders left investment banks and sought other sources of capital. The number of arbitrage hedge funds increased significantly.

The development of the hedge fund industry entered a new phase as the equity bull market drew to a close in 2000. Just as the 1998 liquidity crisis encouraged many traders to leave investment banks, traditional equity fund managers now became economic migrants.

---

13. It has been argued that proprietary trading activities provided traders with a 'free option'. By exposing their employers to large amounts of risk, masked by complexity, traders maximized their potential bonuses. Their personal downside was limited to their dismissal. Arguably, once traders moved to establish their own hedge funds their attitudes altered. As hedge fund managers they became self-employed and they earned fees subject to high water marks that provided them with a greater incentive to preserve capital.

Many had long felt fettered by benchmarking and tight investment restrictions. The end of the bull market saw their bonuses cut dramatically and provided the final push they needed to leave to set up their own hedge funds. So great was this exodus of talent that most traditional fund management companies were forced to review their attitude towards hedge funds. The big fund management firms started setting up hedge funds internally, as a means of retaining talent and in order to generate desperately needed fee revenue.

The demand for hedge funds rose in tandem with supply. Many investors who had once denigrated hedge funds found that their traditional investment approach had lost them a great deal of money. Meanwhile the hedge funds had generally preserved capital well. Indeed, many types of hedge fund continued to generate positive returns through the bear market. This attracted a great deal of attention, and the number and size of investors allocating to the area grew beyond all proportion.

As the hedge fund industry grew, its make-up evolved. Before the 1990s the strategies pursued by hedge funds were often quite fluid. Many equity long–short funds indulged in occasional global macro trades and ran their equity portfolios with relatively loose parameters. Yet because investors increasingly came to look to hedge funds for protection against a reversal in equity markets they demanded greater discipline and conservatism from equity long–short managers. The immense popularity once enjoyed by global macro funds petered out between 1994 and 1998, partly because of poor performance. However, investors also wanted to target their allocations to hedge funds more carefully, and sought to avoid speculative, directional strategies. Consistent with these trends, the appetite for arbitrage strategies increased, in tandem with the growing sophistication and conservatism of hedge fund investors. The few arbitrage funds that existed in the late 1980s generally executed a variety of different arbitrage strategies, switching between them on an opportunistic basis. As the 1990s progressed investors showed a preference for arbitrage funds that specialized in specific areas. This specialization also reflected the division of duties that had emerged within the prop desks of investment banks.

Some of these trends have experienced a mild reversal in recent years. A new breed of more conservative global macro manager has started to gain credibility, implementing tighter risk controls. Multi-strategy arbitrage funds have also regained some popularity. However, investors still demand greater discipline from hedge fund managers and the market continues to mature. (See Figure 1.2.)

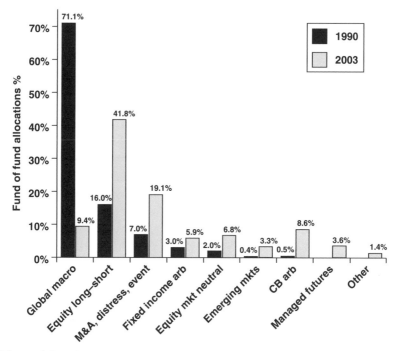

**Figure 1.2**   The changing composition of the hedge fund universe
Investors have shifted their emphasis away from global macro funds towards
equity long–short and arbitrage funds.
Sources: Aurum, Hedge Fund Research, Van Hedge Fund Advisors, Inc,
Tass.

Hedge funds have also been extending their global reach. In 1990
almost every hedge fund was located in the United States. It was in the
United States that equity long–short techniques were pioneered, and
the Americans were also the most adept at developing arbitrage
strategies. Their investment professionals were more advanced and
their vast, complex markets provided more opportunities to develop
such strategies. In the late 1990s, however, the number of equity
long–short funds dedicated to Europe and Asia grew from a small
handful to many hundreds. Growth in non-US arbitrage funds
followed close behind, although there has been slightly less scope for
developing these other strategies outside the gigantic US marketplace.
Despite the globalization of the hedge fund industry, US hedge fund
managers on average still tend to be discernibly more experienced and
sophisticated than their overseas counterparts.

**Table 1.1**    The geographical focus of hedge funds pursuing various strategies

|                        | US    | Europe      | Asia         | Global |
|------------------------|-------|-------------|--------------|--------|
| CTA/Macro              | —     | —           | —            | Many   |
| Statistical arbitrage  | Many  | Few         | Some (Japan) | Some   |
| Equity long–short      | Many  | Many        | Many         | Some   |
| Merger arbitrage       | Many  | Some        | —            | Some   |
| Convertible arbitrage  | Many  | Quite a few | Very few     | Some   |
| Fixed income arbitrage | Some  | —           | —            | Some   |
| Distressed securities  | Many  | Very few    | Few          | Few    |
| Hedged MBS             | Some  | —           | —            | —      |

Despite global expansion, the United States offers the largest and most diverse selection of hedge funds.
Source: author.

# THE RISE OF THE PRIME BROKER

Towards the end of the 1990s another trend developed that played a meaningful role in shaping the hedge fund industry. Hedge funds had originally marketed their services directly to investors or had used small independent third party marketing organizations (often individuals) to promote their funds. The hedge fund world was secretive, and introductions and recommendations were effected by word of mouth. However, in the second half of the 1990s prime brokers came to play an increasingly important role in bringing hedge funds and investors together.

A prime broker is a hedge fund's principal contact with the broking community, providing custody services and being responsible for providing securities on loan for hedge funds to sell short. As the hedge fund industry grew the prime brokerage business became increasingly valuable to investment banks. In a bid to win more prime brokerage mandates from hedge funds, prime brokers started to offer 'capital introduction' services. This meant arranging conferences and effecting introductions with potential investors. While prime brokers have been careful not to refer to these activities as 'marketing', they have nevertheless altered the channels through which hedge funds promote themselves to investors. Now that large numbers of participants meet frequently at various types of function the industry is much more open and

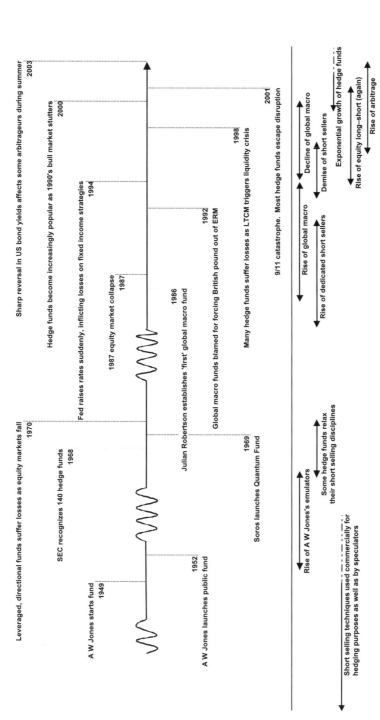

**Figure 1.3** Time line of the evolution of the hedge fund industry (Source: Deutsche Bank, author)

ideas are exchanged more freely. The names of most organizations involved (both hedge funds and their investors) have become widely available.[14]

The desire of prime brokers to grow their client base has had other implications. Prime brokers have established a good understanding of what the investment community looks for in a hedge fund and have started to 'coach' new hedge fund managers about the demands of investors. As a result, the parameters within which hedge funds claim to operate have become increasingly standardized and new trends in hedge fund management methods spread more quickly. While this development may seem cosmetic it has further implications. On the one hand it signals greater maturity and efficiency in the marketplace, suggesting that some of the more extreme activities of hedge funds have been reined in. On the other hand it makes it harder for investors to distinguish between funds because they claim to be so similar. If different funds executing a particular strategy really have become more homogenous then the benefits of diversifying amongst them will have eroded. Likewise, the risks associated with 'herding' amongst hedge funds will have increased.

# HOW PERFORMANCE FEES WORK

Hedge funds pay their managers performance fees, typically at the rate of 20 per cent of profits. The performance fee is almost always subject to a 'high water mark' (HWM) that protects investors from paying performance fees twice on the same gain: when a fund's shares fall in value investors do not pay a performance fee again until the price recovers to above the level where a performance fee was last charged. This is sometimes referred to as a 'loss carry forward provision'. In the absence of such a provision a manager might seek to manipulate a fund's share price lower, in the hope of collecting another performance fee as the price recovered again. This would represent a reward for inducing volatility rather than for generating absolute returns. By contrast, the HWM provision rewards hedge fund managers not only for taking their fund's share price higher but also for keeping it there.

---

14. Note that because the prime brokers do not establish, develop and maintain client relationships, marketing executives and third party marketers still have a valuable role to play in marketing hedge funds to investors.

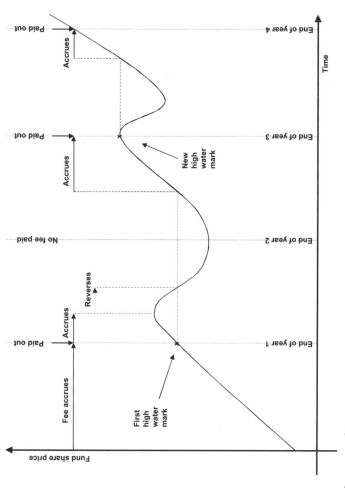

**Figure 1.4** How performance fees accrue

A performance fee that has been accrued but has not yet been paid out will reverse back in favour of investors if the fund's share price subsequently falls, as it does in this example in year 2. The performance fee will not start to accrue again until the fund's share price breaches the high water mark at which a fee was last paid out.

Source: author.

Figure 1.4 illustrates how a performance fee might accrue, assuming it involves a HWM and is paid out (or 'crystallizes') at the end of each calendar year. As the fee is earned over the course of the year it starts to accrue in favour of the manager. However, the fee remains within the fund until the end of the year when it gets paid out. If the fund price starts to fall halfway through a year then any unpaid performance fees start to accrue back to the investors, resulting in the manager losing them. The fear of handing a performance fee back to investors acts as further encouragement for managers to defend their gains.

Performance fees are calculated separately for each investor, so that each investor is protected by his or her own HWM that reflects the performance the investor has enjoyed since he or she invested. This investor-specific calculation is effected either by subjecting each investor's shares to an 'equalization' that reflects the performance fee owed by each, or by issuing each new investor with his or her own series of shares.

'Equalization' is typically used by offshore fund companies while 'series accounting' is the norm for US limited partnerships. Because US hedge fund managers and lawyers are more familiar with series accounting it is sometimes used for offshore vehicles as well. Series accounting often causes confusion among offshore investors and their administrators, who struggle to track down fund prices for their particular series of shares. To add to the confusion, different series are often rolled up and amalgamated at year-end, once their performance fee treatment has become fungible.

Occasionally a performance fee is subject to a hurdle rate, such as the prevailing return on cash. This means a fund manager earns performance fees only on those returns in excess of the hurdle.[15] Few investors insist that a manager incorporates a hurdle rate into the performance fee calculation, although it certainly provides a better discipline and is less greedy. On the other hand, certain performance fee arrangements are considered unacceptable. The absence of a HWM is the most obvious example. A 'limited loss carry forward' is also unacceptable and indicates that the HWM can be adjusted downwards after a period of time. In addition, performance fees that crystallize too often (monthly or quarterly) serve to undermine the capital preservation discipline.

---

15. For example: assume a fund is above its high water mark and earns a 14 per cent return over the year. If LIBID is the set hurdle rate and LIBID has returned 4 per cent over the same year, then performance fees are earned on the excess gain of 10 per cent. Assuming the performance fee is set at 20 per cent the manager pockets 2 per cent.

# A NOTE OF WARNING ABOUT HEDGE FUND INDICES

People seem to write a great deal about hedge fund indices. These are indices constructed from a number of hedge funds, designed to track the performance of the hedge fund universe and its various sub-strategies. Academics value hedge fund index data as the most practical means of analysing the industry and the behavioural traits of individual hedge fund strategies. New entrants to the hedge fund industry also find them a useful way in which to form general views about different types of hedge fund. However, there is a worrying tendency for people to cling to notions of indices as 'benchmarks', against which particular investments can be measured. The very word 'index' seems to encourage such notions. It must be emphasized that the very concept of a benchmark is an anathema in hedge fund land. Hedge funds explicitly target absolute and not relative returns. Furthermore, they deliberately seek to distinguish themselves from one another. Different hedge fund managers often execute the same specialist strategy in very different ways so that an 'index' of all their returns masks considerable diversity. Convertible arbitrage is a good example. It is not a single strategy. It is many.

In addition to the theoretical problems, a number of practical problems plague hedge fund indices. Although academics are conscious of the issues, they may not be obvious to new investors.

- **Survivorship bias:** when they assemble an index for the first time, most providers include only those funds still in existence. The omission of failed funds tends to provide an upward bias to index performance.

- **Reporting bias:** reporting hedge fund performance data is voluntary. Hedge fund managers are less likely to report their data until they have established an attractive track record. Sometimes they only report an (attractive) segment of their record.

- **Inclusion:** many indices are constructed by hedge fund performance data vendors. They only include the limited range of funds they have in their database. Many hedge fund managers, especially the more successful ones, do not report to data vendors because there is little incentive for them to do so. Others only report to one or two vendors but not to all of them. Independent index providers face similar problems, often having to advertise to hedge funds and appeal for them to submit their numbers.[16]

- **Un-investible:** most hedge fund indices are un-investible, meaning they include a large number of funds that are closed to new investors. Therefore hedge fund indices cannot be used in the same way as equity indices.

- **Definition:** there are no clear rules for defining different hedge fund strategies, and different index providers define them very differently. Two indices tracking the same strategy, assembled by different providers, may have very low correlations with one another.

- **Construction:** some hedge fund indices are equally weighted while others are weighted by the size of each fund in the index. Since a few very large funds exist alongside very many small funds, both approaches result in distortions.

This book does refer to indices of various hedge fund strategies. They are a useful means of illustrating broad trends and patterns. However readers should be aware that they only provide rough indications of hedge fund performance. Funds of funds probably provide a more realistic picture of the returns that investors have actually obtained from portfolios of hedge funds. Because many funds of funds charge high fees it seems sensible to adjust for the extra layer of charges. Therefore, as a proxy for overall hedge fund performance this book makes reference to an index of funds of hedge funds, crudely adjusted for fees. Although the average level of fees charged by funds of funds is probably higher, an annualized 1.5 per cent has been added back to the funds of funds index each month.[17]

---

16. Allegedly, Morgan Stanley's hedge fund indices were originally constructed using a database from a single fund of funds advisor. This hardly constitutes a scientific sampling technique because the fund of funds advisor had made conscious choices about those funds it wished to include for monitoring.

17. This is not a very scientific approach to the issue, and many of the difficulties associated with other hedge fund indices may also apply to the funds of funds indices. However a more detailed attempt to correct index distortions would be complicated without guaranteeing accuracy. Funds of funds may not reflect the varying weightings in different hedge fund strategies but they reflect the trends in appetite for different hedge fund strategies over time. For the sake of comparison, the fee-adjusted funds of funds index used here returned and annualized 2.78 per cent less than its equivalent hedge fund composite index (July 1993–June 2003). This adjusted fund of funds index compares with the survivorship bias-adjusted hedge fund index returns constructed by Amin and Kat (2002) that were about 2 per cent below the unadjusted composite index returns. However, the adjusted funds of funds index seems to outperform the composite index on standard deviation, skewness and kurtosis measures. The reverse was the case for Amin and Kat's index.

# 2

# Questioning the merits of hedge funds

Unhappiness is best defined as the difference between our talents and our expectations.

Johanna Spyri

A number of accusations are levelled against hedge funds, some of them based upon misconceptions and some of them valid. As well as critics, hedge funds have fervent advocates. At times they can be a little too fervent, touting some misleading arguments. It is important not to overstate the case for hedge funds and their drawbacks must indeed be recognized. However, dwelling on the risks induces unnecessary paralysis and, on balance, hedge funds represent a very attractive investment opportunity. Above all, hedge funds prove to be different from other types of investment, and this is perhaps their greatest benefit of all.

The case for hedge funds usually goes something like this. Hedge funds are capable of making money in either rising or falling markets. Due to this capability they tend to be better at defending capital in falling markets, the volatility of their performance is lower and their risk-adjusted returns are higher. Furthermore, hedge funds provide investors with access to some of the most talented fund managers in the world. These arguments support the use of hedge funds as a stand-alone investment. Additionally, the pattern of returns they generate differs greatly from those of mainstream asset classes. This gives them valuable diversification properties, so that when they are combined in a portfolio they serve to reduce its volatility.

Against this, detractors have a list of complaints:

- Hedge funds are excessively complex and lack transparency.

- Hedge funds are aggressive and risky.

- They have a propensity to beguile investors with smooth performance but are vulnerable to large losses.

- Their performance fees are outrageous and their redemption terms inflexible.

- Hedge funds are subject to few controls. They utilize excessive leverage and dangerous derivatives.

- Hedge funds are unregulated and frequently fraudulent.

- They are hard to access, either because they are hard to find, or they are closed to new investors, or they are heavily taxed.

- The current enthusiasm for hedge funds is little more than a mania.

Let us now address the main points.

## HEDGE FUNDS: THE RECORD

Although it never pays to put too much faith in past performance, it would be negligent to overlook the past. The last ten years spanning July 1993–June 2003 are worth studying, as they encompass a bull and bear market cycle, as well as a couple of serious setbacks for hedge funds in 1994 and 1998. As discussed in the previous pages, an index of funds of hedge funds (fee-adjusted) provides a more realistic measure of overall hedge fund returns than a composite index of hedge funds.[1]

The principal considerations in assessing the record of any investment are, one, the returns it has generated, two, the risk it has represented and three, its correlation with other assets. During this period the hedge fund universe has produced very attractive returns with limited volatility and little correlation to mainstream equity markets. The hedged nature of these funds caused them to lag equity markets during the 1990s bull-run, something which often amused hedge fund sceptics at the time. However, this hedging provided

---

1. A figure of 4.1 per cent was taken as the risk free rate for this period, representing the annualized compound return on the US one-month T-bill.

valuable protection when the bull market gave way to a bear market at the end of the decade. Although hedge fund returns moderated, losses were slight, while conventional assets suffered terribly. At the end of the period the tortoise (hedge funds) had caught up with the hare (equity markets). These are very positive observations about hedge funds. (See Figures 2.1 and 2.2.) However, this time period is a favourable one and there are always likely to be periods during which hedge funds under-perform conventional assets.

# CORRELATION

Perhaps the most valuable attribute of hedge funds is their low correlation with mainstream asset classes. It seems intuitive that they should be uncorrelated: a large portion of hedge fund returns stem from the relative performance of long and short positions, a source of returns that bears little relationship with holding assets outright.[2] One might even argue that hedge fund returns are derived from a series of activities, such as mastering complexities and decision making. These activities represent a different form of risk and return from traditional investments, where investors expect to be paid for passively owning risky assets. Whatever the reasons, hedge funds are valuable diversification tools and they act to reduce the volatility of a conventional portfolio. Even as stand-alone investments, hedge funds tend to exhibit quite low levels of volatility, so their low correlations make them doubly valuable.

However, hedge funds need not be combined with mainstream assets in order to achieve diversification. Because of their diverse nature, most hedge fund strategies have very low correlations with one another. Given the attractive profile of hedge fund returns, some investors are content simply to diversify across a range of hedge fund strategies that meet their criteria. From Figure 2.3 you will notice that the hedge funds as a group seem to have quite a high correlation to equity markets. This is partly attributable to the high weighting that equity long–short funds have been afforded in funds of funds and the composite index. However, this weighting is a matter of choice for investors, who have the option to select from a range of other hedge fund strategies that are less correlated with equities (as seen in Figure 2.4).

---

2. Most hedge fund strategies involve significant short exposures that inevitably have a negative correlation with markets.

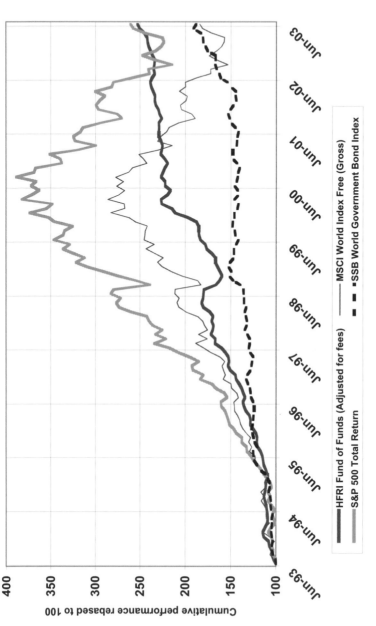

**Figure 2.1** Line graph of hedge fund performance versus mainstream asset classes (July 1993–June 2003)

Hedge funds have matched the returns achieved by the S&P 500 and exceeded those achieved by the MSCI World. Indexes used are HFRI Fund of Funds Composite Index fee-Adjusted, MSCI The World Index Free – Gross, S&P 500 Total Return, SSB World Government Bond Index, all maturities in US dollar terms.

Sources: HFRI, Altvest, PerTrac Indexes.

---

Legend (within chart):

HFRI Fund of Funds (Adjusted for fees)  ——— MSCI World Index Free (Gross)

S&P 500 Total Return  ■ ■ SSB World Government Bond Index

Y-axis: Cumulative performance rebased to 100 (100, 150, 200, 250, 300, 350, 400)

X-axis: Jun-93, Jun-94, Jun-95, Jun-96, Jun-97, Jun-98, Jun-99, Jun-00, Jun-01, Jun-02, Jun-03

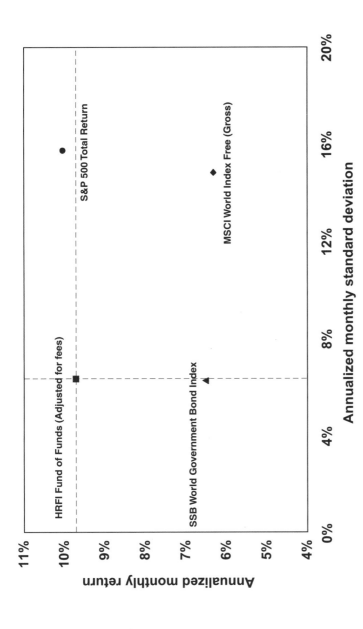

**Figure 2.2** Scatter graph of return versus volatility versus mainstream asset classes

The high returns secured by hedge funds have been obtained with remarkably little volatility. As an investment they have dominated mainstream asset classes.

Sources: HFRI, Altvest, PerTrac Indexes.

**Correlation Jul 1993 – Jun 2003**

| | HFRI FoF F | MSCI World | S&P 500 | SSB WGBI |
|---|---|---|---|---|
| HFRI Fund of Funds (Adjusted) | | 0.56 | 0.51 | -0.15 |
| MSCI World Index Free (Gross) | 0.56 | | 0.93 | 0.06 |
| S&P 500 Total Return | 0.51 | 0.93 | | -0.03 |
| SSB World Government Bond Index | -0.15 | 0.06 | -0.03 | |
| Mean | 0.31 | 0.52 | 0.47 | -0.04 |

**Figure 2.3**  Correlation table of hedge funds versus mainstream asset classes

Not only have hedge funds produced remarkably strong risk-adjusted returns, they also exhibit a relatively low correlation both to bonds and to equities.

Sources: HFRI, Altvest, PerTrac Indexes.

| Correlation Jul 1993 – Jun 2003 | CTA | CB Arb. | Distr. | Eqty. H. | Stat. A. | FI Arb. | MBS | Macro | Merg. | MSCI | S&P | SSB |
|---|---|---|---|---|---|---|---|---|---|---|---|---|
| Barclay CTA | | -0.08 | -0.14 | -0.07 | -0.03 | 0.04 | -0.03 | 0.43 | -0.14 | -0.16 | -0.17 | 0.25 |
| HFRI Convertible Arbitrage | -0.08 | | 0.64 | 0.48 | 0.22 | 0.18 | 0.17 | 0.38 | 0.46 | 0.29 | 0.31 | -0.07 |
| HFRI Distressed Securities | -0.14 | 0.64 | | 0.64 | 0.22 | 0.33 | 0.29 | 0.52 | 0.53 | 0.50 | 0.46 | -0.10 |
| HFRI Equity Hedge | -0.07 | 0.48 | 0.64 | | 0.32 | 0.03 | 0.09 | 0.59 | 0.57 | 0.71 | 0.68 | -0.01 |
| HFRI Statistical Arbitrage | -0.03 | 0.22 | 0.22 | 0.32 | | -0.01 | 0.07 | 0.20 | 0.43 | 0.52 | 0.57 | 0.00 |
| HFRI Fixed Income: Arbitrage | 0.04 | 0.18 | 0.33 | 0.03 | -0.01 | | 0.52 | 0.19 | 0.02 | -0.04 | -0.13 | -0.17 |
| HFRI Mortgage-Backed | -0.03 | 0.17 | 0.29 | 0.09 | 0.07 | 0.52 | | 0.21 | 0.02 | 0.02 | 0.01 | -0.15 |
| HFRI Macro | 0.43 | 0.38 | 0.52 | 0.59 | 0.20 | 0.19 | 0.21 | | 0.32 | 0.41 | 0.36 | 0.04 |
| HFRI Merger Arbitrage | -0.14 | 0.46 | 0.53 | 0.57 | 0.43 | 0.02 | 0.02 | 0.32 | | 0.49 | 0.50 | -0.06 |
| MSCI World Index Free (Gross) | -0.16 | 0.29 | 0.50 | 0.71 | 0.52 | -0.04 | 0.02 | 0.41 | 0.49 | | 0.93 | 0.06 |
| S&P 500 Total Return | -0.17 | 0.31 | 0.46 | 0.68 | 0.57 | -0.13 | 0.01 | 0.36 | 0.50 | 0.93 | | -0.03 |
| SSB World Government Bond | 0.25 | -0.07 | -0.10 | -0.01 | 0.00 | -0.17 | -0.15 | 0.04 | -0.06 | 0.06 | -0.03 | |
| Mean | -0.01 | 0.27 | 0.35 | 0.37 | 0.23 | 0.09 | 0.11 | 0.33 | 0.28 | 0.34 | 0.32 | -0.02 |

**Figure 2.4** Correlation table of various hedge fund indices

Different hedge fund strategies seem to exhibit very low correlations to one another.

Sources: HFRI, Altvest, PerTrac Indexes, Barclay Trading Group Ltd.

Although these low correlations make hedge funds seem very attractive, there are two important caveats. First, there are reasons that the hedge fund universe is always likely to bear some relationship with mainstream markets. Some so-called hedge fund strategies are predominantly long-only in nature. Even if they are managed in an absolute return manner and they involve an obscure specialization, such as distressed securities, mainstream markets are bound to have some effect on them. Even supposedly long–short strategies often entail a 'long bias'. Second, and more importantly, these correlation figures are unstable. Correlations between different hedge fund strategies, as well as between hedge funds and the markets, tend to rise during periods of extreme market volatility. During these liquidity crises, investors are likely to experience losses both on their conventional investments and on their hedge fund investments. Just when investors most need diversification, hedge funds tend to let them down. (See Figures 2.5 and 2.6.)

This drawback does not discredit hedge funds entirely. The average drawdown suffered by hedge funds during these crises merely represents a shock in the context of their usual pattern of returns. It does not compare badly with the sort of drawdown that mainstream assets routinely suffer. Furthermore, hedge funds should be valued for the low correlations they maintain during most periods. During a crisis an investor's long-only equity portfolio is likely to provide the main source of concern.

It seems easy to understand the spikes in correlation between those strategies that entail a long bias. However, the behaviour of supposedly 'market neutral' strategies at these moments does require an explanation. A discussion about the nature of arbitrage a little further on will help cast some light on the issues.

# MARKET ENVIRONMENTS HEDGE FUNDS LOVE AND HATE

Their diversity makes it difficult to generalize about the market conditions that hedge fund strategies profit and suffer from. Later chapters address the market influences that affect each strategy. However, a few very broad observations can be made that are applicable to most types of hedge fund.

- As we have observed, hedge funds suffer during volatility events, be they in equity or fixed income markets.

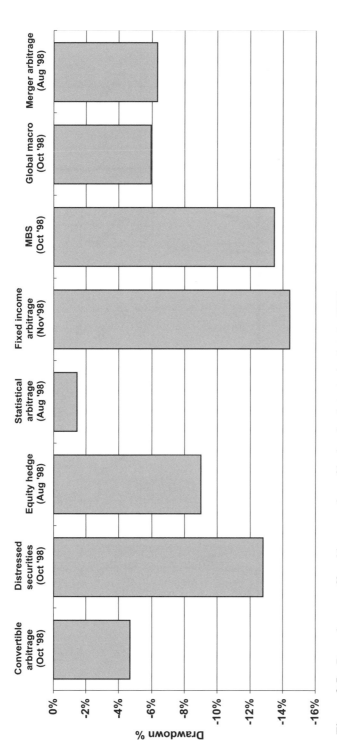

**Figure 2.5** Drawdowns suffered by a number of hedge fund strategies late in 1998
Many hedge fund strategies suffered drawdowns between August and November 1998 as a result of the Russian and LTCM crises.
Source: HFRI.

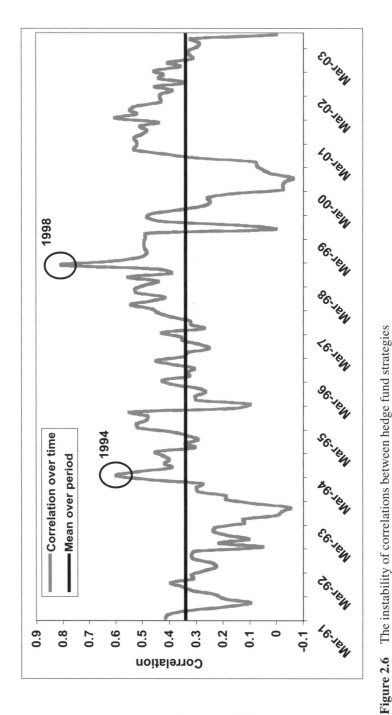

**Figure 2.6** The instability of correlations between hedge fund strategies

The mean of the 9-month rolling correlations between the S&P 500 and a series of eight hedge fund strategy indices (March 1991–June 2003). The list of hedge fund indices excludes global macro and CTAs, which seem to behave differently during such periods.

Sources: HFRI, Altvest.

- Hedge funds engage in specialist activities that are profitable partly because the activities are marginal. Excessive inflows of capital therefore squeeze returns. If trades become crowded they may also become more volatile.

- Rising asset prices in core markets assist hedge funds. Several hedge fund strategies have an overtly long bias whilst others that are supposedly market neutral benefit from rising markets indirectly. This is because rising markets are generally more liquid and they operate smoothly.

- Strong economies help. High levels of economic activity result in more corporate decisions, more takeovers and more new issuance. This benefits strategies such as merger arbitrage, convertible arbitrage and equity long–short.[3]

- Lower interest rates lead to lower returns. There are two reasons for this. First, short exposures earn a meaningful 'short rebate' that falls in line with interest rates. Second, arbitrageurs assess the returns of potential trades in terms of the risk free rate, plus an appropriate risk premium. If interest rates fall the arbitrage community immediately accepts trades that offer lower returns. This squeezes the spreads on offer.

- Hedge funds profit from eradicating inefficiency so markets that operate too smoothly can be a problem. There are times when parts of the market cease to throw up anomalies and money-making opportunities dry up. This phenomenon affects both equity long–short and arbitrage strategies although it is difficult to predict or explain. Sometimes it is caused by the arrival of new hedge fund capital but at other times markets simply go through periods when they work more efficiently.

# THE ATTRACTIONS AND PITFALLS OF ARBITRAGE

The attractions of arbitrage are clear. Arbitrage returns tend to be steady, exhibiting limited volatility given the mean return. Because

---

3. Although stronger economies seem to benefit hedge funds overall, certain strategies favour weaker economies. Distressed securities investing benefits from the opportunities brought by a downturn and fixed income arbitrageurs benefit from a rise in government debt issuance.

arbitrage involves closely hedged positions its returns bear little relationship to mainstream markets and are usually uncorrelated with
them. Owing to these features, arbitrage often generates remarkably
high returns on a risk-adjusted basis, which can be seen from their
Sharpe ratios.

While there is some truth in these observations, they are also
misleading, and the pattern of arbitrage returns exemplifies some of
the pitfalls associated with hedge funds in general. High Sharpe ratios
mask occasional, uncharacteristically large drawdowns. These drawdowns seem to occur during volatility events, so that arbitrage
strategies are often described as being 'short volatility'.[4] The more
statistically minded express these observations by noting that arbitrage returns exhibit high kurtosis and negative skewness. This means
that the distribution of their returns is 1) more peaked than a normal
distribution, implying unusually consistent returns most of the time;
2) has fatter tails, implying a higher incidence of extreme observations; and 3) is asymmetric with a tail extending towards more
negative values. (See Figure 2.7.)

Different theories are advanced to explain why arbitrage returns
behave like this but they all add up to the same thing. The first relates
to the liquidity. Occasionally arbitrage opportunities arise from
genuine aberrations in the pricing of related securities. However in
many cases these 'aberrations' have arisen due to the market's preference for one security over another, possibly mild and possibly
temporary. These preferences are often linked to liquidity. Cause and
effect may be hard to distinguish. Perhaps the degree of the preference
results in a liquidity differential or perhaps a liquidity differential
causes the preference. Either way, it is surprising how often an arbitrage trade consists of a long position in a slightly less liquid security
and a short position in a slightly more liquid security. The onset of a
volatility event is likely to accentuate liquidity preferences considerably, causing price spreads between arbitraged securities to widen
against the arbitrageur. (See Table 2.1.)

The same phenomenon may also be expressed in terms of
complexity. Many arbitrage trades involve long positions in slightly
more complex securities, against short positions in simpler ones.
Arbitrageurs profit from the small discount available on securities that

---

4. Comparisons are therefore drawn between arbitrage strategies and selling uncovered options, an activity
that generates steady and attractive returns for prolonged periods before a spike in volatility results in a
sudden and dramatic loss. Although these comparisons imply that arbitrage strategies are more risky than
experience suggests, the profile of returns is comparable.

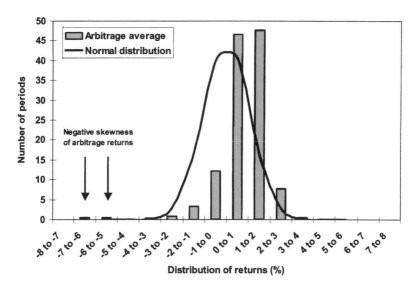

**Figure 2.7**   Distribution of arbitrage returns (July 1993–June 2003)
While the monthly returns of arbitrage strategies are usually fairly
consistent, on rare occasions they are sharply negative. The proxy for
'arbitrage returns' used here is the mean of HFRI Relative Value Arbitrage
Index, HFRI Merger Arbitrage Index, HFRI Fixed Income: Arbitrage Index
and HFRI Convertible Arbitrage Index.
Source: HFRI.

are harder to value. Once again, investor preference for simplicity
increases during a volatility event, undermining the relative prices of
more complex securities.

The second explanation concerns the efficiency of markets.
Arbitrage techniques take advantage of temporary pricing inefficiencies in related securities (regardless of their relative complexity or
liquidity). The efficiency of the market (the weight of arbitrage
activity) routinely irons out such discrepancies when they occur,
closing up pricing anomalies. During periods of dislocation, however,
the increasingly chaotic behaviour of investors serves to exacerbate
inefficiencies and to widen anomalies. The irrational behaviour that
causes pricing discrepancies is therefore likely to increase during
market panics.

Whatever the explanation, once an arbitrage spread starts to widen
the move can quickly become self-feeding. The risk control mechanisms of arbitrageurs cause them to exit their positions, encouraging a
spread to widen further. Because many arbitrage strategies require

**Table 2.1**   The long and short positions that constitute a variety of arbitrage trades

| Arbitrage type | Long security | Short security | Short liquidity? | Short simplicity? |
|---|---|---|---|---|
| Convertible arbitrage | Convertible bond | Equity (sometimes a Treasury) | Yes | Yes |
| Merger arbitrage | Equity of target (usually smaller) | Equity of bidder (usually larger) | Yes | Yes |
| Fixed income arbitrage | Cheaper bond | Dearer bond | Often | Depends |
| MBS arbitrage | Mortgage backed security | US Treasury, other MBS | Yes | Yes |
| Statistical arbitrage | Equity | Equity | Depends | No |
| ADR arbitrage | ADR/local equity | ADR/local equity | By definition | No |
| Closed-end fund arbitrage | Closed-end fund at a discount | Index or equity basket | Yes | Yes |

Source: author.

leverage to secure sensible returns, widespread de-leveraging by arbitrageurs accelerates the process.

It is also important to appreciate the asymmetric nature of arbitrage opportunities. These can be envisaged in terms of pricing differentials between related securities, or spreads, that are expected to close over time. Since these securities are related, one would expect the spread to be reasonably narrow. In most instances the best that can be expected from a successful outcome is for this spread to narrow to zero. This is the limit of a trade's upside potential. Most of the time a trade's downside potential is significantly greater: the extent to which a spread might widen is typically much greater than the extent to which it might close. (See Figure 2.8.)

Another feature of arbitrage is the unusual behaviour of its risk–reward trade-off. In most areas of financial markets higher returns are associated with higher levels of risk and vice versa. Arbitrage sometimes exhibits an inverse relationship. When more arbitrageurs try to profit from an anomaly, or when they apply more leverage to it, an arbitrage spread becomes compressed. Thus the potential gain from the spread narrowing is smaller and the potential loss from the spread widening is greater. The likelihood of it widening also seems greater. This situation reflects lower return and higher risk.

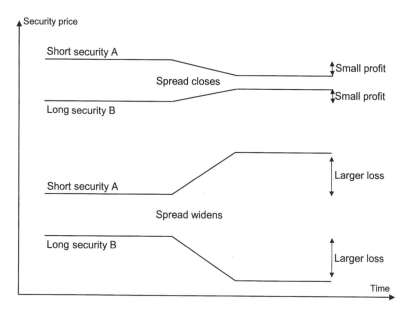

**Figure 2.8**    The asymmetry of risk and return in arbitrage
The potential positive return if an arbitrage spread closes is generally
outweighed by the potential loss if the spread widens, even if spread
widening is the less probable outcome.
Source: author.

By contrast, once a market shock has forced arbitrage spreads to
widen (and inflicted losses), the returns offered by such spreads are
greater and the risk of them widening is lower, as they have widened
already. This opportunity offers greater potential return and lower
risk. In the wake of sudden arbitrage spread widening, therefore, these
strategies typically enjoy a period of outsize returns as spreads narrow.
Ironically, it is immediately after such market shocks that the
perceived risks of these arbitrage strategies are at their highest and
expectations for return are at their lowest. (See Figure 2.9.)

Arbitrage strategies are criticized by many investors and academics
for the asymmetric nature of their returns and for their vulnerability to
market shocks. However academics and investors who level these crit-
icisms often do so when they have first 'discovered' these features.
Investors who are familiar with arbitrage are well aware of the risks
and are prepared to assume them. Carefully executed arbitrage
strategies produce attractive, steady returns most of the time but do
suffer on occasions. Skilled arbitrageurs are able to limit the size of
these occasional drawdowns so that the overall profile of returns
remains attractive, particularly when compared with equities. Note

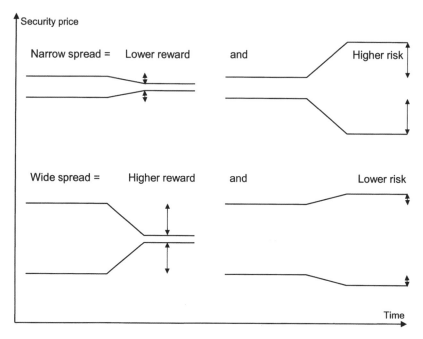

**Figure 2.9**    The nature of risk and reward when arbitrage spreads are narrow

Narrow spreads entail the prospect of lower positive returns, while risking disproportionately high losses should spreads widen. Wide spreads offer the prospect of higher positive returns in relation to the comparatively modest risk of the spreads widening further.

Source: author.

also that arbitrage strategies are not the only forms of investment that suffer from an asymmetric return profile. Investing in credit has an asymmetric return payoff too. Most of the time a credit instrument pays out a coupon and generates a steady return. The potential upside is often limited, perhaps being no more than the instrument's yield to maturity. However, credit investing inflicts severe losses on those occasions that an instrument defaults. The potential losses greatly exceed the potential returns, even if they are less frequent. As with credit investing, the asymmetric returns associated with arbitrage must be understood but they are not a reason to reject the strategy.

Most hedge fund strategies are criticized for the negative skewness of their returns, not just arbitrage strategies. However over the past few years the pattern of returns generated by the S&P 500 index has come to exhibit the same phenomenon. In theory the returns of this 'efficient' equity market ought to be normally distributed. Over the past 10 years they have not been. Given that both hedge funds and the S&P have exhibited this negative skewness, hedge fund returns appear to have been the more attractive. Hedge funds have provided more consistent, positive returns. (See Figures 2.10 and 2.11.)

# THE COSTS AND BENEFITS OF HEDGING

It is difficult to hedge a portfolio, reduce its risk and still generate an attractive return. What is more, we have seen from arbitrage strategies that hedging does not provide protection from every scenario. It would be impossible to hedge every risk in a portfolio. There are always sources of risk for which no hedging mechanism is available and others for which hedging would be too expensive. To hedge every risk would be to eliminate the potential for any return in excess of cash. Hedge fund managers therefore need to identify the risks present in their portfolio and subsequently to decide which risks should be hedged and which risks should be accepted. By accepting the risks of their choice, hedge fund managers should be able to concentrate their attentions on those risk factors that offer them higher returns for the level of risk taken. Furthermore, they can carefully isolate sources of risk and return that have a different profile from those commonly available from buying and holding assets long-only. If anomalous market conditions permit them to hedge tightly and still to generate a high return, then so much the better. They will have cheated the risk–reward equation.

Although hedging helps to reduce certain risks it does create its own issues. One of these is the risk of over-hedging a portfolio, which is likely to choke off its returns. Indeed, all hedging involves an opportunity cost. Investors who hedge an asset cannot expect to enjoy the full appreciation of that asset's value. Hedging costs money. Hedging also enhances 'manager', or 'decision' risk. A hedged portfolio reduces the risks and returns of owning an asset class but it increases the risks and returns arising from the decisions of its managers (decisions over which securities to be long of and which to be short of). Thus a hedge fund has the capacity to make money in both rising and falling markets if the managers make the right choices, and the capacity to lose money in both if the managers do not. This transfer of risks is not necessarily an improvement. It rather depends on the abilities of hedge fund managers. However it is most certainly a change.

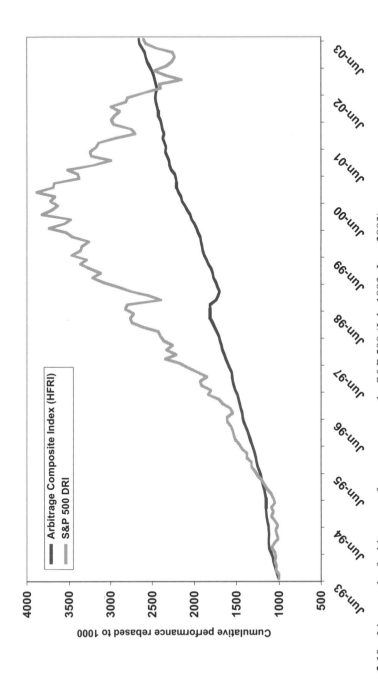

**Figure 2.10** Line graph of arbitrage performance versus the S&P 500 (July 1993–June 2003)

Although arbitrage strategies suffer the occasional sharp drawdown, the seriousness of these drawdowns should not be exaggerated, particularly when placed in the context of equity markets. The proxy for 'arbitrage returns' used here is the mean of the HFRI Relative Value Arbitrage Index, HFRI Merger Arbitrage Index, HFRI Fixed Income: Arbitrage Index and HFRI Convertible Arbitrage Index.

Sources: HFRI, Altvest.

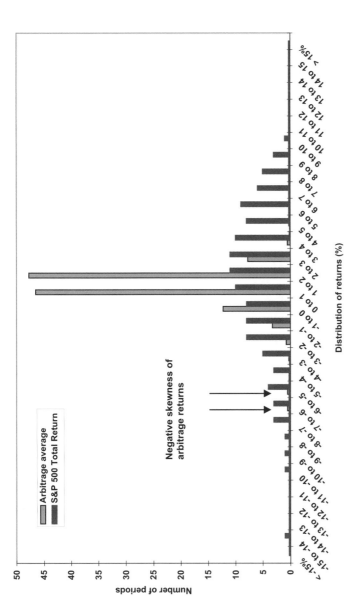

**Figure 2.11** Distribution of arbitrage and S&P 500 returns (July 1993–June 2003)

Arbitrage strategies are criticized for the negative skewness of their returns. However, these negative events are relatively infrequent and arbitrage strategies should be valued for the consistency of their returns under most circumstances. The proxy for 'arbitrage returns' used here is the mean of the HFRI Relative Value Arbitrage Index, HFRI Merger Arbitrage Index, HFRI Fixed Income: Arbitrage Index and HFRI Convertible Arbitrage Index.

Sources: HFRI, Altvest.

Once again we are led to conclude that hedge funds are not in them-selves good or bad but that their value lies in that they are different.

# RISKS OF LEVERAGE AND DERIVATIVES

A favourite investor concern about hedge funds relates to 'their wanton use of leverage and derivatives'. Since a number of serious hedge fund losses have indeed been linked with leverage and deriva-tives investors have every reason to be cautious. The complexities involved can be off-putting. However these are valuable investment tools when they are used carefully in support of low risk strategies.

## Defining leverage

First of all let us clarify what we mean by 'leverage'. A basic definition of leverage relates to investments made with borrowed funds. This is some-times referred to as 'financial leverage'. However hedge funds take in cash as a result of short sales and this cash can be used to purchase additional long positions. Short sales that are sufficiently large can fund long positions that are worth many times a portfolio's net assets. All this can be achieved without any 'financial leverage' at all. Derivatives may also be used to generate such leverage. Therefore most hedge fund investors refer to 'leverage' in terms of their investment exposures as a percentage of their portfolio's net asset value (NAV).

Depending upon the type of strategy, a fund's exposures are usually expressed in terms of:

- long exposure (longs as a percentage of NAV);
- short exposure (shorts as a percentage of NAV);
- net exposure (long minus short exposure);
- gross exposure (long plus short exposure).

Thus a manager with 100 per cent of NAV invested on the long side and 80 per cent of NAV sold short would be 20 per cent net long and 180 per cent gross exposed. Managers generally reflect the underlying market exposure arising from derivatives when they communicate these numbers. This is straightforward for those derivatives whose exposure has a unitary, linear relationship with their underlying reference assets (such as futures or CFDs). Other derivatives leave more room for interpretation. Option exposures can be quantified in very different ways. Most managers give an option's current delta-adjusted exposure but some managers quote the market value of an option premium or the full underlying nominal value to which the option contract relates. These three numbers are often very different. It is therefore worth clarifying with hedge fund managers what they mean by leverage and how they like to express their derivative exposures.

Investors must also be clear about what managers mean by their 'cash position'. Conventionally, a high cash level is taken to imply that a manager is 'underinvested' and is therefore assuming relatively little market risk. This is not necessarily the case in the context of hedge funds because they take in cash as a result of short sales. Therefore an equity long–short fund might claim to have 80 per cent in cash, while also having 80 per cent invested long and 60 per cent short. However, for the equity long–short fund concerned this 140 per cent gross exposure may constitute a fully invested position. Alternatively, arbitrage managers may describe themselves as having plenty of 'spare cash'. This merely means they have far more cash on their books than is strictly necessary in order to meet their margin requirements. In terms of exposure they may be leveraged many times, possibly up to their own internal limits.

Whether leverage is risky depends entirely upon the context in which it is used. To leverage an isolated directional bet on an equity would be highly risky. However, a leveraged and hedged position may prove less risky than holding the equity outright without leverage. If the hedging is sufficiently effective it may reduce both the volatility and the returns of the position to very low levels. Adding modest leverage may therefore be required in order to amplify the position's volatility and its returns. This raises two questions about any leveraged hedge fund:

Is the leverage applied appropriate for the targeted levels of risk and return?

Is the hedging of each position effective?

Because there is a connection between hedging tightly and needing more leverage, discussing exposures in the context of highly leveraged arbitrage strategies becomes tricky. Leverage levels do not properly express the risks being taken. Certain trades in a portfolio may involve less leverage but more risk than other trades that are more leveraged but hedged more effectively. Therefore many managers attempt to convey their risks in terms of VaR measures that encapsulate the historical volatility of the trades they have in their portfolio. They allocate an overall 'risk budget' for their portfolio, which is a total VaR measure. They then describe the size of their allocation to each trade in terms of a percentage of their total risk budget. This seems a better portrayal of how a portfolio is allocated than a simple description of the exposures involved.

Although VaR measures are an improved way of expressing exposures, describing or justifying leverage using VaR may lead to a false sense of security. If the hedging mechanisms used merely work most of the time, leverage can become a real problem on those occasions that hedging fails. VaR measures rely heavily on historical correlations that often break down during times of crisis. This temporarily alters the implications of leverage. In practice highly leveraged funds seem to experience adverse moves in breach of their risk limits more often than their VaR measures would have predicted. The demise of LTCM has been attributed to such problems. Therefore it tends to be harder for investors to understand the risks involved in those hedge fund strategies that require more leverage.

Another caveat about leverage relates to the temptation to use too much of it. During periods when the returns on a strategy fall, a minority of hedge fund managers compensate by increasing the amount of leverage they apply to their portfolios. This response is often fatal. When excessive capital is applied to a strategy it tends to drive down returns even further and to increase the possibility of a sudden reversal. The correct response under such circumstances is usually to apply less leverage and to be patient, an approach that most managers favour.

Hedge funds are also criticized for their use of derivatives, which are assumed to be risky owing to their complexity and the leverage they create. These issues are valid. However, hedge fund managers are unlikely to use derivatives unless they understand them properly. Furthermore, derivatives tend to be hedges for reducing risk rather than a means of assuming more risk. Managers are unlikely to use derivatives to establish directional investment positions unless they represent the most liquid or cost effective means of replicating a position.

In practice, the most common derivatives-related problems experienced by hedge funds involve over the counter (OTC) derivatives. At times OTC pricing leaves room for interpretation, room that unscrupulous hedge fund managers may take advantage of. These contracts may also be constructed in a complex manner that some hedge fund managers may not convey fully to their investors. Additionally, there are times when OTC contracts prove illiquid.

Hedge funds that rely heavily on derivatives may be putting themselves at greater risk from a systemic collapse across derivatives markets. Derivatives exchanges tend to match and diversify their risks very well, so once again the concern focuses more on the OTC derivative markets. It is hard to be sure whether the investment banks that act as OTC counterparties have properly matched their enormous derivative books. This is the start of a much longer discussion but it is worth pondering on it before investing in hedge funds that rely on OTC derivatives. However, one should also bear in mind that a collapse of OTC derivative markets would have implications way beyond the world of hedge funds. The entire financial system is at risk.

# TRANSPARENCY ISSUES

Hedge funds are rarely transparent organizations, and investors have reason to be concerned if they are not properly informed of the risks in a portfolio. They need to understand the extent of a fund's risks so that they can put its returns in context. They need to understand the nature of the risks in order to fit the fund into a portfolio. Where a manager pursues a complex strategy or uses complex instruments, investors have more grounds for concern about transparency.

These concerns need to be balanced against the practicalities of managing hedge funds. For example, it is inappropriate for equity long–short managers to publish the names of short equity positions in a monthly newsletter. If the company executives find out, they might seek to make life difficult for the hedge fund. If other market participants find out, they might seek to manipulate the hedge fund, perhaps by trying to squeeze them out of their short. Many arbitrageurs are unwilling to give their positions away to competitors, since too much money in an arbitrage trade erodes the profit opportunity and adds to risk. Unfortunately a small minority of investors in hedge funds seem prepared to share the reports they receive from one hedge fund with the manager of another. It only takes a little of this behaviour to make managers very secretive. Investors must therefore be prepared to accept the trade-off between a manager's success and a manager's openness.

Yet the secretiveness of hedge funds should not be exaggerated. This is a relationship business in which investors typically have a dialogue with fund managers. Managers are usually happy to show investors their portfolio in a face-to-face meeting and to run through their positions. They are normally willing to conduct such discussions over the telephone as well. A minority of managers will even release their full portfolios on a monthly basis as long as investors sign a confidentiality agreement. However, full transparency does not necessarily provide investors with an understanding of a portfolio. Complex arbitrage positions may not be comprehensible to investors unless they are discussed with the manager. Despite the obstacles, some investors attempt to drill down to the underlying holdings of all their hedge funds. However, attempts at consolidated analysis of all these positions are usually undermined when a number of managers refuse to release the information.[5]

The managers' own descriptions of their portfolios, their allocations and their risk exposures are usually the most informative. Their honesty, accuracy and openness are of course important. Proper transparency acts as a check and a balance on managers, and dissuades them from straying into areas beyond their remit or stated risk. For example, a surprising number of hedge fund managers decided that Russian bonds provided an excellent investment opportunity in the spring of 1998 and quietly added some to their portfolios. At the time this may have seemed like a good idea but some managers failed to inform their investors properly, and later in the year the investors were surprised to find out how much inadvertent exposure they had to Russian bonds. Had managers been more transparent, investors would have been better placed to make informed decisions of their own. Today, this sort of mass misunderstanding seems less likely to occur. Investors in hedge funds have been demanding greater transparency and increasingly hedge funds have been providing it.

## THE VALUE OF PERFORMANCE FEES

Hedge funds charge large performance fees. Some investors find this distasteful and object on principle. This is an emotional rather than a logical reaction. Investors ought to make economic decisions based on whether performance fees improve the size and shape of their net returns.

Performance fees are designed to distort the behaviour of hedge fund managers. Some of the distortions that result are favourable to investors while others are not. On the one hand, performance fees provide a valuable incentive:

- Performance fees align the interests of managers more closely with those of investors. Both benefit directly from positive returns.

- Performance fees result in the accumulation of wealth by managers, which aligns their interests with investors more closely

---

5.  This is an expensive exercise, even if it works. It is not a reliable means of preventing fraud either. Many managers insist on sending reports after a time delay, making them easier to fabricate. Full transparency is often overrated.

still. It is normal for managers to leave their performance fees invested in the funds that they manage. Often the managers become a fund's largest investors.

- High water marks create a focus on capital preservation and absolute (rather than relative) returns. Ultimately, this is what all investors want.

- Performance fees encourage managers to make the additional effort required to gain and maintain an edge over the rest of the market.

- Performance fees attract the best investment professionals and allow them to hire the best analysts.

- They encourage managers to limit assets under management rather than to gather more assets than they can manage successfully. Managers are better compensated for producing higher returns off a lower asset base.

Most investors in hedge funds accept and encourage performance fees. However performance fees are a blunt instrument that can have undesirable side-effects:

- Performance fees can encourage reckless behaviour instead of capital preservation. Managers may choose to treat a performance fee as a call option. Adopting an aggressive stance, managers may shoot for very high returns with the aim of amassing large performance fees. If the strategy fails large losses are borne by the investors. The managers have lost their reputations but little else. In practice this attitude is rare because managers tend to invest heavily in their hedge fund businesses and any left-over wealth goes into their funds. They therefore have much to lose from failure.

- When hedge funds fall well below their high water marks the incentive mechanism breaks down. Managers and their employees become enervated if performance fees seem a distant prospect. This can result in desertions by analysts, and induce some managers to close their funds down. More dangerously, some managers react by assuming inappropriately high levels of risk in an attempt to recover lost ground.

- Occasionally hedge fund managers bypass this situation by closing their funds down and restarting new ones a few months later. This is equivalent to resetting a high water mark, and undermines the principles along which performance fees are meant to work, belittling the importance of capital preservation.

- Some managers accumulate astonishing wealth from these fees, to the point where the incentive to accumulate further wealth evaporates. This 'affluenza' can result in a number of different symptoms. Some managers shut down their funds and retire to the beach to enjoy their millions, which is a shame for investors but does them little harm. Others are so excited by their job that they barely have time to notice how rich they have become, which does little harm either. However, others surreptitiously take more time off, gradually losing their focus.[6] This may be hard to spot and puts investors at risk. Conversely, some managers remain focused but become increasingly risk-averse with their hedge funds. Having accumulated so much wealth within their funds they become terrified of losing it. As a result they cease to target the return profile that their investors had come to expect of them.

- Performance fees may encourage managers to manipulate their fund prices in the run-up to the date that their performance fees are paid out. This is a particular risk with strategies that invest in less liquid securities, since their prices are more vulnerable to manipulation. Against this, managers who 'bring forward' their performance are merely stealing from their performance fees in subsequent periods. This reduces their incentive to behave in this manner.

- Managers who have accrued a performance fee have an incentive to defend capital, lest subsequent losses result in the fees accruing back to investors before they are due to be paid out. Performance fees usually 'crystallize' (get paid out) once a year. However, some fees crystallize more often, perhaps quarterly. This reduces the incentive for managers to preserve capital in the ensuing period because the managers have already banked their profits (the investors have not).

- Most performance fees are a flat 20 per cent of profits, with no hurdle rate of return. This means that the portion of the return that one might attribute to the risk free rate is subject to a performance fee, not just the excess returns generated by the managers.

---

6. One successful manager started commuting to Los Angeles in an attempt to start a second career as a scriptwriter. He left his fund in charge of his moderately experienced analysts, eventually handing the reins over entirely. The results were not good – both the fund and the scriptwriting proved disappointing.

- Likewise, investors must accept the possibility that managers might under-perform conventional asset classes, or simply generate very low risk-adjusted returns, and still earn performance fees. The only sanction for weak performance is a swathe of redemptions by investors (in the world of hedge funds, investors tend to be pretty good at exercising this right).

- Other managers may operate hedge funds that are closet long-only vehicles, riding bull markets without hedging their portfolios properly. This means investors are charged performance fees for 'beta exposure' which they can very well add themselves at much lower costs.[7]

- Performance fees sometimes act to smooth the pattern of a hedge fund's returns, although when it occurs the effect is mild. When a fund is above its high water mark its gains are dampened by 20 per cent. Subsequent losses may also be dampened because any performance fees accrued to the manager are reversed, accruing back to the investors. While this effect may serve to flatter volatility figures, it is unlikely to flatter Sharpe ratios or other measures of risk-adjusted return. This is because performance fees dampen return by as much as they dampen volatility.[8]

Regardless of these arguments for and against performance fees, the net returns to investors from hedge funds have been very good. More contentious, perhaps, are the fees charged by funds of funds. To analyse hedge funds properly takes quite a bit of effort and good funds of funds managers do add value. However, the vast majority of 'hedge fund value' is added by the hedge fund managers themselves. Although they vary greatly, some funds of funds charge remarkably high fees for their services. Some funds of funds products charge management fees as high as 3.5 per cent and add their own performance fees as well.[9] Additional fees this high result in much lower returns for the investors purchasing these funds of funds, without there being a commensurate reduction in risk.

---

7 . It is worth noting that performance fees originated with long-only strategies. Initially, performance fees were paid to venture capitalists. In the 1970s family offices started paying them to the managers of their listed equity portfolios as well. They were considered a bonus in recognition of the additional research managers made into small listed companies not covered by Wall Street research. Shorting followed later.

8. If anything, Sharpe ratios are likely to be lower, since the performance fee would reduce volatility as a whole but detract disproportionately from the excess return over the risk free rate, having a greater impact on the numerator than the denominator.

9. Source: Economist (2003).

# THE ACCESSIBILITY OF HEDGE FUNDS

Most hedge funds offer infrequent redemption facilities, only allowing investors out on a monthly or quarterly basis after a notice period of a similar length. Many managers also impose a one year lock-up so that new investors are unable to withdraw their capital for their first 12 months. These features make hedge funds relatively inflexible vehicles, suitable for longer-term investors only. However, the resulting portfolio stability improves fund managers' ability to perform.

A small minority of managers impose a very long lock-up, sometimes three years. This does their investors a disservice. Long locks-up give managers a 'free option' to collect management fees without fear of facing redemptions for poor performance. Although managers need to ensure the stability of their portfolios and their businesses, investors must also retain the threat of redemption as a sanction for poor performance. They must also reserve the right to make their own asset allocation decisions.

Unfortunately many investors, typically 'onshore' and small investors, are effectively barred from using hedge funds because of tax considerations. Structured products can be used to navigate through certain tax issues but many of these vehicles charge large additional fees. In certain jurisdictions, legal restrictions on marketing hedge funds may also reduce the information available to investors, sustaining the secrecy that surrounds the industry. Unfortunately there is little consolation on offer for potential investors subject to such tax or regulatory hurdles.

Complexity is also a barrier to entry. Many investors are uncomfortable investing in strategies they do not understand. On the other hand, complexities give hedge fund managers their edge and secure them excess returns. Those investors who tackle the complexities of hedge funds may expect to share in the benefits.

# LACK OF REGULATION

Hedge funds are subject to regulation at two separate levels. First, the hedge fund vehicles (the offshore limited companies and US onshore LPs) may be regulated in their domicile, and second, the investment management firms that run these vehicles may be regulated where they are located, generally a financial centre.

The hedge fund vehicles are barely regulated at all, which is the source of their opportunity. They are free to employ investment techniques that many other market participants are barred from using. The playing field is therefore uneven in their favour. If the regulation of mutual funds, pension funds or other such investment vehicles were loosened it might impinge upon hedge funds. Likewise, tightening the rules for hedge funds would choke off their opportunity set. Regulators are unlikely to restrict the investment activities of hedge funds because they would be unable to define boundaries for such complex and fluid strategies.

By contrast, the activities of hedge fund investment management firms are often regulated quite tightly, notably in jurisdictions such as the UK, Hong Kong and Singapore. This regulation ensures that hedge fund managers conduct their affairs with integrity without restricting their investment parameters. However, most hedge funds are managed in the United States, where so far managers have been left to apply for regulation on a voluntary basis. Those that have volunteered have been overseen by the SEC in a casual manner, which has shown limited concern for protecting wealthy or professional investors. This is an unsatisfactory state of affairs for investors in hedge funds. While hedge fund fraud has been relatively rare given the size and complexity of the industry, those frauds that have occurred have generally been in the United States. The lax attitude of the US authorities must surely have been a contributing factor.[10] More recently, the interest in hedge funds shown by US retail investors seems to be spurring the SEC into action.

In the future US regulators may enforce higher standards of conduct, but they will not be able to prevent hedge fund managers from making serious investment mistakes. From this aspect the hedge fund industry will always be 'self-regulating'. It is up to the managers and their investors to ensure that these unconstrained funds avoid inappropriate investment activities. In the wrong hands hedge funds are dangerous weapons.

## GREAT HEDGE FUND DISASTERS

The hedge fund world does experience the occasional disaster, or 'blow-up'. Investors define these disasters in various ways, but most

---

10. Anecdotal evidence suggests that many hedge fund frauds are conducted on a relatively small scale in provincial America. They are preventable ponzi schemes in which local dentists are persuaded to part with their savings for a non-existent hedge fund.

count any incidence of losses from 30 per cent to 50 per cent. This definition would classify the entire US equity mutual fund industry as a disaster. Yet most types of hedge fund are designed to avoid losses of this magnitude, so the definition seems fair. Hedge fund investors also count any meaningful loss that results from theft or the mispricing of a portfolio.

These disasters are a very real feature of hedge funds, and investors must prepare themselves for the possibility of their occurring. Yet such events must be kept in perspective. They are rare considering the size of the hedge fund universe, and their frequency compares favourably with the traumas suffered elsewhere in the investment world. The financial consultant Capco estimates that to date there have been 140 of these dramatic failures.[11] This is an average of about 12 a year. In the context of an industry that is now estimated to contain more than 5,000 funds this does not seem so bad. When considering the impact of such failures, review once more the results produced by funds of hedge funds, quoted earlier in the chapter. Funds of hedge funds have been victims of these disasters but they have still produced attractive results. We should also recall the financial pain inflicted by fraud and speculation in mainstream investments, be they individual telecom companies, technology mutual funds, or split capital trusts in the UK.[12] In the context of all this, dwelling on isolated disasters is a disingenuous way to tarnish the entire hedge fund universe, which has provided relative safety as a whole.

---

## Some famous hedge fund disasters

**LTCM (excessive leverage):** the largest and most famous of all hedge fund disasters. Astonishing levels of leverage left little room for error. When securities started to behave in a 'statistically impossible' manner during the 1998 Russia crisis the enormous arbitrage portfolio suffered terrible losses. Unwinding its positions moved markets across the globe.

**Manhattan (hidden losses):** the most famous hedge fund fraud, conducted by one Michael Berger, who falsified portfolio statements in a bid to convince investors his US $500 million short-selling fund was making money. In reality, he had lost almost everything. He stood trial, skipped bail and is still on the run.

---

11. As cited by Taylor (2003).
12. Thomson Venture Economics and the National Venture Capital Association suggest that venture capital funds as an entire group suffered a one-year loss of 29.1 per cent in the four quarters ending 1Q03. Morningstar reports that the wave of mutual fund closures and mergers reduced their number by 865 in 2001. See Taylor (2003).

**Beacon Hill (mispriced portfolio):** this leveraged MBS arbitrage fund suffered serious losses after hedging failed in its complex MBS derivatives book. The managers had been mispricing the portfolio.

**Blue Water (price manipulation):** a US $160 million fund, found to have manipulated the prices of thinly traded stocks.

**Brown Simpson (Reg D implosion):** strong performance during the technology boom caused warrants in the portfolio to shoot up in value, sucking speculative investors into the fund. When the technology bubble burst in 2000 the fund's value reversed sharply and investors tried to redeem. However, the underlying Reg D and warrant investments were illiquid and it was impossible to sell them.

**Princeton Economics (fraud):** managed by a maverick technical analyst, this hedge fund posted excellent returns that were never audited. In 1999 they turned out to be mythical. A number of eminent investors had been subscribers to his technical analysis newsletter.

**Askin Capital (hedging failure):** an early hedge fund failure that was triggered by the sudden rise in interest rates in 1994. The manager was not properly hedged against this eventuality and his counterparties withdrew their leverage, causing the portfolio to be liquidated at an inopportune moment.

**Ellington and MKP (withdrawal of leverage):** two MBS funds that entered into a pricing dispute with their prime broker during the darkest hours of the 1998 crisis. The prime broker demanded additional margin, forcing them to liquidate their portfolios at the worst possible moment. The funds later sued and the prime broker's behaviour was widely criticized.

**Lipper (mispriced portfolio):** a renowned convertible arbitrage firm that was discovered to be grossly exaggerating the valuation of the securities in its portfolios.

**Maricopa (theft):** a US $60 million case of outright theft conducted by the 'fund manager' David Mobely.

**Eifuku Fund (excessive leverage):** this improbably named fund was managed by the equally improbably named John Koonmen. The US $300 million Tokyo-based fund was almost entirely eradicated when concentrated, leveraged, directional positions moved against the manager.

# THE HEDGE FUND BUBBLE

Over the past few years assets have flooded into hedge funds and it is predicted that they will continue to do so. In 1993 it was estimated that hedge fund assets amounted to just US $50 billion and it is projected that by 2010 they will have reached US $2,000 billion. This astonishing growth has prompted some observers to reject the rise of hedge funds as a temporary phenomenon, likening it to the Internet bubble. Indeed, the speed with which these strategies are being embraced has got a little out of control. The barriers to entry are comparatively low and far too many hedge funds have been established by mediocre managers. Success has given way to excess.

Yet the comparisons with the Internet boom can only be stretched so far. This is not a new area. Most hedge fund strategies have been widely practised for decades and seem likely to endure for many more. In the past they have been conducted more discreetly and it is the manner in which they are perceived that has changed. This is not an asset price bubble doomed to end in disaster. The massive inflows of capital into hedge funds will not force any asset valuations into the stratosphere or result in heady, self-feeding returns. If anything, capital inflows are likely to drive down rates of return for a period and dissuade other investors from participating. Hedge funds go through these periods of increasing and declining popularity but they tend to be self-correcting.

## WHAT THE ACADEMICS SAY

Financial academics tend to support the view that core markets are highly efficient, even if mild inefficiencies linger. Perceived wisdom holds that fund managers are unable to produce excess returns on a consistent basis, and that the risk–reward trade-off cannot be cheated. Hedge fund managers, however, claim to be able to do both these things. Many academics react with disbelief, dedicating research to demonstrating that the returns reported by hedge funds are an illusion. Starting with this sort of premise, early academic studies tended to 'discover' attributes of hedge funds that were already intuitively understood by industry practitioners. Their research observed that:

- hedge fund returns are negatively skewed;

- the returns resemble the pay-off from selling options;

- hedge fund index data tend to over-state the returns actually achieved;

- those hedge funds invested in less liquid securities report artificially smooth returns.

These observations are consistent with the findings of investors. However, investors are unlikely to concede that they undermine the attractions of hedge funds. These observations merely remove the gloss from the hedge fund record. Investors who have held portfolios of hedge funds over the last decade know they have enjoyed remarkably attractive returns, even accounting for the drawbacks highlighted above. In the view of investors, academics are yet to discover how hedge funds perform their prestidigitation.

Although academics in this field seem a little too intent on proving that there is no such thing as investment skill, there are no real grounds for criticizing them. They have only turned their attentions towards hedge funds relatively recently, and it is particularly difficult to conduct robust academic research in this area because the investment strategies are complex, varied and ever-changing. Academics have no access to information on underlying hedge fund portfolios and are therefore relegated to dissecting hedge fund performance histories. This return data is of questionable quality and the nature of the relationships identified tends to be non-linear and difficult to encapsulate. Despite these challenging conditions, academics are obliged to validate all their findings, often using immensely complicated equations and reams of dirty data. This contrasts with investment professionals, who content themselves with sweeping empirical observations. Now that the groundwork has been laid and more academic attention is being paid to hedge funds I suspect that more revealing findings may shortly be on their way. A selection of the more interesting academic papers in this field is referred to at the end of this chapter.

# CONCLUSION

Sadly, the debate about hedge funds usually takes place at a low level, with battle lines that reflect the interest groups involved. Proponents of hedge funds are often biased and selective with their arguments. There is a great deal of money to be made in hedge funds, and their most fervent advocates tend to be the intermediaries, consultants and funds of funds managers who sell hedge fund products on to mainstream investors. The fiercest critics of hedge funds also have their judgement clouded by various factors:

- Many critics are ignorant about how hedge funds work.

- Conventional investors recognize that the success of hedge funds undermines their own competitive position.

- Some investors suffer from conservative, narrow-minded attitudes.

- Many fund managers are too cowardly to risk their careers by taking decisions that appear 'different', even when they believe those decisions would benefit their clients.

- Academics behave as though they feel threatened by hedge funds: they like to explain market phenomena with equations and many believe markets are efficient. Although we owe thanks to academics for disproving a number of myths about hedge funds, as a group they seem biased against the asset class.

A balanced approach to the debate is boring but provides investors with a better understanding of what hedge funds really are. First of all we must acknowledge that hedge funds are structured to meet specific objectives that make them inappropriate for certain investors, even in theory. Hedge funds have absolute return objectives, so they are unsuitable for investors with a relative return mentality. Those investors seeking strong capital appreciation may also find them disappointing: hedging techniques are a drag on returns even though they help to smooth them. The natural buyers of hedge funds are therefore 'stay rich' investors rather than 'get rich' investors.

Even when hedge funds appear to meet an investor's objectives we must recognize the drawbacks. Investors face a number of logistical hurdles, such as secretiveness, complexity, lack of regulation and illiquidity. Furthermore, hedge funds do not always meet their stated goals. They sometimes suffer periods during which their returns are disappointingly low or even sharply negative. Yet with a little effort and research the logistical problems of the asset class can be overcome. Occasional losses have been suffered but they have been a price well worth paying given the overall pattern of returns. Hedge funds have attracted some of the most talented individuals in the financial industry and have offered them incentives to deliver results. The results have indeed been delivered. Any objective observer is likely to conclude that hedge funds have been a great success.

Of course, hedge funds do involve risks. But investors have no right to expect returns without taking some risks. A careful examination suggests that the risks are lower than one would expect given the returns on offer. More importantly, the risks seem to be of a somewhat different nature to those that investors are exposed to elsewhere in their portfolios.

There are no guarantees for the future. Given that there are now so many converts to their cause, hedge funds may attract more money than they can accommodate. For the time being, however, they remain an invaluable investment tool.

# APPENDIX 1: THE FINDINGS OF SELECTED ACADEMIC PAPERS

Details of papers cited are in the References section on page 394.

### Amin and Kat (2002) *Stocks, Bonds and Hedge Funds: Not a free lunch!*

- The addition of hedge funds to a portfolio improves its mean–variance characteristics but also results in greater negative skewness and kurtosis.

- Hedge funds do not mix particularly well with equities.

- In order for an allocation to hedge funds to have an impact upon a portfolio it needs greatly to exceed the 1–5 per cent being considered by many institutions.

- Survivorship bias leads to an overstatement of the mean hedge fund index return by approximately 2 per cent. It also serves to dampen estimates of standard deviation, to moderate the impact of negative skewness and to lower kurtosis. A survivorship bias-adjusted index return series can be used to correct such distortions.

### Argarwal and Naik (2001) *Characterising Hedge Fund Risks with Buy-and-Hold Option-Based Strategies*

- An empirical study suggesting that hedge funds have non-linear exposures to traditional asset classes. Linear factor models are therefore an unhelpful means of assessing the risk–reward trade-off.

- Adding factors representing option buying and writing strategies increases the proportion of equity-oriented hedge fund returns that can be captured by a factor model.[13]

- Thereafter, higher R-squared results can be achieved than for the buy-and-hold model Sharpe used to describe long-only asset classes.

---

13. Note that the properties of hedge fund returns are not as extreme as those from holding and selling options, merely comparable in nature.

- Results imply that many hedge funds claiming to be market neutral actually involve non-linear systematic risks.

- Correlations between hedge fund strategies and long-only strategies increase under materially adverse conditions.

- The nature of the option-like exposures changes over time and with manager styles.

## Attari, Mello and Ruckes (2002) *Arbitraging Arbitrageurs*

- Margining is less safe when positions are large because the potential price impact of liquidating a position may exceed the value of the margin.

- Market participants often know which arbitrageurs dominate open-interest, leaving these arbitrageurs open to manipulation.

- If large arbitrageurs are capital constrained, other participants have the opportunity to trade against them in anticipation of trades that large arbitrageurs will be forced to make in order to satisfy their margin requirements (that is, liquidating a portion of their existing position).

- If the securities are illiquid or the arbitrageurs have a high price impact then partial liquidation of an existing position may not be viable. Arbitrageurs are faced with a choice of having to liquidate their entire position at a loss or increasing the size of their position (thereby manipulating the price in their favour in order to meet their margin requirements).

- Other participants (perhaps banks) may be able to manipulate such crises to their profit, encouraging a troubled arbitrageur into deeper water by lending capital to them to help them meet margin requirements. The potential losses the banks may incur if these loans default may be exceeded by the trading profits they make.

## Baquero, ter Horst and Verbeek (2003) *Survival, Look-Ahead Bias and the Persistence in Hedge Fund Performance*

- Before measuring performance persistence it is advisable to model first for hedge fund attrition and then for look-ahead bias.

- Hedge funds appear to exhibit greater performance persistence than mutual funds. This may be because, unlike mutual funds, there are hurdles to investing in hedge funds. Therefore investors are unlikely to compete away excess returns by making additional allocations, as it is suspected they do with mutual funds.

- The top performing 20–30 per cent of hedge funds are likely to produce above average returns in the ensuing quarter. The persistence is not apparent from one year to the next.[14] Nor does it seem to apply to the top decile of funds, whose performance appears to slip in ensuing periods.

## Brooks and Kat (2001) *The Statistical Properties of Hedge Fund Index Returns and their Implications for Investors*

- Many hedge fund indices exhibit unusual skewness, kurtosis and serial correlation.

- They have attractive mean–variance properties, but less so once their other statistical features are accounted for.

- Sharpe ratios over-estimate the true risk–return benefits of a portfolio containing hedge funds and mean–variance optimizers tend to over-allocate to hedge funds.

- The benefits of hedge funds appear to vary greatly depending upon the index provider used.

- Funds of funds managers under-perform the aggregate hedge fund indices and fail to add alpha in excess of the fees they charge.[15]

- Many hedge fund indices exhibit surprisingly high correlations, both with one another and with equity indices (particularly smaller companies indices).

- Assuming that markets are efficient, high serial correlation implies hedge funds indulge in return smoothing. Convertible arbitrage and distressed securities appear to be the worst culprits. This high autocorrelation serves to flatter standard deviation figures (and therefore Sharpe ratios also).[16]

---

14. This is a shame, since investors in hedge funds find it difficult to shift their portfolios on a quarterly basis, while on an annual basis they may be able to do so.

15. Given the fees some funds of funds charge this seems inevitable. However the difference between fund of funds performance and index performance must also be attributed to survivorship bias.

16. Deliberate smoothing is a real issue with regard to less liquid securities, such as convertibles and distressed securities. However it is unlikely to explain autocorrelation for most other hedge fund strategies, which tend to invest in liquid securities. Furthermore the assumption that autocorrelation is the result of smoothing simply because markets are efficient is not constructive. Hedge funds claim to be able to smooth their returns through legitimate investment techniques, and this claim needs to be challenged more directly.

- High Sharpe ratios are usually offset by negative skewness and do not necessarily imply superior performance.

- Analysing quarterly returns helps to mitigate these distortions.

## Fung and Hsieh (2001) *Asset-based style factors for hedge funds*

- Use of asset returns to explain the returns of various hedge fund styles (focusing initially on trend following), as an extension of Sharpe's 1992 model for mutual funds.

- Found that the Wilshire 1750 Smaller Companies Index, CSFB High Yield Bond Index and IFCI Composite Index were good explanatory variables for many hedge funds.[17]

## Getmansy, Lo and Makarov (2003) *An Economic Model of Serial Correlation and Illiquidity in Hedge Fund Returns*

- There is far more serial correlation in returns from hedge funds than from traditional investments. Serial correlation can be considered a violation of the random walk hypothesis and therefore needs explaining.[18]

- Hedge fund managers who enjoy some predictability in their returns should in theory increase or reduce their positions in accordance with their expectations, until such predictability is eliminated.[19]

- Serial correlation can therefore be attributed to the illiquidity of the assets that hedge funds invest in and the stale prices they use for valuations.[20]

---

17. The explanatory power of the IFCI index highlights the limitations of such exercises. Emerging markets equities are unlikely to be a driver of hedge fund returns. The relationship probably exists because both emerging markets and many hedge funds exhibit symptoms of the influence of a third force, perhaps the prevailing market appetite for risk.
18. Arguably, many hedge fund strategies ought to be characterized as investing activities rather than as assets. Gamma trading a convertible bond is not an asset, it is an activity. Yet it generates returns. While the prices of liquid assets may follow a random walk this does not mean that the returns from investing activities need do so.
19. This is a slightly impractical theory since managers do not behave in this way. Even if they believe they can predict their returns for a subsequent period they tend to be bound by risk considerations that prevent them from expanding positions beyond a certain size, regardless of their level of conviction.
20. The problem with this argument is that it assumes markets are efficient and therefore serial correlation must be attributable to the illiquidity of assets. The higher serial correlation exhibited by strategies using less liquid assets seems to confirm the theory (CB arbitrage and distressed securities). However, illiquidity and inefficiency go hand in hand, confusing matters. Many CB issues and many distressed securities trade surprisingly actively. It can be argued that the markets for them are more inefficient than they are illiquid.

- Even mild performance smoothing can significantly affect Sharpe ratios. Exposure to illiquid assets can be modelled in order to generate a smoothing-adjusted Sharpe ratio.

## Kat (2002) *Taking the Sting out of Hedge Funds*

- The addition of hedge funds to a portfolio improves its mean–variance characteristics but also results in greater negative skewness and kurtosis.

- These highly undesirable attributes of hedge fund returns can be mitigated by purchasing out-of-the-money put options on a relevant equity index, sacrificing a significant portion of the return in doing so.

- However the option purchases become significantly cheaper if one simply seeks to combat the additional negative skewness resulting from the inclusion of hedge funds in a portfolio. This cost may be as low as 1 per cent per annum.

## L'Habitant (2001) *Assessing Market Risk for Hedge Funds and Hedge Fund Portfolios*

- A hedge fund's return data can be used to identify its asset allocation and to measure its effective risk. The problem of non-linearity of returns can be addressed by using hedge fund indices as factors in a multiple regression model.

- Although the use of hedge fund indices as factors may be less useful than other assets as a means of explaining a hedge fund's returns they are better for quantifying its VaR.[21]

## Mitchell and Pulvino (2001) *The Characteristics of Risk and Return in Risk Arbitrage*

- Merger arbitrage returns display a positive correlation with equity markets during severe corrections and no correlation in flat or positive markets. They can therefore be likened to selling index puts.

- An index of mergers can be created to test this theory.

- Transaction costs prove to have a substantial impact on returns.

---

21. Such an exercise is inevitably limited by the fact that a fund's historical returns reflect those assets it used to hold in its portfolio, rather than those assets currently held.

- The excess returns available, an annual 4 per cent in excess of the risk free rate, are lower than those suggested by other studies.

## Schneeweis, Kazemi and Martin (2001) *Understanding Hedge Fund Performance*

- Review of the problems associated with hedge fund performance data.
- Multi-factor models can be constructed to analyse hedge fund strategies and to assess their consistency.
- Some strategies can be described in terms of traditional market measures, whereas others cannot. This may reflect the degree to which they are skill-based return enhancers or simply diversifiers.
- Numerous fund-specific characteristics, such as a fund's age and size, also influence returns.

## Weisman and Abernathy *The Dangers of Historical Hedge Fund Data*

- Owing to the statistical biases of hedge funds, risk budgeting exercises do not work for them.
- Returns of individual hedge funds may be described using 'generic model decomposition'. This tests potential factors that are selected to fit managers on the basis of qualitative considerations.
- Selecting hedge funds using a mean–variance optimizer tends to maximize both risk and illiquidity.[22]
- Hedge fund performance records are rarely long enough to be able to characterize their behaviour through varying market conditions.
- Incorporating a non-parametric, non-linear objective function helps to capture the non-linear nature of hedge fund returns.
- Several hedge fund styles exhibit short-option-like exposure and managers appear to smooth their reported returns.[23]

---

22. This is because an optimizer expresses a preference for hedge funds with a low standard deviation and a low correlation to other investments. However, these characteristics are often associated with strategies that are illiquid and short volatility, resulting in negative skewness of returns (that is, their low standard deviation masks their propensity to suffer from catastrophic drawdowns).

23. This paper makes interesting reading, although it seems to assume that the authors' model is more accurate than a reported hedge fund NAV. It also suggests that failure to explain a hedge fund's returns in terms of other securities should lead one to believe they have been fraudulently reported. This inference is made in conjunction with MBS arbitrage, a highly complex strategy that must be almost impossible to model. Therefore one must remain open to the possibility that hedge fund returns are both real and difficult to describe with a model.

# APPENDIX 2: STATISTICS ON HEDGE FUNDS

**Table 2.2**  Comparative performance statistics for various hedge fund indices (July 1993–June 2003)

| | Yearly returns | | | | | | | | | | | Cumulative | Other return statistics | |
| --- | --- | --- | --- | --- | --- | --- | --- | --- | --- | --- | --- | --- | --- | --- |
| | 2H93 | 1994 | 1995 | 1996 | 1997 | 1998 | 1999 | 2000 | 2001 | 2002 | 1H03 | | Annualized | Mean monthly |
| Barclay CTA | 2.2% | −0.7% | 13.6% | 9.1% | 10.9% | 7.0% | −1.2% | 7.9% | 0.8% | 12.4% | 4.2% | 87.91% | 6.51% | 0.56% |
| HFRI Convertible Arbitrage | 6.7% | −3.7% | 19.9% | 14.6% | 12.7% | 7.8% | 14.4% | 14.5% | 13.4% | 9.1% | 6.6% | 195.73% | 11.45% | 0.91% |
| HFRI Distressed Securities | 12.4% | 3.8% | 19.7% | 20.8% | 15.4% | −4.2% | 16.9% | 2.8% | 13.3% | 5.3% | 15.6% | 208.96% | 11.94% | 0.96% |
| HFRI Equity Hedge | 13.9% | 2.6% | 31.0% | 21.8% | 23.4% | 16.0% | 44.2% | 9.1% | 0.4% | −4.7% | 7.3% | 331.00% | 15.73% | 1.26% |
| HFRI Statistical Arbitrage | 3.3% | 4.7% | 14.3% | 19.6% | 19.4% | 10.1% | −0.2% | 8.9% | 1.6% | −3.2% | 0.5% | 108.66% | 7.63% | 0.62% |
| HFRI Fixed Income: Arbitrage | 9.5% | 11.9% | 6.1% | 11.9% | 7.0% | −10.3% | 7.4% | 4.8% | 4.8% | 8.8% | 4.9% | 87.96% | 6.51% | 0.53% |
| HFRI Mortgage-Backed | 7.8% | 11.6% | 16.6% | 17.1% | 17.3% | −9.2% | 11.3% | −1.4% | 21.2% | 8.6% | 3.8% | 162.40% | 10.13% | 0.82% |
| HFRI Fund of Funds (adjusted) | 13.3% | −2.1% | 12.7% | 16.0% | 17.9% | −3.7% | 28.3% | 5.6% | 4.3% | 2.5% | 6.0% | 152.63% | 9.71% | 0.79% |
| HFRI Macro | 20.8% | −4.3% | 29.3% | 9.3% | 18.8% | 6.2% | 17.6% | 2.0% | 6.9% | 7.4% | 9.8% | 211.87% | 12.05% | 0.98% |
| HFRI Merger Arbitrage | 10.0% | 8.9% | 17.9% | 16.6% | 16.4% | 7.2% | 14.3% | 18.0% | 2.8% | −0.9% | 3.6% | 192.60% | 11.33% | 0.90% |
| MSCI World Index Free (gross) | 6.7% | 5.6% | 21.3% | 14.0% | 16.1% | 24.8% | 25.2% | −12.9% | −16.5% | −19.5% | 11.5% | 84.36% | 6.31% | 0.60% |
| S&P 500 total return | 5.0% | 1.3% | 37.6% | 23.0% | 33.4% | 28.6% | 21.0% | −9.1% | −11.9% | −22.1% | 11.8% | 160.37% | 10.04% | 0.90% |
| SSB World Government Bond | 4.5% | 2.3% | 19.0% | 3.6% | 0.2% | 15.3% | −4.3% | 1.6% | −1.0% | 19.5% | 7.1% | 87.87% | 6.51% | 0.54% |

**Table 2.2**  *continued*

| Risk table | Maximum drawdown | Standard deviation | Down dev 0% | Gain deviation | Loss deviation |
|---|---|---|---|---|---|
| Barclay CTA | −6.74% | 8.66% | 4.76% | 6.00% | 4.41% |
| HFRI Convertible Arbitrage | −4.84% | 3.47% | 1.71% | 2.24% | 3.48% |
| HFRI Distressed Securities | −12.78% | 5.71% | 3.28% | 3.55% | 5.75% |
| HFRI Equity Hedge | −10.30% | 9.58% | 4.43% | 7.07% | 5.34% |
| HFRI Statistical Arbitrage | −5.40% | 4.03% | 1.96% | 2.65% | 2.39% |
| HFRI Fixed Income: Arbitrage | −14.42% | 4.28% | 3.10% | 2.05% | 5.86% |
| HFRI Mortgage-Backed | −13.48% | 4.89% | 3.68% | 1.94% | 8.67% |
| HFRI Fund of Funds (adjusted) | −12.44% | 6.33% | 3.25% | 4.58% | 4.47% |
| HFRI Macro | −10.70% | 8.14% | 3.83% | 6.20% | 4.67% |
| HFRI Merger Arbitrage | −6.32% | 3.74% | 2.19% | 1.97% | 4.64% |
| MSCI World Index Free (gross) | −46.31% | 14.83% | 10.14% | 7.86% | 10.23% |
| S&P 500 total return | −44.73% | 15.75% | 10.33% | 8.32% | 10.56% |
| SSB World Government Bond | −7.94% | 6.25% | 3.11% | 4.72% | 3.17% |

**Table 2.2** *continued*

**Drawdown table**

| | | Worst drawdown | 2nd worst drawdown | 3rd worst drawdown | 4th worst drawdown | 5th worst drawdown |
|---|---|---|---|---|---|---|
| Barclay CTA | Drawdown | -6.74% | -6.13% | -5.63% | -4.87% | -4.77% |
| | Peak | Oct-01 | Jul-93 | Jun-99 | Mar-01 | Jan-96 |
| | Valley | Apr-02 | Feb-94 | Jun-00 | Jul-01 | Feb-96 |
| HFRI Convertible Arbitrage | Drawdown | -4.84% | -4.69% | -1.28% | -0.72% | -0.57% |
| | Peak | Feb-94 | Jul-98 | Jun-02 | Oct-00 | May-03 |
| | Valley | Apr-94 | Oct-98 | Jul-02 | Dec-00 | Jun-03 |
| HFRI Distressed Securities | Drawdown | -12.78% | -4.04% | -3.92% | -2.20% | -1.71% |
| | Peak | Jun-98 | Aug-00 | May-02 | Mar-00 | Oct-94 |
| | Valley | Oct-98 | Dec-00 | Oct-02 | May-00 | Nov-94 |
| HFRI Equity Hedge | Drawdown | -10.30% | -8.98% | -6.53% | -3.58% | -2.83% |
| | Peak | Aug-00 | Apr-98 | Mar-00 | May-96 | Jan-94 |
| | Valley | Sep-02 | Aug-98 | May-00 | Jul-96 | Jun-94 |
| HFRI Statistical Arbitrage | Drawdown | -5.40% | -4.29% | -4.25% | -1.86% | -1.42% |
| | Peak | Mar-02 | Dec-98 | Jan-01 | Sep-93 | Jun-98 |
| | Valley | Sep-02 | Apr-99 | Sep-01 | Nov-93 | Aug-98 |
| HFRI Fixed Income: Arbitrage | Drawdown | -14.42 | -1.89% | -1.71% | -1.54% | -1.31% |
| | Peak | Jul-98 | Aug-95 | Apr-95 | Aug-01 | May-98 |
| | Valley | Nov-98 | Sep-95 | Jun-95 | Sep-01 | Jun-98 |
| HFRI Mortgage-Backed | Drawdown | -13.48% | -5.12% | | | |
| | Peak | Mar-98 | Aug-02 | | | |
| | Valley | Oct-98 | Sep-02 | | | |

*continued overleaf*

**Table 2.2** *continued*

**Drawdown table**

| | | Worst drawdown | 2nd worst drawdown | 3rd worst drawdown | 4th worst drawdown | 5th worst drawdown |
|---|---|---|---|---|---|---|
| HFRI Fund of Funds (adjusted) | Drawdown | −12.44% | −5.24% | −4.66% | −3.31% | −1.97% |
| | Peak | Apr-98 | Jan-94 | Mar-00 | Aug-00 | May-02 |
| | Valley | Oct-98 | Apr-94 | May-00 | Nov-00 | Jul-02 |
| HFRI Macro | Drawdown | −10.70% | −7.32% | −5.93% | −4.54% | −2.23% |
| | Peak | Jan-94 | Feb-00 | Jul-98 | Jan-96 | Feb-03 |
| | Valley | Apr-94 | May-00 | Oct-98 | Jul-96 | Mar-03 |
| HFRI Merger Arbitrage | Drawdown | −6.32% | −3.39% | −2.72% | −0.84% | −0.75% |
| | Peak | Apr-98 | Mar-02 | Aug-01 | May-01 | Feb-01 |
| | Valley | Aug-98 | Jul-02 | Sep-01 | Jun-01 | Mar-01 |
| MSCI World Index Free (gross) | Drawdown | −46.31% | −13.44% | −6.83% | −5.72% | −5.67% |
| | Peak | Mar-00 | Jun-98 | Jul-97 | Dec-99 | Oct-93 |
| | Valley | Sep-02 | Aug-98 | Oct-97 | Jan-00 | Nov-93 |
| S&P 500 total return | Drawdown | −44.73% | −15.37% | −6.96% | −6.82% | −6.24% |
| | Peak | Aug-00 | Jun-98 | Jan-94 | Dec-99 | Jun-99 |
| | Valley | Sep-02 | Aug-98 | Mar-94 | Feb-00 | Sep-99 |
| SSB World Government Bond | Drawdown | −7.94% | −5.75% | −5.72% | −3.44% | −2.27% |
| | Peak | Dec-98 | Nov-96 | Oct-01 | Jul-95 | Dec-95 |
| | Valley | Oct-00 | Apr-97 | Jan-02 | Aug-95 | Apr-96 |

**Table 2.2**   *continued*

| | Data patterns | | Risk-adjusted returns | | |
|---|---|---|---|---|---|
| | **Skewness** | **Kurtosis** | **Sharpe**<br>**–4.10%** | **Sortino**<br>**–4.10%** | **Sortino**<br>**0.00%** |
| Barclay CTA | 0.25 | –0.13 | 0.31 | 0.43 | 1.33 |
| HFRI Convertible<br>  Arbitrage | –1.29 | 3.46 | 2.00 | 3.38 | 6.37 |
| HFRI Distressed<br>  Securities | –1.62 | 8.44 | 1.31 | 2.01 | 3.45 |
| HFRI Equity Hedge | 0.25 | 1.48 | 1.16 | 2.16 | 3.32 |
| HFRI Statistical Arbitrage | –0.30 | 0.16 | 0.85 | 1.36 | 3.77 |
| HFRI Fixed Income:<br>  Arbitrage | –2.86 | 14.15 | 0.56 | 0.67 | 2.04 |
| HFRI Mortgage-Backed | –4.03 | 23.75 | 1.18 | 1.43 | 2.63 |
| HFRI Fund of Funds<br>  (adjusted) | –0.18 | 3.59 | 0.87 | 1.42 | 2.86 |
| HFRI Macro | 0.19 | 0.67 | 0.95 | 1.71 | 2.99 |
| HFRI Merger Arbitrage | –2.47 | 11.46 | 1.82 | 2.72 | 4.92 |
| MSCI World Index<br>  Free (gross) | –0.55 | 0.31 | 0.22 | 0.20 | 0.61 |
| S&P 500 total return | –0.57 | 0.31 | 0.43 | 0.51 | 0.93 |
| SSB World Government<br>  Bond | 0.43 | 0.46 | 0.40 | 0.62 | 2.03 |

**Table 2.2**   *continued*
**Correlation July 1993 to June 2003**

| | CTA | CB Arb. | Distr. | Eqty. H. | Stat. A. | FI Arb. | MBS | Macro | Merg. | MSCI | S&P | SSB |
|---|---|---|---|---|---|---|---|---|---|---|---|---|
| Barclay CTA | — | –0.08 | –0.14 | –0.07 | –0.03 | 0.04 | –0.03 | 0.43 | –0.14 | –0.16 | –0.17 | 0.25 |
| HFRI Convertible Arbitrage | –0.08 | — | 0.64 | 0.48 | 0.22 | 0.18 | 0.17 | 0.38 | 0.46 | 0.29 | 0.31 | –0.07 |
| HFRI Distressed Securities | –0.14 | 0.64 | — | 0.64 | 0.22 | 0.33 | 0.29 | 0.52 | 0.53 | 0.50 | 0.46 | –0.10 |
| HFRI Equity Hedge | –0.07 | 0.48 | 0.64 | — | 0.32 | 0.03 | 0.09 | 0.59 | 0.57 | 0.71 | 0.68 | –0.01 |
| HFRI Statistical Arbitrage | –0.03 | 0.22 | 0.22 | 0.32 | — | –0.01 | 0.07 | 0.20 | 0.43 | 0.52 | 0.57 | 0.00 |
| HFRI Fixed Income:<br>  Arbitrage | 0.04 | 0.18 | 0.33 | 0.03 | –0.01 | — | 0.52 | 0.19 | 0.02 | –0.04 | –0.13 | –0.17 |
| HFRI Mortgage-Backed | –0.03 | 0.17 | 0.29 | 0.09 | 0.07 | 0.52 | — | 0.21 | 0.02 | 0.02 | 0.01 | –0.15 |
| HFRI Macro | 0.43 | 0.38 | 0.52 | 0.59 | 0.20 | 0.19 | 0.21 | — | 0.32 | 0.41 | 0.36 | 0.04 |
| HFRI Merger Arbitrage | –0.14 | 0.46 | 0.53 | 0.57 | 0.43 | 0.02 | 0.02 | 0.32 | — | 0.49 | 0.50 | –0.06 |
| MSCI World Index Free<br>  (gross) | –0.16 | 0.29 | 0.50 | 0.71 | 0.52 | –0.04 | 0.02 | 0.41 | 0.49 | — | 0.93 | 0.06 |
| S&P 500 total return | –0.17 | 0.31 | 0.46 | 0.68 | 0.57 | –0.13 | 0.01 | 0.36 | 0.50 | 0.93 | — | –0.03 |
| SSB World Government<br>  Bond | 0.25 | –0.07 | –0.10 | –0.01 | 0.00 | –0.17 | –0.15 | 0.04 | –0.06 | 0.06 | –0.03 | — |
| **Mean** | **–0.01** | **0.27** | **0.35** | **0.37** | **0.23** | **0.09** | **0.11** | **0.33** | **0.28** | **0.34** | **0.32** | **–0.02** |

Sources: HFRI, Altvest, PerTrac Indexes, Barclay Trading Group Ltd.

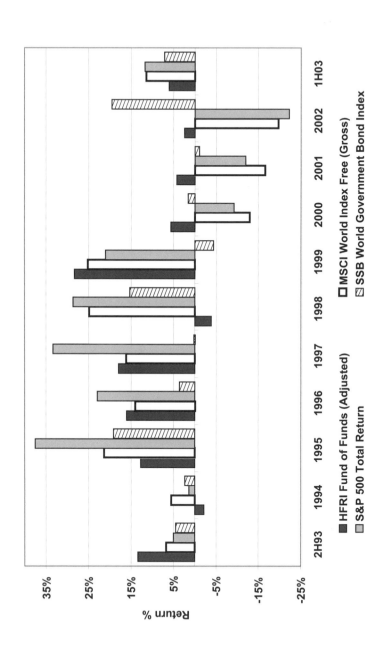

**Figure 2.12** Bar chart of hedge fund performance (July 1993–June 2003)
Sources: HFRI, Altvest, PerTrac Indexes.

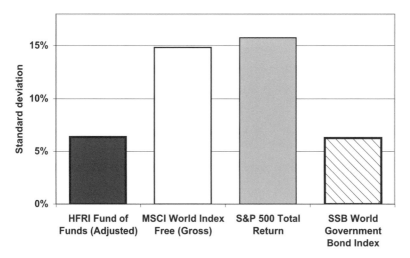

**Figure 2.13**   Bar chart of volatility (July 1993–June 2003)
Sources: HFRI, Altvest, PerTrac Indexes.

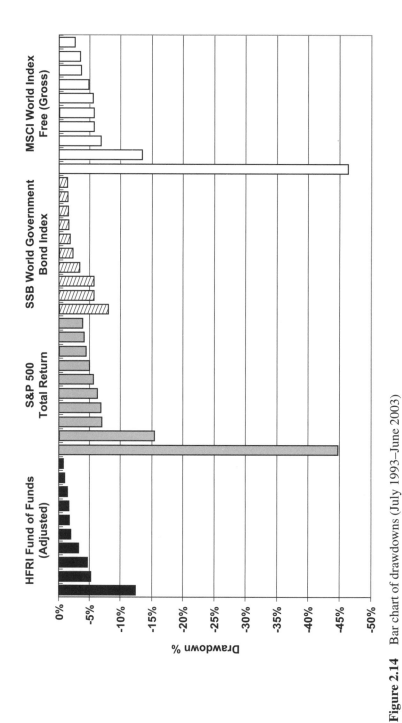

**Figure 2.14** Bar chart of drawdowns (July 1993–June 2003)
Sources: HFRI, Altvest, PerTrac Indexes.

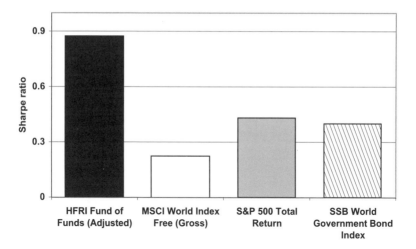

**Figure 2.15** Bar chart of Sharpe ratios (Risk free 4.10%) (July 1993–June 2003)
Sources: HFRI, Altvest, PerTrac Indexes.

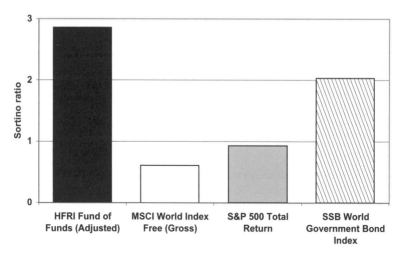

**Figure 2.16** Bar chart of Sortino ratios (Risk free 4.10%, Mar 0%) (July 1993–June 2003)
Sources: HFRI, Altvest, PerTrac Indexes.

# 3

# How to select a hedge fund

The function of the expert is not to be more right than other people but to be wrong for more sophisticated reasons.

David Butler

Superficial analysis of a hedge fund is straightforward. Armed with a basic understanding of a manager's strategy and an accompanying track record, a fairly simple decision can be taken about whether or not to invest. The manager will then do the rest. Thorough analysis, on the other hand, involves a great deal of work. It is worth the effort because mistakes can be costly. Behind all research, however, lies one simple question. Will the managers generate returns that are attractive, given the risks they are taking? We can break this question down into two further questions: are the managers following a promising strategy, and are they able to execute it effectively?

This chapter provides an introduction to hedge fund selection and explores these questions. It walks through an investment process, focusing in turn on the key areas of strategy assessment, sourcing hedge funds, qualitative analysis, operational due diligence, quantitative analysis and manager monitoring. Portfolio construction and management are covered in a separate chapter. At the end of the chapter you will find a section on how to organize an effective hedge fund research effort, plus an appendix with a long list of considerations that are relevant for selecting most hedge funds. You are unlikely to address every one of these points with every manager but the list provides a menu of issues to be aware of. Later in the book there is a series of chapters dedicated to specific hedge fund strategies, and each of these ends with a series of considerations particularly pertinent to that strategy.

# AN INVESTMENT PROCESS FOR SELECTING HEDGE FUNDS

There are not that many ways to approach the hedge fund selection process. In broad terms the philosophical choice is whether to emphasize quantitative or qualitative analysis. However, this choice should not be too difficult.

Some investors rely on quantitative analysis at all stages of the process. They allow statistical screens to define their investment universe, and when they have identified investment candidates they place too much faith in managers' track records. They then compound these misdeeds by constructing their portfolios using quantitative techniques, such as mean–variance optimization. Although a quantitative approach appears exact it is in reality somewhat vague because the statistical analysis of hedge fund returns is so fraught with difficulties. Investors who emphasize statistical analysis often do so because it impresses their employers and their clients. In truth, the availability of statistical software makes it relatively easy to generate extensive statistical reports. Relying on performance analysis is a lazy and misguided approach which ducks the essential work of thorough qualitative analysis. Thorough statistical analysis should form an essential component of the process, it is a prerequisite, but it rarely provides the investor with clear-cut answers. Instead, it should be used to furnish a series of questions, the answers to which illuminate the past and cast some light on the future. These answers can only be unearthed through qualitative research.

A sensible approach to hedge fund selection might look something like this:

1. **Establishment of investment policy:** analyse the macroeconomic environment, markets and different asset classes in order to establish views on the prospects for each.[1]
2. **Strategy assessment:** assess each specialist hedge fund strategy to ascertain whether the future environment will be conducive to it. This establishes priorities for finding new types of manager.
3. **Sourcing hedge funds:** draw on a variety of sources to find interesting hedge funds, including industry contacts, publications and quantitative screens.

---

1. This element of the investment process is not specifically addressed here, not because it is unimportant but because it is considered to be widely understood by investment professionals.

4. **Qualitative manager selection:** conduct thorough qualitative analysis of investment candidates, concentrating on priority areas.
5. **Quantitative manager selection:** concurrently, perform statistical analysis of investment candidates and their track records to support and illuminate the qualitative research.
6. **Operational due diligence:** once a fund has been approved on quantitative and qualitative grounds, conduct due diligence on the fund vehicle, the investment advisor and the fund's counterparties.
7. **Portfolio construction:** blend complimentary hedge funds to build a portfolio that reflects top-down expectations, risk–return targets and diversification requirements.
8. **Monitoring:** repeat earlier stages of the process in an iterative manner, monitoring the environment, conducting ongoing qualitative and quantitative research of managers and reviewing the portfolio.

# STRATEGY ASSESSMENT

Hedge funds encompass a wide variety of specialist strategies and the success of each is driven by its own set of factors. The specialist strategy pursued by a hedge fund must be thoroughly understood, together with the economic and market forces which affect the strategy's success. Armed with this understanding a hedge fund investor can start to form judgements about the likely success of each strategy given the prevailing environment. Some of the specialist strategies pursued by hedge funds are described in separate chapters of the book. Each chapter touches on some of the factors that affect that strategy specifically.

Making predictions about a particular strategy's prospects can be difficult. Most hedge funds profess to make money regardless of the direction in which mainstream markets are moving. Therefore traditional sources of top-down investment research can rarely be relied upon. There is currently no specialist research dedicated to the specific requirements of the hedge fund investor. Investors must cobble together information from a variety of sources in order to form a picture. The first step is to maintain a good understanding of the general economic and market environment. In addition, there are a number of specific indicators that provide some insights into the forces affecting hedge funds. These are often available from

Bloomberg or other conventional sources, and they provide a partial insight into what is happening. These indicators are unlikely to be predictive but they provide a picture of current conditions and they sometimes alert investors to alarming developments early on.

A far more valuable source of information is the hedge fund managers themselves. They have the best understanding of what is driving performance in their area. Because they are usually specialists they can be a little over-optimistic about their own strategies. Multi-strategy managers, who are engaged in more than one type of activity, are more likely to be objective about the relative merits of each of their areas. However even single-strategy managers are aware of the need to explain their performance to investors. It reflects badly if events appear to have taken them by surprise. Hedge fund managers can therefore be quite objective about the outlook for their own strategies. With a little reading between the lines investors can usually build up a good picture of consensus expectations.

A more technical approach to analysing hedge fund strategies is to model their performance quantitatively against a range of economic and market factors. For example, merger arbitrage returns might be modelled against factors such as interest rates, the number of mergers announced and completed, the level of GDP, equity market returns or credit spreads. Such a model would probably illustrate how crucial interest rates are to merger arbitrage returns. Constructing these models is a useful exercise that can improve an investor's understanding of what drives a strategy. The risk is that the investor becomes mesmerized by a model and loses sight of its limitations. These models are discussed further in an appendix at the end of this chapter.

## SOURCING HEDGE FUNDS

Finding the best hedge funds is not always easy since there is no definitive database of hedge funds available. A few years ago it was even harder as investors had to rely on word of mouth and third party marketing agents. More data is now available and things are now a little easier. However, investors must still be both reactive and proactive in their search.

By being reactive investors will leverage off the efforts of others. Hedge fund investors can quickly plug into the hedge fund network. They are approached by third party marketing agents, and directly by some hedge funds. Various prime brokers keep them informed about which hedge funds are trying to raise more money. The prime brokers invite investors to presentations given by these managers and arrange free conferences at which investors and managers can meet one another. Investors can subscribe to industry journals and attend commercial, independently arranged hedge fund conferences. As with all things in life, someone who signals a desire to spend money is soon approached by people offering to lend a hand.

Yet it is also important to be proactive, as this will uncover hedge funds that would otherwise have remained unknown. Those funds that seek out investors most actively are sometimes newer or sub-standard. Many of the best hedge funds keep a very low profile and are selective about the type of client they wish to attract. Some are altogether closed to new investors. One of the best ways to seek out hedge funds is to ask the hedge fund managers themselves. If you are already invested with a manager and are unlikely to allocate any more, there is no reason why the manager should not recommend admired competitors. Investors who regularly ask hedge fund managers about their competitors quickly discover the names of most respected practitioners in each field, as well as those of promising newcomers. Hedge fund investors should also make an effort to swap ideas with each other. Since the better managers tend to limit the size of their funds investors do not always wish to give away the names of their best finds, for fear that they may lose out on capacity. As long as they get ideas in return, however, most investors are prepared to do a little horse trading.

The search for ideas is likely to include the odd statistical screen.[2] This approach suffers from the various limitations associated with historic performance and with statistical measures, and it entirely fails to identify promising hedge funds with short track records. Screens also exclude managers who have made mistakes in the past but have permanently changed their approach for the better. However, it can sometimes bring good funds to light. Screens should be tailored to the type of fund required by defining appropriate performance and volatility characteristics. If a specific strategy is being reviewed, all the funds in the database will have to be accurately categorized. This can be quite a task because definitions are often a matter of dispute and most investors have databases that include thousands of funds.

---

2. This is not inconsistent with an emphasis on qualitative research. Some investors make the mistake of relying on statistical screens to narrow down the massive universe of hedge funds to a more manageable number that can then be examined qualitatively. While this approach is frightfully convenient, it may result in an investor missing all sorts of opportunities that might have been found through other means. Statistical screens should therefore be used in parallel with other ways of sourcing funds.

# QUALITATIVE ANALYSIS

Qualitative analysis is arguably the most important aspect of hedge fund selection. It is essential for predicting success. Unfortunately it involves subjective judgements and these can be difficult to justify. Therefore steps must be taken to establish an analysis structure that improves objectivity. The first step is to identify the qualitative factors that distinguish a good hedge fund and to use these as the basis of the assessment process. The following characteristics are among the most desirable:

- a fund strategy backed by a solid investment case;

- managers with an identifiable 'edge' that acts as a sustainable source of returns;

- investment parameters that avoid latent risk;

- a genuinely 'hedged' portfolio, when required by the strategy;

- managers with honesty, integrity and expertise;

- well-resourced managers with a stable business model;

- transparent and accurate pricing.

Having done this, one can then break qualitative assessments down into carefully defined areas. 'Compartmentalizing' the assessment process improves the investor's ability to articulate what is attractive about a particular hedge fund and makes it easier to contrast the qualitative attributes of different funds. Qualitative assessments can be divided up into the following broad areas:

- **Investment process and strategy:** managers must be able to convey how and why their funds make money. They must also explain why they will continue to do so. Managers who cannot explain themselves clearly may be hiding or overlooking important aspects of risk within their strategy.

- **Top-down considerations:** the investor must appreciate how different economic and market environments will affect the specific strategy as it is pursued by each manager. This understanding affects both the decision of whether or not to invest in a particular hedge fund and how it should be combined within a portfolio.

- **Past performance:** managers must explain their funds' past performance, concentrating on notable events, how they were dealt with and what changes were made as a result.

- **Management and staff:** investors should review managers and their supporting staff to understand who they are and how they operate together.

- **Personal qualities:** as with all actively managed funds, the success of hedge funds relies on the decisions made by the lead managers. Their personal qualities affect their decision making abilities.

- **Risk management:** various aspects of risk management need reviewing, including leverage levels, diversification, hedging and other risk systems. Hedge fund offering documents rarely impose tight investment restrictions. Instead, practical investment considerations mean that managers operate according to internal guidelines and investors need to understand how these work.

- **Transparency and reporting:** investors must ascertain the level of transparency they will be given, whether it is appropriate and whether it is sufficient to maintain an understanding of the strategy. Many managers take greater risks than they admit to, and one has to ask why a manager wants to restrict the flow of information. Higher levels of transparency can reduce the possibility of managers straying from their stated methodologies, particularly in periods in between reporting.

- **Terms:** a fund's terms must be acceptable to its investors, including the level of fees and the rights of investors to withdraw their capital.

It is worth dwelling a moment longer on a manager's personal qualities, since these are so crucial to the success of a hedge fund. The hedge fund industry is predicated on harnessing the talents of individuals but it can be difficult to define what qualities are required. I would suggest there are nine essential attributes that a hedge fund manager should have:

- Intelligence: this is obviously a prerequisite for someone managing large sums of money in a sophisticated manner.

- Good judgement: without good judgement, intelligence can be dangerously misapplied. Fascinating and intelligent theories do not make money unless they prove to be right. Managers must be realistic.

- Technical knowledge of their specialist strategy: to be able to sustain an advantage over the broader market, managers must demonstrate a superior understanding of their field.

- Experience within their specialist strategy: sometimes recently trained individuals have a better technical understanding of a specific area. Yet nothing can replace the experience of executing a strategy through bull markets, bear markets and liquidity squeezes (investment teams that combine youth with experience may work the best).

- Humility: this characteristic is often missing from hedge fund managers. One of the benefits of experience is that individuals are reminded of their own fallibility. Past experience that does not include mistakes may result in hubris (unless a manager has the modesty to distinguish luck from brilliance). Arrogance is a form of investment risk.

- Integrity: some investors refuse to place money with managers they dislike. This sounds ridiculous, especially since many of the most talented individuals on Wall Street are aggressive. However, investors must trust these people with large sums of money. What sort of respect will managers have for the millions of dollars with which you entrust them? Might they stretch the truth here and there? How will they behave in a dispute?[3]

- A stable personality: managing hedge funds can be very stressful and expectations are high. A robust character is required. Managers who lose their temper or their nerve in difficult situations are more likely to make bad decisions.

- Discipline: a well-ordered mind takes clearer investment decisions. Disciplined managers are more likely to generate alpha on a repeatable basis.

- Ambition: generating 'excess returns' is a competitive business. Those without ambition need not apply.

---

3. All this is hard to judge. One of the things I do is to perform the 'cat test': would I trust this person to look after my cat for the week? Would he or she remember to feed it? Would he or she kick it out of the way? Individuals who fail the cat test might not deserve custody of clients' money.

# QUANTITATIVE ANALYSIS

While careful interpretation is required, quantitative analysis of a manager's performance record is an essential component of the research process. The interpretation of specific statistical measures is reviewed in detail at the end of the chapter. However the general characteristics that define an attractive record are:

- an attractive level of returns, meeting the fund's objectives;

- consistency of returns;

- tolerable 'risk' as defined by volatility, downside volatility and drawdown;

- low correlation, both with core markets and other investments in a portfolio.

Performance statistics should be interpreted with a sense of curiosity and a degree of caution. Rather than providing straightforward answers, performance statistics tend to throw up a series of questions (Why has volatility fallen? What went wrong in the summer of 2002? Why are returns negatively skewed? Why has the correlation with US equities increased over time? and so on). At the beginning of the chapter we alluded to the fact that the statistical analysis of hedge funds is fraught with difficulties. The principal limitations to bear in mind are as follows:

- Whilst we are repeatedly warned against it, it is remarkably easy for expectations to be influenced by historical returns. This is driving in the rear view mirror. Statistical analysis itself suggests that relying on statistics is an unreliable method of predicting future fund returns.

- Attempts to capture the concept of 'risk' in a numerical form are futile. The notion of 'risk' relates to the potential for adverse events in the future. Numbers highlight the occurrence or non-occurrence of adverse events in the past. They do not highlight the imminent implosion of an investment strategy or the presence of fraud or the forthcoming departure of a team of analysts.

- Statistical analysis of hedge fund performance data is often mathematically flawed. The data set is often too small to be significant and the patterns within the data present further problems.[4] Hedge

---

4.  Performance measures generated with less than three years of monthly returns are unlikely to be statistically significant. Some investors place inappropriate faith in measures relating to shorter periods, measures that statisticians would dismiss as invalid.

fund data is renowned for being non-normally distributed, sometimes by design and sometimes by accident.

- Steady historical returns are commendable but they often mask underlying risks that, while inherent in a manager's strategy, lie dormant until a market dislocation triggers sudden losses. It is most unwise to be reassured by low historical volatility without developing a thorough understanding of a manager's strategy.

- A number of hedge fund strategies invest in some illiquid securities. Where this is the case, the monthly pricing may be the subject of 'smoothing' which flatters risk-adjusted return statistics.

- Periods of poor historical performance should not necessarily result in the rejection of a fund. In some cases managers have been through an important learning process (perhaps at the expense of other investors) and have taken corrective measures that mean repetition is unlikely. Perfect records are not always ideal, especially if they cause managers to become overconfident.[5]

- Unlike long-only funds, which often suffer frequent changes in manager, most hedge funds enjoy continuity of management. However, in many cases hedge fund managers adapt their investment style to changing market conditions. This may not be clear from their string of monthly returns.[6]

- Because they are active absolute return vehicles it is difficult to compare hedge funds with indices. Sometimes indices are useful for comparison purposes but never as benchmarks. Alternative investment funds are expected to provide returns which are an 'alternative' to conventional assets. Even comparisons with relevant peer groups, or indices of hedge funds, must be conducted with care. While some types of hedge fund strategy are reasonably homogenous, most incorporate large variations in style.

## OPERATIONAL DUE DILIGENCE

Investors are more likely to avoid a hedge fund disaster by conducting operational due diligence than by analysing a fund's investment

---

5. It is not a good idea to get too obsessed with monthly returns. This is an artificial performance measurement period favoured by many hedge fund investors that is not necessarily consistent with the underlying strategies pursued by hedge fund managers.
6. Equity long–short managers may alter their net and gross exposures and convertible arbitrageurs may shift their bias from traditional carry trading to gamma trading.

strategy. There are four main avenues for due diligence: checking for fraud, verifying a fund's details, reviewing operations, and assessing the business model.

## Fraud

Sadly there have been a number of cases of hedge fund fraud. Considering the size of the hedge fund industry, the number of funds in existence and the lack of regulation, instances of fraud are comparatively rare. The area has been no more prone to scandal than other parts of the investment world. Nevertheless, it is worth taking preventative measures because the financial consequences are devastating when it does occur. Furthermore, hedge funds are obvious and fertile ground for fraudsters (a glossy presentation, a prospectus, a convoluted but convincing story and some wiring instructions can appear quite credible).

While some frauds are direct thefts via ponzi schemes, the vast majority of situations are less straightforward. Most hedge fund frauds result from managers 'stretching the truth' when pricing their portfolios. An overvalued portfolio constitutes indirect theft of assets by the managers because performance fees are earned on the overvaluation. Overstating performance allows managers to grow their investor base and to continue earning 20 per cent of the profits. In some cases, managers push for an unreasonably optimistic pricing methodology for securities that are genuinely difficult to value. In other instances managers are tempted to understate their losses, particularly if they fool themselves that they can make the money back again (archetypal rogue traders). However managers rationalize it, when investors are misled about the value of their assets managers stand to profit from the deceit.

Fraud is difficult to spot, especially if managers are fooling themselves that they are not fraudsters. Nevertheless, steps can be taken to reduce the risk. Fraud usually involves a tangled web of deceit, so that one big lie might be spotted through a number of smaller ones used to support it. Investors are therefore advised to check a number of the details given by managers, particularly their backgrounds (genuinely talented individuals do not have to embellish their backgrounds, so there should be no inconsistencies). Some investors hire private investigators to perform background checks. This is not an unreasonable measure, although it is worth remembering the managers concerned may become aware of the fact. American managers seem less inclined to take offence than Europeans, for whom it seems unusual.

Investigators generally check publicly available tax, bankruptcy, regulation and law court records. They can also verify educational and employment histories.[7]

## Verification

It is easy to develop misunderstandings about funds on the basis of meetings with managers or by reading marketing material. Small but crucial details, such as the notice period for redemptions or fee calculations, all require checking. Managers may not have been forthcoming about those details that disadvantage investors and it is incumbent on investors to understand all aspects of a fund. There are a number of details investors should check in a fund's offering documents. However investors should also ask to see the investment management agreement that governs the relationship between the fund and the investment advisor, as this usually takes legal precedence over the offering documents. On occasions the two differ on important points (I have known them to contradict each other on performance fee calculations) and the management agreement may cover issues not included in the offering documents.

If available, it is also worth reading the administration agreement that governs the duties of the administrator. This will confirm pricing sources and policies (which are particularly important for funds investing in complex or illiquid securities). Some administrators are simply not equipped to price complex portfolios. Investors must be absolutely sure they understand what happens under such circumstances because very often managers are left with responsibility for marking the book. To be really thorough, an investor may also wish to see the prime brokerage agreement, as this too is a material contract.

## Operations

Reviewing the operational capabilities of a small firm is a fairly obvious measure. Investors should look to see proper administrative, compliance, client relations and IT personnel in place. The managers' premises should therefore be visited before an allocation is made to ensure the level of resources is sufficient for the strategy being implemented.[8] Some strategies, such as fixed income arbitrage, require far

---

7.  Investigation firms conducting background checks include Kroll Associates, NCO Financial Services, Back Track Reports and Citigate Global Intelligence and Security. They may be hired to conduct checks on an organization as well as on individuals.
8.  Visiting the manager's offices also offers insights about how a manager and his or her team relate to each other. It is a good idea to get a feel for the atmosphere prevailing within an organization.

more resources than others, such as equity long–short. It is also important to consider the nature of the fund's counterparties to verify they are as stated, as well as being happy that they can do a good job (the administrators, prime brokers, auditors and lawyers). They vary in quality and with a little experience investors get to know which ones are the least efficient.

To someone used to investing in regulated mutual funds this may seem to be going too far. However, many funds are obliged by their domicile to have their administration performed in small islands. Many of these offshore centres issue a strictly limited number of work permits while others attract very few experienced individuals. After a decade of rapid growth in the hedge fund industry during the 1990s many of these offshore administrators struggle to keep up with their workload, resulting in delays and errors. But even administrators in Dublin, Luxemburg or New York should be questioned. Fund administration is a low margin business and it is not always conducted carefully, even for complex portfolios.

## Business model

The management firm's business model has implications for the success of a hedge fund. It is reassuring to see assets under management and fee revenues at levels that comfortably sustain operations. Where revenues are low, a business must have sufficient capital backing to support operations for long enough to gather assets under management. Furthermore, the nature and concentration of the client base affects the 'quality of earnings'. Certain types of investor have a reputation for withdrawing capital very quickly, and a concentrated investor base also leaves a hedge fund vulnerable to redemptions. Equally important to the business model is the experience of support staff, and their remuneration must be sufficient to ensure they are locked into the business. Hedge fund managers who are distracted by business considerations will pay insufficient attention to managing money. Few managers have had business responsibilities before setting up a hedge fund, and they can come as a shock.

# MONITORING

Manager selection is not merely about finding new investments. The selection process continues even after a hedge fund has been incorporated within a portfolio, since a fund must continue to justify its inclusion. Ongoing monitoring of each hedge fund is therefore required in case the original investment criteria cease to be met. Reasons for selling a hedge fund might include:

- The fundamentals for the hedge fund strategy have weakened from a top-down point of view (perhaps following a period of abnormally high returns).

- An alternative hedge fund has been found which executes the same strategy more proficiently.

- Key personnel have left the firm.

- Assets under management have grown to such high levels that the managers' ability to execute their strategy has been impaired. Alternatively, assets under management may have fallen to levels where the strategy is difficult to execute or where the managers' business model is threatened.

- The managers have drifted in their investment style in an inappropriate manner. An evolution or change in investment style is not necessarily a concern, so long as it is a conscious decision, declared to investors and supported by sufficient in-house expertise.

- The managers have loosened their risk parameters. This is a particular threat during quiet periods for a strategy when some managers 'stretch for returns'.

- There has been a sustained decline in risk-adjusted returns.

- There has been a sudden drawdown which has uncovered weak adherence to the stated strategy or inherent flaws within it (as opposed to being the result of an improbable exogenous event). Even when the managers are beyond blame, sharp drawdowns can prompt investors to redeem from a hedge fund for fear that its business model will break down (a sharp drawdown can reduce assets under management, force the share price well below the performance fee high water mark and induce employees to leave in search of better remuneration).

- The managers are failing to respond promptly to communications or are obfuscating in some other manner.

Monitoring hedge fund investments involves many of the same methods used in selecting them. Managers should be interviewed periodically and telephoned in the interim. Their performance should be tracked both on a monthly basis and intra-month where possible. Attempts should be made to predict likely future returns and changes in correlations with other investments. Regular investment commentaries from hedge fund managers should be screened for changes in their investment outlook and important organizational developments. Their exposures should be monitored and assessed within the context of the other hedge funds within a portfolio.

Monitoring hedge fund exposures is important, lest individual managers stray from their strategies or groups of managers display signs of herding into the same investment ideas. It is not a straightforward exercise, particularly if efforts are made to consolidate reporting from different hedge funds to assess the underlying exposures of an entire portfolio of hedge funds. Most equity long–short funds circulate summaries of their month-end long, short, net and gross exposures. However, they present these summaries in various ways, using their own sector and regional definitions. By the time investors get this information it is generally hopelessly out of date and it does not necessarily reflect a manager's behaviour intra-month. While most managers are prepared to release the names of their largest long positions, few will declare their short positions in print. Furthermore, it is very difficult for managers of arbitrage funds to convey their exposures in this manner. The dollar values of their long and short positions are poor indicators of their alignment and of the risk levels in their portfolios. Investors must therefore tailor their approach to analysing the exposures of each of their hedge fund holdings.

Finally, it is worth pointing out that prime brokers usually monitor the portfolios of the hedge funds they act for, subjecting the portfolios to extensive risk analysis. Many hedge fund managers find their prime brokers' risk systems to be so comprehensive that they too come to rely on them for their own risk monitoring purposes. Investors must not allow this independent risk monitoring to give them comfort. The interests of prime brokers are not aligned with those of a fund's investors. Prime brokers make money from providing leverage and are inclined to encourage a hedge fund to take on as much leverage as they consider 'safe'. Prime brokers can lend a great deal of money to a hedge fund 'safely' because the assets in a fund are generally very good collateral. These assets belong to the fund's investors, and by encouraging hedge fund managers to borrow against them the brokers place these assets in jeopardy. Thus, if anything, the risk monitoring activities of prime brokers serve to undermine the interests of a hedge fund's investors.

# ORGANIZING HEDGE FUND RESEARCH

## Features of a successful research effort

Although it is decidedly less glamorous, researching hedge funds involves many of the same disciplines as military intelligence gathering. Both involve collecting information from a wide variety of sources, interpreting it, communicating it and acting upon it. Imposing some of the disciplines used by military intelligence is therefore quite a useful exercise.[9] There is nothing particularly revolutionary about these disciplines but adhering to them improves efficiency.

Effective research is well organized, accurate, timely, honest, objective and complete. We can break down the 'research cycle' into this series of activities:

1. **Requirement.** At all times bear in mind the 'research requirement'. The overriding aim is to ascertain:
   - whether a fund will make money and under what circumstances;
   - what pattern these returns will take;
   - the extent and nature of the risks involved.
2. **Collection.** Decide what information to gather to satisfy this requirement and what the sources are. Then collect the information.
3. **Collation.** Once collected, information must be drawn together into good order, so that it can be referred to, interpreted and stored for future reference.
4. **Interpretation.** Information for its own sake is useless. It must be interpreted and conclusions drawn from it.
5. **Communication.** Information is only useful if effectively communicated to the decision makers, be they a team or an individual.
6. **Action.** Conclusions must be acted upon, not ignored.

## Collection

Anyone who has been investing in hedge funds for a while has a good idea of what information is needed and how to find it. For those new to the area things may not be so obvious. Before starting a new project, military intelligence identifies its 'essential elements of information'

---

9. See Hughes-Wilson (1999).

and then designs a 'collection plan' to gather them. In case it helps, here is a collection plan for hedge funds. The table illustrates that research into hedge funds requires investors to draw upon a wide range of sources. No single source can be relied upon to provide the full picture.

Manager meetings are the most important means of establishing a good understanding of a hedge fund. When managers respond to a question it is not so much the answer they give that matters, as how sensibly the answer is given. Managers of different funds are likely to disagree on investment policy, which is healthy and to be encouraged. Yet it would be unsettling if a potential investor in a hedge fund, coming from a position of relative ignorance, raised an issue that had not already been addressed in a manager's mind. Managers are obviously very busy and some discretion is required when investors call upon their time. It is also worth being careful how meetings are conducted. It is the investors' duty to establish a good understanding of how a fund is managed and awkward questions must be asked, so long as they are asked courteously. Antagonizing a hedge fund manager must be avoided, as it is only by maintaining a good relationship that information continues to flow.

Questionnaires are rarely a good substitute for a meeting and they can overlook important issues specific to a manager. Busy fund managers fit their responses to the questions asked. Face-to-face meetings allow investors to interpret more accurately the answers given by managers and to delve deeper when necessary. Many successful hedge fund managers limit the number of clients they deal with and do not have time to fill in questionnaires. Investors who want them completed should fill them in themselves, using information gathered from a range of sources. Any unanswered questions they should save for a manager interview.

Collecting monthly performance data is another key task for the hedge fund investor. Estimates of the number of hedge funds in existence vary but by some measures it is as many as 6,000. Unfortunately there is no easy way to collect performance data on these funds. There is a range of data vendors collecting figures for slightly different but overlapping groups of funds, yet none covers the entire universe.[10] This is partly because different hedge funds each choose to report to a slightly different selection of vendors and partly because some hedge funds choose not to report to data vendors at all. Because many hedge

---

10. Data vendors include MAR Hedge, HedgeFund.net, Altvest, TASS Tremont, Van Hedge, Eurohedge, HFR and Hennessee.

Essential elements of information — A collection plan for hedge funds research

| Essential elements of information (Sources) | Manager meetings | Routine phone calls to manager | Client relations executive | Manager newsletters | Manager website | Prospectuses | Monthly performance data | Mid-month performance | Industry contacts/rumours | Presentations/conferences | Industry journals/websites | Third parties | References/private investigators | Top-down strategy indicators | Prime brokers | Questionnaires |
|---|---|---|---|---|---|---|---|---|---|---|---|---|---|---|---|---|
| **Fund strategy and process** (Idea generation, Research approach, Decision making, Implementation, Instruments used, Portfolio construction, Portfolio monitoring, Degree of directionality, Style) | X | X | X | X | X | X |  |  | X | X |  |  |  |  | X | X |
| **Outlook for strategy/asset class** (Define favourable/dangerous market environments, Current expectations for environment, Current fund strategy) | X | X | X |  |  | X | X | X |  | X | X |  | X |  | X | X |
| **Historical performance** (Periods of strong and weak performance, Changes made, Example trades, Target return profile) | X | X | X | X | X | X | X |  |  |  |  |  |  |  |  |  |
| **Business model** (AUM, Investor concentration, Revenue, Firm capital, Parent/owner, Overheads, Use of Deferral of incentive fees, Consultants or sub-advisors, Back-up arrangements, Accounts, Other business interests) | X | X | X | X | X | X |  |  |  |  |  |  |  |  | X | X |
| **Management and staff** (Decision making structure, Lead managers, Analysts, Operations, Changes, Remuneration, Ownership) | X |  |  |  | X |  |  |  |  | X |  |  |  |  | X | X |
| **Personal qualities** (Intelligence, Judgement, Technical knowledge, Experience, Humility, Integrity, Stability of personality, Discipline, Ambition) | X | X |  |  | X |  |  | X |  |  |  | X |  |  |  |  |
| **Risk management** (Leverage: net/gross, Borrowing, Derivatives, Limits & diversification: Country, Theme, Sector, company, liquid positions, Asset cap, Hedging: risks hedged, methods used, Other: system, risk manager, Stop-losses, Time to liquidate) | X | X | X |  | X | X | X | X |  |  |  |  |  |  | X | X |
| **Reporting and transparency** (Prices, Reports, Portfolio transparency, Availability of manager) | X | X | X | X |  | X | X | X |  |  |  |  |  |  | X | X |
| **Operations and due diligence** (Dealing, Administration, Custody, Prime brokerage, Legal, Auditor, Compliance, Regulator, Pricing, References Background verification) |  | X |  |  |  | X | X |  |  |  | X |  |  |  | X | X |
| **Fund structure** (Legal entity, Domicile, Fee structure, Dealing, Open/closed) |  | X |  |  |  | X |  |  |  |  |  |  |  | X |  | X |

**Figure 3.1** A collection plan for hedge funds research
Source: author.

funds have limited capacity to accept new investors there is often little incentive for them to broadcast their results. Other hedge fund managers distrust the ability of data vendors to report their results accurately, and mistakes are indeed fairly commonplace. Investors must therefore rely on a mix of data purchased from a selection of vendors and data received directly from the managers with whom they have established contact. Collecting these monthly performance figures can amount to a full-time job. In addition to monthly performance figures, many investors choose to collect weekly performance estimates directly from those managers with whom they have investments. These provide an early warning of unfolding problems and enable investors to monitor whether intra-month volatility exceeds volatility on a month-to-month basis.

## Collation

The 'collection plan' above illustrates just how many sources of information there are. These need to be drawn together so that they can be interpreted and communicated. Piling bits of paper into a file is not an efficient way to approach this task. The larger the team of analysts, the greater the need for standardized written reports that incorporate both qualitative analysis and written interpretation of quantitative analysis. Formal reports have a number of advantages:

- Large amounts of information from numerous sources can be collected and stored efficiently, rather than being forgotten. This ensures that subsequent research covers fresh ground.

- A standardized layout allows different members of the team to read each others' reports quickly, knowing where to look for specific items of information.

- Standardizing the reports also acts as a research discipline, ensuring that each key issue is addressed on each occasion.

- The reports should be a fluid work in progress, regularly being updated to reflect changing circumstances.

Just as qualitative information needs to be carefully arranged, monthly performance figures need to be stored in a database attached to a statistical software package.[11] This data needs to be carefully categorized to allow each hedge fund's performance to be compared against an appropriate peer group.

---

11. Packages currently on the market include PerTrac, LaPorte and FinLab.

## Interpretation

Decision making is assisted by written reports that are conclusive rather than ambivalent. While interpretation should always be distinguished from fact, interpretation should be included. To this end, scoring systems based upon a series of criteria may prove useful. There is no need to attach much importance to total scores, as it is the act of highlighting a fund's strengths and weaknesses that really counts. The exercise imposes a degree of objectivity on an assessment process which can otherwise be completely subjective.

Once considerable efforts have been made to collect performance data it is important to study and question it. Maintaining a focus list of hedge funds and studying their results as they are published each month helps investors to build a feel for how specific managers and hedge fund strategies are behaving. An 'exceptions report' that automatically highlights monthly performance numbers that break a fund's usual pattern of returns is a useful device. It acts as a prompt for the investor to call the managers for an explanation. Routinely screening the entire database and specific peer groups is useful for generating the occasional investment idea and as a means of monitoring the performance of existing investments. In addition to these quantitative studies of groups of funds, interpretation of statistical analysis should be incorporated into qualitative reports on specific managers.

## Communication

There is a natural tendency for teams of busy individuals, each swamped with information, to fail to keep each other fully appraised of important issues. All too often relevant facts get stuck within the brains, files or computers of information gatherers without being transferred to decision makers. The larger the team, the harder it is to communicate with everyone within it. Poor communication wastes effort and increases investment risk. Glancing once more at the 'collection plan' above reminds us just how much information flies around a team of hedge fund investors. Establishing methods that ensure good communication within the team is therefore essential. Written reports on individual hedge funds are one example of this. However these can grow to be large documents. They are useful when decision makers pause to consider a specific investment in detail, but additional mechanisms are needed to handle the day-to-day news flow. Simply bringing the team together for regular meetings is not enough. People forget what they wanted to say and there is not time for everyone to say it. One answer is to circulate a weekly log of news items to which all members of the team contribute. This log can be used to capture:

- news flow that is particularly relevant to the team's current and prospective investments, including points from articles in trade journals, telephone conversations with managers, conference speakers or gossip from other industry practitioners;

- a short summary of each manager meeting held by a member of the team over the week;

- concise points drawn from the monthly newsletter received from each fund in which the team is invested.

Drawing key points from manager newsletters is particularly useful. If a team oversees a relatively large number of investments it should not be necessary for every team member to read every monthly report. Yet if these news logs are circulated the whole team's attention is drawn to the key issues faced by every one of its managers.

## Organizing a team

It is not always necessary to employ large numbers of analysts to establish an effective hedge fund research effort. The number of employees required is proportionate to the number of investment positions being taken. This is in turn linked to the size of assets being allocated.[12] More important than the size of the team is the experience of its members. Remember the research cycle at the beginning of the chapter. A large team of analysts can collect large amounts of information. Without experience, however, they will be less able to interpret it and to draw the appropriate conclusions.

It is currently fashionable to divide teams of analysts into hedge fund strategy specializations. This means they are likely to develop a greater understanding of their specific areas, which can be particularly useful if they are less experienced or have prior experience in their field of specialization. However specialization by strategy weakens analysts' perspectives and makes it harder for them to contribute to the asset allocation process.

---

12. Because it can be difficult to allocate very large sums to hedge funds, a larger pool of assets generally forces investors into a larger number of positions. Therefore the size of the assets being managed generally determines the size of the team required.

# CONCLUSION

The appendices to this chapter provide a more detailed list of issues that might be addressed as part of the analysis process. An analyst's work is never complete, but limits have to be set and it would be impractical to address every single issue in every single instance. Some discretion is required. However, the chapter illustrates that cursory analysis of hedge funds leaves many questions unanswered, and that proper analysis requires considerable effort. Hedge funds are complex creatures and it is worth examining them properly in order to prevent unpleasant surprises.

# APPENDIX 1: EXAMPLE MARKET INDICATORS FOR STRATEGY ASSESSMENT

For various fixed income strategies:

- US swap spreads, as a measure of market stability;
- credit spreads, across the range of credit ratings;
- yield curve steepness;
- total returns for high yield, distressed and bankrupt bond indices;
- MBS option adjusted spreads, MBS spreads over LIBOR and MBS average life;
- TED spreads;[13]
- swaption volatility.

For convertible arbitrage:

- historic equity price volatility and implied volatility (such as the VIX index);
- convertible bond indices by region (broken down to show total return, yield, premium and equity price return).

For equity strategies:

- trading volumes;
- put to call ratios;

---

13. The spread between the prices of the US T-bill future and the Eurodollar future.

- advance–decline line;
- level of short interest;
- equity indices;
- value, growth, largecap, midcap, smallcap indices and their relative performance.

For merger arbitrage:

- merger volumes (US and Europe);
- daily returns published by various merger arbitrage funds and daily merger arbitrage indices.

For CTAs and global macro:

- trends in currencies;
- trends in bond and equity markets;
- trends in commodity prices.

General:

- hedge fund indices by strategy.

# APPENDIX 2: QUALITATIVE ANALYSIS CONSIDERATIONS

## Strategy and process

- What is the basic investment strategy and focus of the fund?
- How does the manager describe the investment process? How rigidly is this 'process' adhered to and is this appropriate?
- Within this context, what is the manager's particular investment philosophy and style?
- What methods does the manager use to generate investment ideas and are they effective?
- How is research conducted, what does it consist of and what are the sources? Is it sufficiently detailed given the investment strategy? Does either the approach to research or the depth of research suggest that the manager will be better informed than the general marketplace?

- Is use made of external research partners or consultants?

- How are investment decisions taken, when and by whom?

- When investment decisions are taken, how are they implemented, when and by whom?

- Does decision making appear decisive or rash, indecisive or cautious?

- How is the fund's investment universe defined? What is the range of financial instruments used? In what contexts will different types of instrument be used?

- What approach does the manager take to portfolio construction? How concentrated is the portfolio, what defines the largest positions and what is the manager's approach to correlation between positions?

- How are investments monitored and managed? Are there defined entry and exit strategies and how strictly are they applied?

- What is the level of portfolio turnover and why is it appropriate to the strategy being followed? Does higher portfolio turnover imply paucity of research or does it help to diversify the risk associated with specific investment decisions?

- To what extent is the strategy either 'hedged' or 'directional'? Under what sort of circumstances might the hedging become less effective, causing the fund to behave in a more directional manner?

- When the manager describes example investments in detail does this illustrate analytical depth and cast light on the manager's approach?[14] Are the examples consistent with the manager's stated investment process? How sensibly has the manager dealt with both successes and failures? Have entry and exit policies been adhered to?

- How has the investment strategy changed over time, how might it change in the future and under what circumstances? How do past changes cast light on past performance?

---

14. Depending on the type of strategy employed it is often useful to discuss just one or two investment positions at considerable length, examining all the research relating to them and discussing the events that led up to the establishment and liquidation of the position. This procedure illustrates the investment strategy that has been described and often raises important questions. In addition it often endorses or undermines a manager's claim to in-depth research. Some managers bring out large files or written research documents accompanied by appropriately detailed financial models. Others seem unable to demonstrate that they have verified their simple investment thesis and a flaky research process is shown up.

## Top-down considerations

- What types of market environment are favourable or dangerous for the fund, given the general strategy employed and its specific style? In what sorts of circumstances might the fund face extreme difficulties and how large might the resulting drawdown be?

- What are the warning signs of impending trouble for the fund and how can these be monitored by the investor?

- Given the fund's specific style within the strategy it follows, how will the movements of certain key variables affect the fund (interest rates, bonds, credit spreads, volatility, currencies, equities, growth equities, value equities, specific sectors and so on)?

- Does the fund offer the potential for positive returns in a bear market?

- What is the manager's outlook for the strategy and on what factors does this outlook depend?

## Performance comment

- How does the manager explain periods of past performance that were noticeably weak or strong?

- Were changes made as a result and do they seem sensible? Does the manager seem to have foresight or do past events make the manager seem reactive?

- Have any particular positions or allocation policies been responsible for driving periods of positive or negative performance? How repeatable are these decisions, positive or negative?

- Does the manager have stated target ranges for return, volatility and correlation with other assets? Have they been met and how have these targets been changed?

- What sort of drawdown does the manager consider a disaster?

- Were early performance numbers generated from a fund that was small in size? Is the fund now larger and has growth in assets under management jeopardized the manager's ability to sustain the level of returns? What are the expectations for the future in this regard?

- Is the manager's stated performance record continuous? Have the records of different investment vehicles been strung together or performance numbers simulated in any way?

- Is the offshore fund's performance record similar to that of the onshore fund? If there are meaningful differences then why?

- Is there such a thing as an appropriate benchmark or comparison index for the fund?

## Management and staff

- Who are the lead managers and what are their backgrounds?

- Who are the analysts and what are their backgrounds? Are there enough and are they sufficiently qualified?

- How is the investment team structured and where does decision making responsibility reside?

- If there is a single lead manager for a fund, is there a number two capable of taking over in the event that the lead manager is travelling or incapacitated?

- What operational personnel support the fund and who are they?

- Have there been significant changes in the investment team since the fund was launched and what explanation is given for them? What is the general level of employee turnover and what plans are there for changing the team?

- On what basis are key employees remunerated? Is ownership in the management firm on offer to managers and analysts? Is the performance fee shared by the lead managers with employees? On a discretionary or fixed basis? Do different investment teams share the profits of their business units with each other? Are analysts rewarded on the basis of their individual contribution or as part of a team? Are these arrangements likely to be sufficient to retain and incentivize the employees?

- To what extent do the lead managers and analysts invest in their funds and into which specific products (on or offshore)? What percentage of their liquid net worth is invested in their funds? To what extent are performance fees deferred and kept within the funds?

- Given the fund's performance and its high water mark, do performance fees provide a realistic and attractive incentive?
- Is any part of the portfolio farmed out to third parties?[15]

## Personal qualities

- How are the staff viewed by their peer group?
- How committed are they to their enterprise? How involved do they seem?
- Might they seek to sell their business?
- What are their career plans? If they are approaching retirement are there suitable plans for a handover of control?
- Do the lead managers have the nine essential attributes: intelligence, good judgement, technical knowledge, experience, humility, integrity, a stable personality, discipline and ambition?

## Risk management (leverage)

- Is leverage used and on what basis?
- How does the manager define leverage?
- What are typical and maximum exposures on a long, short, net and gross basis?
- If relevant, are these exposures very different on a beta-adjusted basis?
- Is this leverage appropriate, necessary and safe given the strategy being pursued?
- How is leverage achieved (through borrowings, investing the proceeds of short sales or through derivatives)?
- If derivatives are used how is their contribution to the fund's overall exposure being calculated and communicated to investors?[16]

---

15. Some hedge fund managers farm out small portions of their portfolios to smaller independent fund managers. Sometimes these are talented former employees who have left to set up on their own and whose idea flow is considered valuable. At other times it can be a sign that a fund has reached a size where the manager struggles to get it invested.
16. For example, are exposures derived from option positions stated in terms of their delta-adjusted exposures or in terms of the notional underlying exposure?

- What limitations are imposed by the fund's leverage providers and is the fund well within its borrowing limits?

- What are the risks of a sudden withdrawal of a borrowing arrangement or a sudden increase in margin requirements? Does the firm keep enough unencumbered cash to meet margin calls under extreme circumstances? Have leverage providers ever withdrawn lending suddenly or sharply increased margin requirements for the fund? How much care have the managers taken in reviewing leverage agreement documentation?

- With how many different leverage providers does the fund have a borrowing arrangement?

- Are borrowing arrangements sufficiently secure in relation to the liquidity of the securities into which the fund invests (is the fund 'borrowing short term and lending long term')?

## Risk management (limits, diversification and liquidity)

- What is the manager's general approach to diversification?

- What concentration limits are specified in the fund's offering documents?

- In practice, what concentration limits does the manager impose (by issuer, by individual position size, by theme, by sector, by market cap, as a percentage of a day's trading volume, or by country)?

- To what extent does the fund contain illiquid positions? How does the manager measure position liquidity?

- To what extent are the fund's more liquid positions likely to become illiquid in adverse conditions?

- Without incurring significant cost, how long would it take to liquidate the portfolio under both current and adverse conditions?

- What might the cost be if liquidation had to be effected very rapidly, after accounting for the effect of any leverage used?

- What limits are placed on the size of the fund and on similar funds managed by the same firm? Bearing in mind that trading volumes can decline, do these limits preserve the manager's ability to manoeuvre the portfolios? Is the size of the fund likely to restrict the managers' ability fully to invest the fund in attractive opportunities?

- To what extent does the fund invest in OTC products? How easy is it to liquidate these positions?

- What were the greatest redemptions experienced by the fund, what caused them and what was the effect?

## Risk management (hedging)

- What sources of risk does the fund hedge against (such as equity specific risk, broad market risk, interest rate risk, yield curve risk, credit risk, prepayment risk, or currency risk)?

- How tightly are specific positions and the overall fund hedged?

- Which methods or instruments are used for hedging purposes? What are their limitations and dangers?

- What sources of risk (and return) does the manager deliberately leave unhedged and why?

- Is the fund left exposed to elements of risk which the manager has failed to identify?

- Does the manager employ or rely on 'cross hedging' (and is this appropriate)?[17]

## Risk management (other)

- Are potential investments assessed for their contribution to a portfolio's risk before they are added to the portfolio (or is the impact apparent only as part of a later monitoring process)?

- What systems are used to measure risk exposures within the fund (do the managers use VaR, stress testing or scenario analysis)? Are the limitations of these systems acknowledged or do the managers place undue faith in them?

- How frequently is the portfolio reviewed in these ways?

- Is there a designated risk manager? If so what powers does he or she have to rectify risk within the portfolio or to prevent it from arising?

---

17. 'Cross hedging' refers to an attempt to hedge a position with an indirectly related security. For example, a team of Asian equity long–short managers may decide that a weakening Yen will undermine the competitiveness of exporters in Asia ex-Japan, where they have investment positions. They may decide to hedge their investments in Asia ex-Japan by shorting the Yen, the principal threat to their investment thesis. The limitations of this hedge are obvious. Their investments may be negatively affected by issues other than the weakness of the Yen, the Yen may strengthen without a corresponding benefit to the Asia ex-Japan exporters, a relationship between the two may be non-linear and it may change over time. Very often cross hedging is a poor excuse for proper protection where more appropriate hedges have proven difficult to find.

- Are stop losses employed? If so, how are stop losses set and what are the procedures once a level is breached? How strictly are such procedures observed in practice?

- Do the managers set target levels when they establish new positions? On what basis are such targets set and how strictly are they observed?

- Do the managers think laterally in a search for other hazards that have not been highlighted by market history or personal experience?

- How do the managers react in the absence of sufficient investment opportunities? Would they maintain high cash levels, increase their position sizes in the few remaining opportunities, add leverage to a portfolio of modestly performing positions or stray into new areas?[18] If they were to move into new areas, how would they reassure investors they had sufficient expertise to do so?

- What is the extent of counterparty risk and what measures do the managers take to limit counterparty risk? (See also 'Due diligence considerations'.)

## Reporting and transparency

- What methods are used to communicate performance results to investors and how promptly is this information disseminated? Are mid-month performance estimates available and how accurate are they likely to be?

- What reports are sent to investors (monthly or quarterly investor letters)? How thorough and informative are these reports? What level of detail do they provide in terms of the portfolio (position names and portfolio breakdown by country, sector or other relevant categories)? How promptly are these reports sent?

- What level of transparency does the manager provide? Are full portfolios available on a current or delayed basis?[19] Would these be informative?

---

18. The best response is almost always to maintain high cash levels until opportunities present themselves once more. The investors can then decide whether or not to wait with the fund for the environment to improve. Concentrating positions or adding leverage tends to be dangerous.

19. Many managers are understandably wary of publishing their portfolios as they fear being manipulated by other market participants. They are most often reticent to disclose their short positions. However managers who publish their portfolios, even on a delayed basis, reassure investors greatly. Publishing their portfolio acts as a check and balance on their behaviour. Because they know that at least some of their investors will review their portfolio some of the time they are less likely to stray from their stated investment parameters.

- Are the managers available for reasonably regular meetings with their investors?

- Is there a client relations executive with a good understanding of the portfolio to field questions in the interim? Is there an informative Web site for investor communication?

- Do the managers supplement such meetings with regular conference calls?

- How does the manager keep investors informed during periods of extreme market turbulence?

## Terms

- What are the fund's fees and are they acceptable (including management fees, incentive fees, administrative fees, custodial fees)?

- Is there a fee for early redemption and if so how is it applied? If there is an early redemption fee, is it payable to the fund or to the manager?

- Are the fees calculated in an acceptable fashion? Does the incentive fee incorporate a high water mark? Is there a hurdle rate before incentive fees are payable?

- At what point or points in the year does the incentive fee crystallize? How might this affect the amount of fees paid and how might it affect the manager's investment policy in advance of those points?

- What is the minimum investment and minimum size for additional allocations? Is this minimum sufficient given the manager's client relations resources and the possible need to interact with many small investors?

- What are the subscription dates and arrangements for the fund?

- What are the redemption dates for the fund? How much notice is required for redemptions? What is the minimum period for which an investor must remain with the fund (lock-up period)? Does the manager enforce redemption restrictions rigidly or flexibly? Does the explanatory memorandum permit the manager to limit the percentage of the fund redeemed at any one redemption date? Once investors have redeemed, what sort of delay precedes the return of their cash?

- Are the redemption provisions sufficiently strict to protect loyal investors from the effects of a sudden wave of redemptions? Are they sufficiently lenient to provide investors with sufficient flexibility?

- Have any other investors arranged alternative terms through a side letter? If so what are these terms and why has the manager agreed to them?[20]

## Overview and conclusions

- What is the basic investment strategy and focus of the fund?

- Within this context, what is the particular investment philosophy of the managers?

- What is the background of the managers?

- Can key strengths and weaknesses of the managers' strategy be identified?

- How do the managers differentiate themselves and what is their edge over the competition?

- Who is the competition and what sort of threat does it pose? Are competitors better?

- Can specific risks be perceived in relation to the managers' particular approach?

- What can be concluded about the attractiveness of the fund as an investment candidate?

# APPENDIX 3: OPERATIONAL DUE DILIGENCE CONSIDERATIONS

## Verification

Can the following be verified by studying the fund's documentation and material contracts (principally the offering documents but also the investment management agreement, administration agreement, prime brokerage agreement, articles of association and audited accounts):

---

20. Some investors place 'rolling redemptions notices' with their managers and then cancel them before every month-end. Effectively this shortens their notice period for redemption on that month when they decide not to cancel their rolling redemption (perhaps reducing it from a quarter to just a few days). This can be disruptive to a portfolio and is unfair on other investors. Be sure your managers do not tolerate this practice.

- The fund's domicile and where it is listed (if anywhere)?

- The fund's operating currency?

- The fund's promoter or sponsor?

- The administrators (including address, telephone and fax)?

- The prime brokers and the nature of the services they offer (which may include introductions to investors and rented office space)?

- The custodians (if different from the prime broker)?

- The fund's auditors and lawyers?

- The regulators for both the manager and the fund itself?

- Bank account details?

- The purpose of different share classes, if they exist?

- The fund's inception date, assets under management in the fund and the firm, contact name and contact details (including Web site)?

## Operations[21]

- Has the fund (or the manager) ever been involved in litigation?

- Does the manager have insurance to protect against litigation or gross error?

- What trade entry processing and allocation procedures are in place? If trades are not allocated *pari passu* between accounts what method is used for their allocation? In particular, what allocation differences are there between the onshore and offshore equivalent funds?

- What restrictions are made on employee trading?

- Besides managing the hedge fund, what other investment or management responsibilities does the manager have? How is time allocated between them?

- Does the manager have other business or personal commitments and how much time do they entail?

---

21. A 2002 study into hedge funds by Capco concluded that 50 per cent of hedge fund failures could be linked to operational issues. However, this figure relates principally to business model failures and frauds that operational due diligence might have uncovered. Only 38 per cent of failures were caused by investment risk alone.

- What trading and accounting systems are in place? How are the front and back offices separated? Is there an operations manual or other written policies?

- What are the firm's IT resources and are they sufficient?

- Does the firm have a good investor relations capability, either externally or in-house? Are these investor relations executives conversant with the details of the fund's strategy and the contents of its portfolio (or do they act just as intermediaries between clients and the manager)? Will these investor relations executives effectively reduce client demands on the manager's time while still providing clients with good access to information?

- What other office locations does the firm have and what are their functions in relation to the management of the fund?

- Does the manager have back-up facilities off-site and recovery procedures (particularly relevant in certain locations, vulnerable to extreme weather or terrorist attack)?

- If the lead manager is incapacitated, are there arrangements to hand over portfolio responsibility to a competent second in command or to liquidate the portfolio in an orderly fashion?

- Is there a nominated compliance officer or external compliance consultant? What is the scope of his or her authority?

- Does the administrator independently monitor compliance with the fund's offering documents?

- What procedures are in place for efficient margin and collateral management? Has the fund established netting agreements with counterparties?

- What source does the administrator use for corporate actions and what is the procedure for notifying the manager (particularly important for event driven strategies)?

- Has the fund ever suspended or delayed dealing? If so, what were the circumstances? Were redemptions ever made in specie?

- Has there ever been a meaningful dispute between the managers and their counterparties?

- Does the administrator have off-site back-up capabilities (particularly relevant for administrators located in areas vulnerable to hurricanes)? Are important documents routinely scanned by the administrator?

- Is the administrator regulated and by whom?

- Who owns the administrator and in what form?

- Does the administrator use electronic price feeds or does it rely on manual input (increasing the possibility of error)?

- Are there direct electronic links between the administrator and prime brokers for reconciliation and trade entry purposes?

- Does the custodian segregate assets in the name of the fund?

- How are the fund's cash balances held? At what banks and in what concentrations? (This is a particularly important issue for certain strategies where significant short sales may result in large cash balances and the associated credit risk of the banks where the cash is held. An offshore fund is particularly unlikely to receive compensation if its bank fails.)

## Business model

- What other funds or segregated accounts do the managers run?

- What are the fund's and the firm's assets under management? What is the approximate revenue given conservative return expectations? How much of this is paid away to third party marketers or a parent firm?

- Does the firm have soft dollar arrangements and how are these handled?

- What are the firm's approximate overheads and running costs (given office location, number of staff at various levels, costs associated with the particular strategy being pursued)?

- Is the firm likely to be profitable on the basis of its management fee alone? Is it relying on future growth in assets under management or securing a performance fee in order to reach profitability?

- Does the firm have its own capital reserves and of what magnitude?

- If the firm is operating at a loss, for how long will the managers be prepared to support the venture and how well equipped are they to do so?

- What is the investment management firm's competitive position? What are the prospects for demand for their services? What is the marketing strategy for the fund?

- Is the management firm owned by a larger organization? If so, how is the ownership split and what is the nature of the relationship with the parent firm? Does it provide stability or does it drain away profits?

- Are consultants or sub-advisors employed in the management of the fund and in what capacity?

- Who are the key investors in the fund and do they represent 'hot money'?

- How concentrated is the investor base? (Investor concentration leaves the manager more vulnerable to redemption orders from just a few clients. However an over-diversified client base makes it difficult for the manager to keep clients individually well informed.)

- Do other large hedge funds allocate money to the manager? (Some of the 'big name' hedge funds struggle to get their portfolios fully invested. They often parcel out portions of their portfolio to talented smaller managers. This can be very disruptive if the larger hedge fund piggy backs on the smaller manager's investment ideas, investing much larger sums in the same positions using the larger hedge fund portfolio. In this way smaller managers can find their small portfolios become unwieldy and illiquid. Where they exist, the basis of such relationships with larger hedge funds should be explored.)

- Likewise, does the manager provide any consulting services to other hedge funds?

## Fraud

- Is the investment management firm regulated? If so by whom and when was the last inspection? Are there any issues outstanding with regulators? Have there been any reprimands in the past?

- Can the backgrounds of the lead managers be checked, either directly or with the help of a private investigator?

- Can references be obtained from prime brokers, past employers, former colleagues, investors or competitors?

- Does the administrator confirm the fund's counterparties are as stated? (The prime brokers, custodians, bankers and auditors should all be as stated.)

- Does the fund have more than one prime broker or administrator? If so, why, and does this represent a risk?

- If the fund is new, has an auditor been appointed and are monthly NAVs being independently calculated?

- Has either the administrator or the auditor changed over the life of the fund and if so, why? Have the offering documents been redrafted over the life of the fund and if so, why?

- Does the administrator reconcile positions carefully with all custodians or prime brokers?

- Can the managers' leverage levels be verified by the administrator?

- Does the administrator employ suitable methods for pricing the portfolio? Are all prices obtained from independent sources and what are these sources? Does the manager provide prices for any of the assets within the portfolio, particularly unlisted securities or OTC derivatives? If so, why and what measures are taken to verify these prices? If brokers provide prices, what guarantees the independence of the brokers?

- Does the strategy or the pricing policy provide the scope for smoothing monthly performance figures and artificially lowering the volatility of results?

- Do the audited accounts highlight anything unusual or include any qualifications?

- Are ordinary shareholders granted voting rights (usually not)?

- Does the fund have heavyweight independent directors (usually not)?

- Does the fund centralize its trading? How are trades authorized and how is unauthorized trading prevented?

- Who has authority to move cash and securities? Are there limits imposed or are double signatures required?

- Are there clues about a manager's personal spending habits? Are these expenditures consistent with fund performance or personal background?

# APPENDIX 4: THE APPLICATION OF QUANTITATIVE PERFORMANCE MEASURES TO HEDGE FUNDS

It is helpful to consider each performance statistic from a number of different angles:

- The value for a statistic, expressed as a number, is relevant both since the launch of a fund and over other time periods. It can be illustrative to assess time periods that are both cumulative (one year, three years, five years and so on) and discrete (1998, 1999, 2000 and so on). To put them in context it is preferable to view each of a fund's statistics alongside those for appropriate comparison indices and peer groups.

- The results are easier to interpret when presented as bar charts. Bar charts without the exact numbers are vague, so they should not be a substitute.

- Performance statistics are often unstable over time. The causes of such instability are of interest to investors, perhaps reflecting the influx of assets under management or changes in a strategy's efficacy. It is therefore useful to compare certain statistics graphically on a rolling basis.

## Measures of risk

### Standard deviation
The standard deviation of monthly returns is a measure of volatility commonly used as a proxy for risk. By measuring the average difference between each monthly return and the mean monthly return, standard deviation illustrates the dispersion of returns and thus the volatility of a fund.

Standard deviation is usually used as a measure of 'total risk' because it reflects the contributions of market risk, security specific risk and other sources of risk within a single measure. It is therefore intended to measure the risk of entire portfolios rather than their individual components. Historical volatility should not be used in isolation as a measure for risk. It is important to place a fund's standard deviation in context by comparing it with that of other similar funds or with a reference index over an identical period. This illustrates whether managers have produced a lower-volatility alternative to investing conventionally (or to investing with a competitor).

Higher standard deviations reflect a greater dispersion of returns and therefore higher 'risk'. However some absolute return investors dislike the measure, because a fund that has a high mean return but few losing months may display high volatility due to variance in its positive performance. As absolute return investors, they do not equate upward volatility of returns with the concept of 'risk'. However it is worth considering the volatility of all returns, both positive and negative, because experience shows it is difficult to sustain volatile positive returns without incurring significant losses at some stage.

Absolute return investors have concerns other than straightforward volatility. One of the main concerns is significant drawdowns, which sometimes accompany smooth return profiles. The way in which standard deviation is calculated means that these large individual drawdowns are often 'averaged away' by otherwise steady returns. A single 10 per cent drawdown buried within a long track record can get lost within the averaging (that is, standard deviation does not always reflect negative skewness).

### Downward deviation

Downward deviation is a calculation similar to standard deviation which accounts only for those returns falling below a defined level (the minimum acceptable return, or 'MAR'). All returns above this level are discarded for the purposes of the calculation and the variance of returns from the defined level is measured (as opposed to measuring the variance about the mean). The defined level most often used is 0 per cent, since this allows investors to focus on a fund's 'negative volatility'. However some investors prefer to use a risk free rate as their MAR level, since they consider it unacceptable to under-perform cash. As with standard deviation, higher numbers indicate greater downward volatility.

Downward deviation is a popular alternative to standard deviation used by those investors who are unconcerned about upward volatility. However it seems unreasonable to suggest that volatile upward returns can be achieved without assuming risk. Therefore a low downside deviation figure can provide a false sense of confidence about the future. Many funds have had very few months in which they have underperformed the defined MAR level. Their downside deviation will have been calculated using very few data points and the measure will therefore illustrate very little.

### Loss deviation

The loss deviation is a measure of the volatility of negative months. The calculation is very similar to that for downside deviation but for two features. It refers strictly to negative returns rather than returns below any other defined level. In addition, the variance is calculated around the mean of the negative returns rather than around the defined MAR level.

This is quite a useful statistic but the fact that it measures the variance about the mean losing month means it is a little meaningless when viewed in isolation. It is best viewed in conjunction with the 'gain deviation', as this enables the investor to contrast the respective volatilities of the fund's positive and negative returns. If there is a clear disparity between the two it is worth asking the manager for an explanation. It is difficult to place either measure in context without clearly taking note of the mean negative month and the mean positive month.

### Gain deviation
The gain deviation is a measure of the volatility of positive months. The measure represents an equivalent to the 'loss deviation'.

### Maximum drawdown
The maximum drawdown is the largest 'peak to trough' percentage loss over the given period. This means the figure could span a period of performance including positive months that were followed by further negative months, taking the fund to new lows. The maximum drawdown shows the worst possible period an investor could have chosen to be invested in the fund.

When analysing hedge funds, maximum drawdown is an important complement to standard deviation because it highlights the sharp corrections that are often hidden within the standard deviation figure. It is sensible to examine not only the maximum drawdown but also a number of the largest drawdowns experienced by the fund. These should be compared with the performance of reference indices and competing funds over the periods that correspond to each drawdown. It is important to have these drawdowns explained by fund managers and to understand what has been done to reduce their occurrence in the future. It is worth reiterating that the absence of large drawdowns in the past does not mean they will not occur in the future.

### Beta
Beta measures the extent to which the returns of an investment reflect the returns of the market. After the historical returns of the investment have been plotted on the y-axis against the corresponding returns for a market index on the x-axis, beta represents the gradient of the line of

best fit. Therefore a beta of 0.8 infers that for every 1 per cent rise in the market the investment has tended to rise by 0.8 per cent. A higher beta is taken to infer that an investment incorporates more market risk, since large market moves are likely to be accompanied by large corresponding moves in the investment. Because beta is intended as a measure of market risk alone it is not intended to be used to assess entire portfolios, merely their components (it is assumed that other sources of risk are diversified away when investments are combined together to make a portfolio).

Beta is sometimes used when examining long-only funds to indicate the level of market risk that has been taken by a manager. However it is not a particularly useful measure to use in conjunction with hedge funds because the entire concept of a market index is an anathema. Hedge funds are designed to provide a return profile that substantially differs from a market index. A hedge fund's beta (or exposure to the market) is likely to arise from its net exposure, being the degree to which long positions exceed short positions. Many hedge funds maintain minimal net exposures and therefore the concept of beta to the market becomes meaningless. Even those hedge funds that typically maintain net long exposures are likely to manage their funds very actively. Their security selection differs greatly from 'the market' and net exposures (and thus the funds' betas) may be radically adjusted to reflect the managers' outlook. The beta of the historical returns of an actively managed fund is not a useful figure if the portfolio has changed in this way over time. It is more useful to ask the manager for the beta of the fund's portfolio as it is currently constituted. It can be useful to examine the evolution of a fund's rolling beta over time, as this may raise questions as to how the manager changed the way in which the fund was managed.

### Tracking error

Tracking error measures the standard deviation of a fund's returns relative to the returns of its benchmark index. It is used as a measure of risk: greater tracking error resulting from active management reflects greater deviation from a benchmark and an increased possibility that the benchmark will be underperformed. A perfectly indexed portfolio would have a zero tracking error and therefore no 'tracking risk'.

This is not an appropriate risk measure for hedge funds. First, they have no benchmark to under- or over-perform. Second, hedge funds are absolute return vehicles and risk is defined in terms of the possibility of incurring absolute losses, irrespective of how other assets are performing.

## Measures of risk-adjusted return

### Sharpe ratio

The Sharpe ratio measures how much a fund has returned for each 'unit' of risk taken. Although there are a number of ways of trying to express risk numerically, the Sharpe ratio incorporates the most common, standard deviation. The Sharpe ratio is calculated by taking a fund's excess return over cash and dividing it by the fund's standard deviation:

Sharpe ratio = (Fund's return – Risk free rate) / Fund's standard deviation

Higher Sharpe ratios are more favourable, indicating that a fund's return is sufficient to justify the associated volatility. Because standard deviation is considered to be a measure of 'total risk', the Sharpe ratio is usually considered appropriate for measuring entire portfolios, rather than components within them. If an investor is considering combining a series of funds together then it may be theoretically more correct to use the Treynor ratio to assess individual hedge fund investments. This is because the specific risk associated with individual hedge funds should be diversified away (the Treynor ratio uses beta as its measure of risk). However because of the meaninglessness of betas in relation to hedge funds the Sharpe ratio is a far more sensible tool to use at both the individual constituent and the portfolio levels.

The usefulness of the Sharpe ratio is limited by the use of standard deviation as a measure of risk. It is considered to be a particularly controversial measure when used with hedge funds because occasional severe losses may be hidden within a standard deviation figure. Because standard deviation has a number of competitors the Sharpe ratio should be used in conjunction with other risk-adjusted return measures.[22]

It is difficult to prescribe values that count as 'high' to these ratios because they greatly depend upon the environment. Therefore a fund's ratios are best compared with those of other assets. Ratios incorporating a risk free rate are usually quoted in conjunction with the rate used in their calculation, which should be appropriate to the time period involved. Without this notation it is not clear whether two different ratios should be compared at all. Note that for the Sharpe ratio a negative number should be disregarded. This is because once the numerator (or return) is negative, a higher denominator (risk)

---

22. Professor Sharpe recommended that his ratio be used in conjunction with 20 years of data. He would not approve of how the investment community applies his theories.

serves to reduce the extent of this negativity. It is would be unclear whether a less negative Sharpe ratio was the result of greater volatility (more unfavourable) or a less negative return (less unfavourable). You will observe that this also applies to the other measures of risk-adjusted return mentioned here (with the exception of the Jensen measure, which is not a ratio).

### Sortino ratio

The Sortino ratio is an alternative to the Sharpe ratio, using downward deviation as a measure for risk in place of standard deviation. The Sortino ratio is calculated by taking a fund's excess return over cash and dividing it by the fund's downward deviation. In doing so the Sortino ratio does not reflect the entire volatility of a fund, merely the 'adverse' volatility represented by those returns below the defined minimum acceptable return.

Sortino ratio = (Fund's return – Risk free rate) / Downward deviation

The pros and cons of using the Sortino ratio in preference to the Sharpe ratio are very much related to the relative merits of standard deviation versus downward deviation. Because it can be argued that upward volatility reflects risk, the Sharpe ratio may be the better measure. Furthermore, Sortino ratios are not very effective when used to analyse funds with very low volatility. Assuming the minimum acceptable return used to calculate the downward deviation is zero, the downward deviation may have been calculated using very few data points. Perhaps the Sortino ratio is a more illuminating measure for comparing more volatile investments. When using the Sortino ratio it is particularly important to be consistent. Both the risk free rate and the minimum acceptable return used for downward deviation need to be defined and held constant.

### Sterling ratio

The Sterling ratio is another competitor to the Sharpe ratio. It attempts to capture maximum drawdown as a measure of risk. The Sterling ratio is calculated by taking a fund's annualized return over the past three years and dividing it by the mean of the maximum drawdowns in each of those three years. The mean drawdown is reduced by an arbitrary 10 per cent as a means of scaling the ratio in a user friendly manner.

Sterling ratio = Fund's 3 year annualized return / (Mean of max drawdown in each year – 10 per cent)

The Sterling ratio can be a useful complement to volatility-based ratios because it encapsulates the risk of drawdown. However it is only of use in certain circumstances, and while it is important to examine drawdown figures they do not lend themselves to incorporation within ratios. The Sterling ratio is further limited by its three-year timeframe which may exclude significant positive returns or a large drawdown shortly before this period. In other circumstances it is rendered entirely redundant by the complete absence of a drawdown within the previous three years. This is a particular problem with some of the lower volatility arbitrage strategies. There may also be a distortion when a significant drawdown spanning a year-end is excluded from the calculation.

### Calmar ratio

The Calmar ratio is constructed in a similar manner to the Sterling ratio. However, in place of the three largest drawdowns in each of the past three years it uses the single largest drawdown over the entire three year period.

> Calmar ratio = Fund's 3-year annualized return / Max drawdown over past 3 years

The Calmar ratio is tainted by the same three-year restriction that affects the Sterling ratio. The question whether the fund experienced a particularly large drawdown within the last three years creates an even greater distortion in this instance. Calmar ratios for the period 1998–2001 would have changed beyond recognition during the period 1999–2002 as the events of 1998 rolled out of the data range.

### Treynor ratio

Similar to the Sharpe ratio, the Treynor ratio measures how much a fund has returned for each unit of risk it has taken. However the Treynor ratio uses a fund's beta as an appropriate benchmark as a measure of risk. It is calculated by dividing the fund's excess return by its beta.

> Treynor ratio = (Fund's return – Risk free rate) / Fund's beta

Since beta is intended as a measure of market risk alone, the Treynor ratio (and not the Sharpe ratio) should theoretically be used to assess individual hedge funds that are components of a broader portfolio. This is because of an assumption that non-market risks can be diversified away. In practice, however, the inapplicability of beta within a hedge fund context means that it is not a useful measure.

### Jensen measure (Jensen's alpha)

The Jensen measure differentiates between investment managers who have enhanced returns through active management and those who have simply increased returns by sustaining high betas during rising markets, thereby assuming additional market risk. The measure shows the difference in return achieved by the fund and that achieved by a benchmark portfolio that has the same beta ('market risk') as the fund. The beta-adjusted benchmark return is calculated using CAPM.

> Jensen measure = (Fund's return) – (Risk free rate + Fund's beta × (Market return – Risk free rate))

The Jensen measure is intended for assessing long-only mandates within a broader portfolio in situations where the level of market risk was specified within the mandate. Where an entire portfolio is being assessed the fund's beta can be substituted with a term reflecting total risk (the standard deviation of the entire portfolio divided by that of the market index). Both the Jensen measure and its amended alternative are difficult to apply to hedge funds because hedge funds are so difficult to compare with indices. Nevertheless the measure raises interesting issues, particularly with regard to equity long–short funds. Many equity long–short managers aggressively adjust their net exposures to reflect their expectations for the markets. Sometimes investors mistake these 'beta adjustments' for alpha generation. 'Beta adjustments' are far more risky than stock selection because the effect of the decisions is far more concentrated.

### Information ratio

The information ratio is a measure of risk-adjusted returns commonly used to assess long-only funds. The ratio treats deviance from a benchmark as the adoption of risk. It is calculated by taking the fund's annualized return, subtracting the benchmark's annualized return (the 'active premium') and dividing it by the fund's tracking error. The tracking error is defined as the standard deviation of the fund's returns relative to the benchmark. It is used as the term for risk on the basis that greater tracking error denotes greater inconsistency with and deviation from a benchmark. A higher information ratio implies a fund has outperformed its index in a consistent manner.

> Information ratio = Active premium / Tracking error = (Fund's annualized return – Benchmark's annualized return) / Annualized standard deviation of fund's relative returns

If a fund has consistently fallen by less than its index in a falling market then it is likely to have a high and positive information ratio. Bizarrely, it would be deemed to have delivered favourable risk-adjusted returns. The information ratio may be useful for analysing conventional investment portfolios, particularly if they are mandated to hug a benchmark. However, it is not a suitable measure with which to analyse a hedge fund. Absolute return investors do not consider consistently negative returns to be 'low risk' simply because they are similar to but less negative than those of an index.

## Measures of relationship

### *Alpha*

Alpha represents the element of a fund's return that is achieved regardless of the movement of the market. After the historical returns of the investment are plotted on the y-axis against the corresponding returns for a market index on the x-axis, alpha can be measured as the point where the line of best fit dissects the y-axis. If alpha is +0.5 per cent it implies that even in periods when the market index returns zero the investment still tends to return 0.5 per cent. Funds exhibiting high levels of alpha are recognized for their ability to generate positive returns without necessarily assuming market risk.

Alpha is sometimes employed when examining long-only funds to indicate the extent to which a manager's stock selection has added value over and above the manager's assumption of market risk. However the applicability of alpha in a hedge fund context suffers from the same problems as beta: it is very difficult to apply the concept of market indices to hedge fund strategies. A hedge fund may deliver high alpha in relation to a market index but this is probably because it is passively assuming a number of risks that are quite unrelated to a market index. It does not necessarily reflect 'stock selection skills'. Nevertheless, the fact that many hedge funds generate high alpha is commendable, however they achieve it. High alpha against conventional benchmarks indicates the funds are providing an alternative source of returns which is not the product of assuming conventional market risk.

### *Correlation*

Correlation measures the strength of relationship between two variables. If two variables tend to rise and fall simultaneously they are considered to be strongly correlated. If they tend to move in opposite directions they are considered to be negatively correlated. Correlation only measures the degree to which two variables move in the same direction and not the extent to which they move. Were two variables to be plotted against each other on a graph, highly correlated data points would lie close to the line of best fit.

Correlation is an important measure for hedge fund investors. One of the principal reasons for investing in hedge funds is their low or negative correlation with mainstream markets and with each other. Correlation is therefore a crucial means of assessing their usefulness as a diversification tool. However, investors must be particularly aware that correlations against mainstream markets and between different hedge funds often rise sharply at inopportune moments, such as during liquidity crises. It is therefore advisable to gain an understanding of the nature of different hedge funds and hedge fund strategies and how their correlation features are likely to change in the future. Because of the unusual and diverse nature of hedge funds, high historical correlation figures should be treated with extra care. The correlation may have been coincidental rather than the result of a real relationship. Historical changes in correlation should also be examined and interpreted.

Note that a fund producing consistent positive returns will have positive correlation to markets as they are rising and a negative correlation to markets as they are falling. The correlation to markets may be zero over the entire period and yet none of these three readings is meaningful. They may appear to indicate that there is no market relationship or risk. However, the strategy could nevertheless be 'at risk from the market': a sudden market shakeout might lead directly to a sharp disruption for the strategy.

A further correlation issue arises when a fund exhibits less correlation short term but more correlation in the medium term. Investors may get a false sense of security from a fund that exhibits a low monthly correlation with their portfolio, only to find that its quarterly correlation is somewhat higher. Where less liquid instruments are involved, this may well prove to be the case.

### R-squared
R-squared is simply the correlation figure squared. It is another means of expressing the closeness of a relationship between two variables but it does not distinguish whether correlation is positive or negative. With a long-only fund an R-squared of 0.8 is supposed to indicate that 80 per cent of the movements of the fund (the dependent variable) are the consequence of the movements of its market index (the independent variable). However this way of looking at things is generally

unconstructive with hedge funds: like teenagers, hedge funds are desperately seeking to gain their 'independence' from the 'independent variable'.

### Beta

Beta, referred to earlier as a measure of (market) risk, can also be thought of as a measure of relationship. In the hedge fund context beta is not very useful as a measure of market risk because most hedge funds are designed to neutralize market risks and to assume non-market risks in their place. However it can still be useful as a measure of relationship to complement correlation. Correlation merely indicates the extent to which two variables move in the same direction rather than how far they move. It reflects how close data points lie to the line of best fit. Beta indicates how far one variable moves in relation to the other. It reflects the slope of the line of best fit. As long as a meaningful correlation has been identified, beta can be useful when comparing a hedge fund with another asset (possibly another hedge fund).

### Comparisons with an index

Various measures can be used to compare a fund's returns with those of an index. 'Up capture' measures the extent to which a fund moves up during positive months for the index, expressed as a percentage of the index's positive gain. 'Down capture' measures a fund's loss during an index's negative months, expressed as a percentage of the index's loss. Investors can also examine the percentage of occasions in which the fund outperforms a falling market or a rising market. Such measures will not be useful unless there is some meaningful relationship between the fund and the index concerned. They can be interesting when examining the effectiveness of hedging in a long–short fund.

## Descriptions of data patterns

### T-statistic

T-statistics are a means of verifying the statistical significance of the product of a calculation. The measure takes account of the amount of data used and its dispersion. T-statistics are literally tests to show the extent to which a calculation's product is unlikely to be the result of a coincidence. In the context of fund analysis, using a minimum of three years of monthly data tends to increase the likelihood of statistical significance. This is an important measure as it can alert the hedge fund investor to an inadequate or unrepresentative data set.

### Skewness

Skewness characterizes the degree of asymmetry of a distribution around its mean. If a hedge fund's returns were plotted as a bell curve, positive skewness would indicate an asymmetric tail extending towards positive values. Negative skewness would indicate the opposite. This is an important measure for hedge funds because a number of hedged strategies typically exhibit positive mean returns but negative skewness, reflecting unusually severe negative months on occasion. Skewness can be used in conjunction with the analysis of drawdowns to complement Sharpe ratios.

### Kurtosis

Kurtosis reflects the extent to which the distribution of a fund's returns is peaked or flat relative to a 'normal' distribution. Positive kurtosis (leptokurtosis) is associated with return distributions that are more peaked in the centre (indicating consistency most of the time) but that have fatter tails (indicating a higher incidence of outlier months). Negative kurtosis (platykurtosis) reflects a relatively flat distribution and suggests that the fund's returns are 'all over the place'.[23] Many hedge fund strategies feature positive mean returns, positive kurtosis and negative skewness, reflecting consistently positive returns most of the time, punctuated by the occasional uncharacteristic losing period.

# APPENDIX 5: FACTOR ANALYSIS OF HEDGE FUND STRATEGIES

## Multiple regression

- A means of explaining the movement of a dependent variable (in this case a hedge fund strategy) in terms of the independent variables that drive it (such as the S&P 500 Index and credit spreads).

- The structure of a regression equation may be reasonably straightforward but arriving at an equation that fits well is a little more complicated. Given a set of factors, a programme can run through an iterative process that arrives at the most accurate fit. Then a series of different factors can be tested, using trial and error, in order to improve the results.

- A simple equation may be drawn up as shown in Figure 3.2.

---

23. The kurtosis of a normal distribution is 3. Kurtosis in excess of 3 signifies leptokurtosis and kurtosis below 3 signifies platykurtosis.

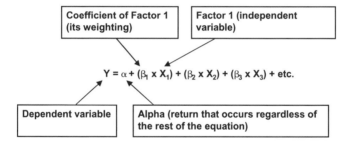

*Or, for example:*

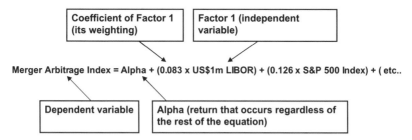

**Figure 3.2** Multiple linear regression explained
Source: author.

## How this might be useful

Clearly these equations are subject to all sorts of limitations. However, this sort of analysis can be a thought-provoking exercise, serving a number of purposes.

- **Factor identification for strategies (strategy analysis):** hedge fund strategies may be studied to ascertain which factors they are most sensitive to. This should improve investors' understanding of what drives each strategy.

- **Factor identification for funds (fund analysis):** this may also be an interesting exercise to conduct for individual funds, highlighting unusual influences that may contradict the picture that a manager has painted.

- **Factor forecasting for strategies (asset allocation):** drawing on their top-down views of the world, investors can make forecasts for a range of factors. These forecasts can be put into an equation to produce forecast returns for each hedge fund strategy. This can serve as an asset allocation tool, improving investors' understanding of the implications that their market expectations have for hedge fund strategies.

- **Portfolio factor exposures (risk control):** the make-up of a portfolio may be analysed in terms of the factors associated with the strategies (or funds) within it. For example, a study might highlight the undue sensitivity of a portfolio to movements in high yield.

- **Mid-month performance estimates (monitoring):** HFR now publish daily performance figures for a range of hedge fund strategies. However, they do not cover all strategies. Investors can use multiple regression models as a simple guide to the mid-month performance of those strategies that are not covered.

These modelling techniques are crude and they work better for some strategies than for others. In most instances investors will be unsurprised by the results of the exercise but from time to time unusual results may give investors pause for thought.

## Measuring an equation's explanatory power

The simplest measure of an equation's effectiveness is its $R^2$. An $R^2$ can be expressed as a percentage to indicate how much of the variations in a hedge fund strategy index can be explained by the movements of the factors. An $R^2$ in excess of 0.5 (50 per cent) starts to look quite powerful and can be achieved for a number of hedge fund strategies.

Those factors that have the most dependable relationships with each hedge fund strategy exhibit high 'T-statistics'. T-statistics measure the statistical validity of a relationship, and any number below –2 or greater than +2 is taken to indicate a dependable relationship.[24]

Factors that may prove to have informational content for hedge fund strategies include:

- CCC yields;
- the credit risk premium;
- the slope of the yield curve;
- Russell 2000;
- the spread between small and largecap equity performance;
- swap spreads;
- swaption volatility;

---

24. Investors who are going to embark on this exercise seriously ought also to consider a number of other tests of statistical significance, such as standard errors, F-statistics, and the adjusted $R^2$. They should also take steps to address MALTHS.

- 1 m LIBOR;
- the US$ trade weighted index;
- the spread between value and growth equity performance;
- VIX index.

## Some limitations of factor analysis

- Some strategies are relatively homogenous and straightforward and lend themselves to such modelling. Merger arbitrage may be one of these. Other strategies are much more difficult to model. For example, different convertible arbitrageurs employ a range of investment approaches and some vary their methods according to the environment.

- The factors in an equation are intended to be 'independent variables', meaning that they are the drivers of hedge fund strategy returns. However, a number of these factors are likely to be driven by other forces, such as general market-wide confidence levels. The independent variables may themselves be 'symptoms' rather than 'causes'.

- As a group, some strategies are likely to exhibit strong relationships with different factors over time. However, as per the previous point, these factors are themselves likely to be the prevailing manifestation of the market's appetite for risk (technology stocks, credit spreads and so on). This makes it harder to use such models for forecasting.

- Although relationships with various economic and market factors can be identified for hedge fund strategies, the nature of these relationships is often non-linear. It can be difficult to capture this non-linearity within a multi-factor model. Unless factors are included that reflect this non-linearity, these equations are likely to understate a hedge fund strategy's reaction to extreme market moves. The standard deviations of the returns predicted by a model are also likely to be lower than those actually realized.

- If a model is to be used for prediction then it may be necessary to forecast some of the model's factors, such as interest rates or equity market returns. Such forecasts are difficult to make with conviction. It may be necessary for investors to restrict themselves to simple factors that they feel more comfortable taking views on.

- Some of the factors that one would wish to include in such a model might not be available as a string of data.

- It is very easy to 'fit' these models and many of the suggested relationships may be spurious.

- Equations used to model a particular hedge fund strategy may not be good for explaining the returns of many of the individual funds that execute that strategy.

- There is a range of mathematical obstacles associated with multi-factor models that must be negotiated.

# 4

# Portfolio construction and management

Honesty pays, but it doesn't seem to pay enough to suit some people.

Kin Hubbard

A portfolio of hedge funds may be constructed and managed in a broadly similar manner to one made up of other assets. However, investors should adapt their approach to account for the particular liquidity and performance characteristics of hedge funds. A traditional portfolio construction approach would combine investments on the basis of their expected returns, expected volatilities and expected correlations. These might be estimated partly by examining historical figures and partly through predictions arising from fundamental analysis. As we shall see, this traditional approach is not as appropriate for portfolios of hedge funds as it is for portfolios of other assets.

## OBJECTIVES

Earlier in this book we discussed the risks and merits of hedge funds in an attempt to establish some realistic expectations for them. Later chapters will serve to highlight the diversity amongst different hedge fund strategies. It seems that hedge funds, in various combinations, can be used to meet four different types of portfolio objective:

- to diversify away from a mainstream portfolio, seeking positive returns but prioritizing low correlation with mainstream assets;
- on a stand-alone basis, as a capital preservation tool, seeking positive returns but prioritizing low volatility;
- as a means of gaining exposure to equity markets with less volatility than traditional long-only equity investment;
- on a stand-alone basis, for capital appreciation, seeking high returns whilst tolerating high volatility.

The chosen objective will influence the level of diversification required and the choice of hedge fund strategies.

# PORTFOLIO CONSTRUCTION IN THEORY

## Expected return and expected volatility

Traditional portfolio management theory calls for an estimation of the expected future returns and expected volatility of each investment within a portfolio. Quantitative analysis of past returns provide investors with a good insight into a hedge fund's history, but to judge its future one must supplement this with qualitative analysis.

Investors have a duty to devote time and energy to predicting which hedge fund will generate the most attractive returns in the years to come. In practice it is notoriously difficult to make such predictions with confidence. Instead, many investors in hedge funds find themselves constructing a portfolio by default. Specialist strategies are perceived to offer an inherent return to skilled practitioners, so that investors find themselves preoccupied with excluding those hedge funds whose approach is particularly flawed. This type of hedge fund selection is akin to credit work, whereby a portfolio's risk-reward is maximized by avoiding big mistakes rather than by identifying big winners.

Standard deviation is traditionally used as a measure of volatility for portfolio construction. This is problematic in the hedge fund context. The negative skewness of returns associated with many hedge funds can be obscured by the standard deviation measure because occasional but significant negative periods are likely to be averaged away. Negative skewness means that long periods of consistent returns belie the latent potential for sharply negative episodes. For this reason past and forecast measures of drawdown may be a more appropriate manner in which to consider risk.

## Correlation

The correlations between many hedge fund strategies appear to be negligible, which seems a good reason to combine different strategies within a portfolio. Often hedge funds pursuing the same strategy also exhibit low correlations with one another, so that it makes sense to diversify across funds within a strategy as well. These modest correlations seem to hold throughout most environments.

However, during periods of extreme volatility a number of otherwise unrelated hedge fund strategies suffer in tandem. Convertible bonds, distressed securities and asset backed securities become illiquid, forcing out bid–offer spreads and causing mark-to-market losses. Spreads on merger transactions widen, as uncertainties about deal completion increase and as arbitrageurs withdraw capital from the strategy. Some statistical and fixed income arbitrageurs suffer because normal relationships break down, exacerbating inefficiencies. Those CTA and global macro managers who are aligned with long-term trends will also be hit if the trends break. Some equity long–short managers may also suffer a correction if their positioning did not anticipate the shock. There is therefore a tendency for correlations between hedge funds to rise sharply as volatility spikes and returns plunge. At the very point investors most need hedge funds to provide capital preservation and diversification they may be let down. This tendency is pretty unappealing if the investor is seeking to meet the first three of the objectives listed above.

Therefore investors should not rely on correlation arguments to combine volatile investments in a portfolio in the hope that low correlations will result in modest portfolio volatility. Rather, when assembling portfolios it is sensible to forecast the likely maximum drawdown of each hedge fund. In the event that correlations between investments rise at inopportune moments the portfolio is likely to suffer a loss equivalent to the weighted average of these drawdowns. Accordingly, the risk and size of each portfolio component must be consistent with the risk profile targeted for the overall portfolio.

There is no mathematical formula for forecasting a hedge fund's maximum drawdown in a future liquidity crisis. Even if a fund's track record spans previous episodes of this kind it would be wrong to assume that similar performance could be expected in the future. Managers change their investment procedures in reaction to prior crises and yet each new crisis tends to present fresh challenges. Investors have no option but to conduct thorough qualitative research into each hedge fund and its risk controls. By combining this research with some fundamental understanding of each hedge fund strategy investors should be able to estimate a fund's potential drawdown.

This does not mean that correlations should be altogether ignored in portfolio construction. Reverting to our earlier observation, modest correlations seem to hold in most environments, so diversification on this basis does contribute to reducing portfolio volatility most of the time. Attempts should be made to forecast how correlated funds are likely to be in the future, on the basis of how they implement their investment strategies. However this should be part of a two-pronged approach that also considers the cumulative risk of the portfolio's components.

## Optimizing portfolios

Some hedge fund investors construct portfolios on the basis of mean–variance optimization. Although the technique appears scientific the approach is misguided. Mean–variance optimization is predicated on forecasting returns, standard deviations and correlations for each investment being considered for a portfolio. It would be impossible to place much confidence in such forecasts. In place of forecast figures many investors substitute historical figures for return, standard deviation and correlation. Yet these historical statistics tend to be unstable, especially the correlations between hedge funds. To complicate matters further, there is often insufficient data to run the model with confidence. Even if one had faith in the method, one would often find that small moves up or down the resulting efficient frontier suggested radically different combinations of hedge funds. In this context the optimizer is not an aid to decision making.

It is not only mathematics that makes optimizers inappropriate for hedge funds, it is the distinction between hedge funds and traded securities. Hedge funds are managed investment pools and their performance characteristics are deliberately manipulated over time by fund managers. They are also illiquid. Optimization may be helpful for constructing portfolios of liquid securities, particularly over short periods during which relationships are likely to hold steady. Yet hedge fund portfolios must be constructed for much longer periods, increasing the likelihood that the results of optimization become invalid over time.

This is not to say that investors must avoid the use of optimizers altogether. It simply means they should not be used for allocating portfolios mechanically. Reflecting on optimization studies can stimulate thought and occasionally illuminates hidden relationships. As with many quantitative techniques, optimization is better for posing questions than for answering them.

# PORTFOLIO CONSTRUCTION IN PRACTICE

Some broad generalizations can be made about the types of hedge fund strategy that are consistent with each of the four portfolio objectives mentioned earlier.

- Diversification: fixed income arbitrage; merger arbitrage; distressed securities; asset backed securities; statistical arbitrage; convertible bond arbitrage; equity long–short funds that assume low net exposure; CTAs and global macro funds.

- Capital preservation: conservative funds within fixed income arbitrage; merger arbitrage; distressed securities; asset backed securities; statistical arbitrage; convertible bond arbitrage and equity long–short.

- Low volatility equity exposure: conservative equity long–short and statistical arbitrage funds.

- Capital appreciation: aggressive distressed securities funds; aggressive convertible arbitrage; CTAs; global macro and aggressive equity long–short funds.

Portfolio construction should also reflect an investor's economic and market outlook and the hedge fund asset allocation decisions that spring from these views. Further discussion of how each strategy fares in different market conditions can be found in the chapters dedicated to each hedge fund strategy. Due to the illiquidity of hedge funds, asset allocation and fund selection decisions must be taken on a long-term basis.

Because they hedge their market exposures, it is not generally appropriate to allocate to hedge funds on the basis of their geographical focus. While many funds do profess to have a geographical focus, this simply reflects the pool in which they are fishing for absolute returns. The manner in which they generate these absolute returns and their assumption of risk define hedge funds, rather than the location of their investments. Furthermore, the geographical bias of hedge funds is lopsided. Most hedge funds focus their portfolios on the US markets. The United States was the birthplace of hedge funds and is arguably the world's most sophisticated financial market. The hedge fund talent pool is still concentrated in the United States and most arbitrage strategies are easier to execute there.

# DIVERSIFICATION AND RISK MANAGEMENT

The level of diversification appropriate for portfolios of hedge funds is a matter for debate. Each hedge fund is itself a diversified pool of investments, so combining even a few can result in exposure to a very large spread of underlying investment ideas. This point is used to argue against investing in too many funds. A contradictory point can also be used against over-diversification, namely that attractive investment opportunities are limited in number and most capable hedge fund managers identify the same ones. Consequently managers within each strategy tend to construct similar portfolios. Either which way, statistical studies suggest that holding many hedge funds provides little benefit by way of reducing portfolio volatility. Investing in too many funds is likely to result in thinner research into each investment. Mediocre research can contribute to increasing risk as opposed to reducing it. A smaller portfolio could be concentrated in higher calibre, better researched funds.

Against these arguments we must consider the dangers of over-concentration. The sad reality about the hedge fund universe is that it is subject to the occasional disaster. This is sometimes caused by manager error and sometimes by fraud, and it can result in an immediate loss of 50 per cent or more. As with many things in life, it is the least probable outcomes that pose the greatest threats. Thorough research helps investors avoid these accidents but provides no guarantees. Remember that fraud and rogue trading are notoriously difficult to spot from the outside. Using a credit investor's approach we can argue against allocating too much to any one vehicle. A compromise may therefore be the best solution. Investors who allocate less than 2 per cent of a portfolio to a hedge fund may be abrogating their decision making responsibilities. Those who allocate more than 15 per cent might be accused of being reckless. Depending on the portfolio objective, 3 per cent to 7 per cent is usually sensible.

These generalizations need adjusting for the types of fund being included. For example, merger arbitrage is a relatively homogenous strategy. At any one time the portfolios of merger arbitrageurs are likely to contain substantially similar positions. It is the manner in which the positions are assembled and traded that tends to differentiate the managers. Within merger arbitrage, diversification can be achieved by using relatively few managers. Convertible arbitrage, by contrast, can be conducted in a number of distinct styles and it is appropriate to invest across a broader range of managers in order to capture this diversity.

A constraining factor is the size of the assets being allocated. It can be difficult to place very large sums with hedge funds since most make a point of limiting their capacity. This means that the largest investors in hedge funds are forced either to allocate large sums to sub-optimal managers or to diversify widely. Either way, having too many assets to allocate to hedge funds is unwieldy and presents diversification problems. Having too few assets presents the opposite problem. Because minimum investments are usually US $1 million, a portfolio with less than US $10 or 20 million may not achieve proper diversification. Even this may not be enough, since most established hedge fund managers are in practice unwilling to accept investments as small as US $1 million.

Beyond referring to diversification it is difficult to embark on a discussion of risk management without sounding repetitive. Investment professionals who specialize in allocating to hedge funds are above all risk managers. All their efforts at qualitative and quantitative fund analysis, operational due diligence, allocation between hedge fund strategies, and fund monitoring can be interpreted as exercises in risk management. These efforts are primarily aimed at minimizing significant errors.[1]

# MECHANICS

A portfolio of hedge funds cannot be allocated and reallocated in the same manner as a portfolio of securities or mutual funds. Hedge funds are long-term investment vehicles and it is necessary to plan portfolio flows with much greater care. It is usually possible to make an investment into a hedge fund on a monthly basis. Yet because many of the better hedge fund managers have limited capacity for accepting new investors it can take time to place new money with hedge funds of

---

1. Investors may also wish to consider the concentration of their exposure to particular counterparties that arises through their hedge fund investments. Some investors monitor their underlying exposure to particular prime brokers and hedge fund administrators.

choice. Notice of between 30 and 90 days must be given before redeeming, which itself may only be permitted on a quarterly basis. Many funds will not permit redemptions within the first year of investment while others levy penalties for investors who withdraw capital after short periods of investment. Once a redemption has been made there is generally a delay of up to 30 days before capital is returned to investors, and even then just 90 per cent of the sum due is likely to be settled. The remaining 10 per cent may be withheld until after the annual audit is completed in case monthly valuations prove to have been inaccurate.

It is not merely redemption terms that make it difficult to switch in and out of hedge funds. Investors who invest and redeem too frequently will generate ill-feeling between them and their hedge fund managers. Fickle investors may be barred from investing in certain funds altogether. Investors must maintain good relationships with their hedge fund managers so that they can monitor their investments. This improves their access to information and their ability to secure limited investment capacity when required. It is therefore crucial to build a reputation as a fair but loyal investor. Such considerations must be balanced against the need to redeem from hedge funds when there are good reasons for doing so. However, it is advisable to invest in hedge funds with a minimum intended investment horizon of three years.

Asset allocation shifts therefore require a long lead time and should be intended to last for reasonably long periods. If a particular strategy is expected to enjoy dull returns for a limited period it may not be worth withdrawing capital, since the managers may not accept the capital back at the end of the period. It may be preferable to leave the allocation in place in the expectation that the environment will improve again later.

To cope with the illiquid nature of a hedge fund portfolio there must be appropriate restrictions on cash flows in and out, with notification periods that allow redemption and investment requests to be passed on to the underlying hedge funds. Maintaining a 'liquidity ladder' that ranks the investments in the order that they can be turned into cash can help control this process. For each investment this must account for lock-up periods, dealing frequency, notice periods and payment delays following redemption. [2] A further tool for managing cash flows

---

2. Note that in times of crisis hedge fund managers have been known to invoke the 'small print' in their offering documents allowing them to delay the redemption process, particularly when they face heavy redemptions and markets are illiquid.

is a borrowing facility for the portfolio. This need not imply the creation of leveraged investment exposure. It simply facilitates the distribution or reinvestment of cash after redemption from a hedge fund but before the fund has settled. The cash liability created by the borrowing facility is directly offset by cash receivable from the hedge fund. A borrowing arrangement is sensible if a portfolio experiences a certain amount of turnover and where the portfolio's returns exceed the cost of borrowing.

## Nerd's corner: foreign exchange hedging

Most hedge funds are denominated in US dollars and are managed to generate US dollar returns. Non-dollar assets within portfolios are likely to be hedged by those managers concerned about their currency exposures. Yet not all buyers of hedge funds are dollar investors and some will wish to hedge their exposure. The only practical means of doing this is through forward exchange contracts. These are simple instruments when used to hedge liquid assets but hedge funds are illiquid, making accurate hedging a little more complicated.

Under normal circumstances, investors wishing to hedge a portfolio of dollar assets back into euros would sell a corresponding amount of dollars forward against euros. At the end of the period they would renew their position by buying the dollars back spot and rolling the position over simultaneously by once again selling dollars forward against euros. On closing out the initial position the hedge requires rebalancing. If the dollar has weakened over the first period then a profit will have been realized on the forward contract but the euro value of the portfolio of dollar assets will have fallen commensurately. This leaves the portfolio with a cash surplus but underinvested in the portfolio's assets. To rebalance the portfolio it is necessary to reinvest the forward contract profits into the pool of assets. If on the other hand the dollar has strengthened, then a loss has been realized on the forward contract and the euro value of dollar assets has become commensurately greater. This leaves the portfolio with a cash deficit and a leveraged pool of assets. To rebalance the hedge it is necessary to sell assets from the portfolio and to cover the foreign exchange losses.

When rolling over for the subsequent period the dollar sum sold forward must be adjusted to account for:

- the performance of the underlying dollar assets in the previous period, which will have caused the portfolio to grow or shrink in dollar terms;
- the change in size of the dollar portfolio resulting from additions or withdrawals by the portfolio's investors;
- the change in size due to rebalancing the portfolio according to the profit or loss realized on the currency hedge in the previous period.

It should be apparent why portfolios of hedge funds are difficult to hedge in this way. The profit and loss on the forward exchange contract is measured on a tick-by-tick basis and settles almost immediately on closure. By contrast, the underlying assets being hedged are priced monthly after a three week delay and are very difficult to liquidate in a hurry. If a currency profit on the forward needs to be reinvested into the portfolio then there is likely to be a rush getting it reinvested into hedge funds for the end of a month. If there is a currency loss on the forward which requires funding then it is very difficult to extract cash from the hedge funds at speed.

To facilitate this process it is necessary to roll over forward contracts shortly before month-end, leaving time to reinvest forward currency profits or place redemption orders for future periods to fund forward currency losses. A modest cash balance can be maintained with a view to settling forward exchange losses. Yet during periods in which currencies move significantly this cash balance may not be sufficient. Thus the illiquidity of hedge funds can present a real problem unless there is access to additional capital to cover such an eventuality. This is not always easy to arrange.

For funds of funds a possible solution arises when the clients who require hedging represent a small proportion of a much larger pool of investors. In such circumstances a feeder fund can be established for the clients requiring hedging which invests in turn into the broader hedge fund portfolio. Hedging can be conducted at the feeder fund level and the master fund can offer the feeder fund preferential liquidity on the rare occasions when it is forced rapidly to liquidate assets to cover a currency loss. If the size of the feeder is small in relation to the master portfolio then this arrangement need not unduly prejudice the majority of investors. This preferential liquidity is only offered to the extent of the loss on the currency position, which is unlikely to represent more than a few per cent of the feeder fund and in turn a much smaller percentage of the master fund. An alternative solution uses multiple share classes for a fund of funds, denominated in different currencies but relating to the same portfolio of assets. The class requiring hedging holds one additional asset, the forward contract.

These pedantic measures may be necessary in order to hedge accurately. Small inaccuracies repeated a number of times over the year can result in cumulative mis-hedging. It makes sense to roll over forward contracts on a monthly basis. Counterparties like to see profit and loss positions being cleared regularly and monthly periods correspond with hedge fund pricing and dealing. If rebalancing is less frequent then a prolonged imbalance between the forward and the portfolio may result in mis-hedging. Rebalancing more frequently is impractical and results in excessive trading costs.

# 5

# Equity long–short

I don't read the president's message in an annual report. I just look at his picture. If he's smiling too hard, I know the company's in big trouble.

Michael Thomsett

Equity long–short is one of the oldest hedge fund strategies. In its simplest form it consists of a series of long positions in companies that are expected to perform well, combined with a series of short positions in companies expected to perform poorly. Such a portfolio has the potential to generate positive returns regardless of whether equity prices are rising or falling. While equity long–short funds may seem straightforward, running them successfully is a real challenge. Superior stock selection and effective portfolio management are prerequisites, and managers with weaknesses in either department are quickly discovered.

## HISTORY AND EVOLUTION

Alfred W Jones, a former editor of *Fortune* magazine and a sociologist, is credited with the creation of the world's first equity long–short fund. Although he was not the first to use leverage or to sell short, he used these tools to create a portfolio with modest risk. Because Jones acknowledged he was unable to predict market direction he combined long positions in undervalued equities with short positions in overvalued equities, generating returns from both rising and falling prices. He launched a public fund in 1952 which enjoyed astonishing success over a 20-year period.

The success of the A W Jones venture later prompted a number of other players to establish similar vehicles. The drag on returns that short positions created led some equity long–short managers to add significant amounts of leverage to their long portfolios. Others, emboldened by their new-found freedom, added directional macro positions. The use of more leverage reintroduced risk into equity long–short portfolios, while macro positions lay outside the scope of a stock picker's expertise. Managers guilty of either sin were generally punished by market shocks, such as those that hit in 1994 and 1998. These events, combined with the demands of investors, have tended to persuade equity long–short managers to return to their core competence, picking under and over-performing equities within a risk controlled framework.

# THE CASE FOR EQUITY LONG–SHORT

The basic argument in favour of long–short portfolios is the potential to generate returns in both rising and falling markets. The portfolio does not necessarily require the prices of long positions to rise or the prices of short positions to fall. Rather it is the relative performance of the long and short positions that determines whether a portfolio makes a profit or a loss.

Assume that a hedge fund manager buys Company A and sells short Company B in equal dollar amounts. If the market rises 10 per cent over the period then the share prices of both companies are likely to have risen in sympathy. Assuming good stock selection, we might envisage Company A outperforming the rising market and Company B underperforming it. If the share price of Company A rises 12 per cent and the price of Company B rises 8 per cent then the profit generated on the long position exceeds the loss incurred on the short position by 4 per cent. In this instance the hedge fund has generated 'double alpha' by identifying both an outperforming long position and an underperforming short position.

Of course, the hedge fund has only made a 4 per cent profit at a time when the long-only index investor is likely to have made a 10 per cent profit. However, the benefits of the approach become apparent if the market falls by 10 per cent. Assuming good stock selection, we might envisage Company A falling by 8 per cent and Company B falling by 12 per cent. Here the profit generated by the short position exceeds the loss incurred by the long position by 4 per cent. This is quite a satis-

fying result when compared with the 10 per cent loss experienced
by the long-only index investor. If a manager's stock selection is
really effective, then the price of Company A might even rise at the
same time that the price of Company B falls. Obviously this
scenario can generate even greater profits, but we need not rely on it
to justify a long–short portfolio. A hedge fund manager merely has
to identify short positions that under-perform the market in order to
add value.[1]

If this type of result can be obtained reasonably consistently then an
equity long–short fund is likely to generate an attractive pattern of low
volatility returns. This low volatility is not merely cosmetic or short-
term, it reflects genuinely reduced risk over a long time span.
Consider a portfolio subjected to alternating +20 per cent and –10 per
cent returns over 10 successive periods. It will gain about 47 per cent
with a mean monthly return of 5 per cent. Compare this with a portfolio enjoying a steady +4 per cent return over 10 successive periods.
It will appreciate by about 48 per cent.

At this point it seems apparent that combining long and short positions brings wonderful diversification benefits. It is fair to assume that
individual equities are often fairly highly correlated to one another.
This is because they are sensitive to so many of the same risk factors,
such as interest rates and the return of the market as a whole. Their
positive correlation means that combining two long equity positions in
a portfolio only serves to reduce volatility mildly. Yet for the same
reasons, a long position in one and a short position in another would
tend to be negatively correlated with one another. Combining them in
a portfolio would reduce volatility to levels far lower than could be
achieved by combining two long positions. Of course this does not
mean that the long–short portfolio is likely to generate higher returns.
That requires strong stock selection.

Stock selection is the catch. Generating meaningful levels of
'double alpha' is very difficult. The associated risk is 'negative double
alpha', whereby the prices of long positions under-perform the market
and the prices of short positions outperform the market. Long–short
portfolios are therefore risky, although the nature of the risk differs
from that contained within a long-only portfolio. The long-only portfolio is exposed to substantial market risk, and accordingly the
investor expects to enjoy the return associated with holding the asset
(the 'market premium'). The long–short portfolio greatly reduces

---

1. Over and above the alternative, which is selling index futures as a hedge against long positions.

market risk but is instead exposed to stock selection risk. Thus the risk of the market is exchanged for the risk of the manager's decisions.[2] Some observers argue that markets are efficient and that fund managers are incapable of adding alpha on a regular basis. Below we discuss whether this argument is likely to be true. However, it is worth pointing out that if anyone can add alpha then it is probably hedge fund managers. The performance fees they earn act as a very powerful incentive in the stock selection effort and attract the very best stock pickers to the hedge fund game.

# THE EFFICIENCY OF MARKETS

Proponents of the efficient market hypothesis (EMH) argue that freely available information is immediately incorporated into equity prices, so that it becomes impossible to beat the market consistently. However, the case for long–short portfolios rests upon the ability of hedge fund managers to generate positive alpha. There are reasons that this should be possible.

Markets are made efficient by those participants who act upon information, thereby incorporating it into equity prices. Yet it can be argued that, one, the universe of active investors is limited, and two, active investors do not 'act' properly on their decisions. The EMH has now gained so much credence that the bulk of investors have given up stock picking in favour of 'closet indexation'. Supposedly 'active' investors manage equity portfolios on a relative rather than an absolute return basis, so that their investment decisions are reflected in marginal adjustments to position weightings rather than the purchase or sale of positions in their entirety. The mantra of relative returns is so entrenched that deviance from the market index (or tracking error) is frequently cited as the definitive way in which to measure risk.[3] These 'quasi active' investors are price takers not price makers. They conduct in-depth investment research but fail to act decisively on the basis of it. Instead the statisticians working for index providers determine their portfolio weightings. These investors contribute to

---

2. Depending on the magnitude of long and short exposures adopted by a hedge fund manger, the magnitude of this risk is likely to be less than that of the equity market, as are the associated returns.

3. The unfortunate truth is that asset managers use tracking error as a measure of their own business risk rather than a measure of their client's investment risk. The reluctance of conventional long-only managers to take stock selection decisions also applies to asset allocation. A survey of asset allocation within managed funds published in *Investment Strategies* illustrated just how static asset allocation policies were within managed funds between 1999 and 2003 (Roy and Smith (2003), citing figures from Lipper).

inefficiency at both the sector and the market level, investing their cash even when their information suggests a company, a sector or the entire market is overvalued. Meanwhile the truly active investors, such as hedge funds, are busily going long and short, setting prices for equities. It is they who truly act on information and it is they who make the markets efficient.

There are other, well-rehearsed limitations to the EMH. The hypothesis is based upon the notion of 'perfect capital markets' and therefore assumes a number of conditions, some of which are related to the ability of investors to arbitrage prices into efficiency. They include the absence of transaction costs, the readiness of investors to go either long or short, the ability of investors to borrow at the risk free rate, the presence of many buyers and sellers, the absence of taxes, an homogenous product and perfect information. Considering each of these assumptions, it seems that many of them can be challenged but that in general they hold for the largest equities in the US market. However, it becomes much easier to challenge the assumptions when they are considered in the context of smallcap and midcap stocks, either in the United States or elsewhere. Consider these factors:

● Since smallcap and midcap companies offer little profitable investment banking business, the larger institutions provide limited research coverage of them.

● Hedge funds often make extensive use of small research boutiques that specialize in smallcap and midcap stocks. However, large institutional investors tend to be stuck in relationships with the bulge bracket firms.

● In order to remain in line with benchmarks, professionally managed money is almost entirely allocated to largecap stocks. Investment professionals allocate their research efforts accordingly.

● The markets for individual smallcap and midcap equities are more likely to be dominated by a small number of buyers and sellers.

● Mainstream investors show little inclination to employ arbitrage tools such as shorting and leveraging. With smallcap and midcap stocks this inclination is zero.

For these reasons smallcap and midcap stocks are not subject to perfect information and the markets for them do not operate smoothly. Therefore it is not surprising that many equity long–short funds show a strong bias towards the midcap arena, where they find it easier to add alpha. Many funds have significant exposures to smallcap stocks as well, although their illiquidity means they tend to be less favoured.

However, the market cap bias within equity long–short funds is not entirely explained by the ability of managers to spot inefficiencies. If it were, then one would expect to find managers balancing their longs and shorts in the midcap and smallcap spaces. In practice, long–short funds often have long portfolios with a slightly lower average market cap than their short portfolios. This is because the market places a lower equity risk premium on large blue chip companies and therefore accepts a lower return for holding them. Smaller companies offer more growth, represent more risk and offer higher returns. In this way, hedge fund managers can 'ride' the differential in risk premium that the market offers for different sizes of company. They 'pay' the lower equity risk premium on slightly larger companies (through shorts) and 'receive' the higher premium on slightly smaller companies (through longs).

## THE NATURE OF A LONG–SHORT PORTFOLIO

In practice few equity long–short managers allocate equal amounts to long and short positions. Most managers maintain a larger balance of longs than shorts, a 'net long position'. Equity markets have a tendency to go up over time, and like everyone else hedge fund managers are happy to enjoy the ride. At moments when managers have a strong conviction that markets are rising they are likely to establish a particularly 'long bias'. In this way many equity long–short managers engage in a modest amount of market timing, seeking to lower their level of short protection during periods when they feel it is least needed and it is most costly.

Equity long–short managers therefore control two principal sources of risk and return. The first is stock selection, or their 'alpha generation' ability. The second is their ability to manage their net exposure to the market, or their 'beta management'. Their approach to these two issues helps to define their style.

## GENERATING ALPHA ON THE LONG SIDE

Managers of equity long–short funds employ all the same analysis techniques that one would expect of stock-pickers. Indeed, most equity long–short managers started their careers as traditional long-only equity investors, and it was their talent that prompted them to graduate into the long–short world. It would be pointless to enter into a detailed discussion of equity analysis here, but it is worth highlighting some areas that are particularly relevant in the context of a long–short portfolio.

- Equity long–short managers take advantage of rigidities in the institutional market. They enjoy a degree of flexibility and open-mindedness that gives them an edge over other market participants. Mainstream portfolio managers often adhere to the cliché that 'you don't get fired for owning IBM'. That is how they manage their careers. By contrast, if hedge fund managers think Wisconsin Widgets will outperform IBM they will buy the former and short the latter.

- Being hedged underlines the importance of stock selection decisions. In a rising market managers have the wind behind their longs but they are heading into it with their shorts. Thus they need to be more decisive in order to make a profit. Where traditional fund managers decide whether or not to overweight a company, hedge fund managers decide whether or not to buy it at all.

- Performance fees prompt further decisiveness, in sharp contrast to the pressures these managers may once have experienced in the long-only world, where they were encouraged to closet index.

- Performance fees encourage hedge fund managers to gain an informational edge over the market. Hedge fund managers seem more inclined to perform deep 'grass roots' research, contacting a company's suppliers, buyers and competitors in order to gain an accurate understanding of a firm's competitive position.[4]

- Hedge fund managers show a greater tendency to maintain detailed financial models for the companies in which they invest, building on the work conducted by analysts at investment banks.

- Many subscribe to independent analysis services, buy databases of insider trading and hire industry consultants to advise them on specific investments.

- Rather than being discouraged by the paucity of broker research on a particular company, hedge fund managers tend to be encouraged by it.[5] It increases the likelihood that they can add alpha.

---

4. These activities are particularly popular amongst US hedge funds. European hedge fund managers seem to be slower to catch on.

5. Whilst hedge funds can be managed very successfully by small investment teams, larger numbers of analysts relative to the assets managed can be helpful. A fund's performance will be driven largely by stock selection decisions and the extent to which good decisions outweigh bad ones. If this is a probability game, it can be helpful to increase the number of decisions being taken. There is a limit to the number of well-researched ideas that one individual can generate. Therefore a larger team increases the number of informed decisions that can be taken, thereby improving a fund's consistency and reducing its volatility. On the other hand, investment teams that grow too large can become unwieldy and a distraction for the ultimate decision makers.

- Because improving timing greatly enhances returns, a number of hedge fund managers conduct momentum-related technical analysis. Many also insist on identifying catalysts that are expected to trigger price appreciation. Hedge fund managers cannot afford to get bogged down in value traps.

# GENERATING ALPHA ON THE SHORT SIDE

Analysing and implementing short positions requires a different approach from analysing and implementing long positions. Managers need to make the mental transition from optimism to pessimism, from searching for success to searching for failure. They must rely on different forms of analysis in an attempt to identify business weakness, fads, frauds and aggressive accounting practices.

- It is much harder for managers to extract information from company executives if they are shorting the firm's stock, since the executives tend to be hostile to them. Some managers circumvent this issue by posing as long-only investors but most avoid meeting the executives of companies of which they are short.

- Instead, managers may conduct initial screens for short ideas using appropriate ratios and valuation criteria.[6]

- However, very few managers profess to short on the basis of valuation alone. An extended valuation often reflects considerable market enthusiasm for a company, and timing the reversal of a 'hyped' situation is very difficult. Shorting such stocks is therefore risky.

- Timing short positions is even more important than timing longs, since stocks seem to spend less time falling than they do rising. In addition, short positions that move against a manager grow in size, as opposed to losing long positions, which shrink in size. Therefore to short a stock one must identify reasons why the market will take the price down soon. This means the analysis of price momentum and the identification of catalysts become more important.

---

6.  Such as the ratio of intangibles : net assets, EBIT – interest, or WACC > ROCE
    (where EBIT = earnings before interest and tax, WACC = weighted average cost of capital and ROCE = return on capital employed).

- A few managers take this process into their own hands, attempting to create their own catalysts by sharing their negative analysis insights with other investment managers and with brokers. This approach has its own dangers as it can attract unwelcome attention, possibly encouraging other market participants to try to squeeze the managers' short positions.[7]

- In general, managers exhibit particular caution over their shorts, since they learn from experience that shorts that go wrong prove particularly painful. As a result their short book is usually made up of a larger number of smaller positions than they hold in their long book. These positions are likely to be in more liquid companies, so that they can be covered more easily. This often contributes to a size bias in short portfolios.

- Managers often spend more analysis time on their short book than on their long book. This is because managers have more short positions, because short ideas are harder to originate and because short positions are frequently held for briefer periods.

---

### A portfolio's static return

Although the profits generated by short selling are primarily driven by movements in stock prices, there are other important contributors. These are the short rebate, the cost of borrow and net dividend payments. When hedge fund managers sell equities short they take in cash from the buyers of the equities. This cash earns interest (a short rebate), which in higher interest rate environments can be a meaningful return.[8] A short rebate of 5 per cent on an average 50 per cent short exposure would enhance a portfolio's return by 2.5 per cent a year. Of course, if managers spend the cash received from short sales because they wish their long exposure to exceed 100 per cent, they will forfeit this return. However, few equity long–short managers leverage themselves up in this fashion.

Offsetting the benefits of the short rebate are the costs of borrowing shares that are sold short. The short rebate, net of the cost of borrow, typically amounts to 80 per cent of LIBOR rates. However, the cost of borrowing can be significantly higher when shorting a smaller company because fewer long-term investors are willing to lend shares. The cost of borrow also rises when a short is 'crowded', meaning that a large number of investors wish to

---

7. See below, under 'Difficulties'.
8. Equity long–short managers must negotiate hard to ensure they receive their full share of the short rebate. Prime brokers retain a slice of it as payment for arranging the stock borrow. The stock lending business is immensely valuable for prime brokers and they have to be restrained from taking too much of the pie.

sell the company short, outstripping the supply of shares being offered for lending. However, for liquid companies the cost of borrowing tends to be modest in relation to the short rebate.

Short selling involves a further cost, namely the dividends payable on those shares being shorted. Hedge fund managers borrow shares from long-term owners who expect to receive dividends on their shares even when they have lent them. Since hedge fund managers no longer own these shares they must meet this expense out of their own resources.[9] Managers who run larger long exposures than short exposures are likely to receive more in dividends from their long positions than they pay out on their shorts. This is particularly the case if one considers that managers' short positions may well have a lower dividend yield than their long positions, although this can of course vary.

After all the cash flows associated with a long–short portfolio have been considered it seems that higher levels of short exposure are likely to increase a portfolio's static return, except when interest rates are very low:

Static return of portfolio = (short rebate + dividends received from long positions) – (cost of borrow + dividends paid on short positions)

It can be seen that higher dividend yields increase the cost of carrying shorts. However a high dividend yield does not reduce the total returns from shorting a share because the cost of paying the dividend is offset by a commensurate fall in the share price once the share goes ex-dividend. Having said that, a share with a high dividend yield is tougher to short successfully because the yield provides price support and reduces the share's beta. Eastman Kodak is an example of a share where a high dividend yield helped to sustain an overvalued share price.

# RELATING INDIVIDUAL LONG AND SHORT POSITIONS

## 'Market neutral'

Managers have different views about the role of shorts in their portfolios. At one end of the spectrum, some managers carefully pair

---

9.    The Bush Administration's 2003 tax package has cut taxes on dividends and changed the manner in which they are taxed. Subsequent to the package only dividends received directly from a company are subject to a lower tax rate. Those received indirectly from the borrowers of stock are not. Short sellers must therefore compensate lenders of shares if they have suffered a tax disadvantage as a result of lending them. Although this might increase the carry costs of shorting, few lenders of stock are required to pay tax on dividends, so these changes are not expected to have much direct impact. More significant is the expectation that corporations will react by increasing their dividend payout ratios, which will reduce the static return associated with selling short. However, this change in corporate behaviour is likely to increase the dividends managers receive from longs as well as the dividends paid on shorts.

long and short positions, matching them by sector, market cap or other criteria. This can be arranged to minimize market, sector or style exposures and to isolate stock selection alpha. This sort of approach can work well when a winner and a loser can be identified within a sector but when the overall market direction is difficult to ascertain. Such an approach is generally referred to as 'market neutral'.[10]

Market neutral portfolios are likely to have limited correlation to markets and modest volatility, but they leave their managers with very little room for manoeuvre. It is not strictly necessary for equity long–short managers to select individual short positions with a view to hedging specific long positions. Most managers would rather have the freedom to express views on overall sectors or areas of the market. Furthermore, a pairs technique is unlikely to work well if either the long or the short is subject to forces that are highly specific to that company.[11] In such situations the other side of the pair fails to act as a hedge (an apple has been paired with an orange).

## 'Directional long–short'

At the other end of the spectrum, therefore, are managers who do not seek to relate their short positions to their longs. Their short positions are a series of totally independent, company-specific ideas that are treated as 'profit centres' in their own right. This means the managers require each short position to contribute positive returns to their port-folios, regardless of market direction. Given that sector influences act as a major driver of stock returns, managers may altogether avoid having both long and short positions within a single sector, lest the two positions should end up cancelling each other out. Shorts treated in this way are sometimes described as 'outright shorts' or 'naked shorts'. A long–short portfolio managed in this way may not sound like a hedge fund at all, since both longs and shorts are directional positions rather than hedges for each other. However, remember that a diversified portfolio of short positions will provide considerable short exposure to the overall market that will act to hedge the long market exposure embedded within the long portfolio. Therefore the short portfolio will inadvertently contribute to hedging.

---

10. In practice it can be very difficult to achieve market neutrality simply by limiting net exposures. A zero or negative correlation with the market might be more achievable. This would not necessarily mean that the portfolio would lose on average simply because the market gained on average, since correlation measures the relationship after the mean return has been accounted for. See Burns (2003).
11. Either a fundamental or technical issue, such as a 'short covering rally'.

## 'Hedged equity'

The attitudes of most equity long–short managers lie somewhere in between these two extremes. It is usual to show a preference for short positions that relate well to a long portfolio, and managers may concentrate their research efforts in those sectors where they have more longs if they wish to limit their net exposure there. However, they are unwilling to 'force a short' onto their books. They would rather generate absolute returns from both sides of their portfolio than be tightly hedged. Other managers combine a series of pairs trades with 'outright' longs and shorts in a single portfolio. One might refer to this middle ground as 'hedged equity'.

## 'Short sellers'

There is a rare breed of equity long–short manager that specializes purely in short selling.[12] When promoting themselves to investors, the managers of 'short seller' funds emphasize the diversification and hedging benefits that they bring to broader portfolios of long-biased hedge funds. Although short seller funds perform well during bear markets, they typically suffer greatly in prolonged bull markets. There does not seem to be such a thing as a wealthy short seller. Indeed, most seem to have been forced out of business. Even though they can help to hedge long-biased managers elsewhere in a portfolio, the losses they incur as an individual investment tend to be psychologically difficult for absolute return investors to tolerate. Like managers of long-only funds, pure short sellers run the risks associated with unhedged portfolios. They also experience the added disadvantage that comes from fighting long-term trends. A more sustainable business model for specialist short sellers is to concentrate efforts on identifying short ideas but to hedge the alpha they generate with passive long futures positions. If the managers wish to take a negative view on the overall market on a temporary basis they can remove or reduce their long hedge.[13] Although it negates the benefits that a pure short fund brings to a long-biased portfolio, this structure helps to harness their skills as identifiers of short ideas in a less risky manner.

There have been a number of famous dedicated short sellers over time. Among the better known were the Feshbach brothers. They started their short-only fund in 1982, when they represented one of

---

12. Restricted, for the most part, to the United States.
13. This is the approach that Michael Berger of the Manhattan Fund told many investors he was following. Unfortunately he was not. He was outright short and he lost almost all of his fund's assets.

only 50 or so hedge funds in existence. At their peak their assets reached about US $1 billion and they had 80 employees. They ran deeply researched, concentrated portfolios and generated impressive absolute returns despite rising markets. They would lose money during three out of every four quarters but win impressively during one of them, grossing 40–45 per cent for a number of years. However, by 1991 there were about 2,000 hedge funds in existence and about 100 short-only funds. The activity of short selling had become somewhat commoditized. The Feshbachs also suffered from a sharp decline in their short rebate, from which they had been earning 15 per cent a year during the 1980s. The Feshbachs had an appalling year in 1991 in which they lost 55 per cent. Michael Steinhardt, one of their main investors, described the phenomenon as a 'flight to crap'.

# MANAGING EXPOSURES

Managing a hedge fund's net exposure is only one part of a manager's job. The fund's sensitivity to the market will be influenced not only by the balance between long and short positions but also by the nature and size of each.

## The nature of exposures

A fund might be invested 100 per cent long and 50 per cent short, implying a net market exposure of 50 per cent. Disregarding the effects of stock selection, one would assume that the portfolio value should fluctuate half as much as the market. If, however, the overall beta of the long portfolio was 0.8 and the beta of the short portfolio was 1.1, the portfolio's beta-adjusted net exposure would be just 25 per cent.

> $0.8 \times 100$ per cent long = 80 per cent long beta adjusted
> $1.1 \times 50$ per cent short = 55 per cent short beta adjusted
> 50 per cent net long = 25 per cent net long beta adjusted

Therefore a portfolio biased towards lower beta longs and higher beta shorts is likely to surprise pleasantly in down markets but disappoint on the upside. Sharp market rallies may prove quite painful, particularly if betas prove to be unstable or non-linear, meaning that longs and shorts fail to act as expected during larger market moves.

This is the start of a much longer portfolio management debate that equity long–short managers must explore. Beta is just one of many drivers of stock returns. In order to understand the dynamics of their portfolios, hedge fund managers must consider their long and short exposures broken down across a range of risk factors. Net long or short exposure to particular sectors, countries, market capitalizations, value, growth or a fashionable valuation metric, makes a portfolio vulnerable to cross-currents within markets. Net long or short exposures in some of these departments are inevitable, and as long they are consciously adopted they can be monitored and managed. Inadvertent exposures, on the other hand, can give managers nasty surprises.

## The balance of exposures

Some managers maintain fairly consistent net exposures, while others vary their net exposure more, in line with their views on the market. However it can be argued that investors should not be expected to pay performance fees on funds that adopt consistent net long exposure to the market. Investors can assume consistent long exposure to the market themselves more cheaply through other means such as index products. Investors should therefore be willing to pay hedge fund managers to either maintain market neutral positions (isolating alpha generation) or manage their net beta actively on their behalf. Most hedge fund managers do the latter.

However, it is very difficult to assess the abilities of managers who radically swing their net exposure on an occasional basis. If these infrequent but big decisions go well, they may generate very impressive track records. Yet these big swings in net exposure are binary decisions. Because such decisions are taken infrequently it is difficult to judge whether managers possess real skill or have simply been lucky. The investor is left feeling uneasy whether the next big decision will go well or disastrously badly. Experience shows that these 'beta merchants' often run into difficulties after extended periods of stellar performance. Their performance also tends to be more volatile, without a commensurate enhancement to return.[14] It is far easier to assess the success of managers who have maintained relatively steady net exposures. Their track records can be interpreted within the context of their typical exposure levels and the investor is reassured that performance has been generated from a larger number of more frequent stock selection decisions. Assessing the track record of a 'beta merchant' by contrast, requires investors to understand how net exposures were swung at each juncture and to dissect past performance accordingly.

14. See Ruddick (2002).

## The ratio of exposures

In addition to their net exposures, managers must formulate a policy on the size of their long and short exposures combined, their 'gross' exposure. It is sometimes argued that larger gross exposures are preferable if the ratio of longs to shorts is low. Lee Ainsley of Maverick is a famous proponent of this view. In this way a portfolio invested 150 per cent long and 100 per cent short would be deemed safer than one invested 75 per cent long and 25 per cent short. Both have net exposures of 50 per cent. However, the former has a long–short ratio of 1.5:1 and the latter has a long–short ratio of 3:1. Proponents of the 'ratio argument' suggest that a low long–short ratio means the 250 per cent gross portfolio can outperform in both up and down markets. Table 5.1 shows how a 10 per cent rise and a 10 per cent fall might affect each portfolio, assuming both managers can add 2 per cent alpha over the period on both their long and their short positions.

This is rather a cute way to justify large levels of exposure. However, large gross exposure increases the risks and rewards associated with stock selection. Higher exposure levels can be achieved either by sizing up every position (increasing the impact of each decision) or by increasing the number of positions (increasing the number of decisions). Likewise, higher exposure increases the risks of any sector or style bets that managers may be taking. The dangers can be illustrated by running the above comparison again, this time under

**Table 5.1** The implications of long–short ratios when alpha is positive

| Up year for market | | | Down year for market | | |
|---|---|---|---|---|---|
| Long exposure | 150.00% | 75.00% | Long exposure | 150.00% | 75.00% |
| Short exposure | 100.00% | 25.00% | Short exposure | 100.00% | 25.00% |
| Net exposure | 50.00% | 50.00% | Net exposure | 50.00% | 50.00% |
| Long–short ratio | 1.50 | 3.00 | Long–short ratio | 1.50 | 3.00 |
| Market return | 10.00% | 10.00% | Market return | –10.00% | –10.00% |
| Double alpha | **2.00%** | **2.00%** | Double alpha | **2.00%** | **2.00%** |
| Long return | 18.00% | 9.00% | Long return | –12.00% | –6.00% |
| Short return | –8.00% | –2.00% | Short return | 12.00% | 3.00% |
| Dividend yield long | | | Dividend yield long | | |
| (2%) | 3.00% | 1.50% | (2%) | 3.00% | 1.50% |
| Dividend yield | | | Dividend yield | | |
| short (2%) | –2.00% | –0.50% | short (2%) | –2.00% | –0.50% |
| Net short rebate (1.5%) | 0.75% | 0.38% | Net short rebate (1.5%) | 0.75% | 0.38% |
| **Portfolio return** | **11.75%** | **8.38%** | **Portfolio return** | **1.75%** | **–1.63%** |

Maintaining a long–short ratio of 1.5 with a high gross exposure (left-hand column) results in a performance superior to that which can be obtained from mantaining a long–short ratio of 3.0 with a low gross exposure (right-hand column). This holds in both up and down markets, as long as managers can generate alpha on both their long and short positions.
Source: author.

the assumption that both managers generate negative alpha of 2 per cent on both their longs and their shorts (see Table 5.2).

As with net exposure, managers often manage their gross exposure actively, in line with the environment. In difficult market conditions they will struggle to make stock selection decisions with as much confidence. As a result they may decide to take fewer positions or smaller ones. Alternatively, managers may find that higher levels of market volatility mean that positions can be taken in smaller size and still have the same impact on a portfolio as larger positions did in quieter markets. Either of these scenarios might be used as a reason to reduce gross exposure. The dividend yield and interest rate environment will also be factors. If higher dividend yields and interest rates mean that a portfolio has a high static return, the argument may swing back in favour of higher gross exposures. This is because the higher static return generated from having higher gross exposure can cushion the impact of negative alpha.

# INSTRUMENTS, TOOLS AND METHODS

## Index shorts (futures and exchange traded funds (ETFs))

When they struggle to identify a sufficient number of individual short ideas, many equity long–short managers use index futures to hedge

**Table 5.2** The implications of long–short ratios when alpha is negative

| Up year for market | | | Down year for market | | |
|---|---|---|---|---|---|
| Long exposure | 150.00% | 75.00% | Long exposure | 150.00% | 75.00% |
| Short exposure | 100.00% | 25.00% | Short exposure | 100.00% | 25.00% |
| Net exposure | 50.00% | 50.00% | Net exposure | 50.00% | 50.00% |
| Long–short ratio | 1.50 | 3.00 | Long–short ratio | 1.50 | 3.00 |
| Market return | 10.00% | 10.00% | Market return | −10.00% | −10.00% |
| Double alpha | **−2.00%** | **−2.00%** | Double alpha | **−2.00%** | **−2.00%** |
| Long return | 12.00% | 6.00% | Long return | −18.00% | −9.00% |
| Short return | −12.00% | −3.00% | Short return | 8.00% | 2.00% |
| Dividend yield long (2%) | 3.00% | 1.50% | Dividend yield long (2%) | 3.00% | 1.50% |
| Dividend yield short (2%) | −2.00% | −0.50% | Dividend yield short (2%) | −2.00% | −0.50% |
| Net short rebate (1.5%) | 0.75% | 0.38% | Net short rebate (1.5%) | 0.75% | 0.38% |
| **Portfolio return** | **1.75%** | **4.38%** | **Portfolio return** | **−8.25%** | **−5.63%** |

The argument breaks down if managers fail to generate positive alpha. Managers with low long–short ratios will suffer if they have high gross exposures and their stock selection fails.
Source: author.

their longs. Some investors object to this practice because they dislike paying hefty performance fees only to find that managers are abrogating their responsibility to generate alpha on the short side. These objections are understandable, since hedge fund investors could buy an actively managed mutual fund and hedge it with futures, saving themselves 20 per cent performance fees in the process.[15] Furthermore, a number of long positions in a hedge fund are likely to be represented in the index. The use of index shorts means that managers are both long and short a number of the same stocks. Where this happens, managers can increase the size of the relevant longs with a view to establishing the desired net long exposure for each stock. Nevertheless such arrangements appear clumsy.

Managers who rely entirely on index futures for their short exposure do not deserve to be running hedge funds. On the other hand the use of these instruments to top up short exposure should not be ruled out. Remember that in most environments individual short positions are harder to identify than longs, that they are often held for shorter periods and that they are typically kept smaller in size. As a result there are bound to be occasions when managers wish to maintain a level of short exposure that they are unable to reach using their bottom-up idea flow. Supplementing short positions with futures is preferable to forcing questionable short ideas onto the book. Sector-specific futures or ETFs are easier to justify. These products are efficient, cheap to trade, highly liquid and can be targeted at quite specific areas of the market. Given the importance of sector influences in driving share prices these are useful tools for expressing short views, and they circumvent the anxieties caused by the stock specific risks that dominate certain sectors, such as the biotech industry.

## Stock and index options

Some managers use put options to hedge their longs. These may be puts on the companies that have been bought long or they may be outright shorts on different companies. Call options may be used as an alternative to long equity positions. Purchasing puts and calls in this way is designed to limit potential losses and to establish an asymmetric return profile, such as the one described in Figure 5.1.

Sadly, option insurance is expensive. In practice it is difficult to establish an attractive return profile without spending an inordinate

---

15. In practice, buying a mutual fund and hedging it with the index would be no substitute for a hedge fund. Mutual funds are rarely managed as actively and they almost never manage the level of their market exposure.

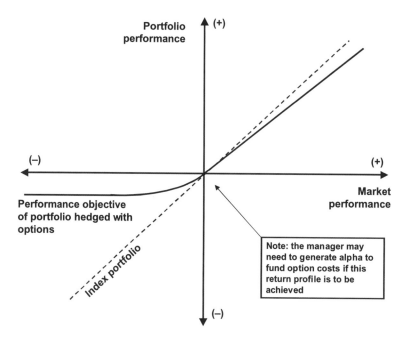

**Figure 5.1**    Protecting a portfolio with options

Hedge fund managers may use option protection in an attempt to create a return profile such as this. Note that this diagram assumes the managers are capable of producing sufficient positive alpha to cover the cost of funding such option protection. Achieving this is difficult in practice.

Source: author.

sum on premium. Hedge fund managers who routinely buy such protection must either:

- accept it a fair way out-of-the-money;

- compensate for the expense by consistently generating large amounts of alpha;

- sell offsetting options that limit their upside but help fund the purchase of option premium.

The market in equity options is notorious for its inefficiency, and opportunities to purchase undervalued protection must at times occur. However, the equity long–short manager's investment decisions are driven primarily by a company's fundamentals rather than by aberrations in its stock options, so such opportunities cannot be relied upon.

A number of equity long–short managers use options in a different way, to establish 'contingent' positions. By selling out-of-the-money puts managers can establish long positions at an entry price that they decide is attractive. If the stock fails to fall to this level they will not establish the position but they will nevertheless collect some option premium. Likewise, managers who identify companies which they would like to short at a higher price can do so by selling out-of-the-money calls, collecting premium even if the price fails to reach it. Of course, these activities should only be conducted using options whose nominal exposures are consistent with the positions the managers are willing to take.[16]

## Boxed shorts

A 'boxed short' is one that has been directly offset with a long position in the same company. This may seem like a strange arrangement but it has its uses. The ability to borrow certain stocks is limited, particularly in midcap or smallcap companies where there happen to be few lenders. Managers may therefore want to arrange stock borrow in advance of shorting the company. While they await the correct timing to actually go short of the stock they can box it with a corresponding long, selling the long at the opportune moment. After a fall in the share price they may wish to cover their short without losing the stock borrowing arrangement that they struggled so hard to obtain (they may anticipate a subsequent rebound in the stock and a fresh opportunity to short it). If this is the case they can purchase the stock again in order to box their short once more.

Boxed shorts can serve other purposes too. In some markets, such as the United States, managers are only permitted to sell short on an up tick. Hedge fund managers can circumvent this regulation by preparing a boxed short that allows them to establish a full short on either an up or down tick, simply by selling their long position.

## Contracts for difference (CFDs)

Contracts for difference are an alternative means of going long or short. These are OTC synthetic positions that mimic the economics of being either long or short of an equity, including the receipt of interest in relation to a short position. These are essentially single stock futures, so the only cash exchanged relates to the profit and loss on the position. Some hedge fund managers prefer to implement their positions using CFDs because they often provide better liquidity, lower

---

16. Risk management tools, such as VaR, must be adjusted to account for the effects of option delta and gamma.

execution costs, greater volume and they save on custody and settlement expenses. Because they are usually executed through a single broker, they also facilitate swift and efficient electronic reporting.[17]

## Cross hedging

One may cross hedge an asset with another instrument that, while indirectly related, is considered to have a meaningful impact on the asset. For example, a manager of an Asian equity long–short fund might own shares in a Taiwanese manufacturer. Because its main competitors are Japanese, the Taiwanese firm's competitive position might be severely compromised by an anticipated fall in the Yen. The manager may therefore choose to cross hedge his Taiwanese equity with a short position in the Yen.

Cross hedging is fraught with dangers and can create a false sense of security. If the Yen weakens the cross hedge may provide some protection. However, it would be easy to envisage a situation in which the Yen strengthened while other factors drove down the Taiwanese manufacturer's share price (such as missile testing by the People's Republic of China). Given the predicted sensitivity of the Taiwanese firm to the anticipated weakening in the Yen, the short Yen position may have to be sized quite generously, increasing the risk if the hedge goes awry. A cross hedge is usually a poor excuse for a more direct hedge, reflecting the fact that a direct hedge is hard to find or hard to implement. In this example, it may have been because shorting stock was forbidden in Taiwan and structures for circumventing the prohibition were too expensive.

## Stop losses

Because of their absolute return focus, equity long–short managers are more likely to implement stop loss mechanisms than long-only managers. The fact that losing short positions grow in size is another good reason for hedge fund managers to use them. Managers implement stop loss rules in a variety of guises. Some mechanistically cover positions whenever a stop loss has been breached ('hard stop

---

17. Note that if a manager does execute all of its trades using CFDs through a single broker, the fund is exposed to one counterparty and hence concentrated credit risk. This risk deserves to be highlighted. However, the counterparties involved are usually solid financial institutions, and a fund is only exposed to the extent of its net profit on its outstanding contracts, plus its margin. As with futures contracts, CFD profits and losses are margined and cleared on a fairly routine basis, so that exposure to the counterparty's credit is unlikely to reach very high levels.

losses') whilst others take the opportunity to pause for thought, leaving the position on if they feel sure their investment thesis remains intact ('soft stop losses'). Some prefer to set their stops close to their entry price ('tight stop losses'), possibly ratcheting them up if the position moves into profit. 'Hard' and 'tight' stop losses are sometimes criticized because markets are prone to sudden bouts of increased volatility that stop managers out of many of their positions. Once volatility subsides markets often revert to their former levels. To prevent being 'whipsawed' in this manner many managers prefer 'soft' or 'loose' stop losses, or they avoid them altogether.

A handful of managers adopt more innovative stop loss policies. They acknowledge that an abnormal percentage move in one company's share price would be ordinary in the case of another more volatile share. They therefore use a measure of a stock's volatility in relation to that of the market as a means of deciding on a stop loss that is appropriate for each position. They may also use a temporary increase in overall market volatility as a reason to widen all the stop losses in their portfolio.

An alternative philosophy involves setting separate stop losses for each lot of shares that were purchased while building a single position. This is intended to counteract the distortions that arise from using weighted average book costs as the basis for protecting profits. Shares purchased recently at a high cost raise the weighted average book cost. Using this to measure profit and loss can result in a manager liquidating an entire position when most of the lots purchased are still showing a profit. Some managers prefer to leave in the portfolio those shares bought early at a low cost, as long as they are still trading above their purchase price.

## The trader

Fundamental investment research is time-consuming and can involve a certain distance from the market. However, managers of long–short funds need to stay in touch with the market noise that determines how and why prices move in the immediate future. Their focus on absolute returns makes timing very important to them, particularly on the short side. For these reasons many long–short managers employ their own traders, in order to ensure efficient execution, to improve the timing of their implementation or to enhance returns on existing positions by trading around them. It might seem disparaging to refer to traders as 'investment tools' but in a way that is what they are.

## Big house versus little house

One of the hedge fund community's favourite debates concerns the relative merits of funds managed by large firms. This discussion most often relates to equity long–short funds because specialist arbitrage strategies generally lie beyond the competence of traditional fund management houses.

Until the late 1990s hedge funds managed by large firms were exceptionally rare. Up until this point mainstream asset managers could generate handsome investment returns using long-only 'closet indexation'. The bull market meant they steadily gathered and grew assets under management, generating handsome revenue streams. It seemed the growth in the pensions and mutual funds industries would continue for decades. The conventional fund management business model worked well and it was dangerous to fiddle with it. 'Hedge fund' was a mysterious and dirty word and any suggestion of involvement could damage a firm's brand.

Thus it was only entrepreneurial individuals, frustrated by bureaucracy and enormous portfolios, who broke away from these parent companies to start their own hedge funds. These were generally the more successful and intelligent stock-pickers who had the vision to see the benefits of equity long–short funds and the skill to make them work. Small hedge fund boutiques therefore contained an element of 'self-selection', whereby the managers were sufficiently talented to have graduated beyond traditional fund management houses. In their own small organization they were freed from the institutionalized mindset and could nimbly allocate smaller portfolios to reflect their investment rationale and to preserve capital. Because the managers owned their own businesses they were more motivated to make them work. Likewise, their employees were offered considerable financial incentives to perform. This ensured that hedge fund managers could choose the most talented analysts to work for them. As organizations these boutiques had few 'moving parts' and from the investor's point of view they were easy to analyse. Equity long–short funds managed by boutiques therefore had a number of advantages.

Clearly they suffered from some limitations. The hedge fund managers themselves were not really entrepreneurs at all. They were fund managers. The burden of managing growing organizations, and increasing numbers of people, often fell on their shoulders. Their businesses could be unstable, with very varied levels of cash flow according to the performance fees they earned. Some managers, thrilled by their unfettered investment freedom, failed to impose upon themselves proper investment controls.

As the bull market of the 1990s drew to a close, large fund management houses suddenly found their assets under management shrinking, through both market action and withdrawals from investors. Their revenues were depleted and their business model was broken. To make matters worse they started to suffer a mass exodus of their most talented managers, whom they could no longer afford to incentivize and who were leaving to manage hedge funds. Clients too were becoming disenchanted, demanding absolute returns now that the markets were falling. The large houses were therefore forced into offering hedge funds as a defensive move, in order to retain key employees and to capture the much higher fees on offer.

Many of the traditional investors in hedge funds distrusted those larger houses who offered equity long–short funds. These were considered to be cynical attempts by larger firms to improve their margins. The investors did not feel they were getting the full benefits of the performance fees they were paying, since the individuals running the hedge funds were often incentivized with only a portion of these fees. Investors had no desire to pay any portion of the performance fees to the parent firms because this did not contribute to incentivizing the investment staff. The manner in which these fees were distributed amongst the various contributing employees was also expected to cause friction and jealousy amongst staff in the large firms. Furthermore, large firms were not considered to have the flexible mindset for equity long–short investing and thus suffered from a 'last mover disadvantage'. Both the senior staff and the professionals running the funds were suspected of suffering from a long-only mentality that was hard to escape. Risk control and compliance divisions initially found the vehicles terrifying, trying to impose inappropriate controls. Large houses also suffered from conflicts of interest. There was pressure for talented managers to continue running huge long-only mandates alongside their hedge funds (the hedge funds often being the concession offered to keep them within the firm). Therefore their time and loyalties were divided. Their hedge funds were made less nimble on the long side because their positions were mirrored in much larger scale in their conventional portfolios. The order in which each fund dealt had to be handled very carefully. The short side could cause them even greater concern. Many of the stocks they sold short in their hedge funds they had been forced to buy for their conventional portfolios in order to limit their tracking error.

Despite all these shortcomings, some investors had good reasons for favouring equity long–short funds managed by larger firms. The bigger firms were considered to have superior oversight and control which would reduce the chance of major mishaps. Importantly, these controls could be exercised independently rather than by the management team themselves. A big firm's excellent infrastructure and support functions meant that hedge fund managers could focus exclusively on investment without the added distractions of running a small fund management business. The size of their investment operations also improved their access to company executives, broker analysts and trading desks. Some firms even argued that their access to stock borrow was improved because they knew their long-only mandates would lend them stock to short, although this too gave rise to other conflicts.

Boutique equity long–short managers have come up with some answers to these points. They point out that equity long–short strategies can be executed effectively with very limited resources and most support functions can be outsourced effectively. These days most employ a chief operating officer to allow them to concentrate exclusively on investment. Stricter codes of conduct, improved risk analysis systems and greater investor transparency all serve to limit the control advantages offered by larger firms. Boutique hedge fund managers also debate the investment advantages of size. They claim that their high levels of turnover mean they punch above their weight with brokers and their analysts. Many managers bring with them excellent connections and relationships from their former incarnations which stand them in good stead when they set up their hedge funds. Large firms too have made moves to offset their perceived weaknesses. Many have chosen to separate their hedge fund management teams from their main operations, often into separate buildings. With time, fewer and fewer are required to continue running their conventional long-only mandates.

## Nerd's corner: measuring performance expectations

It is relatively easy to assess the stock-picking abilities of managers who are long-only and fully invested. Investors can develop realistic ideas about the value long-only managers can add. Assessing the stock-picking abilities of equity long–short managers is much more complex. However, attempts can be made to see whether their claims lie within the realms of possibility. If some broad assumptions are tolerated a model can be built to assess whether managers' return expectations are realistic. This can be done by calculating a range of Sharpe ratios that seem attainable given their typical exposures and comparing these Sharpe ratios with the prevailing ratios achieved by their peer group.

The first of these assumptions is that the prevailing standard deviation of the market can be used as a proxy for the standard deviation of each of the long and the short portfolios. In reality, the standard deviations of each will differ from that of the market. However, if the sizes of the long and short exposures are adjusted for their betas this inaccuracy can be reduced.[18] Second, one must estimate the correlation between the long and short

18. Even after exposures are beta adjusted, the standard deviations of each portfolio are likely to differ from that of the market, reflecting the specific risks adopted. However, hedge fund managers are unlikely to report the standard deviations of their long and short portfolios separately. By contrast, they are likely to be able to quote the betas of each of their long and short portfolios, making this a more practical route for this exercise from the investor's point of view.

portfolios. Given that each is likely to represent significant levels of 'market risk' it is usually fair to assume a high negative correlation, such as –0.75.[19]

Armed with these assumptions one can use managers' typical levels of long and short exposure to calculate likely standard deviation figures for their portfolios, using the Markowitz formula.[20] The portfolios' expected standard deviations can in turn be used to furnish a series of Sharpe ratios that correspond to a series of 'achievable' rates of return. Managers' stated return objectives can then be assessed against the Sharpe ratio they would have to achieve. Given the prevailing Sharpe ratios being achieved by comparable managers one can assess whether the stated return objectives are realistic.

In effect, this is a means of assessing whether managers are making unreasonable claims about their stock-picking abilities. Of course, some managers may seek to outperform their peers not through stock selection but by radically managing their long and short exposure levels. This may invalidate the estimation process. However, large allocation shifts tend not to be a dependable source of returns, and remember that returns other managers secure from allocation shifts will be reflected in the Sharpe ratios achieved by the peer group.

For ease of reference, a table can be constructed showing a series of combinations of long and short exposure against a series of return objectives. Thus managers' stated typical exposures can quickly be measured against their return expectations to see whether they are claiming to be able to achieve Sharpe ratios that greatly exceed those of their peer group. (See Table 5.3.)

# EQUITY LONG–SHORT: OPPORTUNITIES, DIFFICULTIES, REACTION TO MARKETS

## Opportunities

### Incentive to generate alpha

Stock selection is a competitive business and a zero sum game. One person's gain (positive alpha) is another's loss (negative alpha). Hedge fund managers are paid handsomely for winning this game. If they lose they go out of business. By contrast, traditional long-only managers work on a fixed fee basis so their rewards for generating

---

19. Varying the correlation to –0.65 or –0.85 does not make a substantial difference to the outcome of this exercise.
20. Formula for calculating the standard deviation of two investments combined in a portfolio: $\sigma AB = \sqrt{(W_A^2 \sigma_A^2 + W_B^2 \sigma_B^2 + 2 W_A W_B r_{AB} \sigma_A \sigma_B)}$ , where A is the long book and B is the short book, $W_A$ and $W_B$ are the respective weightings of A and B in the overall portfolio, $\sigma_A$ and $\sigma_B$ are the standard deviations of each and $r_{AB}$ is the correlation between the two.

**Table 5.3** Assessing performance expectations

| Expected return | B-Adj L | B-Adj S | Gross | Net | SDp | 6% | 8% | 10% | 12% | 14% | 16% | 18% | 20% | 22% | 24% | 26% | 30% | 35% | 40% |
|---|---|---|---|---|---|---|---|---|---|---|---|---|---|---|---|---|---|---|---|
| High gross, high net | 175% | 75% | 250% | 100% | 21.9% | 0.05 | 0.14 | 0.23 | 0.32 | 0.41 | 0.50 | 0.59 | 0.69 | 0.78 | 0.87 | 0.96 | 1.14 | 1.37 | 1.60 |
| | 150% | 80% | 230% | 70% | 17.7% | 0.06 | 0.17 | 0.28 | 0.39 | 0.51 | 0.62 | 0.73 | 0.85 | 0.96 | 1.07 | 1.18 | 1.41 | 1.69 | 1.97 |
| | 150% | 75% | 225% | 75% | 18.0% | 0.06 | 0.17 | 0.28 | 0.39 | 0.50 | 0.61 | 0.72 | 0.83 | 0.94 | 1.05 | 1.16 | 1.39 | 1.66 | 1.94 |
| | 125% | 60% | 185% | 65% | 15.2% | 0.07 | 0.20 | 0.33 | 0.46 | 0.59 | 0.72 | 0.86 | 0.99 | 1.12 | 1.25 | 1.38 | 1.65 | 1.98 | 2.31 |
| | 125% | 50% | 175% | 75% | 15.9% | 0.06 | 0.19 | 0.31 | 0.44 | 0.57 | 0.69 | 0.82 | 0.94 | 1.07 | 1.19 | 1.32 | 1.57 | 1.89 | 2.20 |
| | 110% | 50% | 160% | 60% | 13.5% | 0.07 | 0.22 | 0.37 | 0.52 | 0.66 | 0.81 | 0.96 | 1.11 | 1.25 | 1.40 | 1.55 | 1.85 | 2.21 | 2.58 |
| High gross, low net | 175% | 150% | 325% | 25% | 19.9% | 0.05 | 0.15 | 0.25 | 0.35 | 0.45 | 0.55 | 0.65 | 0.75 | 0.85 | 0.95 | 1.05 | 1.25 | 1.50 | 1.76 |
| | 150% | 110% | 260% | 40% | 16.9% | 0.06 | 0.18 | 0.30 | 0.41 | 0.53 | 0.65 | 0.77 | 0.89 | 1.01 | 1.13 | 1.24 | 1.48 | 1.78 | 2.07 |
| | 110% | 90% | 200% | 20% | 12.4% | 0.08 | 0.24 | 0.40 | 0.56 | 0.72 | 0.88 | 1.05 | 1.21 | 1.37 | 1.53 | 1.69 | 2.01 | 2.41 | 2.81 |
| | 100% | 100% | 200% | 0% | 12.0% | 0.08 | 0.25 | 0.42 | 0.58 | 0.75 | 0.92 | 1.08 | 1.25 | 1.41 | 1.58 | 1.75 | 2.08 | 2.50 | 2.91 |
| | 95% | 105% | 200% | -10% | 12.1% | 0.08 | 0.25 | 0.41 | 0.58 | 0.74 | 0.91 | 1.07 | 1.24 | 1.40 | 1.57 | 1.73 | 2.06 | 2.47 | 2.89 |
| | 95% | 85% | 180% | 10% | 10.9% | 0.09 | 0.27 | 0.46 | 0.64 | 0.82 | 1.01 | 1.19 | 1.37 | 1.55 | 1.74 | 1.92 | 2.29 | 2.74 | 3.20 |
| Low gross, high net | 110% | 30% | 140% | 80% | 15.3% | 0.07 | 0.20 | 0.33 | 0.46 | 0.59 | 0.72 | 0.85 | 0.98 | 1.11 | 1.25 | 1.38 | 1.64 | 1.97 | 2.29 |
| | 95% | 25% | 120% | 70% | 13.3% | 0.08 | 0.23 | 0.38 | 0.53 | 0.68 | 0.83 | 0.98 | 1.13 | 1.28 | 1.43 | 1.58 | 1.88 | 2.26 | 2.64 |
| | 85% | 30% | 115% | 55% | 11.1% | 0.09 | 0.27 | 0.45 | 0.63 | 0.81 | 0.99 | 1.17 | 1.35 | 1.52 | 1.70 | 1.88 | 2.24 | 2.69 | 3.14 |
| | 85% | 20% | 105% | 65% | 12.1% | 0.08 | 0.25 | 0.41 | 0.58 | 0.74 | 0.91 | 1.07 | 1.24 | 1.40 | 1.57 | 1.73 | 2.06 | 2.48 | 2.89 |
| | 75% | 20% | 95% | 55% | 10.4% | 0.10 | 0.29 | 0.48 | 0.67 | 0.86 | 1.05 | 1.24 | 1.44 | 1.63 | 1.82 | 2.01 | 2.39 | 2.87 | 3.35 |
| | 65% | 20% | 85% | 45% | 8.8% | 0.11 | 0.34 | 0.57 | 0.80 | 1.02 | 1.25 | 1.48 | 1.71 | 1.93 | 2.16 | 2.39 | 2.84 | 3.41 | 3.98 |
| Low gross, low net | 80% | 60% | 140% | 20% | 9.0% | 0.11 | 0.33 | 0.56 | 0.78 | 1.00 | 1.22 | 1.45 | 1.67 | 1.89 | 2.11 | 2.33 | 2.78 | 3.33 | 3.89 |
| | 75% | 55% | 130% | 20% | 8.4% | 0.12 | 0.36 | 0.59 | 0.83 | 1.07 | 1.30 | 1.54 | 1.78 | 2.02 | 2.25 | 2.49 | 2.96 | 3.56 | 4.15 |
| | 65% | 50% | 115% | 15% | 7.3% | 0.14 | 0.41 | 0.68 | 0.96 | 1.23 | 1.50 | 1.78 | 2.05 | 2.32 | 2.60 | 2.87 | 3.42 | 4.10 | 4.79 |
| | 65% | 45% | 110% | 20% | 7.3% | 0.14 | 0.41 | 0.68 | 0.95 | 1.23 | 1.50 | 1.77 | 2.04 | 2.32 | 2.59 | 2.86 | 3.41 | 4.09 | 4.77 |
| | 55% | 45% | 100% | 10% | 6.2% | 0.16 | 0.48 | 0.80 | 1.13 | 1.45 | 1.77 | 2.09 | 2.41 | 2.73 | 3.06 | 3.38 | 4.02 | 4.83 | 5.63 |
| | 50% | 50% | 100% | 0% | 6.0% | 0.17 | 0.50 | 0.83 | 1.16 | 1.50 | 1.83 | 2.16 | 2.50 | 2.83 | 3.16 | 3.49 | 4.16 | 4.99 | 5.82 |

| SDm | R | Rf |
|---|---|---|
| 17% | -0.75 | 5% |

B-Adj L: beta-adjusted long exposure, B-Adj S: beta-adjusted short exposure, Gross: gross exposure, Net: net exposure, SDp: standard deviation of the portfolio, SDm: standard deviation of the market, R: correlation between long and short portfolios, Rf: Risk free rate of return.

Managers' typical exposure levels can be matched against the combinations running down the columns on the left-hand side. These can then be married with their stated return objectives running along the top of the table. This gives some idea of the Sharpe ratios they will have to achieve in order to meet their objectives.

Source: author.

alpha are comparatively small. Because they are punished for breaching agreed tracking errors they only play the game half-heartedly.

### Niche area
The pool of capital dedicated to equity long–short is small in relation to conventionally managed money. Therefore stealing small amounts of alpha from long-only funds can result in handsome profits for long–short funds.

### Diversification
Investing in a long-only fund amounts to investing in the underlying asset class that the fund specializes in. By contrast, investing in long–short funds amounts to investing in a series of decisions. For holders of long-only equity funds, long–short funds can provide an excellent form of diversification. Their reduced exposure to the market and increased reliance on alpha generation reduces their correlation with conventional managers, as well as contributing to capital preservation.

### Superior risk-adjusted returns
Investing long–short tends to result in superior risk-adjusted returns, partly because the correlation between the long and short investments is negative.

### The manager asset allocates
Conventional long-only funds remain close to fully invested at all times. This means the investors in the fund are responsible for deciding the extent to which they are invested in each market. Arguably, it might be preferable for expert fund mangers in each field to determine the extent to which their clients are invested at any one time. The managers of most long–short funds assume this responsibility when they vary their net exposure.

### Less dependence on market timing
Although equity long–short managers assume some of the asset allocation decision from their investors, the structure of a long–short portfolio limits the importance of this decision. Timing markets is difficult for all types of investor, and investing in equity markets through long–short funds reduces the burden of getting this decision right.

## Difficulties

### *The need to generate alpha*

Equity long–short investing relies upon the superior stock selection skills of the managers involved. These professionals must outsmart other market participants. Their gain is another's loss. This burdensome requirement does not apply to all hedge fund strategies. A number of forms of arbitrage provide a return simply for executing the strategy proficiently. Merger or convertible arbitrageurs with appropriate levels of skill and experience can extract returns from their activities without having to steal alpha from their peers.

### *Identifying winners*

So much is demanded of equity long–short managers (in terms of superior stock selection) that it is hard for investors to identify those who will succeed in the future. Assessments of stock selection ability can be very subjective. Managers who can point to particular features of the market's structure that provide them with the opportunity to generate returns generally inspire greater confidence than those who simply claim to be the intellectual superior of their peers.

### *Portfolio alignment*

If managers hedged all their risks they would struggle to make any money. Inevitably their portfolios contain some mismatches that leave them exposed to certain scenarios. It is true that equity long–short managers have the capacity to make money in all environments but by the same token they can also lose money in all environments.

### *Difficult to make money from shorts*

It is difficult to make money from shorts. They require a great deal of research and they can easily go wrong.

### *Crowded shorts*

It is often observed amongst the broking community that most equity long–short funds seem to be short of the same companies. This serves to reduce the diversification properties of a multi-manager portfolio. It also presents challenges to long–short managers. It reduces their ability to obtain the required stock borrow when establishing a position, it may increase the cost of borrow to maintain a position and it threatens their ability to cover the position when they wish to close it out (generally at the same time as everyone else who has the same short on). It is therefore encouraging when managers can demonstrate that they have different short ideas to their peers.

## Short squeeze

A 'short squeeze' occurs when upward price momentum in a particular stock forces investors to cover their short positions. In doing so they must buy back stock in the market, adding further to the share's upward price momentum and forcing yet more short sellers to cover their positions. When it is known that there is plenty of short interest in a stock, market manipulators have an incentive to force the price sharply up with the aim of triggering a frenzy of short covering. However, a simultaneous desire by hedge fund managers to close their positions can have the same effect. Of course, the desire of hedge fund managers to cover a short usually is simultaneous: it occurs once the price has gone down. Sometimes corporate executives who become aware of large short interest in their stock seek to trigger such reversals by improving their relationships with brokers, lobbying for favourable analyst coverage and embarking on a round of investor road shows. Hedge fund managers must therefore remain forever conscious of their need to obtain cover for their short.

## Risk of recall

Selling short involves the risk of recall at inopportune moments, meaning that the lender of the stock demands that it is returned (forcing the manager to cover the short). In practice this is very rare and in the vast majority of cases prime brokers are able to arrange an alternative lender without disrupting the hedge fund manager at all. However, the risk can become more meaningful with small companies where there are few lenders of the stock, with crowded shorts, or in cases where a stock price is falling exceptionally rapidly (causing lenders to wish to sell the stock).

## Managers with opposing views

An inevitable consequence of combining a number of long–short funds within a portfolio is that some will assume opposing positions (that is, some will be short of a stock that others are long of). This is the opposite problem to a crowded short. There is not much that can be done about this self-defeating situation but the benefits of diversifying across decision makers outweighs the reduction in returns.

## Transferring from long-only

Managers who have been successful in the long-only world often struggle when they first transfer to equity long–short funds. They have not had the chance to develop the additional portfolio management skills required of them, such as managing levels of long, short, net and gross exposures. Many are inclined to underestimate the added complexities that shorting involves, including the subtly different psychological pressures caused by shorts that go wrong. These managers need to get a 'feel' for going short and some of them fail to recognize that in their new lives they are beginners and not experts. Of course, new entrants often do extremely well, motivated by their new challenges, and many hedge fund investors make a point of investing in new managers expressly because they often outperform established managers. But the risks are higher too.

### *Delegation*

Some of the larger equity long–short managers parcel out a portion of their portfolio to one or more other managers. Quite often it is the short side that gets farmed out to a specialist short seller. This creates additional complexity for investors, particularly if the manager fails to volunteer the fact that another manager is involved.

## Reaction to markets

### *Rising and falling markets*

Most equity long–short funds aspire to making money in both rising and falling markets but few would claim to be able to do so unless they are amongst the minority who are strictly market neutral. Instead, most equity long–short managers aim to capture the majority of a market's rise and a minority of its fall. This is consistent with their generally net long bias. Over the past 10 years equity long–short funds have generally met these objectives. Whether this pattern of returns can be repeated remains to be seen, as does the amount of value these funds provide if markets move sideways over a prolonged period.

### *Increase in capital pursuing strategy*

As the 1990s bull market has given way to a bear market, the pool of capital dedicated to equity long–short has been growing. At the same time the pool of capital dedicated to conventional equity investment has been shrinking (due to market action if nothing else).[21] This increases the amount of hedge fund capital trying to steal alpha from a shrinking pool of conventional capital, leading to greater efficiency in

---

21. In contrast to the 1990s themselves, in which the pool of equity long–short assets was growing more slowly and the pool of 'quasi-index' long-only assets was still growing quickly.

the pricing of assets and reduced returns from stock selection.[22] Capital inflows also increase competition for stock borrow, cause crowded shorts and result in more frequent short squeezes. Inflows into equity long–short funds therefore threaten their ability to perform. These funds work best if they remain a marginal strategy. Unfortunately the barriers to entering the long–short business have come way down over the past decade. Managers can set up with minimal capital costs and can take technology platforms off the shelf, rather than having to develop their own. However, the barriers to exit are also very low, since the investment community treats underperforming managers brutally.

### Top-down effects

Long–short managers tend to place greater emphasis on stock selection and less on pan-market issues. For periods of time, however, pan-market factors drive the markets (at times of war, for example, or when the market becomes obsessed with technology). During such stampedes, markets sometimes choose to ignore stock specific factors. Because stock selection stops working, some equity long–short managers struggle to generate returns during these phases.[23]

### Relative performance of larger caps

As a group, long–short managers tend to run long positions with a lower average market cap than their short positions. This reflects partly attempts to capture inefficiencies amongst smaller companies and partly their need for liquid short positions. Some studies suggest that over the very long term smaller companies tend to outperform larger ones. However, when largecaps outperform the rest of the market it may have a slight negative impact on the universe of equity long–short funds.

---

22. See points made by Biggs (2002), citing Seth Klarman. Another way of looking at this issue is to compare it with a game of poker, which is also a zero sum game. If a 'fish' (amateur) sits down at the table he (or she) provides the professional poker players with the opportunity to win money off him. If the fish smarts at all his losses, gets up from the table and leaves, the professional players are left to do battle with one other. The competition between them becomes fiercer and their skill no longer guarantees them winnings. Theirs increasingly becomes a game of luck.

23. In Japan, for example, many long–short managers suffer during sharp market rallies, particularly if they are triggered by some form of government support that drives up the prices of badly managed, ailing firms. They tend to be short of these firms, against longs in those Japanese companies showing a willingness to restructure and reform. The Japanese market also tends to be somewhat short-term and suffers from rapid sector rotation.

### Turning points

Equity long–short managers tend to add value during sideways trending markets because they emphasize price relationships over rising prices. During prolonged bull markets they can position themselves with a net long bias, and they can ride down on prolonged bear markets with a net short bias. At major inflexion points their performance is a bit more varied. In any group of managers, some are likely to call a recovery too early and lose money by increasing their long exposure. Others are likely to miss sharp rallies that mark the start of a recovery, maintaining a neutral position. For investors who are concerned by relative returns and opportunity costs these can be frustrating periods to hold equity long–short funds.[24]

### Bear market rallies

Long–short managers often perform particularly badly during bear market rallies. During these phases bombed out stocks in companies with appalling prospects usually rally far faster than the rest of the market. Long–short managers are often short of these companies and they are very rarely long of them.

### Mature bear markets

In mature bear markets it can be tough for managers to identify over-valued companies to short. Moreover, lower valuations across the board increase the risks associated with shorting. The market capitalizations of firms are also lower, reducing the liquidity of potential shorts. It may be difficult for managers to avoid increasing their net exposure under such circumstances.

### Interest rates

Lower interest rates reduce managers' standstill rates of return by cutting back on the short rebate. Higher interest rates increase their standstill rate of return. The extent to which rates affect managers will be influenced by the level of their exposures.

### Equity issuance

During the 1990s, many US equity long–short funds participated heavily in new issue markets, securing attractive allocations to initial public offerings (IPOs). For some hedge funds this activity augmented their returns markedly. There were generally two different share

---

24. For example, many equity long–short managers dedicated to emerging markets failed to participate when emerging markets bounced suddenly off their bottom in 1999.

classes for these hedge funds, catering for those investors who were and were not eligible for hot issues. The importance of new issue activity to a manager's performance could be ascertained by comparing the records of these two share classes. Most investors would probably rather their managers did not rely on new issuance as a source of returns, since it is liable to dry up under adverse market conditions. Those investors who are unable to participate in hot issues are even less keen.[25]

# APPENDIX 1: KEY CONSIDERATIONS: EQUITY LONG–SHORT

- Which market inefficiencies does the manager identify as the source of the fund's returns?

- How does the manager claim to be able to pick stocks better than the competition?

- What is the manager's stock selection process and does it give the manager an informational edge over competitors?

- To what lengths does the manager take company research? How much of it is primary and how much reliant on other sources? Why has the manager chosen this balance?

- What are the manager's policies regarding overall exposures (long, short, net and gross)?

- What is a likely range for long, short and net exposures under both usual and unusual circumstances? How does this differ on a beta-adjusted basis? How has the manager decided that these ranges are appropriate?

- In what manner does the manager seek to identify and act upon major turning points in the market?

- If the fund is subject to large swings in exposures, why is the manager confident that these key decisions can be taken effectively? How have large exposure changes been handled in the past and what bearing does this have on the interpretation of the manager's track record?

---

25. Offshore investors and funds of funds are unlikely to be able to demonstrate their eligibility for hot issues.

- Are shorts used primarily as profit centres or as hedges?

- How does the manager match short and long positions? Are the two considered entirely independent?

- How are style, market cap and other portfolio biases decided upon and monitored? To what extent are short positions in the fund of a larger capitalization than longs?

- What are the relative volatilities of different parts of the portfolio, and will these give rise to unusual performance figures during large market moves?

- Is the manager trapped in crowded shorts? What measures are taken to avoid short squeezes and to initiate original short ideas?

- How does the manager ensure superior access to stock borrow?

- How much research effort does the manager allocate to short ideas versus long ones?

- What particular conditions does a manager require before shorting a company?

- In what circumstances might the manager use index shorts?

- Does the manager implement cross hedges? If so, what are the risks involved and are they sensible?

- Does the manager use options, either as a hedging tool or as a means of establishing positions at other price levels? How does the manager seek to minimize the cost of buying options and the potential risks associated with shorting them? Does the manager have a particular expertise in the options market that acts as a further source of return, or are these simply portfolio management tools?

- Does the manager use stop losses, and if so in what manner? What measures are taken to avoid stop losses whipsawing the fund?

- What other risk control and analysis tools are used?

- Does the manager use a trader? If so, in what capacity? (Is the trader expected to add to returns or simply to enhance execution capabilities?)

- If the manager is an employee of a large organization, how are the associated conflicts addressed? If the manager owns his or her own small firm, can it be run effectively without being a distraction?

- If recently transferred from the long-only world, has the manager truly grasped the added dimensions involved with running a hedge fund?

- Does the relative performance of the fund's different share classes (those that include and exclude hot issues) imply that the manager has been overly reliant on hot issues for generating returns?

# APPENDIX 2: GLOSSARY

**Boxed short:** Maintaining a short position but cancelling it out with a corresponding long, improving the ease with which a naked short can be re-established.

**Contract for difference (CFD):** An equity swap agreement through which a hedge fund manager can simulate the economics of either a long or short position. Similar in effect to single stock futures.

**Cost of borrow:** The fee paid to a stock lender for the privilege of borrowing shares in order to short them.

**Cross hedging:** Hedging a position with an indirectly related asset because it is considered to have a bearing on its performance.

**Crowded short:** A heavily shorted company (a company with high levels of 'short interest').

**Double alpha:** The ability of hedge fund managers to go long of stocks that outperform the market and short of stocks that under-perform it.

**Level of short interest:** The degree to which a company is being shorted by market participants.

**Long bias:** A portfolio in which long exposures typically outweigh short exposures.

**Market neutral:** A portfolio with broadly similar levels of long and short exposure (usually on a beta-adjusted basis).

**Naked short:** A short position which is not acting as a hedge for a long position in the portfolio. Therefore it is itself unhedged.

**Outright shorts:** The use of naked shorts in the portfolio with the intention of generating profits from falling prices (as opposed to implementing shorts as hedges).

**Pairs trade:** Where a long position has been specifically matched with a short position in another company that is considered closely related.

**Risk of recall:** The possibility that the lender of a stock might demand its return, forcing the short seller to buy it back in the market and to return it to its owner.

**Sector neutral:** A portfolio with similar levels of long and short exposures in each sector (which as a result tends also to be market neutral).

**Short bias:** A portfolio in which short exposures outweigh long exposures. May also be taken to infer simply that a manager's forte is the selection of shorts.

**Short rebate:** The interest earned on cash received as a result of shares being sold short.

**Short seller:** A manager specializing in selling short, possibly to the exclusion of long positions.

**Short squeeze:** A rush of short covering in a stock that forces its price up, encouraging yet further short covering ('a short covering rally').

**Static return:** A long–short portfolio's cash flows that occur regardless of share price movements.

# 6

# Merger arbitrage

You can say it was a real love match. We married for money.
S J Perelman

One of the most widely practised forms of arbitrage involves buying the shares of a company that is the subject of a takeover bid. These shares tend to trade at a discount to the price offered by the acquiring company, due to uncertainty over whether the transaction will complete. The merger arbitrageur's job is to buy shares of the target company in situations where, in his expert opinion, merger negotiations are likely to be successful. The arbitrageur captures the spread between the market value paid for the shares and their higher value on the deal's completion. In many mergers the acquiring company offers to pay with its own shares rather than with cash. This means that if the shares of the acquiring company fall, the value of its offer decreases. The arbitrageur can hedge against this eventuality by selling short an appropriate number of the acquiring company's shares for every share of the target company bought. In this way he or she locks in the spread.

The essential principles behind merger arbitrage are relatively simple. First, the arbitrageur must assess the potential return if the deal is completed, as well as the potential loss if it breaks. Second, he or she must assess the risk that the deal is delayed (which will reduce the annualized return) or that it breaks altogether (which will result in a loss). In practice merger arbitrage entails a considerable amount of hard work. Deals often incorporate complexities, so that assessing the true size of the spread is less than straightforward. More importantly, assessing the probability and timing of completion is quite an art. A great deal hinges on making this assessment correctly, since the losses an arbitrageur incurs when a deal breaks are usually a multiple of the profits on offer from a successful transaction. A deal must therefore be judged to have a very high probability of success.

# THE BASICS OF MERGER ARBITRAGE

It is somewhat artificial to discuss return separately from risk. The two are very much interlinked. The spread on offer from a merger trans-action can be viewed as a function of the risk free rate plus a risk premium which reflects the likelihood that a deal completes:

Spread = Risk free rate + Risk the deal is delayed or breaks

In practice this combination (the risk free rate plus a risk premium) has tended to equate to a total return of two to three times cash. Transactions that are considered complex or risky are therefore likely to offer higher returns and involve a wider spread. It is nevertheless worth addressing risk and return individually, since the returns on offer must be established before an assessment of risk is undertaken. Moreover, calculating the size of a merger spread is not always a straightforward exercise.

# ASSESSING RETURN

To understand the components of merger arbitrage return we should first look at a couple of simple deals, one involving a cash offer and the other a share-for-share transaction. With a view to consistency, we will use the word BidCo to refer to the acquiring company and TargetCo to refer to the target company.

The spread that can be captured from a cash deal is simple to calculate. The arbitrageur seeks to buy shares of TargetCo at a price below that offered by BidCo, waiting until completion of the deal to realize the difference. If TargetCo shares can be bought in the market for $95.00 and BidCo is offering $100.00 in cash for each TargetCo share, the spread is $5.00. Transaction costs must be deducted from the $5.00 but any dividend that is due on TargetCo shares before the transaction completes will benefit the arbitrageur. If transaction costs are $0.01 and dividends due are $0.50, the spread after costs and divi-dends becomes $5.49. The arbitrageur must commit $95.00 in capital to the trade because the TargetCo share is bought in the market at that price. The spread is therefore 5.8 per cent ($5.49/$95.00). Assuming that the merger is expected to complete in 181 days this equates to an annualized spread of 12.0 per cent. This is the return on capital the manager expects as long as the deal completes without delay. If the merger completes ahead of schedule the spread will be captured early, the manager will be able to redeploy the capital and the annualized return will be higher. (See Table 6.1 and Figure 6.1.)

The spread on offer from a share-for-share deal can be calculated in a similar fashion. However, there are a few more variables to consider. In a share-for-share deal the arbitrageur seeks to buy shares of TargetCo for a price that is less than the value of the BidCo shares being offered in exchange. In order to hedge against the possibility that the BidCo shares will fall in value he or she simultaneously sells short the appropriate number of BidCo shares. As the transaction progresses the value of the TargetCo shares appreciates until it is equal to the equivalent number of BidCo shares. Upon completion of the merger the arbitrageur receives BidCo shares in exchange for the TargetCo shares. These can be used to cover the arbitrageur's BidCo short position, thereby closing out the transaction.

If BidCo is offering three of its shares, trading at \$33.33, in exchange for each TargetCo share, the offer can be valued at \$100.00 per TargetCo share. If TargetCo shares can be bought in the market for \$97.00 there is an initial spread of \$3.00. From this must be deducted transaction costs for each TargetCo share bought and the three corresponding shares of BidCo sold short (say \$0.04). Let us say that there must also be a deduction of \$0.36 to pay for dividends due on the three shares of BidCo sold short. These deductions are offset by a \$0.80 dividend expected from the long position in TargetCo and a \$1.32 short rebate received from the BidCo shares sold short. The spread net of these costs and dividends becomes \$4.72 or 4.9 per cent (\$4.72/\$97.00). If the deal is expected to complete in 120 days the anticipated annualized spread equates to 15.5 per cent. (See Table 6.2 and Figure 6.2.)

**Table 6.1**   Example 1: cash merger

| | |
|---|---|
| BidCo offer for each TargetCo share | \$100.00 |
| Price paid in market for TargetCo share | \$95.00 |
| Spread | \$5.00 |
| Less transaction costs | \$0.01 |
| Plus dividends expected from TargetCo | \$0.50 |
| Spread net of costs and dividends | \$5.49 |
| Spread in % | 5.8% |
| Spread in % annualized | 12% |
| Expected completion date | 30 June 2001 |
| Date position established | 31 Dec 2000 |
| Days to complete | 181 |

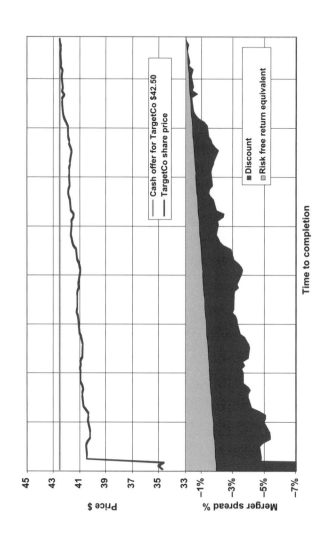

**Figure 6.1** A cash deal

In a typical cash deal the spread between TargetCo's share price and the value of BidCo's cash offer will gradually close as completion draws near. The spread will widen and narrow as confidence in the transaction's success waxes and wanes. The return secured from the closing of the spread over time is likely to represent a multiple of the risk free rate.
Source: author.

There are several points to note from these examples. First, the maximum return on offer is the spread at the time the trade is set up, unless there is a topping bid from a third player. Second, the short sale of BidCo shares can hedge against BidCo shares falling but it also removes the prospect of profit from BidCo shares rising. Third, delaying the transaction dramatically reduces the annualized return on offer. Fourth, it is helpful to have a net dividend inflow to help fund the position. Fifth, transaction costs can have a significant impact on a position's profitability, particularly in share-for-share deals where there are two equity sides to the trade.

## MORE COMPLEX RETURN ESTIMATES

While estimating the size of a transaction's spread may be as simple as the above examples, there are often added complexities. The most obvious example relates to mixed offers, where BidCo makes part of its bid in cash and part in BidCo shares. The offer may even include payment in a range of debt securities. Each of the components of such an offer must be broken down to estimate the return on offer and to arrange hedging. The shareholders of TargetCo are often allowed to opt for one form of payment or another, a choice that is sometimes subject to a limit on the total amount of cash that BidCo is willing to pay. Thus if too many TargetCo shareholders opt for cash they are likely to be 'prorated' to include part payment in BidCo shares. This makes life harder for the arbitrageur who is trying to estimate the size of his or her

**Table 6.2** Example 2: share-for-share merger

| | |
|---|---|
| Number of BidCo shares offered per TargetCo share | 3.00 |
| Price in market of BidCo shares | $33.33 |
| Value of BidCo's offer for each TargetCo share | $100.00 |
| Price paid in market for TargetCo share | $97.00 |
| Spread | $3.00 |
| Less transaction costs (long and short positions) | $0.04 |
| Less dividends payable on BidCo shares sold short | $0.36 |
| Plus dividend expected from TargetCo | $0.80 |
| Plus short rebate on BidCo shares sold short (4%) | $1.32 |
| Spread net of costs and dividends | $4.72 |
| Spread in % | 4.9% |
| Spread in % annualized | 15.5% |
| Expected completion date | 30 April 2001 |
| Date position established | 31 Dec 2000 |
| Days to complete | 120 |

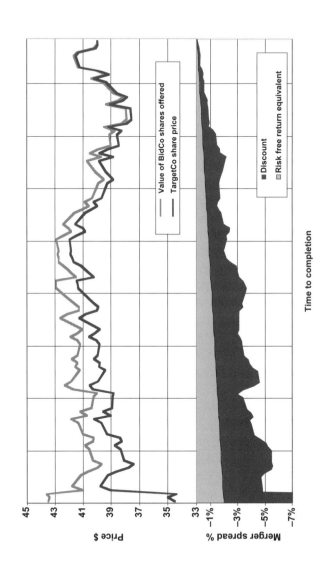

**Figure 6.2**  A stock-for-stock merger transaction

In a typical stock-for-stock merger transaction the spread between TargetCo's share price and the value of BidCo shares offered will gradually close as completion draws near. The spread will widen and narrow as confidence in the transaction's success waxes and wanes. The return secured from closing the spread over time is likely to represent a multiple of the risk free rate.
Source: author.

spread and to assess how many BidCo shares he or she needs to short. The arbitrageur needs to understand enough about the other TargetCo shareholders to predict the extent to which the offer will be prorated.

Share-for-share transactions often involve complications since the participants are often anxious about relative share price movements. If, after the deal is announced, the value of BidCo's shares falls dramatically, TargetCo shareholders may worry they are being underpaid for their shares. Likewise, if BidCo's shares rise dramatically, BidCo shareholders may worry they are overpaying for TargetCo.

To pre-empt such concerns, share-for-share agreements often involve price-related conditions. BidCo may offer a floating exchange ratio, so that the number of its shares offered for each TargetCo share varies, 'fixing' a particular dollar value to the bid. This protects TargetCo shareholders from a fall in BidCo's share price. In these circumstances the arbitrageur may not see a need to short BidCo shares. However, so that neither too many nor too few shares are offered, BidCo often sets a minimum and maximum exchange ratio (a 'collar'). Beyond these bounds the ratio is fixed, and the arbitrageur will again wish to short shares of BidCo to secure the spread. (See Figure 6.3.)[1] To make hedging estimations trickier, variable exchange ratios are often calculated using the average of closing prices over a specified period of time (a 'pricing period').

The merging companies may employ the alternative mechanism of fixing the exchange ratio with a different kind of 'collar' that limits the range of share prices over which BidCo's fixed ratio offer applies. If the BidCo share price rises or falls beyond the bounds of the collar, the participants have the right to terminate negotiations. Such arrangements require the arbitrageur to monitor price movements and adjust the hedge accordingly. The transaction's completion is only anticipated under certain circumstances.

Establishing a deal's expected return can often be done fairly accurately with the aid of a spreadsheet and some sensible assumptions. Yet the arbitrageur must also estimate the potential loss should the deal fail. When a deal is announced, the shares of TargetCo usually jump in the expectation of the sum BidCo is offering. If the market looks favourably on the transaction, the shares of BidCo may also rise on the news. However, often enough the bidding company's shares fall because arbitrageurs are shorting the stock, because the market is concerned about the price being paid for TargetCo or because the

---

1.   If these bounds are breached the risk of the deal's failure may also be higher.

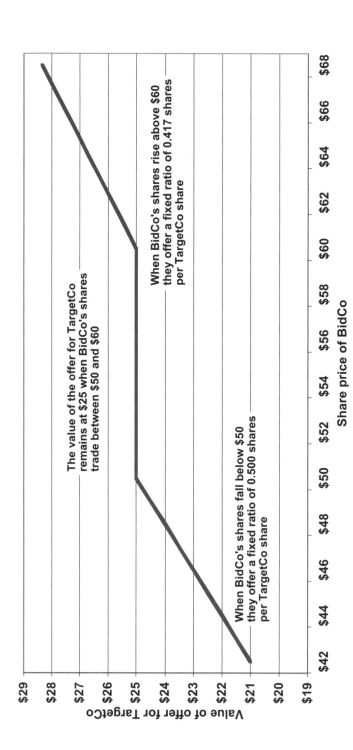

**Figure 6.3**  Illustration of a deal with a collar

A deal with a collar involves a floating exchange ratio that fixes the dollar value of BidCo's offer as long as BidCo's share price remains within certain bounds. Beyond those bounds the exchange ratio fixes, so that the value of the offer fluctuates with the value of Bidco's shares.

Sources: Brencourt Advisors LLC, author.

The following labels appear within the figure:

The value of the offer for TargetCo remains at $25 when BidCo's shares trade between $50 and $60

When BidCo's shares rise above $60 they offer a fixed ratio of 0.417 shares per TargetCo share

When BidCo's shares fall below $50 they offer a fixed ratio of 0.500 shares per TargetCo share

Value of offer for TargetCo: $19, $20, $21, $22, $23, $24, $25, $26, $27, $28, $29

Share price of BidCo: $42, $44, $46, $48, $50, $52, $54, $56, $58, $60, $62, $64, $66, $68 merger will involve dilution. With the BidCo shares already artificially low and the TargetCo shares artificially high, the arbitrageur is entering a trade where the spread between the two securities is already much tighter than usual. If the deal breaks, BidCo shares are likely to rise and TargetCo shares are likely to fall. The arbitrageur must add the rise of the BidCo shares to the fall of the TargetCo shares to estimate the potential total loss from the widening spread. Clearly the larger the premium BidCo has offered for TargetCo, the greater the expected loss if the deal breaks. Sometimes this premium is very large indeed.

The simple approach is to assume that the two shares return to their respective prices before the deal was announced. However, a number of other factors must also be considered.

- Clearly the general level of the stock market is likely to have changed in the intervening period, but this is unlikely to affect the relative attractions of the two securities if the deal was share-for-share. For cash bids, market moves certainly do influence the TargetCo's share price and the arbitrageur must estimate the effect they would have had on the share price in the absence of a bid.

- There may also be company or sector-specific news relating to either party which might affect the levels at which they trade after a deal breaks.

- The pre-announcement trading patterns of each company must also be taken with a pinch of salt. If there were any leaks before the deal was announced there may have been an unexplained rise in TargetCo shares, accompanied by unusually high trading volumes.

- If the deal is heavily arbitraged, a very large proportion of TargetCo shares may lie in the hands of arbitrageurs who will dump the stock on news of a deal breaking. This may drive the share price well below levels at which it traded before the announcement of the deal. If there are few arbitrageurs involved, TargetCo's share price may settle above its former level. This may be because the market at large has started to view the firm as a willing takeover candidate which may attract other offers.

- Equally, the shares of BidCo may rise suddenly when a deal breaks simply because arbitrageurs are covering their shorts. The impact of such short covering is likely to be far less relevant if BidCo was very large in relation to TargetCo, as only a small proportion of BidCo shares would have been required for shorting purposes.

It should be apparent that merger arbitrage returns are asymmetric. The potential returns are usually limited to the closing of the deal spread, while losses tend to be far greater when they occur. This has led many to compare the strategy to 'picking up nickels in front of a steam roller'. A more pretentious way of describing it is to liken the payoff structure to being short of an option: if the deal goes through a modest risk premium is banked. If it fails the losses greatly exceed the option premium. (See Figure 6.4.) The merger arbitrageur is assuming the risk that the deal breaks from the previous shareholders of TargetCo. This is why merger arbitrage is often referred to as 'risk arbitrage'. As the deal progresses, the likelihood of the deal breaking is usually judged to recede, and the risk premium the arbitrageur earns for the remaining period declines (the spread narrows).

The upshot is that the merger arbitrageur simply cannot afford to make mistakes very often. As long as broken deals are avoided a good return is earned. The principal skill of the arbitrageur lies in assessing the risk involved in each transaction.

## ASSESSING TIMING RISK

There are two principal aspects of risk in a merger transaction. The first relates to timing, since delays greatly erode the annualized return that a transaction offers. The second relates to whether the transaction even completes.

While these two risks are distinct they are often related. Delays to a transaction can be a sign that all is not well with negotiations, and delays can actually contribute to a deal breaking. The passage of time can cause psychological strain on the negotiating parties if an element of uncertainty is involved. Delays do give more time for things to go wrong. Whether or not delays end with a deal breaking, the uncertainty causes spreads to widen and mark-to-market losses for arbitrageurs. If the arbitrageur closes the position the losses are realized, but if the transaction completes they will be recovered (albeit reducing the annualized return achieved).

Estimating the timing of a transaction gets more difficult the more complex a situation is. By the time a friendly transaction has been announced due diligence has usually been completed, but it can be difficult to estimate how long any outstanding due diligence will take. Assuming due diligence has been finalized, a share-for-share deal might be completed within 90 days, as long as the regulators do not

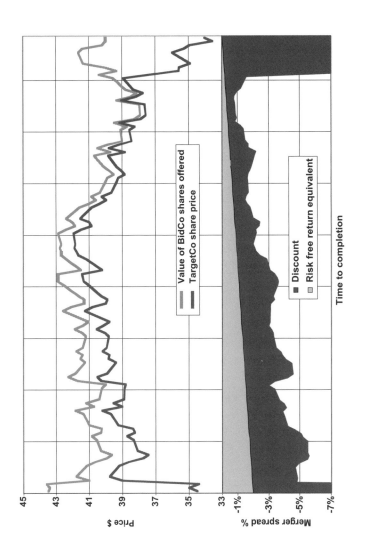

**Figure 6.4** What happens when a deal breaks

When a merger transaction breaks the spread widens dramatically. The losses incurred from a transaction breaking are likely to outweigh the returns that would have been achieved had the transaction completed.

Source: author.

hold the transaction up. For a friendly tender offer the timescale might be as short as 15 to 30 days, again assuming the regulators step aside.

Predicting the behaviour of regulators is both an art and a science. On the one hand there are clear procedures for filing information, and waiting periods that vary for different types of transaction.[2] On the other hand there is a complex code of signals that arbitrageurs pick up from regulatory authorities that help them determine how the authorities are disposed towards a transaction. Requests for further information might be interpreted as routine if they come from one agency, but as a warning signal if they come from another. There are all sorts of regulators to deal with. In the United States alone mergers are subject to oversight from the FTC, the Justice Department, state governments and a range of industry regulators.[3] Where a company has part or all of its operations based in Europe it must gain approval from the EU and a range of authorities within individual EU states. All these authorities have their own procedures, and they are led by individuals who espouse a range of attitudes about how they should perform their duties. Politics can affect these attitudes, both in Europe and the United States. The inauguration of President Bush, for example, heralded a more pro-business environment. Bush made several new FTC and Justice Department appointments that resulted in a more positive attitude towards mergers and increased the speed with which they could be completed. An arbitrageur must therefore have a good understanding of both the rules and the nuances involved in dealing with merger authorities.

## ASSESSING COMPLETION RISK

There is a list of warning signs that may indicate an increased probability of a deal's failure.

- Mergers that have been 'agreed in principle', where there is no 'definitive agreement', are often high-risk propositions. The

---

2. In the United States the timetable and procedures for authorizing a merger are laid down in the Hart–Scott–Rodino Act. This requires a series of filings with the SEC, FTC and Justice Department, followed by a 30-day period in which these authorities may request further information, potentially causing a delay. It is obviously a good sign if no additional information is sought after the original filings. The acceptance of further filings is followed by another 20 days for deliberations, after which the transaction either completes or the authorities challenge it on antitrust grounds. Filings and negotiations may be occurring simultaneously with state governments, industry regulators and overseas authorities. Even after filings have been approved, the US federal government has the authority to halt the merger, although such intervention is rare in practice.

3. Notably for financial institutions, media and natural monopolies.

agreement is only tentative and may have been announced because rumours of negotiations had leaked into the market before the parties were ready to go public. Conservative merger arbitrageurs rarely touch deals before they have been formally agreed, even though the spreads may be attractively wide. They certainly do not get involved in rumours.

- However, even after a definitive agreement is signed there tend to be all sorts of escape clauses written in. A loosely written definitive agreement incorporating wide-ranging terms of abandonment would be perceived as higher risk.

- Onerous performance targets or material adverse change clauses (MAC clauses) written into a merger agreement increase the risk that BidCo will call off an acquisition. MAC clauses are one of the first things arbitrageurs look for when scrutinizing a transaction.

- Any unexpected positives for TargetCo's fundamentals may also threaten the transaction because the merger's terms may have to be renegotiated.

- Personality conflicts can also emerge as negotiations proceed. Squabbles over future management roles in the merged entity often scupper talks.

- If BidCo is seeking to acquire TargetCo with cash it must be able to demonstrate access to financing. Changes in interest rates or in the attitudes of lenders can undermine financing efforts in the period after a deal has been announced. Uncertainties about BidCo's ability to pay do not bode well for a deal's outcome. Clearly an arbitrageur will be more cautious if BidCo is already highly leveraged.

- The financial markets may not approve of the transaction and key shareholder groups may fail to express support.

- Market movements themselves can severely undermine the confidence of the merging parties. Significant shifts in the price of BidCo can lead to fears that TargetCo is either under- or over-valued at the agreed price. Even with floating exchange ratios and collars, concerns are likely to rise on the back of BidCo share price volatility.

- Theoretically, the market price of TargetCo should be relatively stable, at least in relation to the BidCo share price. On the other hand the trading performance of TargetCo will be closely scrutinized in the run-up to completion. Any nasty surprises are likely to cause BidCo to reassess its rationale, so it is a bad sign if TargetCo is struggling.

- As has already been mentioned, outstanding due diligence is a real warning sign because it can cause delays and because there may be unpleasant secrets lurking within financial statements.

- The absence of a 'fairness letter' that independently endorses the offer price is a red flag.

- Each company has its own by-laws and articles of association. It does not help if the burden of shareholder votes and approvals is too great (for either TargetCo or BidCo).

- Regulation is the most important danger of all. Companies that are either very large or that operate within heavily regulated industries may therefore be less attractive arbitrage candidates.[4] When the management of BidCo signals an uncompromising stance about business unit disposals, the arbitrageur can expect lengthy legal battles.

- If either party is involved in material litigation the arbitrageur also has reason to be concerned.

- The impact of a deal breaking is greatly magnified if BidCo has offered a large premium for TargetCo shares. Arbitrageurs may shy away from such situations if they feel the downside is too large.

- Excessively complex deal structures may pose a risk for arbitrageurs, making it difficult to establish a hedged position and creating uncertainty about methods of payment.

- Some deals have unattractive tax implications, particularly if they are cross-border. These can be prohibitive for arbitrageurs if they result in excessive dividends or capital gains. Offshore merger arbitrage funds may have to be particularly careful in this regard, perhaps making a point of exiting some deals before completion. On occasions tax charges can be deal breakers for the negotiating companies themselves.

- A BidCo with a record of 'playing hardball' in merger negotiations may put arbitrage positions at risk.

---

4. For example, some arbitrageurs avoid mergers in the airlines industry because of the regulatory and union issues that often plague such transactions.

- A bid made for the wrong reasons is often a bad bid. The most obvious bad reason is the creation of reserves that can be released over subsequent periods to flatter earnings. A company doing this quickly becomes an addict, but is storing up problems that may resurface in the middle of a future deal.

- Mergers where BidCo might become the target of a bid itself are particularly unattractive. The arbitrageur is likely to be short BidCo shares in a share-for-share deal so an offer for BidCo itself is likely to scupper the original deal and cause BidCo shares to rise rapidly.

All these hurdles seem very off-putting, yet many of these obstacles can be overcome if the parties involved demonstrate sufficient willingness. There are a number of positive ingredients that point to a successful merger.

- The green light from major shareholders is a good sign, particularly if they include company management.

- Above all, arbitrageurs will sleep better if there is a strategic rationale for a merger. Demonstrable synergies, cost savings, cross-selling opportunities, vertical integration, compatible product lines or a good geographic fit are all reasons that help ward off criticism. Shareholder approval means company management is unlikely to abandon its plans.

- It greatly helps if both BidCo and TargetCo are in good financial condition with strong balance sheets. This increases the probability that BidCo will be able to fund a cash acquisition, and will reduce shareholder opposition to a share-for-share deal. Solid TargetCo fundamentals mean that BidCo is less likely to develop second thoughts. In fact, it helps if the entire sector looks healthy.

- In general it makes things easier if BidCo is large relative to TargetCo, as this lessens the possibility that BidCo has been over-ambitious. If BidCo has sufficient cash on its balance sheet to fund a transaction it gives the arbitrageur significantly more confidence than if finance needs to be raised externally.

- A deal is less likely to run into difficulties if a sensible price has been offered for TargetCo. Shareholders of each party are less likely to object and are more likely to retain their shareholdings.

- If the management of BidCo needs a little convincing, a 'golden parachute' sometimes does the trick. Golden parachutes are generous packages for senior executives that are contingent on the deal and that provide reassurance for individuals who fear redundancy or demotion within the merged group. To shareholders they look like bribes, but they give arbitrageurs more confidence in a transaction.

- Various signals confirm the merging entities are committed to a deal. These include a variety of structures such as termination fees and options granted to BidCo by TargetCo.

- Liquidity is an essential ingredient for a good merger, otherwise transaction costs may make arbitrage unprofitable.

- Whilst some arbitrageurs favour smaller deals because they are often poorly researched, most prefer the merging parties to be large. This is partly because the transaction is more likely to be handled by the top lawyers and investment bankers who tend to be more adept at pushing deals through. It also means the securities are likely to be liquid and the merging companies are likely to have a record of doing deals.

## WHAT MERGER ARBITRAGEURS DO

Merger arbitrage is easy to do badly but difficult to do well. Unfortunately, doing it badly is not an option because the penalty for making mistakes is considerable. Therefore a merger arbitrageur has a great deal of work to do. The most obvious job is to perform in-depth research on each deal before establishing a position and as events unfold. An arbitrageur will work frantically to assess a deal's timing and risk in order to gain an informational advantage over the rest of the market. On occasions he or she may have to work fast when a deal is first announced, for fear that other arbitrageurs will close up the spread before he or she gets his/her position on. He or she will attend company meetings, participate in conference calls, comb through financial statements, unpick every sentence of the merger agreement, examine SEC filings, gauge the attitude of key shareholders, read broker analysis, talk to industry specialists, telephone investment bankers, speak to traders, hire lawyers, engage tax advisors, attend antitrust hearings, sidle up to regulators and compare notes with other arbitrageurs. No stone will be left unturned in the arbitrageur's efforts to be reassured that a deal is certain to complete. An arbitrageur must develop a precise understanding of each merging company's business interests in each relevant jurisdiction. He or she must be able to predict where the companies will be asked to dispose of business interests to meet regulatory concerns and whether these requests will be resisted by the merging entities. Thorough antitrust analysis can be a mammoth task.

Of course, complications are not necessarily the arbitrageur's enemy. If he or she is prepared to go the extra mile with research, complications that confuse others can provide great opportunities. The spreads on offer are likely to be wider. Therefore a good merger arbitrageur lifts those stones that others cannot be bothered to look under. Although it is not essential, a big team of analysts obviously helps with this process.[5]

Research is not the arbitrageur's only job. Research is just one part of a risk management process that includes a number of other measures. Careful portfolio construction with good diversification is an obvious example. There is no point in having a concentrated portfolio if a large number of good deals can be researched and identified. An arbitrageur is unlikely to take positions for more than 10 per cent of his or her assets, and many restrict positions to 7 per cent.[6] Exposures are likely to be kept smaller where the potential downside is large or where the manager has less confidence in the probability of completion. The arbitrageur generally calculates and monitors the potential 'total downside' should each and every spread within a portfolio widen to its predicted maximum. This number must be kept within reasonable bounds, and unless it is carefully calculated there will be hidden risks within a portfolio.

Diversification across names should be accompanied by diversification across sectors, otherwise industry-wide anxieties can widen

5. Perhaps the most important research document is the merger agreement. In *Risk Arbitrage: An investor's guide* Keith Moore (1999) highlights a number of important points an arbitrageur should extract. These include: the deadline for completion and the timetable for submitting information to antitrust authorities; confirmation of whether the deal is friendly or hostile; formal correspondence between BidCo and TargetCo (shedding light on the tone of negotiations and the rationale for the merger); the investment bank's opinion on whether the price offered is fair; detailed terms of the deal (including provisions for its termination); the manner and timing of payment (including provisions for adjusting the exchange ratio); the number of shares in issue (including the options and convertibles outstanding); details of the guarantee period in which shares should be tendered; the rights of TargetCo shareholders to withdraw tendered shares (enabling arbitrageurs to change their mind); the effect that dividends paid will have on the price BidCo is offering; the intentions of key employees or shareholders of TargetCo to offer their shares to BidCo; BidCo's plans for raising finance for the deal; discussion of any legal, antitrust or regulatory issues affecting the deal.

6. In the context of merger arbitrage a '7 per cent position' generally refers to the size of the long position in TargetCo. This may or may not be hedged depending on whether BidCo is paying with cash or shares.

spreads across an entire portfolio at once. Since merger activity is often concentrated within certain areas of the economy this is not always easy. It also helps to divide the portfolio up between cash and share-for-share deals, as this may help in periods of stock market volatility. Too many share-for-share deals with collars can make the portfolio vulnerable to changing prices. The arbitrageur should diversify the 'deal duration' in the portfolio too, perhaps aiming to have 20 per cent of the portfolio mature every month. Spreads in early stage deals are often more volatile, so it would not be wise to have the entire portfolio in them. Likewise, it would not help to have all the portfolio's deals maturing at the same time or there might be problems reinvesting the cash.

An arbitrageur's position sizes may well start small and build up as the research progresses and confidence increases. In addition, an arbitrageur may trade in and out of positions. If he or she feels the market has become overconfident about a deal, he/she may take profits on the narrow spread and exit the position. Very often small hiccups cause a narrow spread to widen sharply, and less informed investors are frightened out of the trade. This gives the seasoned arbitrageur the opportunity to re-establish exposure to the deal at a more favourable rate. Most arbitrageurs monitor the spreads in their portfolios on a real time basis.

At times an arbitrageur believes that a deal is likely to fail and wants to bet against its completion. This is referred to as 'reversing' a deal, and consists of going short of TargetCo (and long of BidCo too in the case of a stock offer). This can be a very attractive trade if the spread is very narrow, as the arbitrageur's downside is usually limited to this spread closing. The profits from being short a failed deal greatly outweigh the likely losses, as the spread is likely to widen sharply if it breaks. Reversing deals is not without its risks. If TargetCo is subject to a topping bid from a third party, the arbitrageur's short position may turn out to be painful.[7]

# ATTRIBUTES OF A GOOD MERGER ARBITRAGEUR

Apart from knowledge of law and corporate finance, there are a number of other attributes that an arbitrageur should have. Flexibility

---

7.   'Reversing' is also referred to colloquially as 'Chinese-ing'.

is one. In many instances long and short equity positions are not the cheapest way to access a deal. It may be more cost effective to establish a position using options, and this may limit the potential downside at the same time. A convertible bond may be another alternative route into a deal. This requires close scrutiny of the convertible bond's terms, which is why the instrument is sometimes overlooked and can provide a cheap alternative. Speed is another favourable characteristic. Often a merger spread closes rapidly in the period shortly after the announcement of a deal. It helps to be able to perform research faster than other market participants in order to capture the wider spread without taking too much deal risk. However, not all arbitrageurs have the resources to work quickly, and if a choice must be made it is usually considered to be better to enter a deal later and with more certainty. Critical mass can be a bonus to arbitrageurs if it allows them these research resources and provides for more efficient execution.[8] Then again, smaller arbitrage operations tend to be compensated with access to smaller deals. Although smaller deals can be more risky, the markets are less efficient with them. It is perhaps more worthwhile for smaller firms to devote the time and energy to establishing an informational advantage in obscure situations.

## ASSESSING THE RISK–REWARD TRADE-OFF

It is worth reflecting on how arbitrageurs handle the risk–reward equation. One conventional way of placing deals in order of their attractiveness is by assessing their expected returns as follows:

Expected return = (Probability deal closes × Spread) + (Probability deal breaks × Loss if breaks)

A number of arbitrageurs use this approach to assess the relative merits of different deals. On the surface it appears to capture many of the components of an arbitrageur's investment process (estimates of probability, return and loss). It may be tempting for an arbitrageur to combine a number of transactions on this basis to form a portfolio. Yet this simple approach overlooks a couple of important dimensions. The first of these is time, and the effect it has on annualized returns. If a deal is successful it will complete at the end of an extended period, after which cash can be redeployed elsewhere. The return achieved can be calculated in

---

8. Both access to stock borrow and transaction costs.

annualized terms. However, if the deal fails the losses may be incurred long before the deal's expected conclusion. Therefore positive returns come slow but losses may come fast. This timing difference means that the damage to an arbitrageur's annualized returns caused by losses is greater than the benefit generated by gains.

The second dimension to remember relates to the asymmetric nature of returns. The losses incurred tend to be far more painful than the gains made are joyful. This makes the probability of a deal closing the huge swing factor in determining a deal's 'expected return'. If the perceived probability of a deal closing is 90 per cent for each of 10 deals, and this probability estimate proves accurate, an arbitrageur may generate respectable returns. Yet if just one more deal fails the arbitrageur can finish the period deep into negative territory. Thus the equation above may provide a false sense of security. The overwhelming determinant of success is avoiding failure. By relying on the equation above one might be tempted to enter deals with wide spreads but modest probabilities of success, and be fooled into expecting the same returns as from safe deals with narrow spreads. Cautious managers restrict themselves to deals where they are strongly convinced of the transaction's merits. They do not chase wide spreads.

## Nerd's corner 1: the use of options in merger arbitrage

In most share-for-share transactions a merger arbitrageur goes long the equity of TargetCo and short the equity of BidCo. However, there may be occasions when it is more efficient to use an option strategy. For example, the arbitrageur may decide to buy shares of TargetCo and to simultaneously short a call on TargetCo that is slightly in-the-money. If the merger progresses according to plan for the remaining life of the option, the arbitrageur can expect the call to expire in-the-money or to be exercised by its owner. The arbitrageur can then deliver the shares against the option and bank the premium in lieu of obtaining the merger spread. If the deal fails, the arbitrageur will lose money on the long position in TargetCo. However, if the trade had been structured conventionally, he or she would have lost money both on the long in TargetCo and on the short in BidCo. By using the option strategy the arbitrageur has lost on TargetCo alone, and has been slightly compensated by banking the call option premium.

The potential return from banking the premium may be less than the spread captured from the conventional trade structure, long TargetCo and short BidCo. Many other arbitrageurs may be pursuing a similar strategy, reducing the value of the call premium. Furthermore, implied volatility on stock options collapses if the underlying equity is the subject of a takeover bid. The short rebate from BidCo will also be forgone. However, if the option's life is short the IRR may be respectable.

Another way of using options might be to buy TargetCo shares and short BidCo shares as normal but to add a long TargetCo put position. This would be a means of limiting the downside if the deal breaks. In most instances this is likely to be an expensive form of protection. Options are more likely to be used in conjunction with transactions that involve collars. If an exchange ratio floats in line with the market price of BidCo shares, the arbitrageur may not see the need to short BidCo. The offer has a predetermined dollar value. However, if the floating exchange ratio becomes fixed at certain pre-specified values for BidCo, beyond those bounds the value of the offer becomes subject to the price of BidCo shares. The arbitrageur can set up option positions with strikes that establish short exposure to BidCo shares only if the bounds of the collar are breached.

## Nerd's corner 2: hostile takeovers

Hostile takeovers are 'special cases', and arbitrageurs must consider them separately from agreed mergers. Hostile takeovers are generally much riskier for arbitrageurs since by definition the management of TargetCo is trying to prevent them happening. Because of the risks many conservative arbitrageurs will avoid them altogether, but the more adventurous will partake if they anticipate a successful outcome. Probabilities and time-frames are very hard to judge, but the spreads on offer are understandably wide. The existence of a number of competing bids at attractive prices increases the likelihood that TargetCo's management will be forced by its shareholders to accept one of them. This does not necessarily make life easy for an arbitrageur, as a series of stock offers may leave him or her confused as to which BidCo shares to short to hedge the transaction.

The arbitrageur will also be uncertain as to the true value of an initial offer, as the bidding usually starts low. The uncertainty will be stretched further as TargetCo builds its defence against the unwelcome bid. This defence may merely be a façade aimed at extracting a better price, or it may be the start of a fight to the death. The arbitrageur must assess how long TargetCo is likely to fight and how effective its defences will be. The more control TargetCo's management has over its shareholders, the stronger its position.

Some of the methods TargetCo may use in its defence are as follows:

- A counter-bid by TargetCo for BidCo ('Pac-Man defence').
- Share buybacks by TargetCo which compete with BidCo's share offer and raise the price of shares.
- New debt issuance, which makes TargetCo a less attractive acquisition candidate and increases the overall cost for BidCo.

- Staggered boards, so that only a portion of the board may be re-elected each year. This frustrates attempts by BidCo to gain control of the boardroom rapidly.
- Provisions attached to TargetCo's securities which make their hostile acquisition very difficult or expensive ('poison pill').
- The introduction of awkward new company by-laws, such as more onerous shareholder voting requirements ('shark repellent clauses').
- Legal disputes over antitrust or state takeover laws.
- Sale of shares to a third company or the arrival of a 'white knight'.
- Sale of a crucial business unit that BidCo wanted (selling off a 'crown jewel').

Many of these defences can be challenged in court, but such challenges take time and may be followed by other defensive tactics. If the struggle goes on for years, the arbitrageur's annualized return will start to look very thin, while the likelihood that the deal will break might rise simultaneously. These situations are not for the faint-hearted.

# MERGER ARBITRAGE: OPPORTUNITIES, DIFFICULTIES, REACTION TO MARKETS

## Opportunities

### Low leverage
In contrast with many other 'arbitrage' strategies, merger arbitrage does not require significant leverage. Most managers operate happily with 100 per cent to 150 per cent invested on the long side. Of course, the low leverage required reflects the high volatility of the spreads involved, so the absence of leverage does not necessarily make the strategy less volatile. Yet various other problems associated with leverage are avoided. There is little risk of margin calls being made or funding lines being withdrawn at inopportune moments.

### Self-liquidating
Merger spreads do sometimes blow out in reaction to market crises, causing mark-to-market losses. If a manager receives redemption requests from nervous investors at such a time, these losses will be realized. However, those investors who hold firm are likely to recoup their losses. Experience shows that the vast majority of deals complete regardless of temporary market dislocation, and that spreads do

therefore close up again within a reasonable timeframe. Company executives tend to be less skittish than financial markets, and they usually press ahead with their transactions. In fact, one of the best times to invest in merger arbitrage is during such periods of crisis when spreads have widened unreasonably. Returns in the subsequent period tend to be very strong. Comparisons are sometimes drawn between the properties of merger spreads and those of a rubber band.

### Steady positive returns
Although merger arbitrage has its occasional hiccups and quiet periods, the returns generated by an experienced and talented merger arbitrageur are generally very steady. The strategy tends to generate a favourable Sharpe ratio.

### Event driven
In general, merger arbitrage returns are driven by events rather than the direction of markets. At most times the strategy is an attractive diversifier with low correlation to the main markets and with other hedge fund strategies. Various academic studies have tried to get to grips with the nature of merger arbitrage returns, and they often conclude that the strategy ought to provide lower returns than managers actually report. Within a few short steps these studies often conclude that merger arbitrage managers must therefore be assuming 'covert' directional exposure to equity markets to enhance their returns. Sometimes there is an element of truth in this. For the most part, however, these studies analyse the returns available from every transaction that occurred during the period of the study. Constructing a passive 'merger arbitrage index' in this way is no doubt the academically rigorous thing to do but it is likely to underestimate the returns available to the strategy. In practice it is the arbitrageur's job to pick and chose between transactions, sidestepping deals offering low returns or high risks. There is therefore a 'return to skill'. An index approach to merger arbitrage returns is inappropriate because an entirely separate set of investors suffers the consequences of unattractive deals: the ordinary shareholders.

### Clarity
Merger arbitrage is intuitive and easy to understand compared with many other hedge fund strategies. For this reason, many investors who are uncomfortable with more complex hedge fund strategies favour merger arbitrage.

## Difficulties

### Hard work

Some observers mistakenly dismiss merger arbitrage as a 'simple' strategy. Merger arbitrage requires considerable experience and a good deal of hard work. Even if they are less probable, the risks are greater than the returns and new players who stick to the basics often get burnt.

### Asymmetric risk

As discussed, while most deals complete successfully and produce a modest return, the minority break and produce a much larger loss. A deal might earn the portfolio 0.20 per cent over three months if it completes but lose the portfolio 2.5 per cent overnight if it breaks. This payoff structure is not to everyone's liking and portfolio diversification does not go far in eliminating specific risk.

### Hidden risks

The level of risk within a portfolio can be hidden from a casual observer (such as the investor in a merger arbitrage fund). The arbitrageur may be able to cite the spreads of the deals within his or her portfolio. These may appear to be in line with prevailing market norms, suggesting the manager is taking no undue risks. Nevertheless, the width of spreads can disguise the potential downside in deals. If the bids all incorporate high premiums, the effect of deals breaking is particularly negative. The spread may indicate no more than the probability of completion that the market attaches to a transaction, rather than reflecting all the risks of failure.

### Homogenous

Some merger arbitrage managers pride themselves in playing small and unnoticed deals, yet it is usual to find that most managers are involved in a similar set of transactions and that their portfolios look very much alike. It may not seem very constructive to diversify across several managers as they are likely to contain similar risks. In practice, however, arbitrageurs time and size their positions differently. Because merger arbitrage is all about avoiding losses, the managers' skill accounts for a large portion of returns. Using a number of managers does therefore deliver a degree of diversification against manager risk.

### Quiet periods

Merger arbitrage returns are cyclical because merger activity is cyclical. There are routine quiet periods in which activity is low.

Without this activity the strategy cannot be implemented and returns dry up. These quiet periods tend to be temporary and do not usually cause additional losses. However, the losses that do occur are more frustrating because the prevailing rate of return is lower.

### Limited capacity

Merger arbitrage is an attractive strategy. At times the weight of money chasing merger opportunities is too great, causing the spreads to contract and compressing the returns on offer. This is more of a concern than a lack of merger activity both because returns are reduced and risk is increased. When a spread has tightened too far too fast, it does not mean the deal is any more likely to go through, and if the deal breaks the spread has further to widen. Furthermore, the excess capital chasing merger deals is usually less experienced and more skittish. Marginal players squeeze spreads too tight and evacuate from a deal too fast in the face of bad news. On the plus side, however, this can provide the opportunity to reverse bad deals and to buy into spreads that have blown out.

### Limited upside

Merger arbitrage spreads offer fairly limited returns. There is limited scope for one arbitrageur to outperform the peer group without assuming additional risk (such as leverage or involvement in uncertain deals). Smaller players may add some value by focusing on obscure or complex deals which require additional research. This may not necessarily add to the portfolio's risk although the mark-to-market swings may be a little more volatile. However, few managers are able to restrict themselves to such deals, and for most the upside is limited. What distinguishes them is their avoidance of the downside.

### Adoption of greater risk

Most arbitrageurs are disciplined and allow their returns to decline if the opportunity set withers. Some act irresponsibly. In order to maintain returns and retain investors they enter low-quality transactions, breach sensible diversification limits or add to their leverage. Those managers who maintain strong returns when peers are struggling to invest capital may well be adopting too much risk.

### Regulation and political risk

While governments, regulators and antitrust authorities are generally fairly consistent and predictable in their approach to mergers, they do at times pass surprising decisions. Sometimes the personalities involved can be difficult to read.

### Efficient pricing

Arbitrageurs may disagree on how efficiently specific arbitrage spreads are priced, but in general spreads reflect the risk of each situation. Merger arbitrage is not a secret. It is widely practised and there is no free lunch.

### Timing trade-off

Investing in deals late in the day may give the arbitrageur a strong sense of confidence about a deal's success. However, the spreads are generally narrow late in the day and the returns lower. Yet the loss if the deal breaks is even greater. Being early usually offers better returns but there is less certainty and more spread volatility.

### Transaction costs

Transaction costs weigh heavily on merger arbitrage returns. Short rebates are often a large contributor to positive returns. A large part of merger arbitrage return is therefore at the mercy of transaction mechanics rather than the skill of the manager or the state of the markets.

## Reaction to markets

### Recessions and bear markets (effect on new deal flow)

While merger arbitrage returns may not exhibit a high correlation to markets month to month, the relationship is slightly stronger over the economic cycle. Merger activity and arbitrage returns tend to dry up during sharply plunging equity markets and deep recessions. It is not the rate of economic growth or the level of the markets that kills merger activity, it is uncertainty in the corporate boardroom and operational instability. Corporations are temporarily uncertain about share prices and are uncomfortable launching bids. They are equally uncertain about their own operating performance and that of takeover candidates, causing them to delay acquisitions until prospects become clearer. Merger activity tends to recover once the economy and markets level off, even in the absence of recovery. Indeed, recession often prompts a wave of fully fledged consolidations and bargain hunting.[9] (See Figure 6.5.)

---

9. Company executives often spot a bottom in their sector ahead of the market because they can feel their own operations stabilizing. This will often trigger acquisitions. A particularly bullish sign is a hostile bid, which often heralds a recovery. In a hostile situation BidCo does not have access to TargetCo's books so must be particularly sure of an improving outlook.

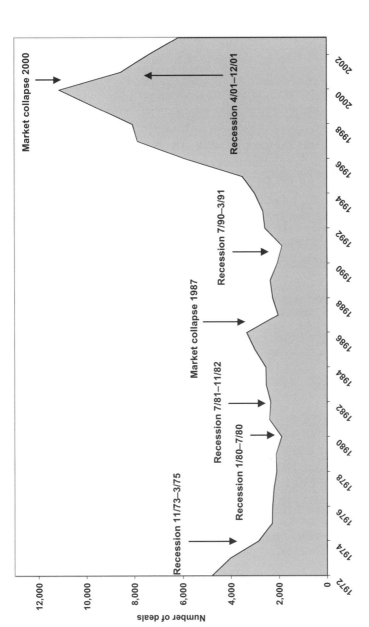

**Figure 6.5** US merger activity during recessions and after equity market crashes

Merger activity tends to tail off temporarily as a result of recessions and sharp equity market corrections.

Source: Mergerstat.

### Recessions and bear markets (effect on existing transactions)

Recessions and bear markets can increase the risk that existing transactions break, particularly if either merger party suffers significant downward earnings revisions. Sharp equity market corrections can also trigger breaches of provisions in a merger agreement, cause participants to have second thoughts and reduce the availability of finance. These risks should not be exaggerated as most deals are driven through despite a deteriorating environment.

### Valuations

When valuations are at higher levels BidCo is more likely to use its stock for takeovers. When valuations are lower cash is a more popular option, particularly if this coincides with lower interest rates.

### Rising interest rates

Rising interest rates affect merger arbitrage on two levels. In the broader sense they can jeopardize the efforts of BidCo to secure finance and can affect the earnings of both merging parties. They therefore increase deal risk. However, the arbitrageur is compensated via the pricing of merger spreads. Merger spreads are usually priced in terms of a risk free rate plus a risk premium. Higher interest rates therefore increase the nominal returns of subsequent transactions. The arbitrager tends to enjoy a double whammy because the short rebate, a major component of total returns, increases with the interest rate. The reverse applies when interest rates fall.

### Sensitive transactions

Certain transactions are particularly sensitive to changes in the environment. Leveraged buy-outs (LBOs) and early stage transactions are particularly vulnerable to a stumbling economy and the threat of weaker TargetCo earnings. They may also be undermined by rising interest rates that may be the by-product of recovery.

### Severe market dislocation

Merger arbitrage spreads tend to blow out during periods of severe market dislocation, due to heightened uncertainty and capital being withdrawn from the strategy. Despite this, the number of deals that break during such periods is not likely to rise by much, if at all. So while mark-to-market losses are incurred they tend to be followed by unusually strong returns thereafter. The result is a pattern of returns that exhibits a very low standard deviation most of the time but with periodic spikes in volatility every few years as drawdowns occur.

## Merger location

Historically, merger arbitrage has been easier to execute in the US market than in many other markets. In the United States, deals have traditionally traded at discounts to the price of the bid. This is usually the case with European deals but they have sometimes traded above par due to speculators buying TargetCo in the hope of a topping bid. The political and regulatory environment in Europe has also been a little tricky at times.

## Evolution of market and economic influences

A study of 'The characteristics of risk and return in risk arbitrage' by Mark Mitchell and Todd Pulvino (2001) examined mergers between 1963 and 1968. It observed a low correlation between arbitrage and equity markets except during sharp market downturns. Another study by Richard Horwitz and Louis Rodriguez of Capital Market Risk Advisors (Horwitz and Rodriguez, 2002) tracked mergers between January 1997 and October 2001. It observed a relatively high correlation between arbitrage and equity markets during equity bull markets and a relatively low correlation during falling and low markets. None of this gets us very far. I would wager that merger arbitrage returns are driven by different factors at different times, not by equity markets. Sharp corrections in equity markets are often accompanied by merger spreads widening out. This does not mean merger arbitrage is correlated to equities. Both the correction in equities and the widening in merger spreads are probably reflections of a temporary third factor, namely panic. Early in a period of economic and market stagnation merger activity is likely to be low and arbitrage funds are likely to have high cash levels. This reduces their correlation to anything other than cash. Later on in an economic and market slump merger activity may recover, once more changing the pattern of arbitrage returns. At other times the level of interest rates or the weight of money committed to the strategy will appear to be the most influential factor determining returns.

# APPENDIX 1: KEY CONSIDERATIONS: MERGER ARBITRAGE

- What methods are used to research the probability of a deal's completion and timing? Who does this research and how quickly?

- Who is contacted outside the firm (lawyers, industry specialists, investment bankers, tax experts and so on)?

- In particular, how much expertise does the manager have in assessing the detailed regulatory implications of a deal?
- What steps are taken to assess a firm's shareholder base and its implications for a deal, including voting attitudes and arbitrage short interest?
- What systems are used for measuring and monitoring deal spreads?
- What steps are taken to assess the expected loss if a deal breaks?
- What is the manager's philosophy regarding the risk–return trade-off? To what extent will the manager invest in risky deals with wider spreads?
- How much of the manager's portfolio is invested in bids with high premiums?
- How does the manager cope with transactions involving different types of collars? What approach is taken to hedging them?
- How are transaction costs minimized?
- Are option strategies used to establish positions or to reduce risk? In what ways?
- How often does the manager access a deal through a debt security rather than equity?
- What are the fund's diversification limits by position, sector, cash versus stock deals, deal size, maturity date and spread width?
- What is the manager's geographic remit? Does the manager have a sufficient understanding of overseas regulatory environments?
- To what extent is leverage employed and in what environments?
- Does the manager invest in unannounced transactions? If so, under what circumstances?
- Does the manager invest in hostile takeovers? If so, under what circumstances?
- What size and complexity of transaction does the manager prefer?
- Does the manager have a particular preference for early or late stage deals?
- Does the manager Chinese deals?
- Under what sort of circumstances will a manager reduce or increase a position size? How actively are spreads traded?

- Does the fund have appropriate redemption restrictions to prevent the manager being forced to realize temporary mark-to-market losses?

- How much experience does the manager really have and how long is his or her record?

- Other than pure merger arbitrage, what other strategies does the manager pursue and in what size?

- How does the manager react to periods of low transaction volume?

# APPENDIX 2: GLOSSARY

**Agreement in principle:** A non-binding agreement between parties acknowledging friendly merger discussions.

**Chinese-ing:** Taking a reverse position from traditional merger arbitrage in anticipation of a deal breaking (short TargetCo).

**Collar:** Conditions in a deal structure that set out its limits. A share-for-share offer may involve an exchange ratio that floats over a specified share price range for BidCo. Alternatively the exchange ratio may be fixed but over a specified share price range for BidCo. Types of collar include 'look back options', 'barriers', 'floors' and 'knock-outs'.

**Corporate raider:** Corporation with a reputation for hostile takeovers.

**Crown jewel:** Key business unit within TargetCo.

**Definitive agreement:** Detailed and binding merger document.

**Exchange offer:** An offer made by BidCo directly to the shareholders of TargetCo, rather than through the management of TargetCo.

**Exchange ratio:** The number of BidCo shares offered in exchange for each TargetCo share in a share-for-share transaction.

**Fairness letter:** An opinion given by an investment bank endorsing the price offered for TargetCo.

**Floating exchange ratio:** A share-for-share offer in which the number of BidCo shares offered for each TargetCo share changes in response to movements in the BidCo share price. The effect is to establish a fixed cash value to BidCo's offer.

**Golden parachute:** A generous settlement offered to senior TargetCo executives on condition that the deal completes. Provides reassurance to those who stand to lose their jobs.

**Greenmail:** The repurchase by TargetCo of its own shares off a corporate raider at a high price. Provides a means of fending off a takeover attempt.

**Hart–Scott–Rodino Act:** The legislation guiding takeover procedures in the US, including the establishment of antitrust clearance.

**Lock-up:** Provisions in a definitive merger agreement granting BidCo advantages over other potential suitors.

**Pac-Man defence:** The launch of a counter offer for BidCo by TargetCo as a means of staving off a hostile bid.

**Poison pill:** The issue of securities specially structured to make hostile takeovers difficult or expensive.

**Premium:** The extent to which BidCo's offer for TargetCo shares exceeded the market value of TargetCo shares before the bid was announced.

**Proration:** The situation in which a TargetCo shareholder's application for a particular form of payment from BidCo is scaled back 'pro rata'. If BidCo has offered a mixture of cash and stock for TargetCo, a TargetCo shareholder might apply to be paid entirely in cash. However, if too many investors opt for cash they may have to be 'prorated'.

**Scorched earth defence:** Damaging attempts by TargetCo to make its company less attractive to a hostile bidder.

**Shark repellent clause:** The insertion of company by-laws aimed at frustrating hostile bids (such as high threshold voting requirements).

**Staggered board:** The re-election of directors in successive years rather than all at once. Aimed at preventing hostile bidders from gaining rapid control of a company.

**Standstill agreement:** An agreement between TargetCo and one of its larger shareholders limiting the extent to which further shares may be bought or sold. Provides reassurance that the shareholder will not become a hostile bidder.

**Walk away provisions:** Provisions in a definitive merger agreement permitting either party to back out under the circumstances specified.

**White knight:** A company favoured by TargetCo as a preferred bidder in preference to a hostile bidder.

# 7

# Statistical arbitrage

'A child of five would understand this'.
'Send somebody to fetch a child of five.'

Groucho Marx

The term 'statistical arbitrage' covers a multitude of sins. In its broadest sense it refers to all tightly hedged quantitative equity strategies. Most investors have some understanding of long-only quantitative techniques, in which the statistical behaviour of financial securities is mathematically modelled. The models of historical patterns are then used to predict the future behaviour of securities and to allocate an investment portfolio. Statistical arbitrage uses such techniques to generate a long–short portfolio. In order to qualify as 'arbitrage', these long–short portfolios are tightly hedged across a range of parameters. In addition, the long and short positions are chosen because historical statistical relationships between them have been violated.

Before investing in a statistical arbitrage fund there are two key questions you should ask yourself. First, will you understand what the manager is doing? Second, do you think the fund will prove consistently profitable? The answer to the first question is usually 'no'. Few investors understand the complex maths that lies behind a statistical model. Even if investors are capable of understanding the maths they will nevertheless not have it described to them, as the systems are usually strictly proprietary. Even investors who play the fool will not be given detailed information, just in case they are clever people masquerading as stupid ones.

Given that the answer to the first question is already 'no', the second question starts to look a little taxing. How can investors determine whether a strategy will work unless they know what it is?

Certainly, a small leap of faith is required. However some comfort can be gained from a manager's track record. Moreover, the basic principles behind a manager's activities may be laid bare. This chapter outlines some of the things that might be going on.

# MULTI-FACTOR MODELS

All sorts of statistical methods might be adopted for their predictive value, but where equities are concerned the basis is often arbitrage pricing theory. This theory suggests that a security's returns are a function of a series of risk–return factors. These factors are observable and measurable and can be used to explain movements in a security's price. A simple regression equation, such as the one below, demonstrates the principles involved. The security is the 'dependent variable' on the left-hand side of the equation. Its value is determined by the collection of 'independent variables' on the right-hand side. Each independent variable incorporates the expected return generated by one 'unit' of exposure to each factor.

$$ER_y = R_f + B_{y_1}(F_1 - R_f) + B_{y_2}(F_2 - R_f) + B_{y_3}(F_3 - R_f) + \ldots\ldots + B_{y_N}(F_N - R_f) + e_y$$

Where
$ER_y$ = Expected return from security 'y' over the period
$R_f$ = Risk free return[1]
$B_{y_1}$ = the beta for factor 1, also referred to as its 'factor coefficient'
$F_1$ = The expected return from factor 1, also referred to as 'independent variable number 1'
$e_y$ = the return unexplained by the model, also referred to as the 'residual' or 'error term'
$N$ = refers to the 'Nth' factor or the 'Nth' factor coefficient

So that the security's expected return may be described as:

The sum of the excess returns of a number of factors multiplied by their individual factor betas, plus the risk free rate, plus a random residual that is unexplained by the rest of the equation.

The statistical arbitrageur may identify any number of risk–return factors that appear to drive security returns. All sorts of indicators might be used to make up these factors, depending on what sort of

---

1. Note that arbitrage pricing theory proposes that the single constant at the beginning of the equation is equal to the risk free rate. This is because securities can be combined in portfolios that effectively neutralize exposure to all factors and where the residuals are diversified away. Such portfolios should be effectively 'risk-less' and arbitrage should ensure they only return the risk free rate.

security is being modelled. Many of them tend to be similar to those incorporated within Barra. Managers usually keep their factors secret, for fear that a competitor might reconstruct their model and thereby front run them. Equity models often include factors such as market capitalization, sector, industry group, earnings forecasts, financial ratios, price volatility and price momentum.[2]

Statistical arbitrage relies on identifying small inefficiencies that often exist for very brief periods. Although some models operate very slowly, turning over the portfolio a few times a year, most involve high-frequency trading, possibly turning the entire portfolio over a number of times every day. Models with different time horizons are likely to include different types of factor. In the short term, for instance, optimism and expectation are likely to be major drivers of a share price. Over longer periods fundamentals are more likely to prevail. The frequency with which a model generates trade signals will also be consistent with the frequency of the data used to drive the model. High-frequency trading may require tick-by-tick data while longer term models are likely to run off daily data.

### Earnings forecast revisions

Earnings forecast revisions are often used within arbitrage models as a predictor of future equity prices. Evidence indicates that analysts are reluctant to reverse previous recommendations sharply and are often uncomfortable expressing controversial opinions. Once a sea change begins in the analyst community it tends to continue, with individual analysts gradually bringing their estimates into line with the newly forming consensus. Investors, for their part, do not take decisions simultaneously. Some investors trade actively while others wait for a weekly or monthly investment committee. Earnings forecast information is not incorporated within a security's price immediately. Thus the effects of changes in earnings estimates are not random. Earnings forecast revisions exhibit gradual herding and they are incorporated into share prices over a period of time. Earnings revisions are 'serially correlated' so that returns can be captured by arbitrageurs. A number of statistical arbitrageurs use data from IBES as an input for this type of model.

By modelling a security's sensitivity to a series of factors it is possible to predict its 'normal' reaction to 'changing circumstances' as defined by the factors used. In an efficient market each security would move

2. For bonds, factors might include inflation, GDP growth, changes in the money supply, the prices of other bonds and the steepness of the yield curve. However it is rare for statistical arbitrage techniques to be applied to bond markets, since the efficiency of the markets tends to furnish few opportunities of the size required.

strictly in adherence to a model's predictions. In practice there are occasions when a security temporarily fails to react as predicted, but after a pause the security price 'catches up with events'. Statistical arbitrageurs seek to profit from delayed responses such as these. When their models identify a security which is theoretically over-valued arbitrageurs will short it, and when their models spot a cheap security they will buy it. This type of approach is a 'true' form of statistical arbitrage, although the term is also applied more loosely in the cases of 'mean reversion pairs' and 'quant fundamental' which are discussed later on.

Portfolio construction can be handled in a number of ways. Once a model has identified undervalued securities they can be bought long and the index sold short against them. Alternatively, for each security that is bought a suitable security can be identified as a short hedge, creating a series of pairs. However, in most instances arbitrage models independently identify separate portfolios of longs and shorts which are optimized to 'neutralize' exposure to a range of risks, the most obvious being the market. Equity statistical arbitrageurs might aim to have very low net exposures on the basis of sector, industry, market capitalization, value, growth, level of valuation, level of gearing, level of dividend yield, foreign sensitivity and equity-specific risk. Thereafter, a successful arbitrage model generates numerous buy and sell signals that on balance result in positive returns. In theory these returns bear no relationship to the direction of the market and are completely uncorre-lated to it. Since the portfolio is so tightly hedged it has a market beta near zero and its returns almost entirely represent alpha.

These models are often predicated on very simple ideas but the underlying maths is often ingenious. Some models are comparatively simple linear regression equations but others incorporate non-linear relationships and complex algorithms. Even theoretically straight-forward models are difficult to implement in practice. All the factors must be proposed and tested for their significance. Discovering exactly which factors encapsulate information capable of generating a return is no easy task. Combining a series of them in the correct sizes is even more complicated. For every security, each factor weighting (or beta) must also be arrived at and tested. Sadly, the mathematical relationships that are discovered are rarely enduring over time. Sooner or later arbitrageurs are forced to make alterations to their models to take account of changes in the world around them. Sometimes the inefficiency upon which a model is premised disappears altogether and an entirely new model must be found to replace the defunct one. Usually the research process is continuous, with models generating portfolios on the one hand and the managers refining new and existing models on the other. With so much research going on and so much money at stake, different statistical arbitrageurs often stumble across the same patterns. Then they start eating each other's lunch and arbitrage away inefficiencies. Different arbitrage firms are therefore engaged in an ongoing competition to discover new statistical opportunities, like wartime enemies racing to break one another's codes.

Statistical arbitrageurs adopt different approaches to constructing their multi-factor models. If they all traded off the same inefficiencies in the same manner they would arbitrage away their returns. Distinctions can be made even before a model is conceived. Some arbitrageurs develop hypotheses about market inefficiencies, then set about statistically testing them. If their theories are corroborated they construct a statistical model to profit from the inefficiency. Other 'purists' take a very different approach, reducing the scope for human bias. They screen statistical data at length, searching for patterns. In theory efficient markets should rarely exhibit statistical patterns (other than by chance) because they represent profit making opportunities which can be arbitraged away. If a pattern is identified these arbitrageurs attempt to explain it and construct a model to capture returns from the informational advantage. Not all arbitrageurs manage to explain all the patterns that they incorporate within their models but it is preferable that they do so, since they will be better placed to judge whether there are structural reasons for such patterns to endure. It will also help reassure them that the patterns they have detected are not purely the result of chance (and therefore transient). Many statistical arbitrageurs come from academic backgrounds and have transferred their skills to financial markets. This may influence the approach they use.

Statistical arbitrageurs hold different views about human intervention in their systems. There is always a human element in hypothesizing and designing mathematical models. They can never be purely statistical. Humans must also quantify risks, set risk parameters and determine the timeframes involved. At times humans must retain responsibility for executing trades that cannot be performed electronically. Some statistical arbitrageurs insist that humans check each trade before execution, just in case their systems have failed to detect a crucial issue. Most arbitrageurs will intervene under specific circumstances. For example, models can rarely cope with crucial information on corporate events like mergers or changes in the regulatory environment. Security prices tend to behave uncharacteristically once they are affected by credit issues or the prospect of bankruptcy. Securities are usually removed from the investment universe under such circumstances.

## MEAN REVERSION PAIRS

Using multi-factor models is not the only means of conducting statistical arbitrage. Some managers adopt a far simpler approach. After correlation analysis, pairs of securities can be identified that exhibit a stable relationship over time. On occasions the two securities within a pair become misaligned, often because human behaviour leads people to overreact to both good and bad news. The predictability of the reversion back to their usual relationship can be studied. Pairs that exhibit statistically dependable mean reversion characteristics can be traded in a portfolio. Such pairs are usually sourced from within fairly homogenous sectors, where there are logical relationships between securities. Relationships between mature companies where industry considerations are the dominant driver of price movement are the most likely to be stable. Equities that are subject to more stock specific influences are less likely to form stable pairs.

Mean reversion pairs strategies can be distinguished from multi-factor models that implement trades on a paired basis. First, mean reversion opportunities are identified using much simpler forms of statistical analysis. Second, multi-factor models generally identify a single mispriced security and then find a 'statistically suitable' second security to hedge the position. This is not the same as a mean reversion strategy, where a series of relationships between a number of previously identified pairs is monitored for disparities.

## QUANT FUNDAMENTAL

'Quant fundamental' strategies form another subset of statistical arbitrage. Quant fundamental strategies use multi-factor models that are entirely based on fundamental factors. They employ a series of fundamental factors to predict price behaviour, rather as Altman's Z-Score is used to determine the likelihood of bankruptcy. Quant fundamental strategies therefore employ more human premise than strictly statistical multi-factor programmes.

Any combination of fundamental factors might be incorporated in such models, so long as they are shown to work. For example, a model might track the difference between reported and cash earnings, identifying those companies where earnings numbers are being flattered by aggressive accounting. The approach works well in situations where price behaviour is driven by fundamental factors but where prices are more volatile than the fundamentals. However, these models can be victim to changing market fashions, such as an obsession with growth metrics at the expense of value.

The quant fundamental approach to statistical arbitrage tends to bridge the gap between quantitative and qualitative hedge fund strategies. The managers are often expressing their own investment beliefs through the construction of their models, and moderating their views with statistical evidence for their theories. Because of this blend, quant fundamental portfolios are more likely to contain deliberate exposures in certain areas that reflect a manager's fundamental views. Therefore quant fundamental programmes are often 'partly directional' strategies.

# TRADE EXECUTION AND MARKET MAKING

Given high levels of turnover, good execution is very important. No trade should be executed unless its expected return exceeds the expected trading costs (after incorporating the market impact of the proposed order). The smarter trading programmes electronically monitor prevailing execution costs and signal them back to the model as part of the trade evaluation process. If a trade involves more than one security, all legs of the trade may have to go on simultaneously at a sensible cost. Because statistical arbitrageurs trade with such frequency the volume of their business makes them much more valuable customers for the brokerage community than their assets under management imply. It is therefore reasonable to expect them to receive very competitive rates from their counterparties. Favourable trading terms can be crucial to the workings of a model.

This leads us to consider an important aspect of statistical arbitrage. Statistical models highlight price anomalies within a universe of securities. Often these anomalies are the result of pockets of investor buying or selling that are causing 'pressure points'. Statistical arbitrageurs stand on the other side of these pressure points and act as pools of market making capital. In some instances statistical arbitrageurs have established such efficient execution rates that they buy close to the bid price and sell close to the offer price. It comes as no surprise to discover that some of the earliest statistical arbitrage activities were conducted within banks in support of market making activities. Many statistical arbitrageurs can therefore be described as being 'long liquidity'.

Markets that support electronic trading facilitate much higher frequency trading and enable arbitrageurs to capture much shorter-lived inefficiencies. However, this is a competitive business and electronic trading itself makes markets more efficient, forcing trading systems to become even faster. Most of the larger markets now have fully electronic trading platforms that can support significant volumes. Some electronic trading systems involve human intervention somewhere along the process. Thus a trade that might otherwise execute in a fraction of a second can take several seconds. It may not sound significant but it can mean a great deal in the world of the statistical arbitrageur. A computer model that identifies a mispricing cannot be certain that the price will remain unchanged for several seconds. The model therefore demands a higher level of confidence before sending a trade signal down the wire to a 'semi-electronic' platform.

# STATISTICAL ARBITRAGE: OPPORTUNITIES, DIFFICULTIES, REACTION TO MARKETS

## Opportunities

### Patterns exist

One must not be too cynical about statistical arbitrage. The real world is not so tidy that it can be expressed as an equation, however complex. Nobody would suggest as much. Yet patterns do exist, however vague, and these patterns are lasting through time. An equation can be used to identify the approximate epicentre of a recurring pattern. If a trading model is based upon the predictions of this equation there will be times when profits are generated and times when losses are incurred. All the model needs to do is win more than it loses. There is no question that these inefficiencies do occur and that statistical models can profit from them for prolonged periods. The past returns of many statistical arbitrage funds bear this out clearly. The lingering questions relate to how long a model continues to work and what happens when things start to go wrong.

### Pure alpha

Statistical arbitrage is perhaps the closest an investor can get to neutrality in the equity markets. Most programmes involve very low net exposures across a broad range of parameters. Any return the model generates represents 'pure alpha' and 'zero market beta'. The strategy is non-directional.[3]

## Uncorrelated

Owing to its neutrality, the portfolio is immunized against market risk, sector risk and security specific risk. The remaining source of risk and reward relates to the success or failure of the statistical model itself. Depending upon how well the model was designed this can be either a good or bad thing. Nevertheless the investor has access to a source of return that is inherently unrelated to conventional investments and tends to exhibit little or no correlation to them. Statistical arbitrage can therefore be a valuable component in a diversified portfolio. During sharply falling markets this low correlation does not always hold quite so well (discussed under 'Reaction to markets').

## Long volatility

As long as they are not too extreme, higher levels of volatility tend to create more opportunities for statistical arbitrage to exploit. This makes statistical arbitrage a useful strategy to combine with other strategies that suffer from higher volatility.

## Devoid of emotion

A statistical arbitrage model does not lose confidence after a bad decision. It does not change its behaviour on the basis of market rumour, what Wall Street did yesterday, how much beer it drank last night or whether divorce is imminent. A case can be made for statistical arbitrage simply because it acts to diversify an investor's means of decision making.

## Numbers game

Statistical arbitrage is a numbers game. Conventional investors make far fewer investment decisions than most computer models. They take bigger bets and these matter more. A computer model makes a multitude of small decisions with strict risk controls. The impact of small losses and small triumphs is often imperceptible at the time of their occurrence. Yet all a model needs to do is to win a tiny bit more often than it loses and gradually it will start to clock up the gains.

---

3. This of course assumes that a model has been tightly defined. It seems that a number of short-term models inadvertently develop a long value bias, which becomes a hidden risk.

### 'Wigwam effect'

If a manager is running a number of models simultaneously, their trade signals can be used to reinforce one another.[4] Where different models suggest the same trade for different reasons the confidence in those signals is greater. In efficient markets statistical arbitrageurs may be stuck for good ideas, so having one 'weak signal' reinforced by another can be very useful.

### Access to market making

Where a statistical arbitrage fund is taking on the role of a market maker it can be an attractive investment proposition. Few investors gain access to this lucrative and uncorrelated source of returns.

## Difficulties

### Purely historical

If ever there was a case of 'driving in the rear view mirror' then this was it. Most types of investment decision are grounded in past experience but statistical arbitrage is entirely so.

### Limitations of history (extrapolation)

A simple regression formula can be designed on the basis of historical data. This data lies within certain bounds. The formula can be used to predict a security's return provided that the data for the independent variable lies within the bounds of the historical range used to design the formula. This is known as 'interpolation' and in most instances it works pretty well. Using the formula in conjunction with data that stretches beyond those historical bounds is a shaky exercise. This is known as 'extrapolation'. For example, kittens might be observed to grow by 1 centimetre a week in the first three months of their lives. A formula could be devised to reflect the observation. Yet it would be wrong to assume that cats are more than 2 metres long by the age of four. One can see that a statistical arbitrage model can quickly find itself in unknown territory, where the independent variables are beyond the bounds of the historical data that were used to construct the model. It is common to hear a statistical arbitrage manager explain away a period of poor performance with comments such as 'Our

---

4. The term 'wigwam effect' is a reference to the structure of a wigwam. On their own the wooden poles of a wigwam do not support themselves but when leant against each other they do. Likewise some academics believe they can combine a series of fairly weak arguments to build a strong case. Some politicians like to do the same thing.

model stopped working but we have fixed it now' or 'A very unusual pattern of events occurred and it is highly unlikely to happen again'.

### Limitations of history (data snooping)

The term 'data snooping' is a criticism of the integrity with which some models are conceived and back tested. An arbitrageur may develop a model to reflect an hypothesis. Let us say that this hypothesis relates to how exchange rates behave, and that it sprung from an observation made about a particular set of data, the sterling–euro exchange rate. In order to test the model independently the arbitrageur chooses the Canadian dollar–Swiss franc exchange rate. It is possible that the movements of each of these exchange rates have been driven by developments in a third currency, the US dollar. If that proves to be the case, the arbitrageur has inadvertently reused the same (or related) data to both inspire and test the model. One can see that such an exercise is self-confirming. It is not clear that the model is predictive of the future. 'Data snooping' can be difficult to avoid, and managers are particularly prone to it when they make adjustments to their models in reaction to earlier failures. Updated models are often tested using the very same data that inspired the alterations.

### Limitations of history (interventions and slippage)

As discussed, a number of arbitrageurs occasionally intervene in their models on a qualitative basis. Their propensity to do this calls into question the validity of their back testing. It is not possible to simulate whether the manager would have intervened successfully. Even if back tests are performed on the assumption that the manager never intervened, it provides no reassurance that intervention in the future will improve performance rather than detract from it. A further challenge that all arbitrageurs face is their ability to incorporate into back tests accurate estimates of what their execution costs (slippage) would have been.

### Future execution costs

Some models are sensitive to changes in execution costs over time, and small rises can deplete returns. Some arbitrageurs were negatively affected when Merrill Lynch ceased to offer them programme trading services in the summer of 1998. They were subsequently faced with a prohibitive rise in their execution costs. The potential for such changes cannot be incorporated into models, even if sensible estimates for past slippage have been used for back testing.

### Competition
In many instances the basic theories behind a statistical model are relatively simple. The mathematical details may be complex but there are quite a few PhDs out there with the capability to construct similar models. There is therefore a great risk that competitors will reconstruct an arbitrageur's model and eat up its return. This has been the trend over the past 20 years, during which period data quality and computing power have also expanded exponentially, tearing down barriers to entry. Statistical anomalies have been found to be shrinking over time and they now decay much more quickly. Arbitrageurs have reacted to the 'sophistication inflation' by applying more complex models to shorter time periods.[5]

### Ongoing research requirement
Most models work well in their early days, as they reflect the behaviour of markets at that time. Once change occurs in the markets they can run into difficulties. Managers sometimes argue against tinkering with a model. The model's very reason for existence is to rise above human judgement and to operate off proven statistical patterns. Therefore some arbitrageurs leave models to run until a sudden loss forces them to address the model's weakness. The more successful arbitrageurs are committed to an expensive ongoing research process. They monitor markets for changes that might jeopardize the success of their existing models, and they continuously develop new models to replace their existing ones.

### Secrecy
An investor is unlikely to be given details about a model, and may not even be told of the simple premise upon which it is based. Some investors may be uncomfortable with a statistical arbitrage fund in the absence of a proper explanation of how it works. However, other investors take comfort from the very tight hedging involved which should serve to limit sudden losses.

### Gradual erosion of value
A fund may be tightly hedged but if a model is flawed it may produce negative absolute returns ('negative alpha'). Even if it generates positive alpha, it might not be enough to cover rising execution costs (or 'slippage'). If the model gradually bleeds negative performance, unpleasant losses can build up over a period of time.

---

5.  The pressure for higher frequency trading also increases the impact of transaction costs.

### Infrastructure

Statistical arbitrage requires considerable IT and staffing infra-structure. Although modern PCs often suffice, there was a time when statistical arbitrageurs required mainframe computers to run their maths. The need to import huge quantities of tick-by-tick data faster than other market participants and to send electronic trade signals adds to the IT burden. Extra IT staff are required and many managers insist on running parallel back-up systems offsite. A leveraged port-folio cannot be left without its automatic pilot for long. As important is a statistical arbitrageur's research capability. Every stat arb fund needs a few PhDs beavering away. This is an expensive business.

### Trash in, trash out

A statistical model will never work well unless it has been cleverly designed and tested by humans. Some of them are too simple to be robust. Others prove too complex for their own good.

### Leverage

Because statistical arbitrage portfolios tend to be tightly hedged over a number of parameters they often come close to hedging out all forms of risk and return. Rapid turnover usually gives them a better chance of generating performance. Nevertheless leverage is usually required to secure meaningful returns. In most environments leverage is perfectly safe for a statistical model. Under extreme conditions it can pose a real danger, amplifying losses when normal relationships break down and markets become illiquid. Rare combinations of events can have a similar effect. The strategy has witnessed a number of dramatic losses where leverage was a contributing factor. Risk controls need to be watertight.

### Limited investment universe

The investment universe is limited. Statistical arbitrage only works well with larger liquid securities, even though inefficiencies may be greater amongst smaller issues. Securities must be transparently traded on a continuous and near electronic basis. Furthermore, the securities concerned must 'respond' well to modelling. Only certain securities exhibit clear characteristics and strong relationships with the chosen variables. Those securities exhibiting 'average' or 'weak' relationships with the selected factors are not good material for the model. A security must also display enough pricing efficiency that it can be depended upon to revert to norm whenever it becomes misaligned.

## Complexity

The theory behind a statistical model may be simple but we should not underestimate how difficult it is to make one work in practice. Meaningful factors, appropriate betas and typical correlations must all be established and their development over time understood. Some managers delve into chaos theory, fuzzy logic and neural networks. The risks and rewards of employing these methods become greater as the methods become more complex. Yet the end investors become even further distanced from the means used to allocate their capital. A handful of statistical arbitrageurs have proven astonishingly successful in the past. Yet it is very hard for the investor to determine which will be successful in the future.

## Capacity constraints

Only a limited amount of money can be applied to a particular market inefficiency before it is arbitraged away. Most statistical programmes have capacity constraints. In the wake of periods of poor market performance the demand for such market neutral strategies is liable to rise, increasing the money invested in such a manner.

## Changes in market structure

Decimalization in the United States and the introduction of the euro have been blamed for causing problems for statistical arbitrageurs. Models have needed adjustment in reaction to such developments. More significant has been the reduction in the minimum tick size in relation to the average US stock price. The use of penny tick increments and the fall in equity prices have reduced barriers to trading by other market participants and reduced the inclination of market makers to commit capital to their business. This has contributed to volatility and illiquidity in markets.

## 'Leg' risk

Some arbitrageurs insist that all components (or 'legs') related to a particular trading signal are executed simultaneously. Thus if the model recommends that one security is bought and another related security is sold short against it, both transactions must occur at the same time. Other arbitrageurs take a more pragmatic approach, allowing for a limited time lag and some discretion over trading conditions for each security. In such circumstances the effectiveness of a model may be confused with a trader's skill. It also leaves the fund temporarily exposed to market movements on one side of a trade without being hedged as intended. The more trades in a portfolio that are awaiting completion, the greater these risks are.

# Reaction to markets

## *Sharply falling markets*
Sometimes statistical arbitrage models fare disappointingly in sharply falling markets. Correlations between securities can change in such situations and a number of statistical arbitrageurs have seen their long positions falling faster than their short positions. This has given their overall portfolios a positive beta in sharply falling markets.[6] Changes in intra-market correlations caused by other factors can also prove disruptive to models.

## *Market shocks*
Severe market dislocations can cause securities to exhibit unusual patterns of behaviour. Normal relationships between securities can break down, perhaps because of holdings being 'dumped' on an isolated basis. There is a risk that a model identifies an unusual movement in a security's price and executes a trade on the basis of this. However, the behavioural discrepancy may persist or worsen before reverting to norm, inflicting losses on the portfolio. Bid–offer spreads often widen out under such circumstances and otherwise liquid securities become illiquid. This can cause mark-to-market losses or trap the manager in positions that the model is trying to exit. Because statistical arbitrage programmes are generally levered the effect of small problems can be amplified. Not all statistical arbitrage programmes suffer during market shakeouts. It very much depends on how a model has been designed. Some will benefit greatly from the misery of others, providing desperately needed liquidity and profiting handsomely from the wider spreads on offer.

## *In the wake of market shocks*
It may be tempting to redeem from a statistical arbitrage fund in the wake of losses triggered by a market shock. However, bear in mind that as markets settle down 'normal' relationships tend to re-establish themselves and wide spreads tend to narrow again. This can be when a statistical arbitrage programme makes its strongest returns.

## *Low volumes*
Low volumes can arise from a reluctance of investors to trade. Thin markets affect statistical arbitrage negatively. They reduce the

---

6. Some managers have tried to combat this by overlaying a trend following system onto their statistical arbitrage portfolio. However this may mean they no longer qualify purely as statistical arbitrageurs. They become CTAs.

arbitrageur's scope for providing liquidity to the market, or market making.

### Volatile markets

While a number of statistical programmes suffer from *extreme* volatility, most benefit from reasonably high volatility. Higher volatility creates discrepancies and therefore opportunities that can be traded at a profit. Low volatility is generally associated with a lack of trading signals and low returns. This strategy needs activity.

### Micro risks

Statistical arbitrage models are at risk from micro events. These may be regulatory changes, corporate actions, swift material changes to a company's profitability or to its level of gearing. In such circumstances the investor must rely on good stop loss mechanisms or intervention from an alert manager. Perhaps the most pernicious micro risk comes from insider trading, which distorts a security's behaviour ahead of an event's announcement. In this instance the manager cannot spot an event on a newswire. A wobble in a security price resulting from insider trading is likely to trigger a trading signal from a model. This will ensure the fund is exposed the wrong way before the announcement is made, blowing the price out further. The introduction of 'Regulation FD' should reduce 'wobbly' prices ahead of events but it will not guard against outright insider dealing.

### Rising markets

In theory statistical arbitrage should produce positive returns in both rising and falling markets. The supposition might be made that gently rising markets are more liquid, more orderly and that theoretical relationships are more likely to reassert themselves. Many models do seem to benefit from gently rising markets. On the other hand, it might be argued that falling markets might create more fear, more disorder and more discrepancies to trade. Each model seems to be unique.

### Lower interest rates

Most statistical arbitrage programmes are both leveraged and market neutral. Because of this they involve short exposures that are considerable in relation to the capital invested. It can therefore be surmised that short rebates can make a large contribution to returns. When interest rates are low this valuable source of return is squeezed.

# Nerd's corner: points about multi-factor models

## Finding factors

Factors can be identified using a heuristic approach or through statistical analysis of data. Having identified factors the statistical arbitrageur must find a meaningful way to incorporate them into his model. Each time one of these new independent variables is added to the model the outcome must be tested to ensure it has increased the explanatory power of the model. This can be done by verifying that the multiple regression equation's R bar squared has increased. Computer programmes can add one variable at a time and rank them in order of their explanatory power. Each variable's coefficient, or beta, can be tested separately using standard error and t-statistic measurements. On occasions a factor may need to be 'lagged', as a datum from one period may be found to affect the security price in a subsequent period.

## Measuring factors

While it may be straightforward to identify a series of factors, measuring them accurately can be more difficult. They must be measured accurately so that sensible sizes can be apportioned to factors within a model. Most financial data contains inaccuracies that must be painstakingly addressed. While there may be benefits in 'cleaning up' the data to remove unrepresentative data points, this must not involve the loss of 'real life' outliers which reflect actual events. High-frequency tick-by-tick data exacerbates the problem.

## Number of factors

Opinions are divided on the merits of including many factors within a model. The strict rules of regression dictate that there should be just one factor to represent each 'concept'. For example, the effect of earnings revisions should only be incorporated in a model with a single factor.[7] Many statistical arbitrageurs take the view that the more factors the better, as long as they can be shown to add value.

## Measuring betas

The betas for each factor (or 'factor coefficients') are meant to be predictive of a security's factor sensitivity in the future. A manager may decide this should be derived purely from history. In practice betas often change over time, so a manager must decide on a timeframe to use. One might argue that a longer timeframe would capture a more representative range of betas in a single figure. Therefore it would be more accurate and more stable. Equally, one might weight the calculation towards more recent data on the basis that it better represents the current state of the world. Decisions on this issue will be influenced by the trading timeframes that a model works with. Alternatively, a manager may simply exercise judgement in estimating a future beta.

---

7.   If a model contains factors that are related to each other it will suffer from multicollinearity.

It is difficult to select a single value for beta when in reality the ever-changing figure lies within a range. In some instances the range of beta values spans both positive and negative numbers. Because beta values lie within a range, the end result of a regression model will also lie within a range. It is very difficult to run a statistical arbitrage model on such a basis, so in practice the manager must settle on a specific beta value. Getting the 'wrong' value for beta compounds errors that have occurred when measuring the corresponding factor, since the two get multiplied together. Put like this, it is a wonder that statistical models ever get the right answer.

## Linear versus non-linear

It is easy to envisage situations where factors predict performance but the relationship is uneven. Straightforward linear regression may not work well in such circumstances. For example, it might be supposed that a company's level of gearing influences the performance of its equity price. At low or modest levels of gearing the effect might be quite small, while at high levels the effect might be much more pronounced. Simply using a factor value multiplied by its factor coefficient is unlikely to reflect the true nature of this relationship and a more complex non-linear approach might be required. Logarithms might be enough to reflect the elasticities of such relationships, as long as these elasticities are constant.

## Statistical pitfalls

The six common problems with multi-factor models are Multicollinearity, Autocorrelation, Lack of data, Time and cost, Heteroskedasticity and Specification (MALTHS). Multicollinearity refers to situations where the different factors, or independent variables, are correlated with one another. This might cause their coefficients, or factor betas, to become unstable. Autocorrelation refers to correlation between successive data points of a factor. This might undermine a model's predictive ability. Lack of data refers both to short data histories and to the use of data in an inappropriate form. The frequency of data used must be consistent with the frequency of trading signals the model produces. When using daily data it might not be appropriate to use closing prices because high levels of activity at the end of a trading day might not reflect price action throughout the rest of the day. Some arbitrageurs prefer to use daily data collected halfway through the day, reflecting the time at which their daily trading signals are sent for execution.

Time and cost is a fairly obvious problem, but statistical arbitrageurs tend to be better funded and rewarded for their efforts than most statisticians. Heteroskedasticity reflects situations in which data is more scattered at one extreme than at the other. This may mean that a model is accurate using values at one end of the spectrum but less so at the other. Specification problems may occur if the arbitrageur includes too many variables, too few, or the wrong ones. The model may also prove to be mis-specified if the variables are incorporated in an inappropriate form.

# APPENDIX 1: KEY CONSIDERATIONS: STATISTICAL ARBITRAGE

- How complex is the model and what is its nature? Is it pure statistical arbitrage or a looser quantitative long–short strategy?

- What universe of equities (or other securities) does the model draw upon and why?

- Does the model incorporate many factors or few? Does the manager disclose the variables in the model? (Why won't the manager answer your questions?)

- Was the model designed by testing preconceived hypotheses or was data searched for patterns that were subsequently explained? Were they subsequently explained or do some of them remain unexplained?

- Are the patterns identified by the model enduring?

- Was the model tested using data that was the same (or related to) the data that inspired the hypothesis for the model in the first place (data snooping)?

- How 'neutral' is the model? Across which parameters is it neutral?

- What sort of data was used to establish the model's factors? What was its frequency and does this correspond to the frequency with which the model issues trading signals? If not, does this matter?

- When the model was designed, what period of historical data was used, one, to establish factor sizes and their coefficients, and two, for back testing? Do the market conditions in these periods reflect current and future conditions?

- Have the factor sizes and their coefficients been arrived at purely mathematically, using historical data, or have they been adjusted by the modeller to reflect their expected future patterns? If so, on what basis?

- What happens if the variables within the model reach extremes that exceed those within the historical data originally used to construct the model? Is the model permitted to extrapolate?

- What sort of statistical problems have been encountered with the model? What are the implications?

- What are the model's risk controls? How does it cope with event risk? Is intervention permitted and how did back tests account for this?

- How is the portfolio likely to react under different market conditions? In particular, is it likely to benefit or suffer from higher levels of volatility?

- What are the dealing arrangements? Are trades executed electronically or in person? Are the model's trade ideas questioned by the manager or implemented automatically? Under what circumstances do humans intervene with the model's activities?

- How much leverage is required to make the model work? How would it operate with more or less leverage?

- Are there capacity constraints on the model in terms of assets under management?

- When a trade is suggested by the model, how is it hedged (with the portfolio as a whole, with one other security, or with an index)?

- What is the manager's commitment to ongoing research into the existing statistical programme and new ones?

- How often is the existing model altered and under what circumstances?

- What research resources and staff are available to the manager for ongoing work? What are their mathematical backgrounds and qualifications? Have the model's original designers left the firm?

- What are the model's original and ongoing design costs, including IT? How do these marry up with the firm's revenues?

- What IT resources does the manager have in terms of staff and systems?

- What happens to the model if the power fails or if connections with trading exchanges are lost? Are there off-site back-up arrangements? Are there power generators on-site?

- Does the manager employ more than one model simultaneously? If so, do they operate within the same universe of securities and are they interconnected? Are signals from different models used to confirm one another? How correlated are the different models and why?

- What measures are taken to minimize future execution costs and reliability? How was slippage accounted for during modelling and what are the risks of dealing costs rising in the future?

- Is execution of all components of a trade signal simultaneous or do different legs go on in stages? How is this controlled?

# APPENDIX 2: GLOSSARY

**Data snooping:** The testing of a model using data that is related to, or the same as, the data which originally inspired the model.

**Dependent variable:** The variable that is determined by a regression equation's factors, or its independent variables. In the context of statistical arbitrage this is the expected return of a security.

**Error term (or residual):** That part of a security's return that is unexplained by the remainder of the regression equation. If the regression equation is accurate, this residual should be small and random in nature.

**Extrapolation:** The use of a model to determine a security's expected return using factor values that lie beyond the bounds of the historical data that was used in the design of the model. The model has not been designed to make predictions under such circumstances.

**Factors:** The independent variables used to predict a security's return.

**Factor coefficient:** The beta or sensitivity of a security to a given factor.

**Independent variables:** Another term for factors.

**Interpolation:** The use of a model to determine a security's expected return using factor values that lie within the bounds of the historical data that was used to construct the model in the first instance. The model's predictions are more likely to be accurate under such circumstances.

**MALTHS:** Mnemonic referring to six frequently encountered statistical difficulties with multiple regression. Discussed above under 'statistical pitfalls'.

**Slippage:** The reduction in the returns achieved by a transaction that is caused by trading costs.

**Standard error:** Statistical measure used to test the validity of part of a regression equation.

**T-statistic:** Statistical measure used to test the validity of a regression equation.

# 8

# Convertible arbitrage

*The only way to make ends meet is to burn a candle at both ends.*
*Somerset Maugham*

Convertible arbitrageurs buy convertible bonds and hedge away one or more of the risks associated with the instrument, most often the equity, interest rate and credit risks. In doing so they attempt to isolate those aspects of the convertible they think will generate a positive return, such as its yield or the equity option embedded within it. If executed properly, convertible arbitrage can produce steady returns which bear little immediate relationship to the direction of equity markets.

Convertible arbitrage is an extensive subject which merits the attention of an entire book rather than a single chapter, yet to my knowledge there are few books on the subject. Those who know enough about the strategy have been too busy executing it and profiting handsomely. Here is a brief explanation of what they have been up to.

## REVIEW OF THE STRUCTURE OF A CONVERTIBLE BOND

The convertible bond can be described as a straight bond, plus a call option to convert into a company's underlying equity. It is on this basis that most convertible arbitrageurs approach the instrument. Figure 8.1 illustrates how a convertible bond's value is determined by these two elements. The convertible's value is shown on the y-axis plotted against changes in the underlying share price along the x-axis.

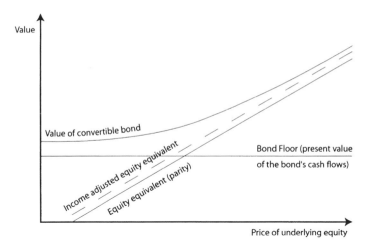

**Figure 8.1** The structure of a convertible bond
The convertible bond offers the potential to participate in the upside of the
equity price, whilst offering some of the downside protection of a bond.
Source: author.

## The bond

The diagram shows the value of the straight bond as a horizontal line
across the graph. The valuation of the straight bond does not change in
reaction to changes in the underlying share price. For as long as the
issuer remains creditworthy the value of the straight bond should
represent the minimum value of the convertible. The convertible is
therefore said to have a 'bond floor'. When the share price is trading at
low levels, far below the convertible's strike price, the value of the
convertible's option will be negligible and the convertible will be
valued close to this bond floor. Of course, the bond floor only provides
limited security. In scenarios when equity prices are plummeting,
corporate spreads are often widening and the value of this bond floor
can decline.

## The equity

The convertible bond includes the option to convert into a number of
ordinary shares. The value of these shares is referred to as 'parity' or
the 'equity equivalent'. Parity can be measured as the share price rises
and falls and is plotted diagonally across Figure 8.1 rising in line with
the underlying share price. When the underlying share price is sufficiently high, 'parity' exceeds the value of the bond floor and provides
a higher minimum value for the convertible bond.

## The convertible

The overall effect is most favourable for owners of convertible bonds. If the underlying equity is trading at low levels, owners enjoy the relative security of a corporate bond, albeit with a fairly modest coupon. If the underlying equity performs well they start to participate in the upside and gain some exposure to moves in the equity price. As an approximation, owners of convertibles expect to enjoy 75 per cent of the equity's upside but just 50 per cent of the volatility. In the past these expectations have proven to be realistic.

Figure 8.1 indicates that the value of the convertible rises in reaction to increases in the underlying share price in a non-linear fashion. This is because the convertible incorporates the option to convert at a pre-specified strike price. As with any option, its value accelerates as the underlying share price approaches the strike price. The rate at which the option price increases is referred to as its 'delta'. When the option is far out-of-the-money, increases in the underlying share price will barely affect the value of the option. The option's delta is very low and the convertible will continue to be valued close to its bond floor. As the share price gets closer to the strike price the option's delta starts to increase and the convertible's value begins to accelerate. After the share price breaches the strike price the option's delta approaches 1. Once the delta reaches 1 any rise in the share price should result in a like-for-like rise in the value of the convertible. In Figure 8.1 the delta can be measured as the gradient of the tangent of the convertible value, since this gradient indicates the rate at which the option value changes in reaction to a move in the underlying equity price. As we shall see, it is due to the convex nature of this slope that most convertible arbitrageurs are able to generate returns.

The difference in value between the convertible bond and its 'equity equivalent' is referred to as its 'premium'.[1] Note that in theory the value of the convertible bond should remain above the value of its equivalent shares (parity) even once the convertible is far into the money. This is because the convertible continues to pay a coupon that usually exceeds the dividend that can be obtained from holding the underlying shares. There is therefore a built-in yield advantage in retaining the convertible bond rather than converting into the underlying equity. This advantage can be described as the 'income adjusted

---

1. Take care with the use of the word 'premium' in the context of convertible bond arbitrage. Be careful to distinguish whether the word is being used to refer to the 'conversion premium' (the value of the convertible over and above the equity equivalent) or the 'option premium' (the value of the option embedded within the convertible). Unless the sense in which the word is used dictates otherwise, the word generally refers to 'conversion premium'. That is how it is used in this chapter.

equity equivalent', marked on Figure 8.1, which shows the value of the 'equity equivalent' adjusted upwards for the additional income provided by the convertible's coupon. In practice, convertible bonds that are far into the money do not always trade in this fashion. A convertible's perceived attractiveness can wane once its optionality has been realized. Its original buyers may therefore sell it in order to move on to new opportunities. Furthermore, convertibles do not always offer an income advantage over their underlying equities.

# THE BASICS OF CONVERTIBLE ARBITRAGE

The convertible bond incorporates a number of sources of risk and return. They include equity risk, credit risk and credit spread risk, interest rate risk, call risk, liquidity risk, takeover and event risk, volatility risk and implied volatility valuation risk. It is not possible to hedge out all of these risks and to do so would leave the arbitrageur without any return. Yet various of these risks can be mitigated, and managers' approaches to hedging distinguish their styles.

Few arbitrageurs wish to be exposed to equity market risk, so most begin by shorting an appropriate number of equities for each convertible bond. Thereafter each of their strategies can differ considerably. Several frequently adopted approaches to convertible arbitrage are discussed below. They have been referred to as 'traditional gamma trading', 'traditional carry trades', 'synthetic calls', 'synthetic puts' and 'discount convertible arbitrage'. Be aware that other investors may refer to similar trading techniques using different terminology. The availability of hedging instruments, the cost of hedging and the effect of market movements can also mean that managers vary their methodologies over time and across their portfolio. (See Figure 8.2.)

## Traditional gamma trading (or volatility extraction)

This has been the most traditional approach to convertible arbitrage in the European market. Gamma trading enables a manager to generate profits from movements in the underlying share price, regardless of its direction. The manager can capture changes in an out-of-the-money convertible bond by routinely rebalancing the equity hedge. This opportunity exists because the convertible contains an option. The technique works as follows.

The convertible arbitrageur wishes to hedge out the equity exposure embedded within a convertible bond. He or she needs to calculate how

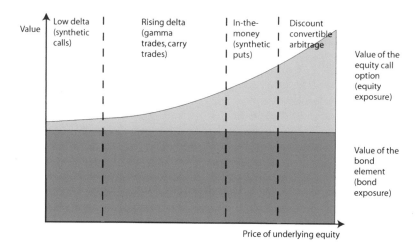

**Figure 8.2**    The basics of convertible arbitrage
Convertible arbitrage may be approached in a wide variety of ways.
Source: author.

much equity exposure there is within the convertible's out-of-the-money option in order to establish a proper 'hedge ratio'. The equity exposure represented by the option can be calculated using the traditional method of multiplying the notional value of the underlying shares by the option's delta. Convertible arbitrageurs use valuation models, based on Black–Scholes, to ascertain the delta of a convertible's option. Having calculated the convertible's delta, the manager sells short an appropriate number of the underlying shares. At this point he or she has hedged out the equity exposure and is 'delta neutral'.

As the underlying equity price rises towards the option's strike price, the delta of the option accelerates. Arbitrageurs find themselves under-hedged. In order to restore a 'delta neutral' position they have to sell short some more shares. But before they have rebalanced the hedge they have made a small profit: on the way up the equity exposure (and value) of the option has accelerated, generating a greater profit than the loss incurred from the short equity hedge. This is the benefit of being long an option. It is important for the manager to rebalance the hedge since this locks in the profit and prevents him or her from being under-hedged in the event of a subsequent fall in the equity price. (See Figure 8.3.)

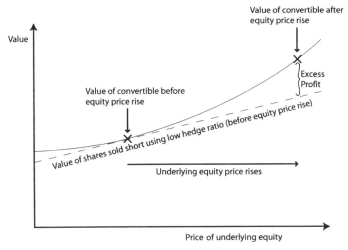

**Figure 8.3** Gamma profits with a rising equity price
Due to the non-linear relationship between the convertible bond price and its
underlying equity, gamma trading profits may be secured when the
underlying share price rises.
Source: author.

If the underlying share price falls, the option's delta falls. Yet owing
to its 'convex' properties it falls at a decelerating rate. Arbitrageurs
finds themselves over-hedged. In order to restore a 'delta neutral'
position they have to buy back some of the shares they have sold short.
Before they have rebalanced the hedge they have made a small profit:
the long equity option has lost less money than the profit generated
from the shares sold short. This is the benefit of being long an option.
Once again, rebalancing the hedge realizes the profit and protects the
arbitrageur from being over-hedged if the equity price subsequently
rises. (See Figure 8.4.)

As the underlying share prices rises and falls, the gamma trader
routinely rebalances the hedge ratio, generating a small profit on each
occasion. Since it does not matter in which direction the equity price
moves the gamma trader is considered to be 'equity market neutral'.
The trader is also 'long of volatility' because more frequent share
price movements furnish more frequent opportunities for rebalancing
the hedge ratio (making 'delta adjustments') and locking in profits.
This is why gamma trading is referred to as 'volatility extraction'.
(See Figure 8.5.)

There are trading costs associated with repeatedly selling shares
short and buying them back again. These costs are mitigated since the

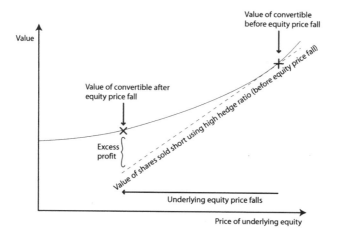

**Figure 8.4**    Gamma profits with a falling equity price
Profits may also be secured when the underlying share price falls.
Source: author.

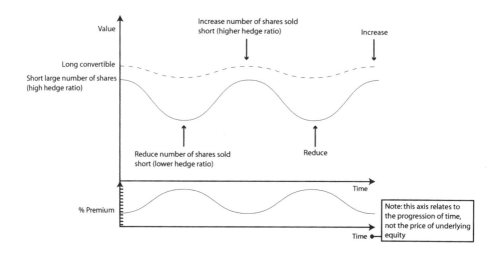

**Figure 8.5**    Gamma trading illustrated in terms of premium
This is a different way of depicting gamma trading. Note that in this
diagram the x-axes refer to the passage of time rather than movements in the
underlying share price. The arbitrageur is short of a larger number of shares
when the share price is high and a smaller number when the share price is
lower.
Source: author.

manager is selling short into a rising market and buying back into a falling one. The arbitrageurs are therefore providing liquidity to the market. Many gamma traders will rebalance their hedge ratios mechanically every time the underlying share prices rise or fall by a set amount (perhaps 1 per cent). Other managers adopt a more flexible approach. For instance, if they determine that a share price is trending in an upwards direction they might set their re-hedging levels at 2 per cent above the current price and 1 per cent below it. Such an approach might lead to greater mark-to-market swings in their portfolio. Regardless of such views arbitrageurs have to set such boundaries sensibly. They must ensure trading costs do not eat up all the profits, that sufficient re-hedging opportunities will occur and that wide boundaries do not leave the portfolio exposed to interim market moves.

Gamma trading centres upon hedging out a convertible's equity risk. Hedging the equity still leaves the arbitrageur exposed to the issuer's credit risk. Most arbitrageurs who focus on gamma trading seek to neutralize this credit risk as well. If this can be done effectively, the trade is truly non-directional. There are a number of ways that the arbitrageur can try to 'ex-out' credit risk and these are described in a separate section below.

Hedging equity and credit risk does leave arbitrageurs exposed to other factors. They remain long of the call 'option' and are therefore vulnerable to changes in its valuation. Changes in implied volatility affect the price that the market is willing to pay for an option, which can either be good or bad news for arbitrageurs. Clearly arbitrageurs prefer to establish gamma trades where undervalued options can be isolated, and it seems these opportunities frequently occur in the convertible markets.[2]

Often there are a number of option-related reasons for buying a convertible in addition to the arbitrageur's ability to extract gamma trading profits. Having hedged out many other factors, arbitrageurs may trade the convertible as if it were just an option, implementing relative value trades that arbitrage the difference between the option's implied volatility and the actual volatility of the underlying equity. Alternatively, they may implement strategies related to the 'term structure of volatility', where mispricings between shorter and longer

---

2. A number of large European issuers used convertibles in the 1990s as a means of divesting themselves of some of their cross holdings. They issued convertible bonds that were convertible into the equity of other companies. The gamma trading arbitrage community liked these bonds because the creditworthiness of the issuer was usually stronger than that of the company into which it converted. This also meant that the equity was more volatile than that of the issuing company.

dated volatility have opened up. This may involve the use of listed or OTC stock options as well as the hedged convertible.

## Traditional carry trades (or coupon arbitrage)

In the US market this has historically been the more traditional approach to convertibles. The initial structure of the arbitrage is similar to gamma trading. Managers buy out-of-the-money convertible bonds, against which they sell short an appropriate number of shares of the underlying company, neutralizing themselves against movements in the company share price. Once set up, the trade should have positive carry and can then be levered. Simply put:

> Positive carry = Coupon from the bond + short rebate from equity sold short – dividends paid on equity sold short – financing costs

Note that this arrangement still leaves the arbitrageur exposed to the credit risk of the convertible. Most formal credit protection mechanisms would eat up the trade's positive carry. However, the structure of the equity hedge provides some protection against sudden credit deterioration. If the creditworthiness of a corporation is seriously brought into question, the value of its bonds may deteriorate but the equity price should fall much faster. In such instances the delta of the convertible's option should fall away sharply, leaving the arbitrageur 'over-hedged' through the short equity position. Excess profits from the short equity position should help offset some of the losses incurred from the deterioration of the bond element. Some convertible arbitrageurs make a habit of maintaining a 'heavy hedge' as a means of protecting themselves against credit deterioration. This involves selling short slightly more shares than the convertible's delta suggests. In addition to a 'heavy hedge' there are a number of other measures convertible arbitrageurs can take to protect against credit problems affecting their performance. These include diversification, minimum credit ratings, monitoring credit derivative markets and proprietary credit research. They are discussed under 'Hedging credit risk'.

As the underlying share price rises or falls, arbitrageurs readjust their hedge ratios to maintain a 'delta neutral' position. There may be an element of 'gamma trading' that generates profits in this delta hedging exercise. However, the 'carry trade' can be distinguished from the 'gamma trade' in one crucial aspect: generating a positive carry is the principal aim, whereas gamma trading profits are secondary. For the dedicated gamma trader, by contrast, positive carry may be minimal or non-existent, as the cost of credit hedging eats it up.

Carry trades are more likely to produce a good static return with high yield convertibles and where the equity dividend is modest. Much of the US convertible market has historically been characterized by such issues. By contrast, gamma trading is easier to effect with higher credit quality bonds, since access to credit derivatives is likely to be greater.

## Synthetic calls (or bond floor trades)

Convertibles that are a long way out-of-the-money can be used to create cheap synthetic call options. In such instances the market has generally overlooked the option element of the convertible and has valued the instrument more or less as a straight bond (at its 'bond floor'). The arbitrageur can buy such a convertible and enter into an asset swap. The asset swap involves selling off the 'straight bond' to a third party but retaining the convertible's 'option to convert' into the underlying shares. Because this option is so far out-of-the-money it can be retained at a minimal cost. Asset swaps are discussed at greater length under 'Hedging credit risk'.

The arbitrageur does not short equities against this call option as the delta is so low. There is a risk that the option's meagre value will disappear altogether, but the potential upside is considerably greater if the underlying share price rises. The risk is therefore asymmetric in favour of the arbitrageur. By asset swapping a number of these out-of-the-money convertibles in this way the arbitrageur can create a portfolio of extremely cheap call options which will benefit from extreme upwards volatility. Because of the structure and complexity of the convertible market such a portfolio can often be created well below its theoretical cost. The strategy employs little capital because most of the convertible has been stripped out of the arbitrageur's balance sheet through the asset swap. (See Figures 8.6 and 8.7.)

## Synthetic puts (or equity substitution)

Synthetic put trades are executed at the other end of the spectrum. The arbitrageur buys a convertible that is a long way into-the-money. Since the option is so far into-the-money it has a delta of 1, meaning every $1 rise in the share price results in a corresponding $1 rise in the convertible. With such a high equity content the convertible trades far above its value as a straight bond. Arbitrageurs buy such a convertible and fully hedge out the equity exposure (using a delta of 1). They do

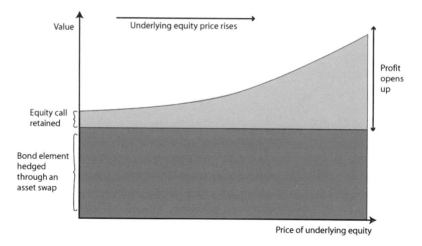

**Figure 8.6** Synthetic call option
On occasions convertible arbitrageurs are able to identify convertible bonds
that entail undervalued out-of-the-money call options. These can be isolated
by stripping out the bond element through an asset swap.
Source: author.

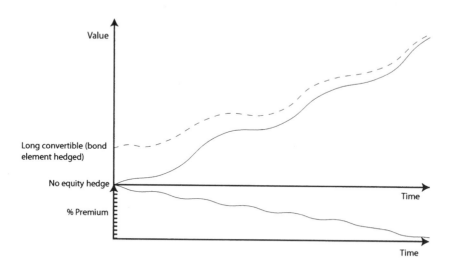

**Figure 8.7** Synthetic call option illustrated in terms of premium
This is a different way of depicting a synthetic call option. Note that in this
diagram the x-axes refer to the passage of time rather than movements in the
underlying share price. As the underlying equity price approaches the
option's strike price the 'call option' starts to rise in tandem with the equity.
Source: author.

not hedge the credit because the convertible is trading so far above the bond floor that it is behaving as a proxy for the equity. Clearly there is little money to be made from such a position day to day, as the long convertible and short equity position negate each other. The delta is stuck at 1 and there is no scope for gamma trading. Carry should be mildly positive, however, as the convertible's coupon is likely to retain a yield advantage over the equity's dividend. (See Figures 8.8 and 8.9.)

The big profits are generated when the price of the underlying equity falls significantly. Under such circumstances the share price may fall back below the convertible's strike price. As this happens the value of the convertible starts to approach its bond floor. As it does so there is a deceleration in the rate at which the convertible price falls, in accordance with the behaviour of the option and the prospect of support that is provided by the bond floor. Meanwhile the short equity position continues to generate a profit that corresponds directly to the falling share price. A difference emerges between the slower rate of descent of the convertible's value and the more rapid rate of descent of the equity price, which has been hedged. This results in a profit.

By implementing a number of such positions the arbitrageur builds up a portfolio of synthetic puts. This strategy uses considerably more capital than implementing synthetic calls because the full value of the

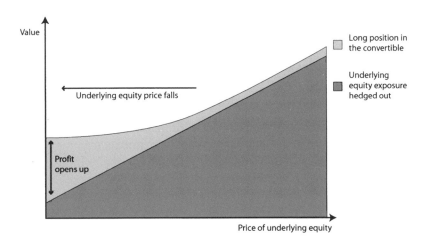

**Figure 8.8**  Synthetic put option
The convertible bond price falls at a gradually decelerating rate, while profits from the short position in the underlying equity continue to accrue in a linear fashion.
Source: author.

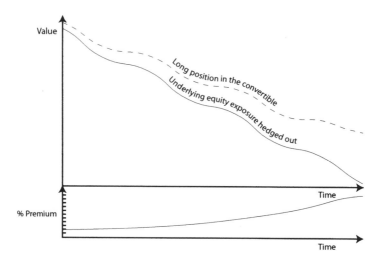

**Figure 8.9**    Synthetic put option illustrated in terms of premium
This is a different way of depicting a synthetic put option. Note that in this diagram the x-axes refer to the passage of time rather than movements in the underlying share price. Over time, the equity price falls at a faster rate than the convertible bond price. The arbitrageur profits from the premium expansion.
Source: author.

convertible remains on the arbitrageur's balance sheet. Because the trade is so capital intensive it might be avoided by those arbitrageurs for whom capital use is a constraint, such as proprietary trading desks in banks. This provides more opportunities for others.

## Discount convertible arbitrage

Discount convertible arbitrage is not a commonly (or easily) executed strategy. On rare occasions supply–demand imbalances mean that convertibles can be found trading at a discount to their equity equivalent. This can present a good straightforward arbitrage opportunity, especially if the convertible is in-the-money (because there exists the simple prospect of converting the bond into the underlying and realizing the difference). In buying the convertible and selling short the equivalent number of shares arbitrageurs can speculate on this discount closing. They may not effect the conversion themselves if there is a yield advantage to owning the convertible rather than the equivalent shares. Besides, arbitrageurs do not want the equity. They simply want to be equity neutral. If they can exit the trade at a profit without converting there remains the prospect of repeating the trade at a later stage. Furthermore, some of the bond's option value will be lost through early conversion, just as it is when a stock option is exercised before expiry.[3]

There is a risk that this inefficiency worsens and the spread widens instead of closing. To protect against this the manager will have to set the trade up at times when the discount is historically wide. In addition, there should always be some protection against the spread widening excessively because the convertible can be 'cashed in' for the underlying shares. (See Figures 8.10 and 8.11.)

In practice such clear price discrepancies rarely occur, particularly with larger issues where the underlying stock can easily be shorted and erroneous pricing would easily get arbed out. If such discounts did appear with larger issues they would usually reflect other factors, such as sentiment about the equity's future, and it would not pay to fight the market. The strategy is only likely to be executable with obscure convertible issues where the inefficiency arises because the underlying stock is difficult to borrow. To get the trade on, the manager must

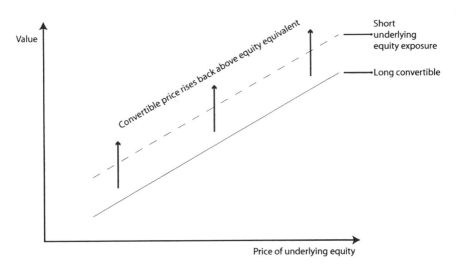

**Figure 8.10**   Discount convertible arbitrage
Arbitrageurs may wish to speculate that a convertible trading at a discount to its equity equivalent will move back to trading at a premium.
Source: author.

---

3.   The time value and implied volatility aspects are surrendered.

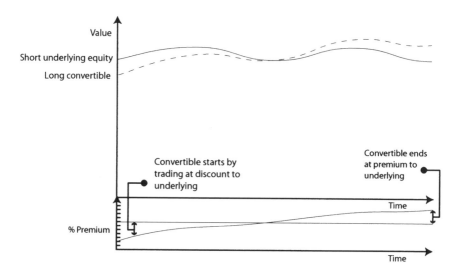

**Figure 8.11**    Discount convertible arbitrage illustrated in terms of premium

This is a different way of depicting discount convertible arbitrage. Note that in this diagram the x-axes refer to the passage of time rather than movements in the underlying share price. Over time, the arbitrageur profits from the convertible moving from a discount to a premium over its equity equivalent.

Source: author.

develop superior access to this stock borrow. Unfortunately, equities that are difficult to borrow are often more likely to be recalled by the lender, so the manager will have to take measures to counter the risk of recall at inopportune moments.

Although it looks similar, discount convertible arbitrage is not quite the same strategy as the creation of a synthetic put. The two may be distinguished by the differing intentions involved. Holders of synthetic puts are hoping that the underlying equity price will fall dramatically in order to trigger a widening of the spread between their equity and their convertible positions. They do not require the convertible to be significantly mispriced when they set up the trade. With discount convertible arbitrage managers need their convertibles to be under-priced in order to assemble their positions. They are not necessarily looking for the underlying share price to fall dramatically. Rather, they want the market to recognize the full value of the convertible, and for the discount between the convertible and the share price to close.

# HEDGING CREDIT RISK

The way managers deal with credit risk is one of their key differentiating factors. Each approach has pros and cons, and how this issue is dealt with can determine success or failure.

## No credit hedge

Leaving credit risk unhedged may sound reckless but it is a legitimate approach. Bear in mind that on a day-to-day basis the bond element of a convertible often makes a minor contribution to the volatility of the convertible's value. All credit hedging mechanisms cost money, and a manager may deem them to be an unnecessary expense. If the manager's primary interest is in establishing positive carry, the expense is likely to be prohibitive. For many convertible issues, particularly those with modest credit quality, credit hedging instruments are either unavailable or expensive. Some managers are sceptical about the accuracy of these devices, while others deem credit hedging to be altogether unnecessary.

However, no convertible arbitrageur can afford to be careless about credit risk. Convertibles are junior instruments, and rarely have the covenant protection enjoyed by more senior paper. A manager who has invested 300 per cent of investors' capital cannot afford a dramatic hit to a position that is 3 per cent of the portfolio, since it represents 9 per cent of investors' money. The short equity exposure will only partly offset a big hit to a bond, even if the manager has used a heavy hedge ratio.

In the absence of credit hedging managers have to diversify their portfolios to minimize the likelihood that isolated problems with individual credits cause significant damage. They need to set minimum credit standards for the components of their portfolios, and include strict limits on how much can be allocated to lowly rated credits and particular sectors.[4] Monitoring credit standards can be delegated to ratings agencies, or managers can build up their own credit research capability in-house. Note, however, that most convertible arbitrageurs are mathematically minded and until recently few built up their own credit research expertise. Some managers make a point of monitoring the credit derivatives markets. These tend to react much more quickly than ratings agencies if doubts emerge about a firm's

---

4. In July 2001 Moody's RiskCalc noted that TMT accounted for more than half the outstanding convertibles. These sector biases sometimes come to dominate the convertible universe.

creditworthiness. However, credit derivative markets are also heavily influenced by (unrelated) supply and demand factors.

Arbitrageurs may seek to counter a slight weakening in a particular credit by implementing a heavier hedge ratio, as discussed under 'Traditional carry trades'. This means they short a few more shares than the convertible's delta suggests, on the basis that credit deterioration is likely to cause the share price to fall faster than the bond element. In practice this is not always the case. Changes in the credit markets are sometimes ignored by the equity markets and vice versa. The two do not always move in line. If a sudden and severe credit problem emerges, a heavy hedge ratio is unlikely to be sufficient to stem all the losses.

Quite apart from credit risk, the manager remains exposed to interest rate risk. If the government bond yield curve shifts upwards, the bond element of convertibles in the portfolio will suffer. Some managers use short government bond positions as a hedge, but it reduces carry, and credit spread widening can mean they lose money on both their government bond short and their long credit exposure.

## Credit default swaps (CDS)

A credit default swap can be likened to an insurance policy or to a put option on the convertible's credit. Convertible arbitrageurs pay an annual premium to protect themselves against severe credit deterioration in the issuing company. If an 'event of default' occurs the arbitrageur can 'put' the bond to the writer of the credit default swap. With this insurance the arbitrageur can concentrate on gamma trading without becoming too diverted by credit issues. However, the money spent on buying credit insurance will eat up the best part of any positive carry. Counterparties are happy to sell such insurance on a series of reasonably solid credits as a means of enhancing their returns.

Credit default swaps have some drawbacks. Theoretically the arbitrageur remains exposed to small changes in the creditworthiness of the convertible issuer, as it is only if the underlying company experiences serious difficulty that the protection is triggered. In practice, the onset of credit problems increases the value of the default protection, so the CDS can often be sold on to other investors at a higher price. Once the underlying company has defaulted, however, the holder of the credit default swap is still exposed to some credit risk: that of the counterparty in the credit default swap. By definition this counterparty's creditworthiness has been slightly tarnished by the fact that it faces an insurance claim.

The more notable complication of credit default swaps lies in exercising them. The ability of the arbitrageur to 'put' the credit hinges on 'an event of default'. There is room for disagreement on how this is defined, and documentation needs to be carefully negotiated.[5] Early attempts to exercise credit default swaps were plagued by litigation. This has left arbitrageurs owning busted convertibles but uncertain as to whether their credit insurance will prove effective. However, as the market matures precedents are set, documentation becomes more standardized and the credit default swap becomes a more reliable means of protecting against credit risk.

Credit default swaps do not protect arbitrageurs from interest rate risk, meaning adverse moves in the yield curve will affect their positions. More importantly, the CDS has no mechanism for unwinding the protection built into its terms. If the arbitrageur wants to be rid of it, the 'put option' must be sold off into the market. At times this can be difficult. If a convertible bond is called by the issuing company there may be a number of arbitrageurs simultaneously trying to dump CDS protection into the market, forcing the price down.

## Asset swaps

Asset swap agreements are an alternative means of mitigating credit risk. The owner of the convertible effectively 'sells off' the straight bond embedded in the convertible but retains the convertible's option to convert into the underlying shares. The straight bond leaves the arbitrageur's balance sheet, but the call option remains in place. The arbitrageur is then free to concentrate on the properties of this option and on gamma trading activities without the fear of default risk.

With an asset swap the straight bond portion of the convertible is sold off to a counterparty with an appetite for credit risk. This counterparty might be the trading desk that executes the swap, but is more likely to be a counterparty with room on its balance sheet for credit, such as an insurance company. Arbitrageurs must retain the ability to reconstitute the convertible bond in case they wish to sell their position, convert the bond, or in case the issuing company decides to call the bond before its maturity. To ensure the convertible bond can be put back together the arbitrageur retains the right to recall the bond portion at a predetermined credit spread (the 'recall spread'). This may be to the disadvantage of the counterparty who has bought the

---

5. Restructuring and obligation acceleration need to be covered in addition to outright bankruptcy. The terms of the contract are at the discretion of the buyer, so it is the arbitrageur's duty to ensure their cover is suitable.

bond element, so there is usually some sort of penalty for unwinding the swap early (a 'make whole payment').

Because the arbitrageur's right to reconstitute the bond is at a predetermined credit spread, the counterparty who bought the bond element has written the arbitrageur a call option that becomes more valuable with tightening credit spreads. However, for this reason asset swapping eliminates bankruptcy risk without entirely protecting against small deteriorations in credit: if for some reason arbitrageurs are required to make whole the convertible once the credit spread has widened beyond the recall spread, in buying back the bond element they will have to pay more than its true worth. This can be likened to exercising an out-of-the-money option. Clearly arbitrageurs avoid this if possible. They are more likely to recall the bond portion when credit spreads tighten, firstly because it increases the risk of the bond being called by the issuer and secondly because the arbitrageur can profitably renew the asset swap at a tighter spread.

Note that asset swaps can be used to help protect the arbitrageur from the risk of rising interest rates. When the straight bond is 'sold off' to a counterparty the arbitrageur is left without the flow of fixed bond coupons. The arbitrageur owns the right to reconstitute the convertible at a prearranged credit spread but not at a prearranged yield. Therefore if interest rates fall, the cost of buying back the bond element will increase. There will be a benefit if interest rates rise, because the cost of reconstituting their bond will decrease. In most instances arbitrageurs are only able to asset swap part of their books, particularly if they invest in lower quality US convertibles. Therefore when interest rates rise they can use the gains from their asset swapped book to offset losses they are incurring elsewhere in their portfolios.[6]

The decision to use an asset swap or a credit default swap (CDS) may hinge on a cost–benefit analysis. The cost of using each of these credit hedging mechanisms varies over time, often due to temporary supply and demand factors rather than credit issues. While arbitrageurs may have a preference for CDSs, they may use asset swaps instead due to cost considerations. Asset swaps have the advantage of employing very little capital. This is in contrast to the CDS, which requires the arbitrageur to finance the ownership of the entire convertible bond plus a credit put option. (see Figure 8.12) Alternatively the arbitrageur may delay implementing a credit hedge in order to allow the credit derivative markets to settle down.

---

6.  If arbitrageurs asset swap all their books they will be at risk from falling interest rates, and may wish to enter into a separate interest rate swap agreement to reverse this exposure.

Both asset swaps and credit default swaps are easier to effect for credits of higher quality, as counterparties have a greater appetite for the credit exposure. Since the credit quality of US convertible issues has historically been slightly lower than elsewhere, the asset and credit default swap markets have been underdeveloped there. The greater availability of these instruments in Europe and Asia has helped shape the way in which convertible arbitrage has been practised in these markets. Consequently there has been a greater emphasis on gamma trading in Europe and Asia, and more emphasis on traditional carry trading in the United States.

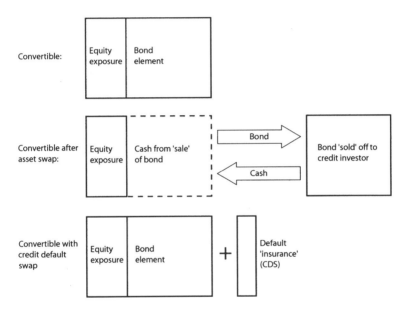

**Figure 8.12**   Asset swaps and CDS

A convertible may be depicted as a bond plus an equity call. By entering into an asset swap an arbitrageur effectively 'sells off' the bond element, leaving behind the equity exposure. This provides the arbitrageur with credit protection and adds cash to his or her balance sheet. Alternatively, the arbitrageur can purchase credit protection by buying a credit default swap, effectively a put option on the credit. This requires the arbitrageur to pay cash for the protection.

Source: author.

## Shorting a credit index

An alternative means of protecting against credit risk is to short a credit index. This acts as a general hedge against systemic credit risk at the portfolio level. There is clearly a potential disconnect between the individual credits held within the convertible portfolio and the constituents of the credit index. A deterioration of specific convertible credits may not be reflected in the index being used to hedge them. Furthermore, the convertible market differs from the market for straight bonds. It is populated by different participants who assess a broader range of factors. On occasions developments in the corporate bond market are not reflected in the convertible bond market. This may result in timing differences between losses on a credit index short and profits from a portfolio of convertibles.

The credit index hedge has certain advantages. The most obvious is simplicity, although this might be offset by the complexities of matching a convertible portfolio to reflect the make-up of the index. Another is the ability to reduce credit exposure in markets where asset swaps and credit default swaps are unavailable, enabling arbitrageurs to focus on gamma trading.

Does such a hedge protect against interest rates as well as credit? If the index hedge relates to credit *spreads* alone, it will only serve to hedge the risk of credit spreads widening. If the hedge is a short on the index in its entirety, it will have the added advantage of hedging interest rate risk as well as credit risk. Of course, the additional cost of shorting the index in its entirety may make it unattractive.[7]

## Puts on underlying equity

In instances where asset and credit default swaps are unavailable, out-of-the-money put options can present an alternative to shorting a credit index. Puts can be purchased on the underlying equity on the basis that a significant deterioration in a company's creditworthiness should result in a significant fall in the company's equity price. These put options can be bought as a proxy for a proper credit hedge, and in addition to any short equity exposure that forms part of hedging the convertible's equity component. They have the advantage that they relate specifically to the issuers concerned rather than to a broad index. However, they will not capture small moves in credit spreads, only dramatic ones. Furthermore, there is the risk that an issuer's equity price does not immediately reflect its credit deterioration. Equity markets are dominated by optimists and credit markets by pessimists. They do not always attend to each other's analysis of a situation.

---

7. Shorting a credit index OTC can take many different forms, including out-of-the-money puts on an index or call options on credit spreads.

The costs of maintaining such put protection are likely to eat up a convertible's positive carry. Yet they may free the arbitrageur to concentrate on gamma trading activities. They will also mean that managers are even 'longer' of volatility and more likely to profit from an increase in implied volatility. This is because they are long two options for every convertible: one call option embedded within the convertible and one listed put option.

### Shorting the issuer's corporate debt

Shorting a corporate bond of the same issuer sounds like a neat credit hedge. In practice it is not so easy. The corporate bond is likely to pay a higher coupon than the convertible, and the short will thus be very expensive. Because it is more senior in the capital structure its price volatility in the face of credit deterioration should theoretically be lower, suggesting the arbitrageur will have to short even more of the senior bond to ensure the hedge is effective. In many instances the issuers of convertibles have no other debt in issue, as the bond markets view the companies with suspicion. Such issuers have turned to the convertible market as the only means of raising affordable debt finance. Note also that corporate bonds are often difficult to borrow and the market for them is not well developed.

# CONVERTIBLE ARBITRAGE: OPPORTUNITIES, DIFFICULTIES, REACTION TO MARKETS

## Opportunities

### *Equity market neutral*
Convertible arbitrage is designed to generate returns regardless of the direction of underlying equity prices. While extreme equity market moves can have implications for equity hedge ratios and creditworthiness, convertible arbitrage is 'equity market neutral' on a day-to-day basis. The correlation of its returns with equity markets is generally very low. It therefore serves as an attractive alternative to equity related investment strategies.

### *Long volatility*
Perhaps the most attractive feature of convertible arbitrage is that participants are 'long of volatility'. They benefit from greater equity

market volatility, regardless of its direction, as it provides gamma trading opportunities. Convertible arbitrage can therefore be a wonderful diversifier for portfolios. Most other investment strategies suffer when equity market volatility rises.

### 'Positive convexity'

A convertible's option value rises disproportionately fast in reaction to gains in the underlying equity price, and falls disproportionately slowly in reaction to losses in the underlying equity price. The convertible's price movements in relation to movements in the under-lying equity exhibit 'positive convexity'. This is a desirable attribute and enables the arbitrageur to extract profits from 'gamma trading'.

### Undervalued time value

The option embedded within a convertible generally runs for a number of years and has a longer life than conventional stock options. Rather than being an option, it is a warrant. The time value of this warrant is often undervalued by the market.

### Undervalued implied volatility

One of the components of an option's value is its 'implied volatility'. The market consistently undervalues the implied volatility element in convertibles. This provides arbitrageurs with cheaper material for gamma trading. Gamma trading techniques could be used in conjunction with listed equity options. However listed options have much shorter lives and the impact of time decay is greater. They are often less liquid in the sizes that convertible arbitrageurs deal in.

### Attractively priced issues

One would expect the attractiveness of convertibles' features to result in fuller prices. In practice convertibles routinely offer investors the opportunity to buy undervalued call options. This is partly because of the manner in which convertibles are first issued. Issuing companies knowingly undervalue convertible bonds at launch, partly to ensure the new issue passes off successfully. The convertible market gives issuers access to cheap subordinated borrowing that is inoffensive to creditors higher up in the capital structure. The prospect of conversion means that it might not have to be paid back in cash, and the ordinary equity owners generally prefer it to immediate equity issuance. Dilution is delayed until the share price has improved, and coupon payments are more tax efficient than dividends. Therefore issuers often consider convertibles to be cheap compromise capital. In adverse market conditions it is altogether difficult to issue either equity or conventional debt. Often the convertible market is the only remaining capital raising alternative, remaining open because the arbitrageurs are unconcerned with the direction of prices just so long as they move in one direction or another.

By issuing a convertible at an attractive price and undervaluing the implied volatility of the embedded option, companies are using the volatility of their share price to access cheap borrowing at little additional cost. Given its cheapness, a convertible bond can be broken up at issue into its two components: a straight bond and an equity call option. On day one, these two components can usually be sold off at a profit over their issue price. This is a rare opportunity in financial markets.

### Complexity advantage in the secondary market

Convertible markets are often dominated by convertible arbitrageurs who use complex valuation models to asses a convertible's worth accurately. However there are often a large number of long-only buyers of convertibles. In many cases these are mainstream corporate bond investors seeking some covert equity exposure. Others are equity investors seeking greater protection.[8] Many of these long-only buyers employ a more simplistic break-even approach to valuing convertibles and do not fully appreciate the theoretical value of the embedded options. This contributes to the continuing cheapness of convertibles in secondary market trading.

## Difficulties

It would be wrong to over-emphasize the difficulties associated with convertible arbitrage, and in friendly markets they can often be ignored. However skilful arbitrageurs must take account of them.

### Leverage

Arbitrageurs hedge out various aspects of a convertible's risk, and in doing so hedge out much of its return. Therefore leverage usually has to be applied. Leverage is not necessarily a danger but when taken too far can leave a manager very vulnerable to severe market disruption. During past market crises the providers of leverage have been inclined to recall their lending at the very time when it is least advantageous to liquidate assets. In such circumstances the leverage provider rarely

---

8. Key participants include equity investors using convertibles as a high yield proxy for equity; fixed income investors using convertibles in lieu of straight bonds but with an equity kicker; dedicated long-only convertible investors; retail investors seeking income; and convertible arbitrageurs.

suffers but the convertible arbitrageur usually does. Even in more normal market environments leverage serves to amplify any individual mistakes within a portfolio, such as sudden credit problems.

### Illiquidity

The convertible bond market is considerably smaller than either the equity or corporate bond markets and it is considerably less liquid. Many of the long-only owners of convertibles take a 'buy-and-hold' approach and many arbitrageurs hold a convertible for long periods. The structure of the convertible market further contributes to its illiquidity. Arbitrageurs dominate the market, particularly in the United States. If a market shock sets off a stampede among convertible arbitrageurs there are few other convertible investors to whom they can sell. Such self-fulfilling stampedes have occurred, triggering swift deleveraging amongst the arbitrageurs. When such selling pressure gets out of hand, the theoretical pricing models normally used by market participants get thrown out of the window, arbitrageurs suffer mark-to-market losses on their portfolios and the providers of leverage increase their margin requirements. This triggers further selling which exacerbates the situation.[9]

### Credit risk

Hedged or un-hedged, convertible arbitrageurs are long leveraged portfolios of junior corporate bonds.

### Declining bond floor

When an equity price plummets the arbitrageurs' exposure to equity 'fades' away and they are left with more exposure to the bond element. However corporate spreads often widen in conjunction with a plummeting equity price. This means the value of the convertible's bond floor falls at the very time it is most needed. Very often the value of this bond floor 'gaps' down suddenly in conjunction with the sharply falling equity price because credit issues are suddenly very serious. In such circumstances the prospect of timely repayment also lessens and the prospective duration of the instrument may extend. (See Figure 8.13.)

### Extreme market volatility

Convertible arbitrage benefits from market volatility. However due to leverage and illiquidity the strategy often suffers during periods of

---

9.  European convertible markets enjoy a broader spread of investors, but convertible arbitrageurs are still very large participants.

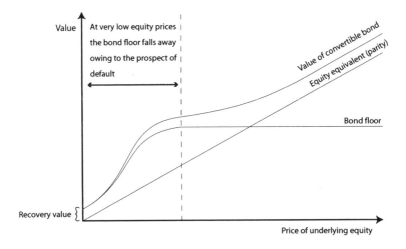

**Figure 8.13**    The declining bond floor
Very low equity prices are consistent with increasing concerns about a
company's creditworthiness. Under these circumstances the convertible's
bond floor tends to fall away, undermining support for the convertible's
bond price.
Source: author.

extreme market turbulence. When markets cease to function properly
and pricing breaks down, convertibles are no place to hide.

### *Stock borrow recall and availability*

Whenever an investor shorts an individual security there is a risk
that the lender will wish to recall it. Usually prime brokers are able
to arrange alternative lending sources without any disruption to an
arbitrageur's portfolio. However, remember that stock borrow is
often more difficult to arrange and maintain for smaller companies
and those whose prospects are less than certain. This can restrict the
ability of arbitrageurs to participate in some converts, particularly
in the US market where issuance has tended to come from smaller
and less established companies.[10] The cost of stock borrow can
be pushed sharply upwards if the issuer bids for another company using its own equity. In such circumstances the merger arbitrage community will wish to short the issuer's stock in significant
quantities.

---

10. Because of the desire of arbitrageurs to short the underlying shares of convertible issuers, new convertible
    issues are often announced very late in the day. Giving the arbitrage community too much notice would
    potentially cause the share price to fall, as arbs would scramble to arrange their shorts in anticipation of the
    convertible's issue.

## Complexity risk

Convertible arbitrage is reasonably complex. Valuation models involve a wide range of assumptions and a good dose of subjectivity. Managers whose valuation models are very different from those of other market participants may find that the market does not price convertibles in the way they expect them to. Most of the convertible community uses valuation models derived from Black–Scholes option pricing theory. In its basic form the Black–Scholes model relies on some unrealistic assumptions, such as frictionless markets, the ability to continuously re-hedge, and normally distributed returns of equity prices. Care is therefore required when convertible arbitrageurs construct their valuation models, as in the secondary market they will pit the accuracy of their models against one another. The complexity of convertible arbitrage also has implications on the operating side. Sophisticated back office and IT capabilities are required to ensure the smooth running of computer models and the maintenance of convertible, short equity and credit derivative positions.

## Risk of overvaluation

No arbitrageur likes their market to get too efficient. If too much money chases convertible arb opportunities or there is insufficient new issuance there is a risk that convertibles will become overvalued. Gamma trading profits will become depressed and some managers may resort to relaxing their hedging disciplines in an effort to bolster returns.

## Call risk

The issue documents of many convertibles give the issuer the right to call the bond. Should a bond be called its price will be affected. Arbitrageurs must account for call risk in their valuation models.[11]

## Takeover risk

Takeovers can be either positive or negative for arbitrageurs. In many instances owners of convertibles are protected by the right to redeem at the bond's par value in advance of any cash takeover (a 'poison put'). If a convertible is trading at a large discount to par this uplift can be very attractive. However, cash takeovers can be very damaging without a poison put, since owners of convertibles are paid parity for

---

11. When calling a convertible, issuers usually force conversion, as they would rather pay out shares than cash. To force holders to convert, bonds are usually called once in-the-money. Because issuers may wish to issue convertibles in the future it is not in their interests to treat the arbitrage community badly.

their bond. This is the value of the equivalent underlying shares, meaning that their entire premium is lost (the value arising from the higher yield offered by the bond). In stock deals the arbitrageur's fate is uncertain, as the bond becomes convertible into the shares of the new company. The shares of the newly merged company may be easier to borrow but if the dividend is higher this will increase the hedging cost. The equity price of the new entity might also be less volatile, reducing gamma trading opportunities and undermining the value of the convertible's vega.[12]

### Special dividends

Some issuers do not compensate the owners of convertibles when they return capital to shareholders via unusually large dividends. In such circumstances arbitrageurs are hit twice. The value of their option is impaired and since they are short the underlying equity they must pay the large dividend to the lender of the stock.

### Risk of mispricing

Convertibles are complex instruments and are sometimes illiquid. Many fund administrators are ill-equipped to second-guess the prices quoted to them. Accurately pricing credit derivatives can also be difficult.[13] There is a risk that investors in convertible arbitrage funds will become victims of fraud related to the mispricing of convertible portfolios.

### Multiple currency exposure

In some instances convertible bonds entail more than one currency exposure. Some European and Asian companies issue US$ denominated bonds that are convertible into their equities (which are traded in the relevant local currency). When such convertibles are trading near the money it might be assumed that they represent local currency risk, in the expectation that they will be converted. Yet should equity prices come under pressure the likelihood of conversion is called into question, and the market might begin to view the bond as a dollar asset. This can make foreign currency exposure difficult to hedge, and can cause the prices of the bonds to be more volatile.

---

12. By the same token, the new entity's credit may well be stronger, increasing the value of the bond element to the arbitrageur's advantage. By contrast, if the convertible issuer takes over another company for cash then its creditworthiness is likely to suffer to the detriment of the bond's valuation.
13. The value of a CDS in the secondary market can vary, and there is no industry consensus on how to mark an asset swapped position. There are costs in reconstituting a bond, and some arbitrageurs may not account for this contingency in their valuations, preferring a theoretical valuation of their equity stub.

### Oversized convertible issues

If a company issues too many convertibles in relation to the size of its equity capitalization, arbitrageurs may starve themselves of volatility. As the underlying equity price rises they will sell more shares short to maintain delta neutrality. As the price falls they will add buying pressure by covering their shorts. They themselves may dampen the volatility they so badly need to make a profit. This problem is more likely to occur with smaller issuers.

### Non-directional equity market risk

Convertible arbitrage should generate profits in both equity bull and bear markets. However there are some non-directional risks. Equity price volatility that is falling or consistently low causes gamma trading opportunities to dry up. Falling equity markets are often beneficial, as profits from equity shorts usually exceed any losses from weakening bond values. However, once equity prices have fallen the options in the convertibles languish so far out-of-the-money that gamma trading opportunities disappear. This problem can only be solved by equity price recovery or new convertible issuance (resetting strike prices to lower levels). Of course, very high equity prices mean that the options trade far into-the-money and the deltas get stuck at 100 per cent. This also scuppers gamma trading opportunities. However, in bull markets new issuance tends to rectify this problem. The ducks quack and they get fed. Because gamma trading requires deltas that are neither too low or too high, it is often the more recent issues that provide the opportunities.

### Risk of mis-hedging

An inappropriate hedge ratio can be costly. Heavy hedges, where a large amount of equity has been sold short, can be painful if the equity price rises. Light hedges can be painful if the equity price falls. Even supposedly accurate delta hedges will fail if a convertible price moves unpredictably. Credit hedging also can be difficult to implement.

## Reaction to markets

The effects that various market trends have on different types of convertible trade depend on how each trade has been structured. The impact is varied, implying that combining different types of trade within a portfolio has considerable diversification benefits. Very often convertible arbitrage managers stick closely to one style, so it is wise for an investor to combine a number of complementary convertible arbitrage managers.

## Strongly rising equities
Strongly rising equities benefit gamma traders by providing good opportunities to lock in delta trading profits. Carry trades are likely to benefit from the expanding value of the convertible's option, but will suffer if managers have used a very heavy hedge ratio. Synthetic calls do extremely well and synthetic puts fail to perform.[14] In-the-money equity arbitrage relies upon the correction of pricing discrepancies and should not be directly related to the direction of equity prices unless they exacerbate discrepancies or cause the bond to be called.

## Rising equities
Mild equity gains may cause carry trades with heavy hedge ratios to experience small losses, but the effect on gamma traders (who use more accurate hedge ratios) should be negligible. Synthetic calls benefit from the prospect of higher equity prices.

## Low equity volatility
Low volatility of equity prices reduces the value of options and has the most adverse impact upon the option related convertible strategies: gamma trading, synthetic puts and synthetic calls.[15]

## Falling equities
Mildly falling equities will cause mild losses on synthetic call positions and mild gains on synthetic puts. Other positions should not be significantly affected.

## Sharply falling equities
Sharply falling equities lead to significant profits for most positions, given that an arbitrageur is generally short the equity but long a bond (which has a lower 'beta' than the equity short). Synthetic puts benefit the most. The value of synthetic calls suffers badly and they can go to zero.

## Rising dividend yields
Rising dividend yields hit convertibles in three ways. First, they tend to reduce the volatility of an equity price. Second, they cause a contraction in a convertible's premium because it loses much of its income advantage over the equity. Third, because of this, they lower the positive carry obtained from being long the CB and short the equity.

---

14. Synthetic puts may lose money if the convertible issuer uses a rising share price as an opportunity to call the bond.
15. Note that gamma trading does not rely entirely on the volatility of equity prices. Gamma trading works as long as equity prices move, even if they do so in a non-volatile manner.

### Low levels of new issuance

Too much demand or insufficient supply is bad for convertible arbitrage. Profitability gets eroded and opportunities get scarcer. At the same time as returns go down, risk can go up, particularly if arbitrageurs react by piling on too much leverage. The hardest hit are the gamma traders, who rely on a good supply of convertibles trading at the right levels. They rely on option deltas being within a sensible range, where they will change significantly in reaction to moves in the underlying equity price (high gamma).

### Low interest rates

Low interest rates are not a direct threat for gamma trades or synthetic calls. They mildly reduce the attractiveness of synthetic puts and in-the-money equity arbitrage by lowering the standstill rate of return. Most importantly they impinge on carry trades, where good positive carry is essential. Although the cost of leverage is reduced, the short rebate and the bond coupon are lower, reducing overall returns.

### High interest rates

The reverse applies for high interest rates.

### Downward shift in yield curve

A downward shift in the yield curve benefits carry traders, since they are long a bond whose price is rising while being hedged against equity price moves. Gamma traders who have used CDS are still exposed to yield curve shifts and benefit accordingly. Those who have used asset swaps will find the cost of reconstituting the bond goes up, and they may wish to account for this in their profit and loss calculations.[16] Gamma traders using credit index shorts will lose money unless they have hedged using the credit spread alone. If a convertible is trading well into-the-money it should behave as an equity proxy, so yield curve shifts are of secondary relevance for synthetic puts and in-the-money equity arbitrage.

### Upward shift in yield curve

An upward shift in the yield curve hurts carry trades because bond values fall. Gamma traders who hedge with CDS will also suffer, but those using asset swaps will find it cheaper to reconstitute their bond if they should wish to. Gamma traders who have shorted credit indices

---

16. Note: the arbitrageur who has asset swapped can recall the bond at a fixed level, but this is based on a credit spread, not the general level of interest rates.

will have immunized themselves against higher yields unless they have shorted the credit spread alone.

### Tightening credit spreads

Tightening credit spreads benefit carry traders in the first instance, but once the initial joy is over their carry will be lower. Gamma traders using CDS will find their bond position benefits but that the value of their CDS in the secondary market will decrease, particularly if tighter spreads induce convertible issuers to call their bonds before maturity. Gamma traders using asset swaps will find that their effective call option on the bond gains value but they are otherwise unaffected.[17] Credit index shorts will lose money, although the convertible markets may take a while to assimilate news from the main credit markets and there could be a delayed reaction.

### Widening credit spreads

Just as upward shifts in the yield curve hurt carry trades, so do widening credit spreads, although once the initial pain is over their carry is likely to be higher. Gamma traders using CDS will find their bond position suffers but that the value of their CDS in the secondary market will increase. Gamma traders using asset swaps will find that their effective call option on the bond loses value but they are otherwise unaffected. Credit index shorts should prove effective, although the convertible markets may take a while to assimilate news from the main credit markets.

### Shakeout / liquidity crunch

All types of convertible position are likely to suffer during periods of extreme market turbulence since all involve being long a convertible bond. Widening bid offer spreads and pricing irregularity can cause mark-to-market losses that trigger coordinated deleveraging. This is the darkest shadow under which convertible arbitrage is conducted.

---

### Nerd's corner: convertible valuation models

It is not within the scope of this book (or the capabilities of its author) to discuss contemporary option or convertible pricing theories at length. However it is important to recognize that these methods are open to question. There is scope for disagreement between different arbitrageurs, and inherent risk in the art of pricing convertibles.

---

17. The arbitrageur has the right to recall the bond element at a fixed credit spread, effectively a call option on the bond.

## Just the option

In its basic form the Black–Scholes[18] model relies on some unrealistic assumptions and some subjective inputs. That these assumptions are made in theory is no reason to criticize. The point is that these assumptions must be accounted for in practice. Different market participants will account for these complexities in different ways, and the results of their pricing models will differ.

Assumptions which must be addressed are:

- frictionless markets (no transaction costs and no taxes);
- the ability to continuously re-hedge;
- normally distributed returns of equity prices (hard to defend for individual equities);
- constant risk free rate;
- continuous stock prices (no gapping);
- no cash dividends paid by issuer;
- European option (exercisable at expiry only);
- no costs or obstacles when selling short.

Inputs that require judgements are:

- the risk free rate (borrowing and lending);
- estimate of future volatility over different time spans ('term structure of volatility');
- the effect of dilution if options and convertibles are exercised.

## The whole convertible

Valuing the entire convertible requires combining the equity option with the bond valuation. This adds further dimensions and additional variables. Among these are the issuer's right to call the bond (this is often envisaged by the convertible owner as being short a call on the bond). The fear of this call option brings into question the time periods used when calculating both the life of the bond and the life of the embedded equity option. The potential for a shortened time period reduces the value of the equity call.

Inputs that require judgements are:

- expected time periods for both the bond and the equity option;
- future credit spreads (or bond price volatility) and their influence on these time periods;
- potential for declining bond floor when equity price falls sharply;

---

18. The basic Black–Scholes formula in summary form: $C = SN(d1) - PV(X)N(d2)$, where C is the call option value, S is the underlying share price, X is the exercise price, PV(X) is the present value of the exercise price discounted at the risk free rate on a continuous basis using the exponential constant, N(d1) is the estimated hedge ratio or delta calculated as a cumulative value on a normal probability distribution bell curve. $(d1) = (Ln (S/X) + (Rf + 1/2 V)t)/$square root of Vt, where Ln(S/X) represent the logarithm to base e of (S/X), V is the variance of the share price. $(d2) = (d1) -$ square root of Vt.

- expectation of full redemption (at par at maturity) or recovery rate after bankruptcy;
- the likelihood of corporate actions.

The need for all these subjective judgements means that models must incorporate appropriate levels of sophistication combined with a trader's practical understanding. Buyers of convertibles may wish to err on the side of caution with their valuations. If this happens implied volatility may always be undervalued by the convertible market. In practice estimating the 'correct' implied volatility can be so difficult that some valuation models simply have it as a residual. Implied volatility is often a poor predictor of events, and often fails to account for levels of observed volatility that are higher intraday than levels at closing prices. Of course, intraday volatility can be captured by gamma traders.

# APPENDIX 1: KEY CONSIDERATIONS: CONVERTIBLE ARBITRAGE FUNDS

- What types of convertible arbitrage strategies is the manager pursuing? What are the sources of return being captured?

- What is the creditworthiness of the portfolio?

- Is credit risk being hedged out? If so, are the methods employed effective?

- If credit exposure is left unhedged, what measures are employed to prevent credit problems? Are they sufficient, particularly in light of the leverage employed?

- Is interest rate exposure hedged, and how? Are these methods dangerous if credit spreads widen?

- Is the manager using a level of leverage suitable to his or her types of convertible strategy?

- What is the liquidity of the portfolio constituents, including the credit derivatives? Accordingly, are the fund's redemption terms appropriate and will a redemption fee be charged?

- What is the current state of the convertible market? (What is the state of: leverage, diversity of participants and dependence on arbitrageurs, option deltas, liquidity, new issues, implied volatility, credit spreads, carry, availability of stock borrow?)

- What sort of hedge ratio is used, and why? Upon what basis is it adjusted?

- What pricing model is used (proprietary or off the shelf)?

- Does the manager invest in busted converts? Does the portfolio contain closet distressed or special situation elements?

- How does the manager predict the portfolio will behave under different scenarios?

- Who marks the portfolio and from what pricing sources?

- How are credit derivatives being accounted for?

- Is stock borrow difficult for the converts being hedged? Is the level of short interest dampening the volatility of the underlying share price?

- Are the operations and trading teams deep enough? Does someone need to trade overnight, and if so is that individual sufficiently senior?

# APPENDIX 2: GLOSSARY

**Asset swap:** Method of credit protection effected by 'selling off' the bond element of a convertible to a buyer of credit.

**Bond floor (or investment value):** The value of the convertible's bond element (equivalent to the present value of its coupons and its terminal payment).

**Conversion price:** The face value of the bond divided by the number of shares into which the bond converts, representing the amount of bond that must be surrendered to get one share.

**Credit default swap (CDS):** Method of credit protection effected by buying insurance against an event of default.

**Delta:** The percentage move in an option's value in reaction to a move in the underlying equity price. The delta accelerates in size as the equity price rises closer to the strike price. The rate of this acceleration is referred to as 'gamma'. The delta is equivalent to an accurate hedge ratio.

**Equity equivalent (or conversion value, or parity):** The value of the equity equivalent, being the number of shares into which the bond converts multiplied by the current share price.

**Gamma:** The rate of change in the delta in reaction to moves in the equity price. As the equity price rises the delta increases at an accelerating rate, reflecting an increasing likelihood that the equity will pass through the option's strike price.

**Hedge ratio:** The market value of the shares sold short expressed as a percentage of the full conversion value or equity equivalent. An 'accurate' hedge ratio will equate to the option's theoretical delta.

**Income adjusted equity equivalent:** The value of the equity equivalent adjusted upwards to account for the additional yield provided by the bond coupon (which exceeds the dividend yield). This adjustment becomes smaller over time if dividends grow, and may even become negative.

**Make whole payment:** Penalty payment made by a convertible manager when unwinding an asset swap ahead of schedule.

**Poison put:** The right to redeem at the bond's par value in advance of any cash takeover.

**Premium (or conversion premium):** The difference between the value of the equivalent number of underlying shares and the value of the convertible bond. Usually the convertible bond will stand at a premium to its underlying equivalent because of the yield advantage. If the dividend has grown sufficiently there may be a conversion discount. (Not to be confused with the word 'premium' when used in the context of the embedded option, which refers to the value of the option.)

**Rho:** The rate of change in an option's price in reaction to a one basis point move in interest rates. (Option pricing models discount back the values of a series of possible outcomes to their present value.)

**Theta:** Refers to the time value incorporated within an option which decays over its life. Theta is the change in an option's value over one day.

**Vega:** The change in an option's value in reaction to a one basis point move in the underlying equity price.

# 9

# Fixed income arbitrage

I handed one of my creditors an IOU and thought thank God that's settled.

Richard Brinsley Sheridan

The term 'fixed income arbitrage' is used in a wide variety of contexts. Some investors incorporate mortgage, municipal, corporate and emerging market sovereign securities within the scope of fixed income arbitrage. However, the added dimension of credit clouds a discussion that is already complicated enough. This chapter refers principally to a fixed income universe of investment grade government and quasi-government securities, where credit issues barely feature. Because it can cause confusion, we should also clarify what we mean by 'arbitrage'. We stretch the term to cover relative value trades between closely related instruments. By 'closely related instruments' we might mean a bond future and one of the bonds deliverable against it. Likewise, a 7 per cent US Treasury maturing in exactly 10 years might be considered substantially similar to another 7 per cent US Treasury maturing in 10.25 years. By contrast, a 7 per cent US Treasury maturing in 2 years is not closely related to one maturing in 30 years. A relative value trade between a 2-year bond and a 30-year bond would not constitute 'arbitrage' because it would be so heavily dependent on the flattening or steepening of the yield curve. It would be better described as a 'global macro' trade.

Fixed income arbitrageurs profit from the small price discrepancies that arise when fixed income instruments violate theoretical principles. Arbitrageurs capture the reversion of securities back to their logical and normal relative valuations. Fixed income arbitrage is one of the most complex and diverse hedge fund strategies. This complexity is partly due to the relative efficiency of government fixed income markets. Because of this efficiency, many arbitrage opportunities arise from technical niceties that the majority of fixed income investors fail to appreciate. These subtle opportunities tend to offer very low returns unless amplified by leverage. Fixed income arbitrage owes its diversity to the wide range of securities and derivatives involved, each of which may have its own implied yield curve. Despite their diversity, all these instruments are closely related in theory. In the United States, the range of fixed income instruments that embody minimal credit risk includes:

- US Treasury bonds;

- US Treasury bills;

- futures on US Treasury bonds;

- futures on US Treasury bills;

- exchange traded options on futures;

- OTC options on bonds and bills;

- repo markets on bonds and bills;

- swap markets;

- Eurodollar deposits (and their associated derivatives) and

- bonds issued by the mortgage agencies (where government support is 'implied').

## HOW ARBITRAGE OPPORTUNITIES ARISE

The government bond markets of G7 nations are highly efficient. Yet their complexity and their diversity often result in modest or fleeting arbitrage opportunities. These opportunities, or inefficiencies, can arise in all sorts of ways.

- The most obvious example is market segmentation. Traditional buyers of fixed income tend to come in three main flavours. The first buyers are the pension funds, who frequently focus their purchasing power and research on the longer end of the yield curve, where they have liabilities that need matching. Second are the money market managers, whose remit rarely permits them to purchase paper with maturities beyond one year. Third are the mutual fund buyers. They usually enjoy greater flexibility in managing duration, but their buying power tends to be considerably less than that of the other two sets of players. These three types of investor are constrained from crossing over into adjacent maturity brackets, which can result in anomalous pricing in certain threshold parts of the yield curve. Securities in the intermediate sector are sometimes under-owned and under-analysed, and there may be unusual pricing just beyond the one-year mark.

- Benchmarking by long-only investors also generates inefficiencies. An index tracking investment approach is theoretically sensible, so long as active investors set prices at the margin efficiently. However, if the vast majority of money invested is index-related there may be times when the active money at the margin is insufficient to correct inefficiencies.

- Even the more active fixed income investors tend to react to inefficiencies over time rather than instantaneously. This is because investment committees take a while to reallocate, short-term traders have limited capital, and because investors are often slow to admit and to reverse errors.

- Regulation exacerbates market segmentation and further restricts the ability of mutual and pension funds to act.

- Traditional investors are ill-equipped to take advantage of small inefficiencies, even if they can identify them. Their execution capabilities are sometimes limited and the leverage required to profit from smaller opportunities is unavailable to them.

- Other anomalies arise from technical factors. For instance, heavy participation in the futures markets can cause price distortions amongst the bonds which are eligible for delivery against them.

- Heavy buying or selling of particular issues by very large buyers can distort prices. Japanese pension funds have developed a particular reputation for indulging in some massive shopping sprees that result in the misalignment of specific bond issues.[1]

- Strong market-wide movements can generate misalignments, since the prices of more liquid issues tend to move faster than those of the less liquid ones.

---

1. In general, event risk is deemed to be relatively high in Japan, despite its status as a leading G7 issuer. Once the local swap market traded through governments, squeezing many players out of the market. During a crisis the market can seem relatively illiquid.

- Political or legislative events can affect the appetite for specific bonds.

- Complexity is another source of opportunity. Arbitrageurs can profit from a superior understanding of the 'finer points' of valuing a particular security. For example, many fixed income instruments involve subtle forms of optionality that some investors find difficult to value or consider inconsequential. Although most investors would appreciate the optionality associated with a callable bond, few would understand the various 'options' associated with bond futures.

- In theory the dealing community should eradicate these sorts of anomalies. Yet even they let opportunities pass on occasions. In order to secure their profits, proprietary traders often pare back their balance sheets towards the end of each quarter and more so at their year-end. As a result they have a tendency to focus on trades that offer an immediate reward with a limited risk of interim mark-to-market losses. They leave many longer-term opportunities to other players, such as hedge funds. Over the end of a quarter, they may even pass up on short-term opportunities.

- A further constraint on the dealing community is their obligation to make markets, which can be a considerable day-to-day distraction.

- Because some discrepancies require large capital flows to correct, there are instances when the dealing community is too small to eradicate a discrepancy, particularly in periods when banks are limiting the capital they allocate to proprietary trading.

## THE NATURE OF FIXED INCOME ARBITRAGE RETURNS

The nature of arbitrage returns, and their associated risks, is difficult to describe. *Some* market discrepancies result from *genuine oversights* by other market participants. Trades based upon these discrepancies can offer attractive returns, as long as the market chooses to recognize and correct the anomaly rather than to ignore and exacerbate it. However, many other arbitrage trades are in reality subtle forms of *assuming risks* from other market participants.

## Not all risk can be eliminated

Arbitrageurs may identify and choose to hedge some of these forms of risk, most notably credit risk and interest rate risk. However, not all risks can be eliminated, either because no mechanism is available or because doing so would eliminate all of the return. Among the risks that may remain within an arbitrage trade are liquidity risk, volatility risk, buy-back risk, changes in the supply or demand for a particular bond, changes in the shape of the yield curve and changes in carry costs. One of the arbitrageur's main roles is to identify the risks embedded in a trade and to choose which to hedge and which to accept.

## Liquidity and volatility risks

Many arbitrage opportunities are subtle forms of assuming liquidity and volatility risks from other market participants. One can illustrate the point with an example. An arbitrage between a pair of near-identical government bonds appears to involve negligible liquidity or volatility risk. However, a discrepancy between such instruments tends to be so small that meaningful leverage must be applied in order to profit from it. This leverage amplifies subtle differences between the instruments. The reason one government bond is marginally cheaper than its neighbour on the yield curve might be that it is less actively traded, or that it represents a smaller issue.[2] In periods of market dislocation the fact that it is marginally less liquid is likely to cause the discrepancy to widen further. During such periods of dislocation the traditional investor might not notice the widening discrepancy whereas the leveraged arbitrageur might incur a severe loss.

## Positive carry means short volatility

If one instrument yields slightly less than another nearly identical instrument, it suggests the market is expressing a subtle preference for the former. When market volatility spikes sharply upwards, this preference is likely to be accentuated further. In this way, an arbitrage position long of a cheap instrument and short of an expensive one may prove to be 'short volatility'. Positions like these are likely to generate a positive net yield (positive carry) because the

---

2. An obvious example is an 'off the run' Treasury, which is likely to yield slightly more than an 'on the run' Treasury. This difference may close during periods of calm but may widen further during times of panic.

arbitrageur owns the higher yielding security and is short the lower yielding one. Investors risk being lured into arbitrage portfolios that have positive carry but that are 'short liquidity' and 'short volatility'. These arbitrage portfolios are likely to provide steady returns in most environments, punctuated by some unpleasant losing periods. This may be acceptable to investors, as long as they understand what they are getting into.

### Certain trades are long volatility

Some arbitrageurs seek to mitigate their vulnerability to volatility events by balancing the trades in their portfolios, including some that are implicitly 'long of volatility'. This might involve the purchase of a marginally *more* liquid instrument that is 'undervalued' against the sale of a marginally *less* liquid instrument that is 'overvalued'. Liquidity shocks and volatility spikes should *positively* impact such trades. They are harder to find and are likely to involve negative carry. However it is logical that it should cost arbitrageurs money to buy volatility. An arbitrage portfolio combining different trades that are both long and short of volatility may produce lower returns but should offer greater stability.[3]

# THE BASICS OF FIXED INCOME ARBITRAGE

Fixed income arbitrageurs can implement a very wide range of trades, and we only refer to a few of them here. It is worth using a 'basis trade' as a detailed case study, since it illustrates a couple of points that investors should bear in mind. First, fixed income arbitrage trades often appear to be straightforward and mechanical. Yet they usually involve technical subtleties that arbitrageurs must appreciate if they are to make a profit. Second, a successful outcome often requires an arbitrageur to make various predictions about the market, even though a trade appears to be market neutral.

---

3. Although it is costly, some arbitrageurs simply buy volatility through options. Being long volatility at the short end of the curve is likely to work well during a crisis because markets will expect central bankers to react, forcing implied volatility higher.

## Case study: basis trading

A basis trade is an arbitrage between a government bond future and the underlying bond that is deliverable against it. The two should trade closely in line, and the relationship between them should be determined by mathematical principles. If the relative prices of the two instruments breach these principles, an arbitrage opportunity exists. Regardless of the mathematics, various factors contribute to making basis trading an art rather than an exact science.

### The mechanics of basis trading

No single government bond is deliverable against a government bond future. Instead, there is a choice of bonds, all of which are deemed to be deliverable against the future. This reduces the possibility that any single bond issue might be cornered as a result of its association with the future. Because of this choice, no single government bond can be used as a means of pricing the future. Instead the future is priced with reference to a non-existent 'notional' bond.

Each of the bonds in the deliverable basket is slightly different and must therefore be adjusted with a 'price factor' before it is delivered against the future. This adjustment brings the deliverable bond into line with the 'notional' bond that is used for pricing the future. Because the price factor adjustment is not entirely accurate, one of the bonds in the deliverable basket is the cheapest to deliver against the future at any one time. The seller of the future retains the right to choose which of the deliverable bonds to deliver against the future and the 'cheapest-to-deliver' (CTD) will always be the bond of choice. Basis trading is therefore an arbitrage between a futures contract and its equivalent CTD.

If the CTD and the future are efficiently priced, each should present equally attractive alternatives throughout the life of the future. In principle, investors who wish to purchase the bond in its physical form must 'carry' it, which means borrowing to finance the purchase or suffering the opportunity cost of not having cash earn interest in the bank. Investing via the future, on the other hand, gives access to the bond with a minimal cash commitment. Therefore holders of the future can leave the underlying cash in the bank and earn interest on it.[4] In an efficient market the prices of the future and the CTD will account for the advantage enjoyed by those investors who mimic ownership of the CTD by using the future. This advantage, the interest differential, is known as 'basis'. The theoretical futures price can therefore be calculated as:

Futures price = (CTD price + net interest paid) / CTD price factor

where

---

4.  Some, of course, is required for margin.

Net interest paid = interest paid on the 'loan' to buy the CTD + accrued interest on CTD at outset – accrued interest on CTD at completion – coupon receipts from CTD over period

If the futures price exceeds its fair value, arbitrageurs will sell futures against purchases of the CTD ('buying the basis'). If the futures price is below its fair value arbitrageurs will buy futures against short sales of the CTD ('selling the basis'). The weight of arbitrage money is likely to bring the two prices back into line. However, the trade is also self-liquidating if held to maturity. As the future nears expiry the carry advantages of accessing the CTD through the future erode, and the basis therefore declines. At expiry the futures and the CTD prices will have converged altogether (after adjusting for the CTD price factor). The passage of time has the effect of entirely eradicating price differentials between the two, naturally securing arbitrage profits.[5]

## The details of basis trading

There is therefore a simple formula for calculating whether a future is fairly valued against the CTD and in an ideal world this would be exact enough for arbitrageurs. In practice there are further subtleties to consider. Most of these relate to the CTD. Sellers of the futures have the right to choose which of the deliverable bonds they deliver against the future and precisely when they deliver it. Market movements mean that among the deliverable basket, the 'cheapest-to-deliver' bond might change over the life of the future. Market movements may also influence the preferred timing of delivery. Because the sellers of futures have these choices they 'own' the 'CTD option'. Arbitrageurs selling the future against the CTD have limited downside. If the CTD changes they can sell the deliverable bond they owned and buy the new CTD. By definition, this transaction results in a profit because the new bond they have bought is a cheaper alternative to the one they sold. The CTD can change regularly and they will profit from the changes.

The reverse holds true when arbitrageurs take the opposite side of the trade, buying the future and shorting the CTD. They are 'short the CTD option'. When entering the trade they must attempt to identify correctly which deliverable bond will be the CTD when the contract expires, otherwise they may incur losses. The need to predict the CTD represents added risks, for which arbitrageurs expect to be rewarded. The level of these risks and rewards changes according to the environment. When interest rates are both low and stable the CTD is likely to remain unaltered over the life of a contract. The returns on offer from basis trading tend to fall

---

5. Note that because the durations of the future and the CTD rarely match, arbitrageurs duration-weight the number of futures contracts to ensure their hedge ratio establishes duration neutrality. Most arbitrageurs are likely to unwind their position before expiration. However if they held their position until expiration they would have to make up the difference in the last few minutes of trading, so that they could make whole at delivery.

commensurately. In less stable environments the CTD may change more often, increasing the value of selling the CTD option. However, due to the increased risks involved, some arbitrageurs may choose to sacrifice a portion of their basis trading profits by implementing options strategies that reduce their CTD risk.

Because these delivery options affect the profit and loss of both the buyers and the sellers of futures, these options have a value which arbitrageurs must estimate. In making such estimates arbitrageurs must forecast the local yield curve's shape and the bond market's volatility, in addition to estimating carry costs and yield levels. The principal options owned by the short seller of a US Treasury bond future are listed below. (The first two identify the CTD and are particularly important for the arbitrageur to analyse.)[6]

- 'Quality option': which of the deliverable bonds to deliver against the future before its expiry.
- 'End of month option': which bond to deliver if the position is held until after trading ceases.
- 'Wildcard afternoon option': the privilege of delivering in the afternoon after futures trading has ended but while the bond markets continue to trade, applicable during the first 15 days of the contract month.
- 'Timing option': the choice of the day on which to deliver, which will be influenced by changes in the carry outlook.
- 'New issue option': the outside possibility that during the life of the future a new US Treasury bond will be issued and that it will become the CTD.

Some arbitrageurs go to great lengths to value these options and to predict their outcomes. The techniques they use include predictions of the yield curve, probability based models and the application of option theory to replicate the delivery option. A certain amount of experience must be as important as a grasp of the maths.

A much 'safer' form of basis trading consists of an arbitrage between the T-bill future and the sole T-bill deliverable against it. However, attractive opportunities of this nature are unlikely to present themselves because the trade is so much more straightforward. The levels of leverage required to secure acceptable returns might be very large. Likewise, basis trading on the two-year Treasury note futures involves a relatively low risk of the CTD changing, and therefore the market is unlikely to proffer attractive opportunities. Markets rarely offer a 'free lunch'.

---

6.  See Wong (1993).

# OTHER FIXED INCOME ARBITRAGE STRATEGIES

## Yield curve anomaly trade

Liquidity flows in particular bond issues sometimes cause them to become cheap or expensive in relation to other bond issues adjacent to them on the yield curve. Arbitrageurs who judge that unusual demand for a 10-year bond has artificially depressed its yield may seek to profit from the temporary discrepancy. They might sell the 10-year bond short against long positions in the adjacent 8- and 12-year bonds, with weightings adjusted to establish duration neutrality. There are risks with such a strategy, the most obvious being that the irregularity worsens rather than corrects itself. Therefore arbitrageurs will generally look for a catalyst to correct the situation, such as the imminent issue of a new 10-year benchmark. Establishing the offsetting long positions in the 8- and 12-year bonds protects against parallel shifts in the yield curve but not against certain changes in the yield curve's shape. If yields at the short end were to rise and cause the 8-year sector to flatten disproportionately versus the 10-year and 12-year sectors, the long position in the 8-year bond might suffer disproportionately. To guard against this risk, arbitrageurs might short some lower maturity bonds or implement an options strategy as a hedge. Alternatively, they might insist on keeping the trade tighter on the yield curve by shorting the 10-year bond against adjacent 9- and 11-year bonds.

## Inter market relative value trades

Inter market relative value trades seek to capture unusual differences between instruments on two closely related yield curves. For example a government futures contract might imply an unusually different yield from a matched maturity swap. The difference might be arbitraged as long as the swap has the same characteristics (coupon, duration and convexity) as the future's CTD. There is a risk that the anomaly might persist or widen further, particularly during market dislocation when swap spreads tend to widen because they involve a modest element of credit risk. Some sort of option protection or offsetting position may therefore be necessary.

## Options related trades

Options in the fixed income markets occasionally present good arbitrage opportunities. Both the listed and OTC options markets can be monitored for anomalies that crop up in their implied yield curves or in their implied volatilities. Arbitrageurs who spot these anomalies can often construct trades to take advantage of them, although they must be wary to avoid mismatches that leave them long of time decay or exposed to unlimited risk. For example the implied volatility of listed options on futures differs at times from that of OTC options on the related CTD. This can present arbitrage opportunities. An alternative options strategy is the conversion trade. This involves using options to create a synthetic future[7] in order to trade discrepancies against an equivalent futures contract or its underlying bond. To complicate matters, the OTC and listed options markets are not directly comparable. Listed options are standardized contracts and are options on the futures, which in turn account for basis risk. OTC options are less liquid, non-standardized and usually relate directly to specific securities, so that changes in financing rates may affect them differently.

## Callable bond arbitrage

On occasions callable bonds become mispriced in relation to similar, non-callable equivalents. This may be because other market participants have failed to calculate the value of the 'call option' correctly, given the outlook for interest rates. Alternatively it may be because market segmentation causes the bond's call feature to be overlooked. A number of traditional investors are prohibited from investing in bonds with long maturities, and will be forced to disregard a bond despite the likelihood that it will be called long before its official maturity. By contrast, other traditional investors seeking longer maturities for portfolio immunization purposes may have to avoid the issue because its likely duration is too low. If any of these factors cause the bond to be inefficiently priced arbitrageurs may be able to profit. The return on offer may be sufficient to fund the purchase of additional option protection against an unforeseen change in the interest rate outlook.

## Roll down strategies

A number of strategies can be executed that take advantage of how instruments change as they roll down the yield curve. These changes

---

7. Long a put and short a call with matching strikes and maturities (synthetic short future) or short a put and long a call (synthetic long future). In such instances the deltas of the put and the call should be the inverse of one another. As long as they are struck at-the-money forward, the combination of the two should generate a position that is similar to a future (with a delta of 1 and a negligible net premium paid).

take place naturally as an instrument's duration shortens, but additional returns can be generated as the instrument crosses into a new market segment. For example, swaps naturally trade at a small yield spread to their equivalent government bonds. This spread tends to narrow as a swap's maturity shortens, and the narrowing process accelerates slightly as it becomes eligible for money market investors. Arbitrageurs can position themselves just beyond this inflexion point in order to capture this narrowing as the swap rolls down the yield curve. Like many other trades, this position is 'short volatility' because it relies on the yield curve shape remaining unchanged and on stability in the markets. Arbitrageurs might adopt option protection to offset volatility and yield curve shape risk. A reverse position (long the government bond against the swap) further out on the yield curve would also help protect against a general widening of swap spreads[8] and it would not experience the same roll-down effects.

## TED spread strategies

The term 'TED spread' refers to the difference between the prices of the 91-day T-bill future and the 90-day Eurodollar future. Being interest rate instruments, the futures prices are quoted in terms of 100 minus the interest rate for the remaining period of the future. The T-bills are considered to be risk-free whilst Eurodollars reflect the credit risk of overseas banks (LIBOR). The TED spread is therefore taken as an indicator of political and credit risk, and it widens during periods of uncertainty. The spread narrows as interest rates fall and investors stretch for the Eurodollar yield (as long as the interest rate fall is not associated with market panic). Conversely, the spread widens as interest rates rise, since the differential between T-bill and Eurodollar rates naturally increases. Arbitrageurs may take positions in TED spreads when they reach extremes and are expected to reverse. However this involves the considerable risk that the extreme may persist or increase. The lower risk alternative is to go long of a very narrow spread in the expectation that it will widen, since there should be a limit to how far it can narrow. This creates a form of 'put option' protection against increasing market volatility, which can be a valuable addition to a portfolio of other arbitrage positions that are

---

8. Swap spreads can be affected by the general level of disquiet in the markets as there is an element of counterparty credit risk involved, even though in most cases the liabilities are restricted to interest payment differentials. However, swap spreads are also affected by demand. If interest rates are low and expected to rise there will be an increased desire to pay fixed and receive floating, causing swap spreads to widen. The hedging activities of MBS arbitrageurs, in particular the agencies, can also cause distortions in the swaps market.

vulnerable to higher volatility. Unfortunately this 'option protection' can be expensive to carry. Each of the futures prices converge to 100 as they approach expiry. Since the Eurodollar interest rate is the higher, its futures price is the lower. The arbitrageur therefore loses money from maintaining the short position in the Eurodollar future against the long in the T-bill future. (See Figure 9.1.)

## Delivery basket trades

CTD-related options open up a range of associated opportunities in addition to basis trading. Such trades may include shorting the CTD, within a hedged structure, in the expectation that the CTD will change. Alternatively, some arbitrageurs will take positions short of a particular deliverable bond in the expectation that it will be kicked out of the deliverable basket, going long of another that they expect will stay in.

---

### Reflection on the use of leverage

The more similar that instruments are and the lower the volatility of the relationship between them, the greater the requirement for leverage when trading small discrepancies. As a result, fixed income arbitrage often requires significant amounts of leverage in order to secure a meaningful return. Some types of trade are able to support 15 times leverage without resulting in undue risk and without generating a particularly handsome return. Other types of trade may involve higher levels of risk with just five times leverage.

This may sound a little frightening. However, as long as leverage is kept to *appropriate* levels it need not be dangerous. If two instruments really are closely related, the historical volatility of the price relationship between them may be so low that the profit or loss on a leveraged trade would be small and stable. Even if the price relationship were stretched beyond conceivable limits the trade's volatility might still seem tolerable when compared with traditional long-only investments in equities.

Investors face difficulty in gauging whether arbitrageurs are indeed applying appropriate levels of leverage to each type of trade. It is difficult for arbitrageurs to convey the risk in their portfolios through a discussion of leverage because it begs the question of what exactly is being levered. Instead, arbitrageurs tend to use other measures to convey the risk in their portfolios, such as VaR and PV01. Portfolios that have a monthly VaR (Value at Risk) of 3 per cent at the 95 per cent confidence level seem unlikely to lose more than 3 per cent in any one month. Every 3.3 years the portfolio is liable to lose more. This is not particularly reassuring. The risk to fixed income arbitrage portfolios usually lies in the tails, and it is the *extent* of

---

losses during the one month in 40 that investors should be concerned about. Furthermore, VaR analysis relies on historical measures of volatility and covariance whose predictive value is open to debate. The use of PV01 (present value of a basis point) also has its limitations. It is a measure of the impact that a one basis point move in government bond yields will have on a portfolio. However, it measures the impact of the *first* basis point move. Given that there is optionality embedded within many fixed income arbitrage portfolios, the impact of subsequent basis point moves might be quite different. To conclude: one of the trickiest aspects of investing in this strategy is understanding how much risk a manager is adopting. Investors must be comfortable that the manager is not misleading or unduly reassuring them.

# FIXED INCOME ARBITRAGE: OPPORTUNITIES, DIFFICULTIES, REACTION TO MARKETS

## Opportunities

### Diversification
In most environments fixed income arbitrage returns exhibit very low correlation to other hedge fund strategies and to mainstream asset classes. The existence of discrepancies in fixed income markets is not reliant on rising bond or equity markets.

### Steady returns
While fixed income arbitrage can become unstuck during periods of severe market dislocation it generally produces very steady returns. The strategy actually benefits from limited amounts of volatility, given that volatility generates more discrepancies to profit from.

### Self-liquidating
A number of fixed income arbitrage trades are self-liquidating, since market forces naturally eradicate some discrepancies over time and generate profits for the arbitrageur in the process. An obvious example might be arbitrage between a derivative and its underlying instrument, whereby the two become almost fungible towards the end of the derivative's life. This is an attractive risk-reducing attribute. (Not all fixed income arbitrage opportunities have this attribute, and even self-liquidating trades can suffer mark-to-market losses during the course of their lives.)

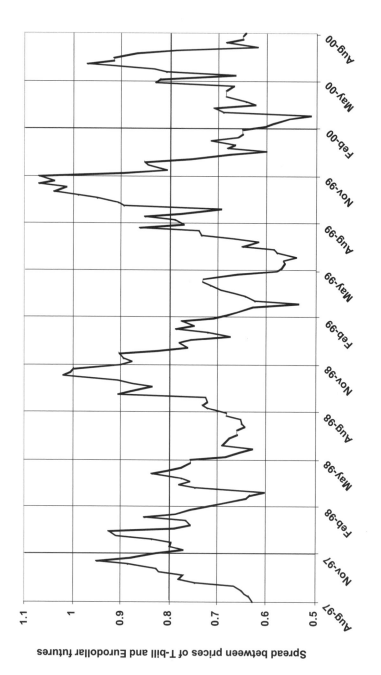

**Figure 9.1** TED spreads (August 1997–August 2000)

TED spreads fluctuate in reaction to interest rate expectations, perceptions of political risk and credit risk.

Source: Bloomberg.

## Liquidity

Most of the securities involved in the type of arbitrage mentioned here are highly liquid (OTC options being a notable exception). They can be traded readily even when significant leverage is applied. Arbitrageurs are therefore unlikely to experience liquidity difficulties when managing their portfolios, other than in the most extreme circumstances. Because the instruments are so liquid they can usually be priced accurately and without controversy. This is important in a leveraged strategy.

## Difficulties

### Multi-dimensional risk

While they may seem market neutral, almost all arbitrage trades rely on particular scenarios either occurring or not occurring. Many arbitrage trades are at risk from changes in interest rates, changes in the shape of the yield curve, changes in carry costs and changes in volatility. It is simply not possible or profitable to protect against all such eventualities without sacrificing all of the returns on offer. Furthermore, certain risk factors are more easily hedged (interest rates, duration, convexity, currency) than others (volatility, liquidity, short recall, funding, event). Those factors that are difficult to neutralize are likely to remain in the portfolio.

### Short volatility

Not all arbitrage trades are vulnerable in periods of dislocation but overall there is a tendency for them to be so. A seductively smooth pattern of historical returns can belie dangers hidden within an arbitrage portfolio. Investors in a fixed income arbitrage fund must make a point of understanding the measures an arbitrageur is taking to offset vulnerability to a sharp increase in volatility.

### Complexity

One of the greatest disadvantages for investors in fixed interest arbitrage funds is their complexity. It can be very difficult for investors to formulate a proper understanding of the underlying strategies and whether they are being executed in a responsible manner. The considerable amounts of leverage involved tend to heighten anxieties. When explaining their trades, many arbitrageurs are inclined to discuss the risks they have hedged but gloss over unhedged risks that may not be apparent to their investors. They are often reticent about detailing complex scenarios that would leave them exposed, even though they are aware of them.[9] It is therefore particularly important for investors to build up confidence and trust in managers of fixed income arbitrage funds.

### Recall of leverage

One of the risks faced by highly leveraged fixed income arbitrageurs is the sudden withdrawal of capital by leverage providers. During periods of extreme dislocation bid–offer spreads in some instruments widen and their pricing becomes more debatable. Simultaneously, leverage providers are under pressure to reduce their capital at risk. In such circumstances leverage providers may be within their rights to increase the margin they require. Arbitrageurs who do not have spare capital may be forced to sell assets quickly into hostile markets at unfavourable prices. This can in turn cause their leverage providers to revise down the valuations of their remaining assets further, triggering additional margin calls. This process can be self-fulfilling, particularly if it is market-wide. Arbitrageurs can protect against such difficulties by structuring their lending agreements very carefully, remaining well within their borrowing limits and borrowing through a diversified range of providers. If they restrict their portfolios to the most liquid government-related instruments, bid–offer spreads should expand relatively little during crises and it will be difficult for leverage providers to challenge the marks in their portfolios. Those fixed income arbitrageurs who incorporate mortgage backed securities within their portfolios may at times find themselves under greater pressure.

### Short squeezes

There are occasions when fixed income instruments get squeezed, and this can be very dangerous for arbitrageurs. There was an instance in the late 1990s when a major European bank was alleged to have cornered the market for the bonds deliverable on a particular future, where the choice of deliverables was small. This must have caused them considerable expense, and few believed that they would hold on to their position. However they did hold on and many investors who were short of the future were unable to deliver against it at the expiry of the contract. As a result they were fined heavily by the relevant futures exchange. It was observed that the major European bank was also a major shareholder in the exchange. This sort of behaviour

---

9. Investors who regress the returns of a group of fixed income arbitrageurs are likely to find a strong relationship with swaption volatility. This is because some fixed income arbitrageurs made money during the later 1990s by betting on the next moves of central banks. They did this using long positions in swaptions, giving them a correlation to swaption volatility. These might be described as subtle macro bets. Note that many of these arbitrageurs were likely to be short of volatility elsewhere in their portfolios.

would be illegal in the United States but was not illegal in the particular European country concerned. However there was a famous squeeze in 2-year US Treasury notes in July 1991, so it can happen there too.

### Mean reversion

Some 'arbitrage' positions are simply mean reversion trades based on historical patterns. An arbitrageur who relies too heavily on historical mean reversion characteristics is risking being caught out by changing circumstances. The more professional arbitrageurs will give careful consideration to the technical and fundamental factors relating to a trade, to reassure themselves that reversion to historical norms is still to be expected.

### Execution

Efficient execution is crucial for arbitrageurs, and the ability to execute may determine whether profits can be made from an opportunity. This can be a real challenge for arbitrage funds below a certain size, unless they already have strong relationships with the dealer community.

### Crowded trades

Some arbitrageurs may find themselves caught in crowded trades. While the G7 fixed income markets are extremely liquid, the arbitrage community as a whole can have a significant footprint in the market once leverage is involved. At times this can be dangerous.

### Concentration

Although most arbitrage portfolios contain numerous individual positions, the positions are often related to one another. There may be only a handful of themes involved, or the overall make-up of a portfolio may reflect and depend upon a particular set of market expectations.

### Resource requirements

Fixed income arbitrage generally requires considerable resources. The discipline involves a wide array of instruments, each of which is subject to its own execution, pricing, accrual, settlement, funding and margin protocols. This requires a good internal administrative function. Because the instruments are so diverse and the arbitrage opportunities are so technical, fixed income arbitrage also requires a large number of investment personnel. Some may be required to work night shifts. These human resources, both front and back office, require sophisticated IT support. On the other hand, these resource requirements are also a useful barrier to entry.

### Pricing technicalities

G7 government securities and their related instruments are generally very liquid, and their pricing is therefore unlikely to be the subject of dispute between fixed income professionals. However the maths can be a little complicated to the uninitiated, particularly given the vast array of instruments on offer. As a result, offshore fund administrators are unlikely to have the skills required to value a fixed income arbitrage portfolio quickly.[10] Many fixed income arbitrage funds are marked in-house and checked at leisure by auditors. This arrangement has the disadvantage of increasing the risk of fraudulent mispricing. This concern is heightened if complex OTC derivatives are involved. Offsetting some of these concerns, we should remember that fixed income arbitrage portfolios tend to experience a high level of turnover, so pricing errors should be revealed quickly. Furthermore, leverage is applied to most instruments, and their value must therefore be confirmed with the leverage provider on a daily basis as part of the margining process.

### Sustained anomalies

Many types of fixed income arbitrage trade are self-liquidating, and as long as mark-to-market losses can be tolerated they are highly likely to produce a profit when held to maturity. In other situations there is no mechanism to close an anomaly other than other market participants forcing it shut. Arbitrageurs run the risk that this sort of anomaly will linger or worsen. Many arbitrageurs seek to identify a catalyst before entering such trades, but these cannot always be relied upon.

## Reaction to markets

### Lower interest rates

As with most arbitrage strategies, fixed income arbitrage returns suffer when interest rates are lower. Most arbitrageurs judge the merits of an opportunity by assessing their expected return in excess of the risk free rate (or in excess of their funding costs). This means they tolerate lower returns when interest rates are lower, forcing spreads to narrower levels. Lower interest rates also lead to a reduction in income from short rebates.

---

10. There are some specialist administrators who are more than capable in this field, most notably GlobeOp, the proficient administration arm that span out of LTCM.

### Dislocation (high volatility)

Many fixed income arbitrage trades rely on a judicious mix of market efficiency and inefficiency. Inefficiency is required so that opportunities present themselves, and efficiency is required so that they correct themselves. A sudden deterioration in the level of market efficiency presents problems for arbitrageurs. Markets become unpredictable and anomalies fail to correct. An existing arbitrage portfolio, with leverage levels set during a more stable environment, is likely to suffer losses as logic breaks down in the markets. These losses may be considerable if the portfolio is dominated by trades that are 'short volatility'. In the wake of spikes in volatility, however, there may be the opportunity to profit handsomely from the reversion of markets to more 'normal' patterns.

### Stable markets (low volatility)

It should be noted that G7 government bond markets are generally very efficient. Calm markets tend to reduce the number and size of opportunities on offer by fostering even higher levels of market efficiency. In such environments it can be very difficult to find opportunities as fiercely competing arbitrageurs steal each other's ideas. Moderate volatility is therefore to be encouraged, since anomalies are thrown up more often.

### Arbitrage capital flows

During market dislocation many arbitrageurs suffer the withdrawal of their capital. Prop desks are reined in by risk managers, and hedge funds experience redemptions from investors. Since markets rely on this capital to enforce efficiency its withdrawal exacerbates the increasing inefficiency. Conversely, if too much capital is applied to arbitrage then it becomes difficult to generate attractive returns without applying so much leverage that the arbitrageur becomes badly exposed to the risk of a sharp spike in volatility. Arbitrage must remain a marginal activity.

### Traditional capital flows

Large capital flows from traditional investors in and out of fixed income markets frequently create arbitrage opportunities. Excessive supply of (or demand for) particular issues gives rise to small mispricings at the margin.

### Economic fundamentals

An unexpected change in economic fundamentals, particularly monetary and fiscal policy, can cause disruption to yield curves. This in turn may cause complications for certain arbitrage strategies that were predicated on yield curve stability or mean reversion. However the disruption caused may also throw up other opportunities.

### Fiscal deficits

During periods in which governments run large fiscal deficits, new bond issues occur more regularly. This generates small disruptions and adds to the number of opportunities available.

# APPENDIX 1: KEY CONSIDERATIONS: FIXED INCOME ARBITRAGE

- What exactly does the manager mean by 'fixed income'? Which instruments are incorporated and why?

- What types of trades are included in the fund? How strictly does the manager define 'arbitrage'?

- How does each type of trade work? How do the opportunities arise? What causes them? Has the nature of the portfolio been properly explained?

- Is the portfolio truly diversified? Are the positions related in some way? How many genuinely independent themes are included?

- What forces the anomalies to close? Are they self-liquidating or do they rely on other market participants?

- What types of risk are left in the portfolio after hedging? How are interest rate, duration, convexity, currency, volatility, liquidity, short recall, funding and event risks tackled?

- To what extent are market views being expressed?

- Does the portfolio have positive carry? What are the implications of this? Which of the trades is 'short volatility'?

- Is the portfolio as a whole vulnerable to volatility shocks? What measures are taken to protect the portfolio from severe market dislocation?

- How is leverage arranged and what measures are taken to prevent the forced liquidation of the portfolio by leverage providers?

- When funding positions with repos, are they matched to the expected duration of the trade or are they extended for as long as possible in order to reduce the risk of increased margin requirements?

- What measures are taken to prevent large, disorderly redemptions by investors from disrupting the portfolio?

- How are crowded trades identified and avoided? Can measures be taken to prevent short squeezes affecting the portfolio?

- What is the leverage requirement for each type of trade? Given the leverage employed what sort of volatility can be expected from the profit and loss on each trade?

- How does the manager convey the levels of risk taken in the portfolio (leverage, PV01, VaR)? Does the manager conduct scenario analysis?

- What dangers have been left unaddressed? Can the manager be trusted to convey the portfolio's risks properly?

- Who marks the portfolio and on what basis?

- To what extent are OTC derivatives used and how are they marked? How easy are these positions to liquidate in times of stress?

- What analytical systems and data links are available to support the investment process? How does the manager maintain an edge over other arbitrageurs?

- What steps are taken to ensure superior trade execution capabilities?

- What research, night trading, IT, administrative, margining and settlements support does the manager have? Is this sufficient?

# APPENDIX 2: GLOSSARY

**Asset swap:** An exchange of the interest streams relating to specific assets. Although the name might seem to imply it, it is not usual to exchange the principal. Not to be confused with the term 'asset swap' when used in the context of convertible arbitrage (see separate chapter).

**Basis:** The difference between the notional values of a bond future (adjusted by its conversion factor) and its cheapest-to-deliver bond. In theory the difference should reflect the advantage in being long of a futures contract instead of paying interest on a loan to buy the bond in its physical form over the remaining life of the future. For this reason, also referred to as the 'implied repo rate'.

**Butterfly:** A trade in which an undervalued bond is purchased and hedged with bonds that lie either side of it on the yield curve.

**Buying the basis:** A basis trade in which the arbitrageur is short the future and long the CTD (also long the CTD option).

**Convexity:** Whereas modified duration measures the rate at which a bond's price changes in relation to a change in yield, convexity measures the extent to which this relationship is non-linear. A bond with positive convexity enjoys a more rapid price increase for decreases in yield at lower levels. It benefits from smaller price declines when yields rise at higher levels.

**CTD:** The cheapest bond to deliver against a future.

**Delivery option:** The privilege of the short seller of a future to deliver any one of the deliverable bonds at the expiry of a futures contract.

**Notional bond:** A fictitious bond with defined characteristics used to price a bond future. In practice a range of deliverable bonds may be used to settle futures contracts as long as they are adjusted by a price factor to bring them into line with the notional bond.

**Price factor:** The adjustment made to a deliverable bond to ensure it is equivalent to the notional bond used to price a future.

**PV01 (PVBP):** Price value of a basis point. A measure of how a single basis point move in government yields will affect the value of a position or a portfolio.

**Selling the basis:** A basis trade in which the arbitrageur is long the future and short the CTD (also short the CTD option).

**Short a swap spread:** Describes a situation in which an investor will profit from a reduction in the spread.

**Synthetic future:** The construction of a trade resembling a futures contract, using options. Purchasing a put and selling a call with matching strikes and maturities mimics a short futures position. Purchasing a call and selling a put mimics a long futures position.

**TED spread:** The spread between the prices of the 90-day Eurodollar future and the 91-day T-bill future. Considered to be an indicator of market confidence.

# 10

# Distressed securities

Bankruptcy is a legal proceeding in which you put your money in
your pants pocket and give your coat to the creditors.

Joey Adams

Distressed securities investors purchase the securities of stressed and
bankrupt companies. The distressed securities universe therefore
includes bonds trading at yield spreads significantly wider than the
high yield indices,[1] as well as the securities of companies that are in
the throes of restructuring. These securities have few natural holders,
and panic sellers are often willing to abandon them for less than their
intrinsic value. Successful distressed investors are expert analysts of
the bankruptcy, restructuring and recovery processes. They understand how value can be released from distressed securities and, unlike
mainstream investors, they are prepared to tackle the complexities
associated with troubled companies.

Distressed investing involves capitalizing on the inefficient pricing
of these securities. The inefficiencies are the result of a number of
factors, all of which contribute to the number of price insensitive
sellers of the securities and an overwhelming excess of supply over
demand (see Figure 10.1):

- Bankruptcy and restructuring are surrounded by technical
  complexities, legal niceties, lengthy negotiations and practical
  politics. Mainstream investors do not have the expertise to understand the proceedings fully.

---

1. During 2003 stressed credits were being defined as those bonds trading at yields in excess of 15 per cent,
   or as those bonds trading at spreads over Treasuries in excess of 1,000 basis points.

- Many investors do not have the time, resources or inclination to monitor the progress of restructuring, let alone to drive the process.

- Brokers and ratings agencies tend to drop their research coverage of companies in distress, which further reduces the ability of mainstream investors to analyse distressed situations.

- A number of investors are obliged to sell securities whose credit ratings have been cut or that have declared an inability to meet their next coupon payment. This obligation may be due to the trust deed of a mutual fund, the guidelines of a pension fund mandate or because a collateralized debt obligation needs to maintain its own credit rating.[2]

- Likewise, various investors are prohibited from holding equity. The prospect of debt being converted into equity as a result of a restructuring process forces them to sell.

- Investors' need for liquid investments may induce them to accept unfavourable prices to secure an exit from illiquid distressed securities.

- Banks must provision heavily for non-performing assets, since they do not contribute to meeting capital adequacy ratios.

- Many credit investors are simply too emotional, embarrassed or risk-averse to keep distressed securities in their portfolios.

Distressed investing has traditionally been conducted on a long-only basis, without the use of short selling. Therefore one might question whether distressed securities funds should classify as 'hedge funds'. Nevertheless, investors have incorporated distressed securities funds into the hedge fund universe. This is because they are alternative, non-correlated, absolute return investment vehicles. The release of value from distressed securities is driven by the restructuring process. The prices of distressed securities are therefore influenced by company-specific events rather than broader market issues. Furthermore, these investment opportunities tend to wax and wane in a counter-cyclical fashion, so that distressed investing often gets combined with merger arbitrage within event driven hedge funds. More recently, distressed securities funds have begun to make greater use of shorting techniques, making it easier to justify their inclusion amongst hedge funds.

---

2. As at December 2002, the US high yield market was 89 per cent owned by insurance companies, pension funds, CDOs, mutual funds and investment grade investors (according to *CSFB Leveraged Finance Outlook 2003*). Bank debt is even less likely to attract unconstrained, speculative investors than corporate bonds.

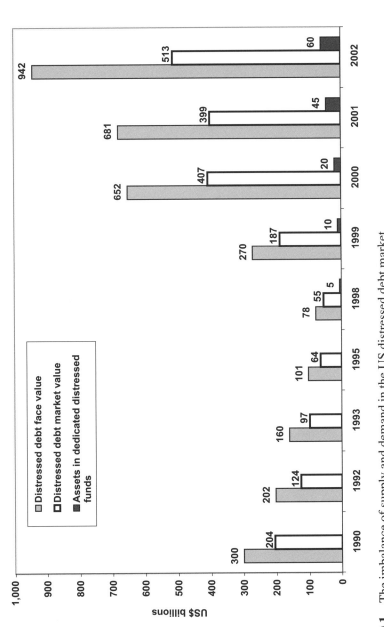

**Figure 10.1** The imbalance of supply and demand in the US distressed debt market

The volume of distressed debt greatly outweighs the pool of specialist capital dedicated to the space.

Source: Professor E Altman, NYU Salomon Center, Avenue Capital Group.

Distressed securities investing is most often practised in the United States, where the bankruptcy regime is clearly defined by the reorganization and liquidation provisions of Chapter 11 and Chapter 7 of the US Bankruptcy Code. Under the US bankruptcy rules, outcomes can be predicted more easily. It is harder to implement this investment strategy in Europe. European companies frequently have subsidiaries in multiple jurisdictions and tend to issue different types of security under different legal systems. Bank debt is often issued under English law, bonds in Luxembourg and equity in a third country where the firm is officially based. The predictability of the bankruptcy legal process varies across Europe. While liquidations in the UK can be relatively straightforward for distressed investors to analyse, French courts have a reputation for favouring employees over creditors, and German accounting is notoriously suspect. Most European legal processes tend to wreak havoc on bankrupt companies, so that in practice restructuring is usually negotiated by the senior lenders informally and out of court. These negotiations are sometimes plagued by political interference. These factors contribute to increasing the uncertainty surrounding the European bankruptcy process. To make matters harder, the senior securities of European companies have generally been difficult for distressed investors to buy because the secondary market for them has been comparatively undeveloped.[3]

A number of distressed investors have been able to participate in Asia ex-Japan, finding that local parties often adopt a pragmatic approach. However Asia ex-Japan is a small and specialized area for the distressed investment community, and in Japan political and cultural factors have tended to hamper distressed investors. For all these reasons discussions of distressed investing are likely to concentrate on the United States, and we now turn our attentions there.

# THE US BANKRUPTCY PROCESS

Liquidations of failed US companies are governed by Chapter 7 proceedings. However, large firms are more often subject to Chapter 11 proceedings, in which the debtor retains control of the assets with a view to rehabilitating the company. In this way viable businesses can

---

3.  The secondary market for bank debt is far more developed in the United States. However it is not without its occasional problems. Accounting regulations have encouraged some insurance companies to hold on to distressed bank debt rather than selling it on to distressed investors. This is because they are allowed to keep it on their books at cost on the assumption that they intend to hold it until maturity. It therefore delays their embarrassment if they do so.

escape liquidation through restructuring, saving valuable jobs and factors of production. Chapter 11 arrangements are motivated primarily by social considerations, and while liquidations might be considered wasteful, sustaining a failing business is sometimes wasteful too.[4] Chapter 11 fails to remove excess capacity from struggling industries and can sow the seeds of further bankruptcies in the future. Given that the company emerging from Chapter 11 has had many of its debts written off, it may be a competitor that is forced under next. On the other hand, many good businesses are forced into bankruptcy by excessive debt, an isolated strategic error or some other operational problem which can be fixed during Chapter 11 restructuring. Chapter 11 proceedings can therefore be the best economic choice, and by law must be undertaken if creditors expect to realize greater value than they would from a Chapter 7 liquidation.[5] On this basis more highly leveraged companies are less likely to be subject to Chapter 7 liquidations than those that are highly equitized. The management of a company whose capital structure is predominantly equity has the leeway to continue executing a destructive strategy until almost all a company's value has been destroyed. By contrast, difficulties trigger restructuring for highly leveraged companies much earlier on because of their need to service so much debt. At this stage most of their value still remains intact.[6] (See Figure 10.2.)

Chapter 11 proceedings may be initiated by company management (voluntary) or by the creditors (involuntary). It only requires a handful of small creditors to invoke involuntary Chapter 11 proceedings, but creditors initiating unnecessary bankruptcy proceedings run the risk of being sued by the company for damage to its reputation. Therefore creditors are unlikely to initiate Chapter 11 proceedings on spurious grounds. Under Chapter 11 rules the debtor is given the first opportunity to propose a restructuring plan and is granted 120 days to formulate one. Thereafter other parties are entitled to file competing plans. The restructuring inevitably involves the transfer of value from equity holders and junior creditors up the capital structure to more

---

4. Note that although the US bankruptcy process is governed by federal law, bankrupt companies may also be subject to procedures at the state level. State laws are often felt to favour rapid resolutions and to encourage creditors to move more quickly against a company. Federal laws are more concerned with the equal treatment of creditors, and providing the debtor with the opportunity to start again.

5. In practice, Chapter 11 can also be used to effect a liquidation and is sometimes chosen in place of Chapter 7 proceedings. This is generally in order to reduce the costs of liquidation, since under Chapter 7 rules a liquidation trustee must be appointed. Trustees generally charge anywhere between 1 per cent and 3 per cent of the sum raised.

6. I am indebted to Phil Schaeffer of Scott's Cove Capital Management LLC for raising this point with me and for allowing me to use his graph illustrating it.

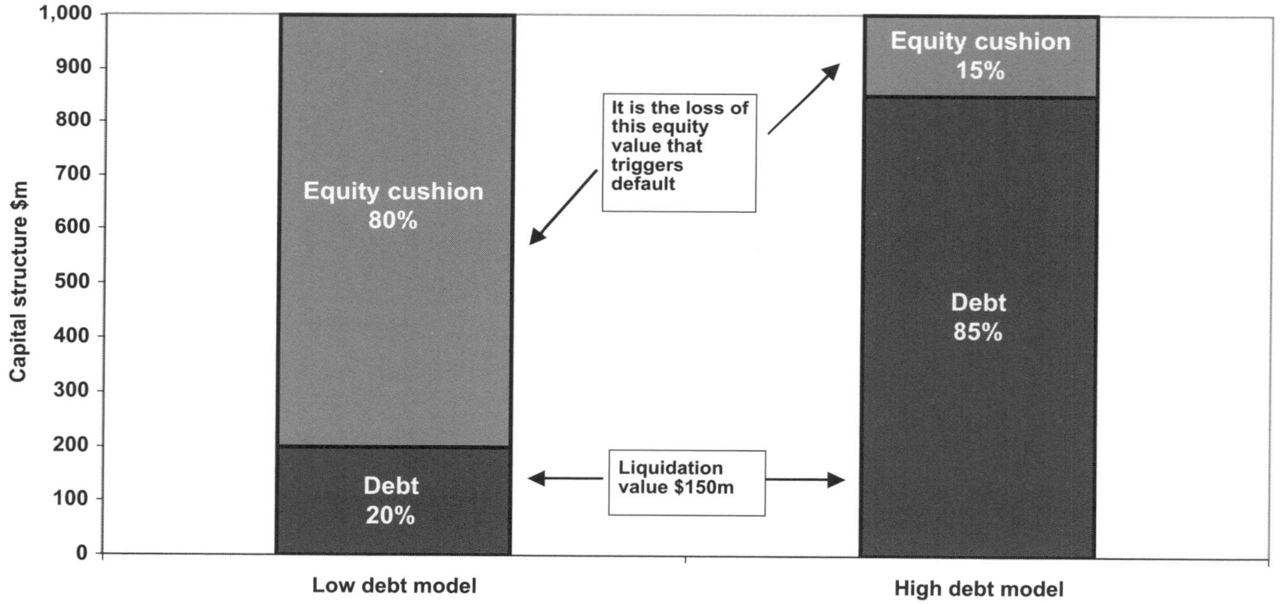
Capital structure $m
1,000
900
800
700
600
500
400
300
200
100
0
Equity cushion
80%
Debt
20%
It is the loss of this equity value that triggers default
Liquidation value $150m
Equity cushion
15%
Debt
85%
Low debt model
High debt model

In a low debt company, management can make poor decisions for a long time before the company is unable to service its debt. By that time, the value of the company may be near liquidation. In a high debt company, management cannot make poor decisions for very long before its inability to service debt provides a catalyst for restructuring. At that stage the company still contains a large amount of enterprise value and the debt may be reorganized to produce a viable entity thereafter.

**Figure 10.2** Why highly leveraged companies make better restructuring candidates
Source: Scott's Cove Capital Management LLC.

senior debt holders. Unless they are prepared to inject further capital, equity holders are likely to see their ownership severely diluted or wiped out entirely. (See Figure 10.3.) While they consider the plan, creditors benefit from enhanced disclosure about the company's performance, including regular, detailed operating and financial information. The creditors then vote on the restructuring plan, generally with separate ballots held for each level of the capital structure because the plan treats each level differently. In theory the plan must be approved by each and every class in order for the vote to carry. The judge in the bankruptcy court then rules on the outcome of the vote, verifying that each party is treated fairly and receives more than they would under liquidation. The judge is tasked with sorting out disputes that arise during these votes.

As part of the Chapter 11 proceedings the judge will rule on obligations and contracts that the firm has left uncompleted, as well as deciding whether damages claims are assumed or rejected. The judge will also set a 'bar date' after which no more pre-Chapter 11 claims may be asserted. Audits will be carried out to verify that there are no other hidden claims or lawsuits unaccounted for.

The entire Chapter 11 process typically takes a couple of years but can drag on for much longer if negotiations get bogged down or become enveloped by litigation.[7] In some instances the management of a company will enter into voluntary Chapter 11 proceedings, having already successfully concluded restructuring negotiations with its creditors. These so called 'pre-packaged bankruptcies' are relatively rapid, they minimize dissent, reduce fees and limit the stigma associated with bankruptcy. If during Chapter 11 proceedings a company's operating and financial position are seen to have sufficiently recovered, the court can dismiss the proceedings altogether. Some distressed companies effect restructuring outside of US courts by informally securing agreement between creditors. This is certainly an economical option if it can be achieved. Distressed investors have to apply many of the same analysis considerations to these situations as they do to Chapter 11 proceedings.

# THE BANKRUPTCY BATTLE

During the Chapter 11 legal process a power struggle unfolds between different types of creditor. Predicting the likely outcome of this

---

7.  Lengthy asbestos litigation plagued many restructurings during the 1990s.

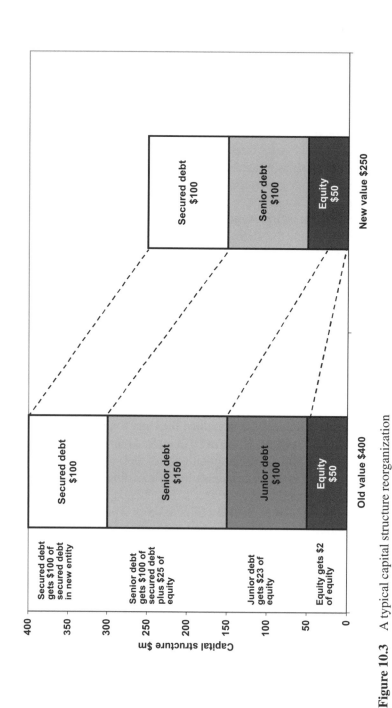

**Figure 10.3** A typical capital structure reorganization

An illustration of how a capital structure might be reorganized.

Source: Scott's Cove Capital Management LLC.

struggle is one of the key elements in distressed investing. In theory the treatment of each type of creditor should be straightforward, based upon their position within the capital structure. The 'absolute priority rule' suggests that each tranche of creditor should be 'made whole' before the next most senior tranche gets paid a cent. In practice there tends to be disagreement both over how much value should accrue to each type of creditor and about exactly where certain types of creditor stand in the capital structure.

While most securities are easily ranked in the capital structure, disputes occasionally arise as a result of inconsistencies in offering documents, small differences between similar debt issues or the ambiguities of hybrid securities. Trade creditors are a frequent source of frustration, generally seeking to be treated between bank debt and subordinated bonds despite the objections of junior bondholders. In practice their treatment varies, being variously placed alongside bank debt, subordinated debt and in-between. The precise treatment of trade claims can make a big difference to distressed investors when the assets are limited and the claims are large.[8]

In order to secure a larger slice of the cake, junior creditors may exploit their ability to disrupt proceedings by slowing negotiations and voting against restructuring plans. They do this in the knowledge that such delays result in additional fees being incurred and in the postponement of the settlement. This impinges on the IRR of other distressed investors. If half the creditors by number, or a third by value, vote against a plan, that class of creditors is deemed to have rejected it. Thus an investor can buy a third of any particular class with a view to blocking an entire restructuring plan. This threat can be used to extract better treatment for that class of creditor, a process known as 'bondmail'. In order to persuade junior creditors to accept a restructuring plan they are usually offered slightly more than their fair share, at the expense of the senior creditors.

In addition to hard bargaining, junior bondholders may have other reasons for wishing to delay the process. If the circumstances of a restructuring mean that many of their more senior bondholders are no longer being paid interest, prolonging restructuring adds value to the juniors. (During the interest holiday a greater portion of the firm's cash flow accretes to them than would otherwise be the case.)

---

8. Trade creditors are those firms from whom the bankrupt company has purchased goods or services and to whom it owes money. They are the only constituency with whom the bankrupt company has ongoing relationships before, during and after the restructuring process. Clearly this can have a bearing on how the company wishes to treat them, as their continued support is vital.

However, there are limits to how far junior creditors can disrupt proceedings. A bankruptcy judge who deems objections from junior creditors to be unreasonable can impose the plan on them against their will (a move referred to as a 'cram down'). In addition, there are a variety of tactics the seniors can use to prevent disruption from juniors:

- Trade creditors can be cajoled into reducing their claim in the interests of maintaining good relations with a customer.

- Seniors can amend a restructuring plan to include junior creditors with them for the purposes of a vote, while maintaining their subordination for the actual settlement.

- They can threaten to convert Chapter 11 proceedings into Chapter 7, implying that the juniors will be treated less well in the event of liquidation.

- Senior creditors can insert a clause in the plan proposing fully to enforce subordination and the absolute priority rule.

- Juniors may be reminded that having dismissed the original plan, subsequent proposals may treat them no better.

- What is most likely to deter junior creditors from delaying a plan is their treatment during the delay. As long as there are the resources to do so, senior secured paper is often paid current during bankruptcy proceedings, or at least their unpaid interest is accrued as part of their claim.[9] By contrast, junior bondholders usually forgo their right to coupons, so their IRR suffers the most by delays to restructuring.

Using their respective bargaining positions, various tranches of creditor jockey for position during negotiations, sometimes delaying them against their own immediate interests as part of a complex game of chicken.

## ANALYSIS CONSIDERATIONS FOR DISTRESSED SECURITIES

The analytical techniques employed by distressed investors encompass those used by both credit and equity investors. This

---

9. As long as secured paper is deemed to be over-collateralized, it will continue to pay interest during restructuring if the company's cash flow covers it. Alternatively, post-petition interest will be paid out upon completion of restructuring to make up for any interest that was not paid. Holders of unsecured senior paper are entitled to petition to be paid current, but are unlikely to obtain it. They are only entitled to post-petition interest if they can demonstrate that the company was solvent at the time it entered bankruptcy.

reflects the fact they may receive varying quantities of both debt and equity as a result of restructuring. Much of this work can be taken as read, including the analysis of the prospects for a business and its forecast financial performance. There is no point in expanding on familiar concepts such as enterprise value, free cash flow, liquidation values or the analysis of comparables. However, because distressed investing is event driven, investors must perform additional types of analysis that are specific to the restructuring process. Predicting how this process unfolds will determine their success or failure. To forecast the returns each tranche of creditor will enjoy investors must ascertain, first, who will get what, and second, when they will get it.

## Assets

The immediate priority of distressed investors is to assess the value of the company's assets, on both a going concern and a liquidation basis. Investors will wish to consider whether these assets are tangible or intangible, whether they are readily marketable, what their age is and what type of discount they should apply to them. Of course, tangible assets are not necessarily more appealing than intangible ones. For example a bankrupt airline may own a number of aircraft outright. Certain models will be readily marketable as long as they are under a certain age and depending on the environment. Otherwise they may be extremely difficult to sell. Some of the airline's intangible assets may be much more valuable and readily marketable, namely its landing slots. The percentage of a security's original face value that is recovered after bankruptcy (the 'recovery rate') typically follows industry-specific patterns. Some industries suffer from notoriously low recovery rates due to the nature of the assets found on their books. Distressed investors may choose to avoid such industries unless the prices of securities are particularly low.

## Claims on the assets

Alongside an examination of the firm's assets, distressed investors must assess the claims on those assets. This involves a careful appraisal of where each claim lies in the capital structure and the strength of each claim, including any liens or covenants pertaining to each. This appraisal will generally involve careful examination of the original offering documents of each security in issue in an attempt to spot material subtleties overlooked by other investors. In addition to the holders of debt securities these claimants may include litigants, tax authorities, employee benefit schemes, trade claims and various providers of services to the bankruptcy process (lawyers, accountants, investment bankers and consultants). Before purchasing any particular claim distressed investors must value it in the context of all the other claims.

## Cause of bankruptcy

The health of a company's underlying business is obviously a crucial factor, so the cause of bankruptcy must be diagnosed.

- If bankruptcy was caused by failure of the underlying business, the value of restructured securities will be limited (unless restructuring includes substantial operating and strategic changes).

- If bankruptcy occurred *despite* a healthy underlying business, the securities may have far more value after restructuring. The closure of loss-making divisions and the restructuring of a balance sheet can transform a failing company into an industry leader.

- Bankruptcies that reflect industry-wide malaise may or not be suitable investment candidates. If Chapter 11 protection sustains excess capacity, the outlook is poor for all concerned.

- Those companies entering bankruptcy as a result of fraud may have sound underlying businesses with a good future. Unfortunately the earlier stages of these bankruptcies are plagued by uncertainty because the extent of fraud is notoriously difficult to quantify.

## Post-restructuring prospects

When analysing the company's business the distressed investor must look beyond the bankruptcy process. Restructuring may result in a significant reduction in the firm's cost base through redundancies and the sale of underperforming business units. Therefore the firm's historical operating history may not provide a good guide to the future. Current performance is also likely to be depressed because of the stigma of bankruptcy. Customers and suppliers are less willing to deal with a company that is in the midst of such difficulties, but usually resume their dealings after restructuring. A great deal of management time is also freed up by the conclusion of proceedings, and capex can be resumed in order to take advantage of immediate business opportunities ('low hanging fruit'). The distressed investor should also consider whether the restructured entity will be an attractive takeover candidate. If so, the firm may be subject to a takeover bid once restructuring is completed.[10]

## Timing

Timing is a crucial factor in the return estimations of distressed investors. Interest payments are suspended for most debt securities during Chapter 11 proceedings, so delaying a settlement directly impacts the investor's IRR. Unforeseen delays reduce the present value of an investment, unsettle the business's suppliers and buyers, and subject the workout to additional fees from lawyers, accountants, investment bankers and consultants.

## Negotiating parties

Predicting who gets what and when requires an understanding of the negotiating parties.

● The judges presiding over bankruptcy courts are considered to be key players. Some judges develop reputations for sympathizing with debtors, some for being incompetent and others for tolerating lengthy workouts. Investors must therefore consider the track record and sympathies of each judge.

● Just as important are the individuals who make up the creditor committee. Investors need to determine whether the committee is experienced or naïve, driven or aimless, acting in unison or squabbling. It is generally a good sign when other experienced distressed investors or experienced bankers take a lead on the committee. However, if they choose to use their position to fight aggressively for their own corner, their experience and drive can be to the detriment of other investors who buy into different parts of the capital structure.

● The mindset of other participating distressed investors and legacy owners must be considered (whether they are aggressive, experienced, short-term, optimistic or fatalistic). Their attitudes will affect the aggressiveness of their negotiating tactics, their voting behaviour and the speed with which proceedings complete.

---

10. Takeover bids before restructuring is completed are comparatively rare (other than for specific divisions) because they tend to trigger in-fighting amongst creditors wishing to renegotiate the proportion of equity attributable to them (whereas they had previously had a preference for debt securities).

## Legal technicalities

The laws surrounding the bankruptcy process are complex, and a wide range of conflicting interest groups attempt to use them to recover as much value for themselves as possible. Many distressed investors come from legal backgrounds, while others routinely employ lawyers to provide a viewpoint on particular bankruptcy proceedings. It is not unknown for distressed investors to attend bankruptcy court hearings in person in order to monitor their progress. Most will resort to direct legal intervention on occasions in order to defend or further their interests.

## Upside and downside

Most types of investor consider upside and downside potential, at least implicitly. However distressed investors must pay particular attention to this type of analysis because specific events radically affect their outcomes.

# DIFFERENT APPROACHES TO DISTRESSED INVESTING

There are a number of approaches to investing in distressed securities. Often these are related to the size of assets under management controlled by investment managers and their inclination to exert influence over bankruptcy proceedings. It would be convenient to split distressed investors into distinct camps but in practice they often adapt their approach to each bankruptcy situation.

## Activism

Some investors like to drive the bankruptcy process, sitting on creditor committees in order to maximize the value obtained for their tranche of securities. Those investors on the committee gain privileged access to information and to company management. However they are made insiders in the process. Unless they establish Chinese walls within their organization their ability to trade the securities during bankruptcy is restricted (other than transactions with other members of the creditor committee). Sitting on creditor committees is also time-consuming, and many distressed investors would rather ride on the coat-tails of others who drive the creditor committee on their behalf. It is usually the larger distressed investors who feel obliged to sit on committees, who have the resources to do so and who have the greatest incentive to keep negotiations on track. Managers of smaller funds tend only to volunteer when they can see no alternative.[11]

## Stage of the process

Early stage investors may capture the greatest risks and rewards from bankruptcy investing. An initial panic sell-off can provide a cheap entry point, particularly if information about the situation is still limited and fearful credit investors scramble to ditch the securities. An entry point may come when Chapter 11 proceedings appear inevitable but before they have been officially been announced. However the lack of information early on involves uncertainty, since early asset valuations are often downgraded. Early stage investors run the risk of bankruptcy negotiations becoming bogged down due to investor fatigue, lengthening the process beyond initial expectations. For these reasons bank debt may be the debt instrument of choice for early stage participants. Bank debt typically remains current (continues to pay interest), providing some protection from delays to the process.

Later stage investors may have to pay higher prices for their securities but they enjoy greater certainty about the timing and the outcome of mature negotiations. Later in the process asset values have been clearly established and the underlying business may have stabilized sufficiently to allow investors to predict post-restructuring cash flows. It is often possible to make respectable returns from distressed securities very late in the day, once the settlement attributable to each debt security has been finalized and scheduled but before it has been paid out.[12]

## Seniority

Senior debt securities are clearly safer investments than junior ones, enjoying the first call on a firm's assets and a superior negotiating

---

11. Managers of smaller funds with a penchant for sitting on committees are sometimes maligned by their peers and accused of being 'ego investors'. It is felt they gain a sense of importance from sitting around the table with larger players, but that their time would be better spent on other activities. While distressed investors will often gain comfort from seeing their peers drive creditor committees on their behalf, seeing them on the board of directors is less reassuring. Industry experts make more useful board members for companies in Chapter 11, and distressed investors are less well equipped to add value.

12. These types of very late situation are analogous to merger arbitrage, whereby the future receipt of a cash flow or security can be purchased at a price which implies a risk free rate of return plus an appropriate risk premium. Indeed, actual merger arbitrage opportunities arise when an outside company agrees to buy the bonds of a distressed company late in the bankruptcy process, on the basis that this gives them control over the equity. This type of merger arbitrage can offer very attractive returns but where the distressed company's viability relies on it being taken over the risk of the deal breaking can be considerable.

position. They are more likely to receive cash (or cash plus debt) from a restructuring rather than to receive equity, whose trading value is less certain. They may also enjoy the right to current interest if it can be paid. Of course investors have to pay higher prices for these privileges. There is therefore no rule saying senior securities are more attractive investments than junior ones. It depends upon the prices at which they can be purchased as well as the recovery expected from each. Some investors express a preference for one end of the spectrum or the other in accordance with the particular risk–return profile they are trying to construct. Most evaluate the opportunity offered by each security on its own merits.

While most distressed investors are happy to consider a range of debt securities, few express an initial interest in a firm's equity because it is generally wiped out by restructuring. Even post-restructuring equity tends to be considered a distraction by many investors. Many distressed players design their portfolios to capture the risks and returns associated with restructuring, and would rather not expose themselves to broader equity market risk. Post-restructuring equities often languish for long periods before being rehabilitated into mainstream equity markets, and some distressed investors would rather move on to the next bankruptcy situation. Banks have a particular dislike for post-restructuring equity because it does not contribute to their assets for capital adequacy purposes. However a number of investors are happy to hang on to the equity they receive from restructuring for a number of years, until its eventual rehabilitation lifts its valuation to attractive levels.

Some investors seek to buy trade claims. Trade claims tend to be small in size, requiring a considerable commitment to administration and sourcing. However, for those managers who succeed in amassing significant amounts of them they tend to be very profitable.

## Cause of bankruptcy

An investment opportunity varies in nature according to the root causes of a bankruptcy (which can include excessive debt, a failing business, litigation and fraud). Most investors prefer situations in which a good underlying business has been driven into bankruptcy by excessive debt, despite the existence of assets and positive cash flow. The balance sheet of such a company can be fixed at the expense of the equity and junior bondholders, creating a series of attractive securities at the end of restructuring. In these situations many of the uncertainties associated with replacing the company's management or turning the business around may be absent. However, the returns achievable may reflect expectations for the company's promising post-restructuring prospects.

A limited number of distressed investors deliberately target a troubled underlying business when they can identify a fix for its fundamental problems. This might constitute a reduction in the cost base, the imposition of new management or a strategic shift. Investors who are large in relation to the size of the firm are better placed to add value in this way, and have greater confidence in their ability to impose changes. They must also be prepared to endure the risk of their long-term commitment. If an operational turnaround fails it is extremely difficult to exit a position.

Although many distressed investors avoid companies plagued by litigation others develop a specific expertise in predicting the outcome of substantial lawsuits. As mentioned before, however, few investors are specifically attracted to bankruptcies caused by fraud because they can be very difficult to analyse in the early stages.

## Size of bankruptcy

Some distressed investors favour the bankruptcies of larger companies because their securities provide greater liquidity and they have a better chance of surviving in some form. Political expediency and the sheer waste of liquidating a large company improve their odds of continuation. Larger bankruptcies also attract more experienced negotiating parties. Creditors are forced to pay closer attention and top advisors are hired to expedite the workout. Investors with large sums of money to allocate to distressed securities may find they have little choice but to invest in these high-profile situations. On the other hand there is a breed of investors managing smaller pools of capital who prefer smaller situations. Smaller situations are more likely to be overlooked by other distressed investors, increasing the chance that they may be inefficiently priced.

## Size of fund

Managers of larger funds argue that they get the first call when large slices of distressed bank debt are being placed. They consider bank debt to be the most attractive security on offer, and there is frequently none available for smaller players, who are relegated to the junior securities. However many smaller distressed funds do manage to include bank debt within their portfolios. Their nimbleness means they are less committed to a situation if proceedings to go according to plan, and there is less requirement for them to get bogged down in creditor committee negotiations. Both large and small distressed funds therefore enjoy certain advantages.

---

### Short selling and capital structure arbitrage

Distressed securities do not typically lend themselves to short selling. Once a company is in difficulty its securities tend to trade at thoroughly depressed prices. The moment for shorting has generally passed. Even if a distressed security is deemed to be trading above its true value it can be a dangerous exercise to short it. Minor news items can cause sharp rallies. Even if the volatility can be tolerated, borrowing a security at such levels is difficult to arrange, particularly if it is a debt security. The cost of carry may be huge if the borrower has to pay the lender a large yield.

In order to hedge their overall portfolios, distressed securities investors occasionally deploy small short positions in equity and high yield indices. These tend to be of limited use because the correlations tend to be low other than for large moves. Other managers diversify their activities by shorting bonds trading at high prices that are expected to fall into distress. These opportunities can arise when mainstream credit investors maintain support for an issue either through misjudgement or because it represents a meaningful weighting in an index. The risk of price appreciation is minimized when a bond already trades close to par, and modest yields reduce the cost of carrying the short.[13] However, even these positions can with time become expensive to carry, so it may be more efficient to set up the short in some other manner. This might involve the use of a credit default swap or an equity option strategy.

In the context of distressed securities, shorting is most often used as part of a capital structure arbitrage. Capital structure arbitrage is a means of profiting from discrepancies between the valuations of securities at various levels of a company's capital structure. The strategy most often involves the purchase of a senior security at a relatively low valuation and the short sale of a junior security at an inconsistently high valuation. For example, if a company's bonds trade at 40 cents on the dollar it suggests the debt holders expect to wipe out all of the company's equity and still suffer a loss during restructuring. In such situations one would logically expect the equities to be trading at zero, but there are occasions when they still change hands for meaningful valuations, sometimes sustaining market capitalizations amounting to many millions of dollars. When this scenario occurs it is clear that either the equity holders are blindly over-optimistic or the bond

---

13. Borrowing high yield securities for shorting purposes used to be difficult and expensive. Recently, however, it seems to have become a little easier. The cost of borrowing high yield securities has fallen from around 1.5–2 per cent to around 0.5 per cent.

holders are excessively pessimistic. The opportunity exists to arbitrage these expectations.

Junior bonds can be used to arbitrage against senior debt. However, in many cases the junior security sold short is equity, since the cost of carrying an equity short is lower and there is less chance that it will reflect the concerns of senior debt holders. For obvious reasons, the price of a junior security is more prone to volatility than that of the senior security. It is therefore necessary to adjust the size of the long and short positions to reflect their respective volatilities. Settling on this hedge ratio can be difficult because the historical relationship between the two securities is likely to be a poor guide to their future behaviour, given the change the company is undergoing. Investors attempt to solve this problem in a variety of ways, relying to various degrees on experience, fundamental valuation work and scenario analysis.[14]

If a hedge ratio is set incorrectly, an improvement in the company's fortunes may lead to a loss on the volatile short position that equals or exceeds the profit on the more stable long position. Even if the arbitrage is set up with a sensible ratio the market forces (or failures) that led to the relative anomaly might persist or worsen. This risk is greater if the anomaly is milder or if the price of the junior security is already quite depressed. The behaviour of the remaining holders of depressed junior securities can be unpredictable and does not always reflect fundamentals. Capital structure arbitrage often gets its best results just as a company descends into Chapter 11, since this forces value up into the senior securities.

The occurrence of capital structure arbitrage opportunities can be attributed to a number of factors. Many of these factors reflect the divisions that exist between equity and debt markets.

- First, job functions in financial institutions are segregated along asset class lines. Analysis, broking and trading in credit markets are conducted by entirely separate individuals from those performing similar functions within equity markets. There is surprisingly little crossover and communication between the two. Even within credit investment there is a series of subdivisions between bank debt, investment grade bonds, high yield bonds and convertible bonds. The divisions are most sharply expressed in the world of investment management, where a bond fund manager is usually prohibited from expressing a favourable view on a company through the equity and an equity investor is barred from purchasing bonds.
- Second, the two types of investor often view the same company through quite different lenses. Credit investors are sometimes accused of being pessimists because their investment instruments offer them limited

---

14. Each security can be valued based upon its claim on the company's cash flows, using a sensible range of scenarios for this cash flow.

upside. Their obsessions relate to avoiding the downside. Equity investors are more inclined towards optimism because they participate fully in a company's success. Each type of investor is prone to analyse a company in a manner reflecting these differing investment philosophies.

- Third, they may have different sources of information. Senior debt holders enjoy privileged access to information about a company's operating finances which are not available to equity holders.
- Fourth, there are times when similar views on a company's prospects are expressed in different ways. Credit investors are quicker to dump securities on signs of deterioration and few credit investors are prepared to step in at low levels. Prices in debt markets can therefore gap down faster than in equity markets, where investors are prepared to embrace a greater spectrum of risk.
- Lastly, some anomalies are simply the result of large capital flows in or out of an entire asset class, be it equities or bonds.

# DISTRESSED SECURITIES: OPPORTUNITIES, DIFFICULTIES, REACTION TO MARKETS

## Opportunities

### Complexity
The market for distressed securities provides an excellent opportunity for specialists to assume complexity risks and to be handsomely rewarded for doing so.[15]

### Supply exceeds demand
Underpinning the distressed securities opportunity is the consistent excess of eager sellers over buyers. This serves to reduce the prices at which investors can purchase these instruments.

### Self-liquidating
The suppression of prices through excess supply would be self-defeating were it not for the bankruptcy process, which releases value and has a defined conclusion. Distressed securities may suffer mark-to-market losses over the course of the bankruptcy process, but they

---

15. Remember that distressed investors are provided with detailed and regular financial and operating information. This contributes to reduce uncertainties about distressed securities. However the bankruptcy process and the vagaries of the markets for these securities may serve to add back any complexities that this information removes.

have a reasonably short 'duration', equivalent to the length of the proceedings.[16]

## Diversification

Day-to-day the prices of distressed securities tend to reflect developments in a restructuring process. They are rarely influenced by small changes in equity or high yield markets. Because this strategy is driven by events, the returns it produces are for the most part uncorrelated with mainstream markets and other hedge fund strategies.

## Countercyclical

The opportunity set for distressed securities tends to expand during periods of economic and market weakness, when other hedge fund strategies such as merger arbitrage are often experiencing quieter periods.

## Modest volatility

If investors wish to invest in distressed securities aggressively, they can do so. However, if approached conservatively the strategy can be managed to produce reasonably low volatility returns. To some extent the low volatility of returns may be illusory, since the assets involved may be illiquid, meaning that fundamental changes are incorporated into prices only gradually. Yet the low volatility is not entirely an illusion because within a certain size the instruments can be actively traded at the quoted prices.

## Difficulties

### Complexity

While complexity provides the opportunity it also presents the challenge. Analysis errors concerning tax issues, listing documents or corporate actions are costly. Negotiations about rankings in a capital structure and the payout afforded to each can turn against the most experienced investor. There is a wide range of legal issues which investors must be aware of, such as the Avoiding Powers that are designed to prevent one debt holder securing an unfair gain through a preferential transfer (such as the purchase of an asset from the company at an unreasonably low fire sale price).[17]

---

16. This does not mean to imply that investors necessarily receive a cash distribution at the end of bankruptcy proceedings. However their deeply discounted non-performing securities are likely to be swapped for performing securities of a higher value.

17. All of a firm's transactions in the 90-day run-up to bankruptcy are subsequently scrutinized for signs that such a fraudulent conveyance has occurred. The buyer of a distressed security must check that the previous owner was not involved in such a fraudulent conveyance, because subsequent owners of the securities are liable for lawsuits.

## Illiquidity

Bankruptcy may reduce the market values of large companies to a fraction of their original size. Bid–offer spreads are wide and trading is often on a matched bargain basis. Many distressed securities are therefore illiquid, and managers of large funds may be locked into a series of long-term views. Bank debt is generally concentrated in few hands and therefore tends to be the preserve of larger investors. Transactions in bank debt can be difficult to arrange, involve considerable paperwork and take a long time to settle. It is therefore important that the redemption terms offered by a distressed securities fund are consistent with the style of distressed investing it is conducting. (Note that distressed securities are not necessarily illiquid, particularly for managers with smaller funds. Many bonds trade actively and are more liquid than many Nasdaq stocks. Liquidity tends to be particularly good at the very beginning and very end of the bankruptcy process.)

## Pricing

These are often illiquid OTC markets with wide bid–offer spreads. For smaller situations the only way to be sure of a security's value is to sell it. It is not possible for fund administrators to mark a portfolio of these securities without assistance. They must rely on a series of marks provided by broker dealers with whom their distressed securities manager conducts regular business. This process is not entirely independent and there is scope for massaging valuations and smoothing performance. It is particularly difficult to compare the performance of different distressed securities managers during periods of extreme market dislocation because their respective marking arrangements are likely to have differed at the time. To some extent the risk-adjusted returns of all distressed managers are likely to be flattered by performance smoothing.

## Diversification within the strategy

Investing across a range of distressed securities managers does not necessarily provide diversification. Depending upon the style of the managers there may be considerable overlap between their portfolios. Combining larger-scale managers with smaller-scale managers (specializing in smaller situations) may go some way to solving this problem.

## Length of time

Distressed investing is not for the impatient. The restructuring process is slow and subject to delays. The possible illiquidity of the securities, and associated high transaction costs, means they are not suitable for short-term investors.

## Reaction to markets

### *Economic and market strength*

During periods of economic and market strength default rates tend to subside, squeezing the flow of investment opportunities available to distressed investors. This generally results in depressed returns. Although the favourable economic environment supports a more satisfactory conclusion to bankruptcy proceedings, the supply–demand imbalance becomes less favourable to the distressed investor. Furthermore, those companies that fall into bankruptcy in spite of the buoyant environment are often seriously flawed.

### *Economic and market weakness*

During weak environments default rates are high, adding to the supply of distressed paper and increasing the flow of opportunities. The pool of companies experiencing distress during difficult periods contains a higher proportion of recoverable businesses with good prospects once their balance sheets have been restructured. With the improvement in both the quantity and the quality of their investment universe, distressed investors generate better returns.

### *Turning points*

High default rates and a good supply of distressed situations are generally good for the opportunity set. In the short-term, however, sharply rising default rates can temporarily swamp the market with distressed paper, depressing pricing. This phenomenon has a temporary mark-to-market effect. Note, though, that the bankruptcy process concludes with payments to investors that are independent of swings in the default rate. Thus the investor who 'holds to maturity' need not be affected by such developments. If a sharp rise in supply does depress the price of distressed paper, it generally provides a good buying opportunity.

### *Default rates*

The key turning point for distressed securities prices tends to come when default rates peak and the supply tap slowly turns off. This is typically followed by a period of outsized returns for the strategy. Studies have shown that default rates tend to peak two to three years after high yield bond issuance has peaked. This reflects the fact that the probability of a high yield bond defaulting is relatively high during the two or three years after it has been issued. Additionally, a peak in corporate bond issuance tends to be symptomatic of a peak in the economic and market cycle. It is therefore understandable that the number of companies experiencing difficulties should rise in the ensuing period, but that the situation should stabilize a few years later. (See Figures 10.4 and 10.5.)

### Sector influences

Peaks in corporate bond issuance influence subsequent returns in distressed securities, but the nature of the bond issuance is also a factor. Booms in bond issuance are often dominated by growth in particular industries, and the dominance of these sectors is reflected in the subsequent supply of distressed paper. Overcapacity in a particular sector is likely to weigh on the recovery rates achievable when those bonds are restructured. If the assets employed by the sector are unmarketable, the recovery rates will be particularly low. In these ways the entire distressed securities market can be affected by the nature of economic growth in prior years. (See Figure 10.6.)

### Liquidity crises

Distressed securities are illiquid instruments. During periods of extreme market dislocation liquidity preferences rise sharply, and the prices of distressed securities can suffer from unpleasant mark-to-market losses. However these losses should ultimately be recouped once the environment stabilizes. This is because the progress and outcome of a restructuring are rarely affected by the market dislocation. A more tangible threat is posed when managers of distressed securities portfolios are for some reason obliged to liquidate holdings when markets are at their extremes, crystallizing their losses.

### Correlation with equity markets

Returns from distressed securities should be independent of the equity and high yield markets. In practice, however, they can be affected by strong moves in either. There is a real element of 'equity risk' within distressed securities because many of them are destined to be partly converted into equity. Even before Chapter 11 proceedings commence, bonds that have traded down to 50 cents on the dollar imply that the bondholders consider themselves the owners of the equity, and that they have the potential to make equity-like returns. The investors are doubtless using various forms of equity analysis and no longer feel directly affected by modest moves in government bond yields.

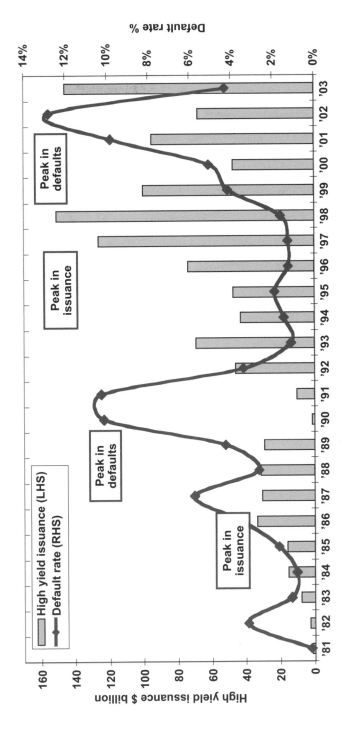

**Figure 10.4** The relationship between high yield issuance and default rates

Peaks in high yield issuance tend to be followed by peaks in the default rate several years later.

Source: Professor E Altman, NYU Salomon Center.

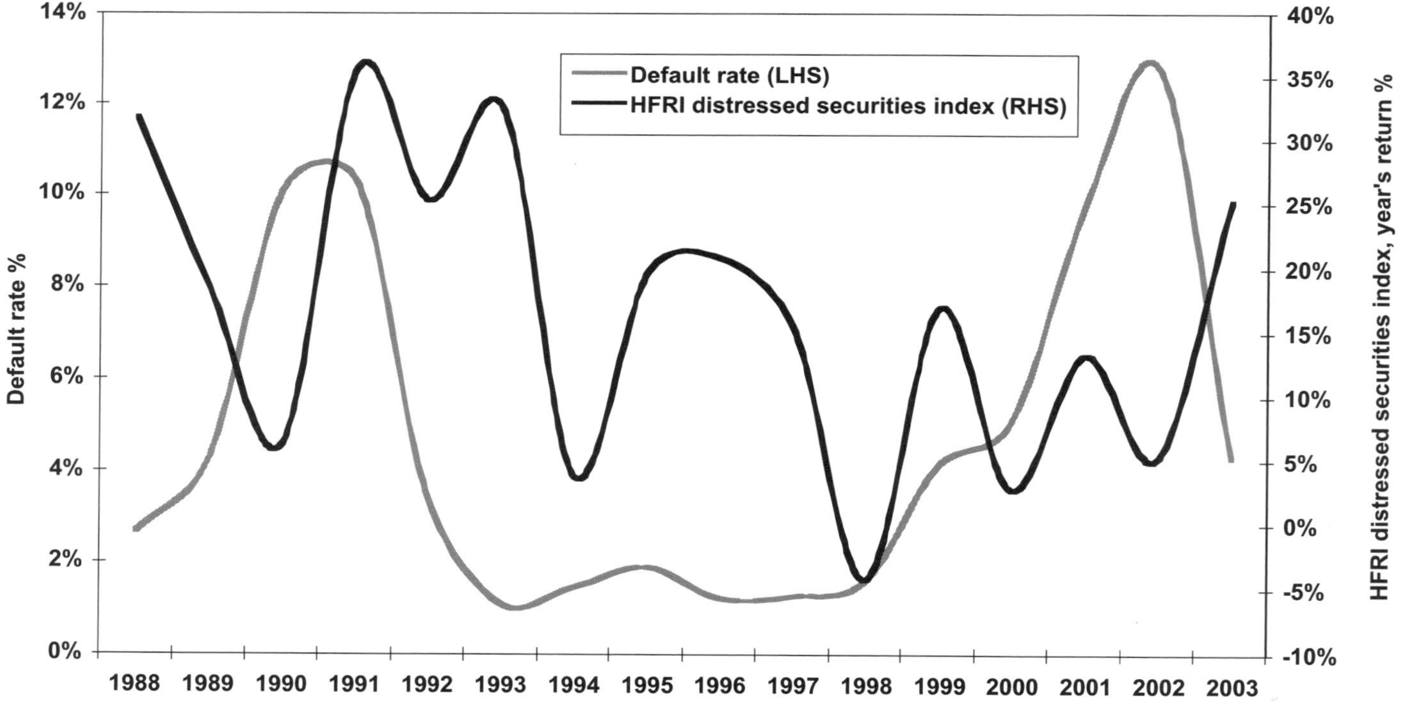

**Figure 10.5**  Distressed investing returns and the default rate

Peaks in the default rate tend to be followed by periods of outsized returns for distressed securities investors.

Source: Professor E Altman, NYU Salomon Center.

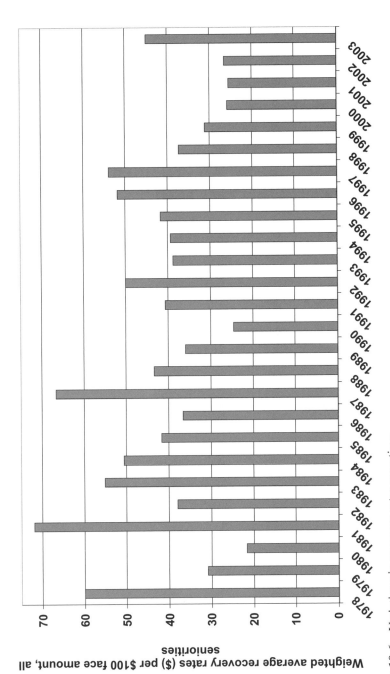

**Figure 10.6** Variations in recovery rates over time

Depending upon the nature of the sectors entering distress at any one time, the prevailing recovery rates achieved by creditors are likely to vary.

Source: Professor E Altman, NYU Salomon Center.

### Correlation with high yield markets

While distressed debt is not driven by minor changes in the yield curve, it is affected by significant changes in credit spreads. A large change in the appetite for credit risk will filter right down to the most stressed of credits. This is not unreasonable, given that debt being restructured will end up in part as new high yield bonds. Those securities still managing to pay some form of coupon will be the most directly affected by changes in credit spreads.

# APPENDIX 1: KEY CONSIDERATIONS: DISTRESSED SECURITIES

- Does the manager have sufficient expertise in the area, including experience of bankruptcy investing, access to legal opinions and other consultants? Is the manager's experience purely legal or bankruptcy related? Does he or she also have the commercial awareness to judge the prospects for the underlying business?

- Has the manager got a good network of contacts within the bankruptcy community, including consultants, bankers, lawyers, accountants and other investors?

- Does the manager have the negotiation skills and determination required to deal with conflicts? Does the manager have a reputation for 'playing hardball', and if so is this appropriate?

- Is the fund strictly invested in bankruptcy situations or does it also include stressed companies that are expected to avoid bankruptcy?

- Is the fund strictly long-only or are other strategies pursued, such as outright short sales or capital structure arbitrage? How are the risks of these situations handled (such as agreeing a sensible hedge ratio)?

- Does the manager have a large pool of assets to allocate? If so, how does this affect the style of investment?

- Does the fund concentrate on, or include, bank debt, subordinated bonds, trade claims or equity? Why? (Bear in mind that investors concentrating on junior securities will use equity biased valuation techniques, while those focusing on senior securities will be less equity biased.)

- How much sensitivity to equity valuations does the manager tolerate? Are duration and credit spread risks being avoided?

- Will the manager sit on investment committees? What is the reason for this policy? How are the restrictions and conflicts that arise managed?

- Is there a preference for investing at any particular stage of the bankruptcy process?

- Is the fund invested long-term? Could it be more actively traded or are its holdings too illiquid?

- Are the fund's redemption terms consistent with the liquidity of its portfolio?

- Does the manager have a preference for a type of bankruptcy situation, such as good business–bad balance sheet, or litigation situations? Does the manager get involved in turnaround situations? If so, how does the manager add value?

- Does the manager deliberately target low volatility, and if so how does this affect investment policies?

- How do the administrators ensure they obtain accurate marks for their valuations? How often is the portfolio audited, and using what methods to verify accurate pricing? What measures are taken to limit performance smoothing?

- How does the manager react to periods of low default rates and a shrinking supply of opportunities? Does this prompt ventures into other areas?

- What particular analysis considerations does the manager consider the most important within the context of distressed investing?

- Is the manager an optimist or a cynic in relation to the asset values and business prospects of distressed companies?

- How thoroughly does the manager appear to analyse the finer points of the offering documents of each security issued by a company in order to decompose its capital structure?

# APPENDIX 2: GLOSSARY

**Absolute priority rule:** Requirement for each class of creditor to be fully repaid before the next class of creditor receives any payment. Negotiations frequently result in this rule not being applied strictly (see 'bondmail' below).

**Avoiding powers:** Measures designed to prevent fraudulent conveyances that effectively provide favoured creditors with preferential recovery rates.

**Bar date:** Date, set by the bankruptcy judge, after which no more pre-Chapter 11 claims may be asserted.

**Bondmail:** Attempts by junior creditors to improve their treatment in the restructuring process by threatening to vote against reorganizations plans, thereby delaying the process.

**Chapter 7:** Rules governing the liquidation of a bankrupt company in the United States.

**Chapter 11:** US rules governing the restructuring of a bankrupt company, leaving the debtor in possession of the company to salvage the business in the hope that creditors will recover greater value by such means.

**Cram down:** Ruling by the judge of a bankruptcy court overriding the objections of junior creditors to a plan of reorganization on the basis that the objections are unreasonable.

**Creditor committee:** A committee drawn from representatives of the creditors that is charged with steering the bankruptcy process, examining the company's plan of reorganization and proposing alternatives if necessary. Generally dominated by larger holders of senior debt, who have a prior claim on the assets. The committee is advised by a law firm and a financial advisory firm, with fees being paid by the debtor. Thus its members are relieved of most of the burden of due diligence.

**Debtor in possession:** A company undergoing Chapter 11 reorganization. Although the firm is bankrupt the assets have been left in the control of the company's management, which continues to operate the firm.

**Fraudulent conveyance:** A transaction between a particular creditor and the company in the run-up to bankruptcy that unreasonably favours that creditor. This would mean that the company is offering a preferential recovery rate.

**Recovery rate:** The value of the cash and securities received at the conclusion of bankruptcy proceedings, expressed as a percentage of their original face value.

# 11

# Hedged mortgage backed securities

There is nothing better for a man that he should 'feel the blessed flow of labour' within him; but because of Usury one man never gets to feel its warmth, and perishes with his powers undeveloped, while another man has so much of it forced upon him that his faculties are shrivelled up, and he is consumed by its excess.

William Ridley[1]

In today's financial markets most lending activities are backed by credit analysis. Yet throughout history lending activities have been backed by assets pledged as security against debts. Lenders would not lend on the basis that a borrower was 'creditworthy'. On the contrary, they would lend to anyone with good collateral and lend to no one with poor collateral. Parts of the lending market, most notably the mortgage market, still operate on this basis. However, a wide range of assets are used to support lending in addition to property, such as commodities, finished goods, commercial receivables and consumer receivables. A number of hedge fund structures have been set up to invest into these loans, most notably into US mortgage backed securities (MBS).

Mortgage backed securities offer excess returns because they are complex. Managers who hedge MBS accurately can extract these excess returns and secure handsome profits. Much of this chapter is

---

1. Taken from Ridley, W (1897) *Interest or Usury: Some thoughts on modern methods of finance and their effect on our national life*, Liverpool. This is one of my esteemed ancestors, who was more than a little irritated by money lenders.

dedicated to discussing the complexities of MBS arbitrage. Investors should not think of these complexities as a reason to avoid this strategy. MBS arbitrage is challenging, as are many specialist investment strategies. However, hedge fund managers have shown themselves to be successful in coping with these challenges, which are an excellent source of opportunity.

# MORTGAGE BACKED SECURITIES

Mortgage backed securities (MBS) are a means of bundling mortgage loans together and securitizing them so that they can be purchased by financial institutions. MBS are by far the largest component of the asset backed universe. Advocates of this asset class highlight a number of its attractive attributes:

- These loans are extremely well collateralized, since they are secured against property.

- The creditworthiness of most of these instruments is also good. Securities packaged by the three main US mortgage agencies are guaranteed by them. These agencies in turn enjoy various forms of support from the US government, either explicit (Ginnie Mae) or implied (Fannie Mae and Freddie Mac).

- Those securities packaged by private entities are generally tranched in order to provide the majority of investors with high grade, senior securities. These are supported by junior securities for those investors who choose to be more speculative.

- Despite their strong asset backing and strong creditworthiness, MBS tend to trade at higher yields than corporate bonds of a similar quality because they entail some complex features. They seem to outperform corporate bonds across most time horizons.

- Structured securities can be derived from MBS that offer a wide variety of characteristics. These are versatile tools for creating and hedging MBS portfolios.

- The US MBS market is the largest fixed income market in the world. During 2003 it was approximately 2.5 times the size of the US Treasury market. The market has a large, diverse, institutionally dominated investor base that includes insurance companies, mutual funds and commercial banks.

Borrowers in the US mortgage market usually have the option to repay their mortgage early, causing MBS securities to miss out on the interest payments they would otherwise have received during the ensuing years. The rate at which mortgage borrowers 'prepay' their loans affects the value of MBS, and it can be difficult to predict. Understandably, the speed of these prepayments is linked to the prevailing level of interest rates relative to the coupons that mortgage borrowers are paying. However, the prepayment speed is also influenced by a number of other factors. It is this analytical complexity that provides hedge funds with their opportunity: it causes MBS to offer their premium yields.

Hedge funds seek to capture this complexity premium by assembling portfolios of attractively priced MBS and MBS derivatives and hedging themselves against as many of the associated risks as possible. This activity is usually referred to as 'MBS arbitrage'. It would be unwise to launch into a discussion of these hedge funds without first considering the unusual characteristics of mortgage backed securities.

# CHARACTERISTICS OF MORTGAGE BACKED SECURITIES

## The MBS pass through

The most basic mortgage backed security (and the most prevalent) is the 'MBS pass through' issued by one of the three main mortgage agencies. These are pools of mortgage loans that have similar characteristics, bundled up and issued as a single security. The cash flows thrown off by the pool of mortgages are simply 'passed through' to the holder of the security. Interest, scheduled principal repayments and early 'prepayments' are all passed through on a monthly basis. For the Wall Street investor this arrangement has a number of attractions. The investor can buy into a large number of small loans with one transaction, originated by an independent agency. The agency administrates, collecting the cash flows together for disbursement and guaranteeing their delivery. As a result the investor can buy a security that resembles a bond and dispenses with the effort and risk of handling numerous private borrowers.

The characteristics of these pass throughs are carefully defined so that the pool of loans is reasonably homogenous. Changes in these characteristics are monitored monthly and published via 'pool factor tapes'. These inform the investor of:

- the date at which the mortgage loans were issued and their overall duration (they will not all be exactly the same);
- the basis upon which interest is paid (e.g. fixed rate);[2]
- the weighted average coupon (WAC) being paid by the borrowers, net of a servicing charge;[3]
- the weighted average loan age (WALA) and weighted average maturity (WAM) of the remaining loans (thereby accounting for past prepayments);
- the original and the remaining size of the pool (resulting in a 'pool factor' that expresses the outstanding balance as proportion of the original).

To improve liquidity, these pass throughs are usually traded on a 'to be announced' (TBA) basis, meaning that the buyer does not know exactly which pass through will be delivered against a purchase until 48 hours before its delivery. A protocol exists that limits its variance from the characteristics agreed at the time of a trade. Pass throughs can also be traded on a specific basis, which increases certainty for the buyer but also increases the price paid. Alternatively, investors may buy combined pools that serve to average out the characteristics of the underlying loans and reduce the burden of administration.

## Analysing prepayments

The essence of MBS complexity lies in measuring and predicting the speed of prepayments because they greatly affect the cash flows accruing to MBS. It is difficult to assess the IRR of a security unless one knows how much cash is coming and when it is coming.[4]

Mortgage prepayments result from:

- homeowners selling and re-mortgaging;
- homeowners refinancing;
- homeowners who partially prepay in order to build up equity in their homes;
- homeowners who default.

---

2. Most mortgages in the United States are fixed rate, although some are adjustable rate mortgages (ARMs) or a hybrid between fixed and floating. These require separate analysis.
3. To improve the accuracy of valuation calculations, investors are also provided with the number of days delay between actual mortgage payments and when they are passed on by the servicing company.
4. The speed at which prepayments occur in a mortgage pool is referred to as the 'single monthly mortality', a figure which is usually quoted in annualized form as the 'constant prepayment rate' (CPR).

The first two (homeowner mobility and refinancing) have by far the greatest impact. Within a pool of mortgages the pattern of prepayments from all four sources progresses with the passage of time, an effect known as 'seasoning'.

Home sales typically result in the prepayment of 3–7 per cent of a mortgage pool every year. However, in the first 30 months of a pool's life this is much lower because the borrowers have just moved and are unlikely to do so again for a few years. Turnover increases in the spring and early summer, and bottoms in January and February. Rising house prices increase turnover because borrowers build up equity in their houses more quickly. The strength of the housing market is in turn affected by the economy, interest rates and regional factors. Over the course of the 1980s homeowner mobility rose steadily, from a trough of 3.3 per cent in the recession at the start of the decade, to 6.8 per cent at the end of the decade.[5]

Refinancing is driven principally by interest rates. It is likely to occur once prevailing mortgage rates fall below the coupon rate being paid by the borrowers in a pool. Refinancing typically accelerates once interest rates fall 100 basis points below the weighted average coupon (WAC) in the pool. However, the pace tends to slow once rates fall a few hundred basis points below the WAC, an effect known as 'burnout'. This is because those borrowers alert to the refinancing opportunity have already taken advantage of it, whereas those remaining seem unable to spot it (the 'dumbo effect'). If interest rates dip below the coupon rate for a second time during the life of a mortgage pool, the increase in refinancing is likely to be muted because the pool will have burnt out already. When interest rates reach levels deemed historically low, media discussion tends to improve borrower awareness, resulting in unusually high rates of refinancing (the 'media effect').[6] The pace of refinancing is not just influenced by prevailing interest rates. Low income borrowers, such as those represented in Ginnie Mae pools, show a weaker inclination to refinance when rates drop because they are less well positioned to negotiate improved terms. Likewise, borrowers who have been lured by discounted rates during the early years of their mortgage are unlikely to refinance or move home during the discount period. Borrowers with low loan balances also display less motivation to refinance.

---

5. Salomon Smith Barney (1999).
6. There are various other interest rate nuances. Fixed rate mortgages issued when the yield curve is flat are likely to prepay more quickly because a number of the borrowers who are naturally inclined towards adjustable rate mortgages were probably lured into fixed rate mortgages by relatively attractive 30-year rates.

Partial prepayments (or curtailments) are a relatively minor contribution to a pool's prepayment speed, as are defaults.[7] The default rate is particularly slow after an initial seasoning period, partly because the gradual build-up of equity makes homeowners keener to avoid default.

There are therefore quite a number of factors influencing prepayment speeds, many of them relating to human behaviour. This human behaviour follows certain patterns, on the basis of which some fairly good generalizations can be made. MBS investors therefore compare each pass through's prepayment speed with a 'base case' level of prepayments calculated by the Public Securities Association (PSA).[8] The Public Securities Association has plotted a curve that averages market-wide prepayment speeds, adjusting for a pool's age and the degree to which it has seasoned. A particular pass through's prepayment speed can therefore be quoted as a percentage of the speed on the PSA curve. Because of burnout, the PSA curve generally has an S-shape, although its precise appearance changes with seasoning. (See Figures 11.1 and 11.2.)

## Analysing the option-adjusted spread

Non-callable fixed income securities are conventionally quoted in terms of the spread they offer over comparable US Treasuries. If one were to examine a pass through in this way one would compare it against the US Treasury whose duration most closely matched the weighted average life (WAL) of the pass through concerned. However, yields on pass throughs cannot be directly compared with US Treasuries. Treasuries repay their principal at maturity and pay coupons semi-annually in the interim. Pass throughs pay coupons and amortize their principal on a monthly basis, together with an uncertain volume of prepayments. The cash flow timings are thus so different that straightforward comparisons between pass throughs and Treasuries of similar durations would be of limited interest. For greater accuracy, each monthly coupon, principal payment and expected prepayment may be individually discounted at its own forward rate.[9] Using this more accurate pricing method, a pass

---

7. Remember that these loans are backed by assets, which are liquidated in the event of default. Therefore defaults represent accelerated repayments rather than a loss of capital. Note that agency pass throughs are guaranteed by the agencies, who assume the burden of restructuring the loan or recovering the collateral. The pass through owner simply experiences a prepayment. However, this does still mean that interest payments due in the ensuing years are lost.
8. Now called the Bond Market Association.
9. Monthly forward rates can be extrapolated from a generic Treasury yield curve.

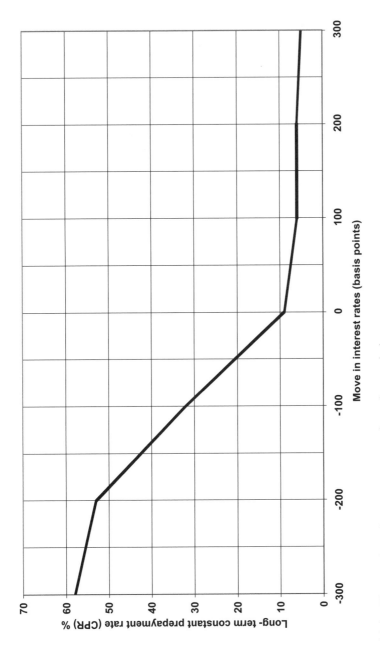

**Figure 11.1** The reaction of prepayment speeds to changes in interest rates

Prepayment speeds are inclined to rise as interest rates fall. This diagram provides an illustration, although different pass throughs will react in different ways.

Source: Salomon Smith Barney.

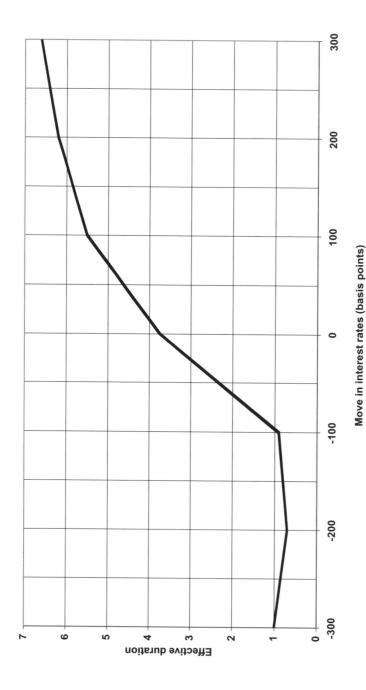

**Figure 11.2**  The reaction of effective duration to changes in interest rates

As interest rates fall and prepayments rise, a pass through's effective duration falls. This diagram provides an illustration although different pass throughs will react in different ways.

Source: Salomon Smith Barney.

through's yield curve spread (YCS) can be calculated, facilitating more appropriate yield comparisons with US Treasuries.

Although the YCS represents an improvement on a simple spread over the nearest Treasury, it fails to encompass the full implications of investing in pass throughs. Changes in interest rates affect Treasuries and MBS very differently. The homeowner possesses the option to prepay if rates fall, whereas the US government usually does not.[10] Pass through cash flows vary with interest rates because of this prepayment option. The cost of these variations in cash flows (the cost of the prepayment option) needs to be incorporated into the measurement of a pass through's value. To rectify this, the impact of interest rate volatility can be acknowledged using another calculation, one which derives the option-adjusted spread (OAS).

The failing of the YCS is that it values a pass through on the basis of a single path for interest rates and it assumes zero interest rate volatility. The solution is to value the cash flows from a pass through on the basis of all possible interest rate paths.[11] Each of these interest rate scenarios must incorporate the pass through's cash flows associated with each interest rate path, reflecting the results of a prepayment model. A pass through can then be valued using the average of its present values under all these scenarios. From that valuation an average spread can also be calculated. This is the option-adjusted spread.

Thus we can value a pass through using three different methods that are increasingly informative:

1. A pass through may be compared against the US Treasury most closely matching its weighted average life (WAL).
2. A series of forward rates that match a pass through's cash flows may be used to calculate its yield curve spread (YCS).
3. A whole range of forward rates that match a pass through's cash flows under all possible scenarios for interest rates may be used to calculate the average of its different spreads for each path. This is the option-adjusted spread (OAS).

---

10. The owners of MBS are thus short of this call option, and part of the yield curve spread represents the premium for this option. Conventional option theory cannot be applied to valuing these options because so many factors determine whether the holders of the option decide to exercise them. Some borrowers exercise the option when it is still out-of-the-money (such as on selling their home), while others fail to exercise it even when it is in-the-money (as with the dumbo effect). Instead, MBS investors calculate the value of the option by 'backing it out' of an OAS calculation. The cost of this option (paid by the borrowers) is generally considered to over-compensate lenders for the risk they take when they buy MBS.
11. This exercise is conducted using Monte Carlo simulation, incorporating a term structure model that depicts the evolution of interest rates over time. Generally these models are designed to keep the 'possible' paths for interest rates within realistic bounds, such as limiting the range of possible interest rate moves and acknowledging the different volatilities of different US Treasuries in different parts of the curve.

The OAS highlights the cost of the homeowner's option to prepay. This cost can be calculated by subtracting the OAS from the YCS. For example, in March 1999 Salomon Smith Barney referred to Ginnie Mae 6.5 per cent pass throughs that had a spread of 153 bp over their nearest US Treasury. Their YCS was 134 bp and their OAS was 75 bp, implying an option cost of 59 bp. The OAS is a useful measure of relative valuation between different MBS, fulfilling a similar role as the standard spread for non-callable bullet bonds. It also helps investors compare the value of MBS with all other types of bonds, be they callable or non-callable.

# THE NEGATIVE CONVEXITY OF MORTGAGE BACKED SECURITIES

At this stage it is worth pausing to consider the central risk associated with mortgage pass throughs. As with most fixed income securities, a rise in the general level of interest rates eats into the present value of a pass through's cash flows, reducing their value. Unfortunately the opposite cannot be said for a fall in interest rates. Falling interest rates accelerate prepayment speeds and reduce a pass through's effective duration.[12] The early receipt of principal serves to improve returns, as do lower discounting rates. However, these influences are offset by two factors that are usually more powerful. First, the owner of the MBS security misses out on coupon payments for the remainder of the loan's life. Second, the owner is forced to reinvest the capital at a lower rate of interest. Faster prepayments therefore serve to reduce a security's value.[13] Because of these features, many mortgage securities suffer from negative convexity, meaning that their price falls in reaction to both rising and falling yields. (See Figure 11.3.) This negative convexity is likely to be at its worst when a security is 'at-the-money', meaning that the loan pool's coupon rate is the same as prevailing mortgage rates. It is here that the risk of rising prepayment speeds is greatest. The owners of MBS therefore require the premium OAS yield as payment for negative convexity and for complexity. Historically, the additional returns offered by MBS have more than compensated for the risks involved.

---

12. Depending on interest rate expectations and the make-up of a mortgage pool, a pass through with a 30-year life might have an expected duration of just 2 years.
13. A measure of this risk can be found in the 'prepayment duration', the measure of a security's price sensitivity to an instant 10 per cent change in the prepayment rate.

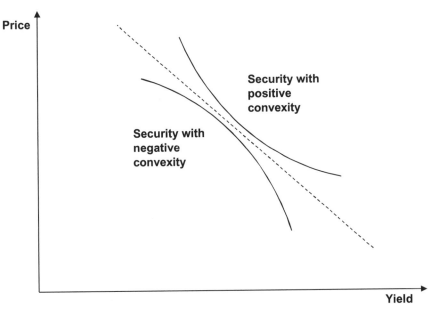

**Figure 11.3**   Crude illustration of the concept of negative convexity
If a security has positive convexity, we would expect its price to rise at a
faster rate when interest rates rise to higher levels but for its price to fall at a
decelerating rate when interest rates fall to lower levels. The reverse holds
true for securities with negative convexity.
Source: author.

# STRUCTURED SECURITIES

Agency pass throughs are not the only form of mortgage backed
security. Several hundred pass throughs can be collected into a portfolio to create a more diversified entity, a collateralized mortgage obligation (CMO). Backed by the cash flows from its portfolio, the CMO
can then issue a series of 'sequential bonds' with a range of maturities.
A class of short-term securities can be retired using the CMO portfolio's initial principal cash flows. The timing of cash flows for all
classes is likely to be affected by changing prepayment speeds in the
underlying portfolio. As the deals season, prepayments may become
more volatile, causing the structure of the CMO deal to alter from its
original schedule. These changes need to be managed by MBS hedge
funds. However, later classes are provided with some buffer from
prepayments by the earlier classes, and portfolio diversification
averages out geographical variations.

These CMOs can be structured in a variety of ways in order to meet investor preferences. These frequently include the issue of one or more planned amortization class (PAC) bonds. These are attempts to create securities that resemble conventional non-callable bonds. As long as prepayment speeds in the underlying portfolio remain within predefined bounds, each PAC bond will stick to a specified repayment schedule.[14] This can be arranged by issuing support or companion bonds, which assume some of the slack and keep the PAC bond repayments on schedule. Another security frequently issued by CMOs is the 'floating rate bond', which provides some protection against rising rates. This can be achieved by pairing it with the issue of another security whose coupon moves in the opposite direction from that of the floating rate bond, an 'inverse floater'. The inverse floater is generally issued in smaller size and so contains considerable leverage to falling interest rates.[15]

The cash flows from CMOs may also be divided up to provide varying proportions of interest or principal payments to different CMO securities. The extreme examples are the strips, interest only (IO) and principal only (PO) securities. These are exceptionally sensitive to changes in interest rates and prepayment speeds. Falling interest rates and accelerating prepayments result in principal being paid back early, greatly enhancing the rate of return achieved by holders of POs. However, such prepayments also result in the curtailment of interest payments, which is immensely damaging to holders of IOs. By contrast, falling prepayments imply that borrowers will continue paying interest on their loans for longer periods than was previously expected and will therefore be paying more interest coupons. IOs rapidly go up in value under such circumstances. Conversely, the prospect of delays to principal repayments means that POs suffer.[16] IO and PO securities can be used to hedge MBS portfolios, or may be combined with other securities to create a synthetic

---

14. Perhaps a range of 100–300 per cent of the PSA curve.

15. Limits must be set defining the extent to which a floater's rate can float up, since the inverse floater's rate can fall no further than zero. The floater's rate will be defined in terms of LIBOR plus 'x' basis points, while the inverse floater's rate will be 'y' per cent minus 'z' times LIBOR. The leverage incorporated within an inverse floater clearly varies greatly according to its structure.

16. The loss of coupons when interest rates fall greatly outweighs the effect of falling discount rates. IOs therefore have a negative duration in periods of falling interest rates, particularly if the loans involved are at or just below-the-money, where refinancing is most likely to accelerate in reaction to falling rates. They also have a negative duration when rates rise because the additional coupons greatly outweigh the effect of the higher discount rate applied to them. At much higher interest rates prepayments stop slowing, and the effect of the higher discount rate starts to take effect. POs have a high positive duration because falling interest rates mean both a reduction in the discount rate applied to principal repayments and a reduction in time until they are received. POs also have positive convexity, although both their duration and convexity properties are dampened once the underlying loans are further out-of-the-money.

portfolio with the managers' desired attributes. They can also be used to bet on prepayment speeds, although their sensitivity means managers must have a very good understanding of prepayments. (See Figure 11.4.)

CMOs and their derivatives therefore permit a wide range of investors to use MBS to meet their needs more closely, reducing uncertainty about the timing of cash flows, providing diversification and facilitating hedging. CMOs also involve a fresh layer of analytical complexity. All these types of CMO security (sequential bonds, PAC bonds, floating rate bonds, inverse floaters, IOs and POs) react differently to changes in prepayment speeds. Both their structure and the underlying collateral, namely the pass throughs, require careful analysis.

# NON-AGENCY SECURITIES

Agencies are not the only entities to issue residential mortgage backed securities. A variety of commercial organizations also issue pass throughs, each focusing on particular segments of the borrowing community. 'Jumbo loans' are pools of larger loans borrowed by the more affluent, 'alternative-A loans' are of moderate credit quality, while 'subprime loans' and 'home equity loans' feed through to less creditworthy borrowers. Each of these constituencies exhibits its own behavioural tendencies that affect the pattern of prepayments. Jumbo loans tend to be more reactive to changes in interest rates because the borrowers are well informed, well placed to refinance and have larger loan balances. These pass throughs are therefore more sensitive to interest rates than agency pass throughs, and they exhibit strongly negative convexity. Many alternative-A loan borrowers have failed to arrange a loan through the main agencies, and their propensity to refinance is therefore driven not so much by falling interest rates as by improvements in their personal circumstances over time. There is less negative convexity to these securities. Subprime loans are even less interest rate sensitive, since the borrowers have even fewer refinancing options available and they suffer prepayment penalties.

Non-agency MBS securities cannot provide the guarantees offered by the main agencies, but they compensate for the risks involved through attractive yields. The credit risks can be mitigated by investing through a CMO structure, and of course there is underlying collateral. Like agency CMOs, non-agency CMOs provide

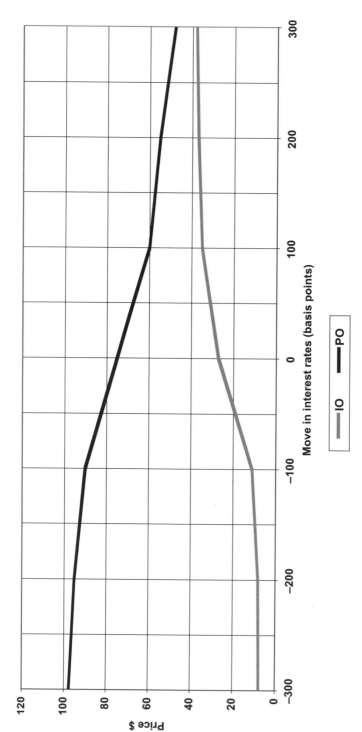

**Figure 11.4** The reaction of IOs and POs to changes in interest rates

As interest rates fall the value of IOs falls sharply in reaction to higher prepayment speeds and the expectation of interest payments forgone. The value of POs rises sharply because faster prepayments accelerate the payment of principal and increase the present value of the cash flows. The reverse forces are at work when interest rates rise.

diversification. However, they tend to be constructed in a senior-subordinated structure, with a number of tranches ranked by seniority rather than by their exposure to prepayments. Thus junior tranches, representing up to 20 per cent of the capital, provide enhanced security for the more senior issues and assume the role of the agency guarantee.

Another non-agency security is the commercial mortgage backed security (CMBS). Here the corporate world mingles with the MBS world. CMBS are generally loans to real estate developers and REITs that are backed by retail, office, hotel and multi-family property. They are quite different from residential MBS because the borrowers are unable to prepay without paying proper yield maintenance and penalties. Therefore CMBS do not exhibit the negative convexity of residential MBS. Instead their principal cash flows more closely resemble those of a non-callable bond.[17]

# HEDGING MORTGAGE BACKED SECURITIES AND MANAGING RISK

The MBS markets incorporate a diverse range of securities that spans the full spectrum of risk and reward. Although MBS involve some complexities, they offer a high return that more than compensates. MBS hedge fund managers attempt to isolate this excess return by identifying and hedging the particular risks associated with MBS, and the underlying duration risk. This hedging transforms the nature of the risk and return offered by the portfolio. Instead of being exposed to the price volatility of a traditional portfolio of MBS, managers are exposed to the excess spread offered by MBS, to their security selection and to their portfolio management capabilities.

Hedging a portfolio of MBS involves a series of discrete exercises:

## Assembling a portfolio

The first task is to assemble a long portfolio by selecting from a range of attractively priced MBS pass throughs, CMO securities or CMO derivatives. The portfolio can be constructed in order to diversify away a number of specific risks, such as regional biases, credit differentials and relative prepayment differences between securities. MBS arbitrageurs are equipped with a number of sophisticated modelling

---

17. CMBS are also non-recourse, meaning that in the event of default the lender is entitled to no more than the property collateral.

tools that facilitate their analysis of relative valuations between different securities. Separate models are used for assessing prepayment patterns, for estimating OAS and for analysing the structures of different types of security. Once a portfolio of cheap long positions has been constructed, the next step is to select a series of short positions that are correlated with the longs. This short portfolio acts as a hedge, and isolates the relative value embedded within the long portfolio.[18] Once these hedges are in place, leverage is judiciously applied in order to secure acceptable levels of return.

## Hedging MBS-specific risks

Portfolio diversification alone cannot remove all prepayment-related risks. This requires hedging against interest rate risk, changes in the slope of the yield curve, interest rate volatility and negative convexity. Falling interest rates (rising prepayment speeds) can be hedged against with long positions in POs, which benefit disproportionately from falling rates and have a high positive convexity. Options on interest rates or on US Treasuries may also be used to counteract the asymmetric nature of MBS.[19] Arbitrageurs may wish to protect themselves against increasing prepayment speeds due to other factors, such as increased homeowner mobility, greater alertness to refinancing or rising default rates. This is difficult to do on a security by security basis, but some measures can be taken at the portfolio level. Long positions in POs may serve this purpose, as might short positions in other MBS.[20]

## Neutralizing duration

Having mitigated many of the risks particular to MBS, arbitrageurs may then choose to neutralize their underlying duration exposure. Protection against rising interest rates can be obtained by shorting US Treasuries, interest rate swaps or interest rate futures. In addition to parallel shifts in the yield curve, arbitrageurs must develop strategies

---

18. Note that the models used by hedge funds are well tested and accurate (to the extent that they can be on the basis of the latest information). The models are not used to make predictions about the future path of interest rates, their likely affect on prepayments and their consequent price impact on specific MBS securities. Instead, they are used to assess relative values between securities. The hedging is designed to protect the portfolio from interest rate and prepayment outcomes, so that these relative value differences may be isolated without undue concern about interest rate changes.
19. Note that having long option positions means paying for interest rate volatility, so arbitrageurs must be sure they are paying less for the implied volatility in these instruments than the implied volatility they are receiving from the homeowners.
20. Short positions in other MBS cannot be used too extensively to hedge long MBS positions or else it will be impossible to capture the excess spread offered by MBS securities.

to protect against a steepening or flattening of the yield curve, or a change in its curvature. Some MBS derivatives can be used for these purposes, and a portfolio's sensitivity to yield curve pivots and other changes can be monitored.

## Hedging the spread

Despite these measures the arbitrageur is still exposed to variations in the yield spread between MBS and Treasuries. This exposure is measured as 'spread duration', referring to a security's price sensitivity to a 100 basis point widening in the OAS. Because arbitrageurs are both hedged and leveraged they are particularly exposed to changes in this spread, which has been known to range from 100 basis points to almost 500 basis points at extremes.[21] Further hedging may therefore be desirable at times when spreads are expected to widen. This may be difficult unless one counts on simultaneous spread widening in other areas of the fixed income world. Short positions in interest rate swaps, agency bonds, other MBS and interest rate derivatives should help. It is difficult to eliminate the threat of widening spreads completely, but any pain from widening spreads is followed by higher carry in ensuing periods.

## Rebalancing hedges

Even new expectations for interest rates result in new predictions for prepayments speeds, which alone is enough to alter a security's profile (including its expected duration and its convexity). All hedges must therefore be dynamically adjusted on a regular basis. In addition, many arbitrageurs employ an options overlay to protect them against sudden and extreme moves that dynamic hedging alone might not cover.

## Trading relative values

For the most part, mortgage backed arbitrageurs concentrate on buying MBS and hedging them. This enables them to isolate the excess return available. But there is also a wide range of attractive relative value trades they can execute between mortgage securities. These trades generally have the benefit of being uncorrelated with one another. Managers may add alpha by capturing anomalous spreads between:

---

21. By some estimates OAS briefly peaked around 480 basis points during 1998.

- similar securities issued by two different agencies;
- the differential between AAA corporate bonds and CMBS;
- the relationship between a CMO and the pass throughs in its underlying portfolio;
- credit differentials between agency and non-agency securities;
- or similar securities that have different liquidity, prepayment or volatility characteristics.

# HEDGED MORTGAGE BACKED SECURITIES: OPPORTUNITIES, DIFFICULTIES, REACTION TO MARKETS

## Opportunities

### Credit quality

MBS enjoy strong credit quality because they are well secured, they are monitored monthly and because many of them are guaranteed by agencies. Their credit quality improves over time because home-owners make monthly repayments. These increase the amount of the borrowers' equity and shrink the value of their loans (lowering the loan to value ratio). Rising house prices often enhance the equity further.

### Diversity

The diverse nature of mortgage backed securities provides an opportunity to build portfolios with a wide variety of characteristics. Investors can combine securities that are uncorrelated with one another and achieve considerable diversification.

### Complexity premium

Those investors who tackle the complexities of MBS enjoy the privileges of niche investors and are rewarded with higher returns. Although many different investors buy MBS, hedge funds tend to take a more sophisticated approach to modelling them, and are more inclined to use complex securities. This complexity premium is supported by significant barriers to entry. A very rough estimate would suggest that in 2003 only US $25 billion of hedge fund capital is committed to an MBS market of about US $5 trillion.

### Low correlation

MBS exhibit fairly unusual patterns of behaviour even before they are hedged. A hedged portfolio can provide attractive, steady returns that are for the most part non-correlated with mainstream asset classes and other hedge fund strategies.

### Clear issues

The issues involved with MBS securities are relatively clear-cut. The cash flows due from a pass through are clearly identifiable, and the solidity of the credit means the cash flows are dependable. The key variable is the prepayment rate, and the MBS market tends to approach this issue scientifically. By contrast, it can be argued that equity markets and credit markets involve a variety of amorphous, opaque issues that are difficult to assess (earnings estimates, business models, sector influences and so on).

## Difficulties

### Hedging risk

Managing and hedging the cash flows from MBS is challenging, but many hedge funds have demonstrated their ability to do it. Those who fail to take proper care over their hedging put their investors at considerable risk, particularly given that these portfolios involve leverage. In practice it may seem too expensive to hedge against every eventuality. Too much of the return might be eroded. Some managers choose to leave themselves exposed to sequences of events that they consider highly unlikely, especially if the hedging would cost too much. These managers may continue to generate attractive, steady returns for prolonged periods while all the while remaining vulnerable to particular interest rate scenarios. However, the time may come when they get found out. The collapse of Askin Capital was attributed to this type of mis-hedging.

### Policy risk

Changes in government policy might undermine the value of MBS. An example might be a reduction in the tax advantages associated with mortgage payments. A new government attitude towards the three main agencies would also undermine agency securities. Currently Ginnie Mae is the only one of the three main agencies to enjoy the explicit guarantee of the US government. Fannie Mae and Freddie Mac receive certain tax breaks but have been privatized and do not have the explicit support of the government. Wall Street likes to think that government support is implied simply because the institutions are so large and so important to the US economy that the failure of either would require government intervention. Although they do not openly concur with this view, it suits the government not to dispel this belief. US depositary institutions have a very high proportion of their capital base invested in mortgage-related securities so the collapse of this marketplace would indeed be tantamount to a collapse of the global financial system. However, from time to time various individual legislators question the status of Fannie and Freddie, and this seems to unnerve the markets for their corporate debentures.

### Agency investing activities
The large mortgage agencies are themselves highly leveraged investors into MBS, and they have extensive hedging programmes. The agencies act as gigantic hedge funds and they are not particularly transparent, so that from time to time their solvency comes into question. These fears can usually be allayed but the effects of one of these institutions failing are hard to countenance. The large-scale activities of the agencies can cause disruption for MBS hedge funds. The agencies compete for the use of many of the same hedging mechanisms, sometimes causing huge pricing distortions. This can also provide opportunities.

### Financing risk
Because of the risk of pricing disputes during times of crisis, MBS investors must pay particular attention to the security of their financing. If a leverage provider withdraws support during a market crisis it can force the liquidation of positions at the least favourable moment. After the 1998 crisis very serious allegations were made against Salomon Smith Barney in this regard by two well-known MBS hedge funds (MKP and Ellington) that had reason to believe they were mistreated by their prime broker. Today, most MBS hedge fund managers have their financing quite well locked up. Depending upon the complexity of their instruments and their own need for flexibility, a fair portion of their portfolios is likely to be subject to Evergreen agreements that secure financing for a year, with 60 days' notice.

### Lack of transparency
It is very difficult for a manager to convey the risks embedded within a hedged MBS portfolio, even if investors are given access to all of its positions. For example, knowing that a manager has invested in IOs provides limited information, since it is possible that the structuring of these IOs significantly alters the leverage inherent within them.

## *Pricing risk*

Pricing the less liquid and more complex MBS securities can leave room for disagreement. Even vanilla MBS securities need to be priced carefully during times of upheaval, given that leverage amplifies otherwise small variations. It is important that MBS hedge funds demonstrate fair and independent pricing methods because mispriced securities have caused problems in the past. Accurate pricing is important both for the manager and to reassure investors that they are not the victims of fraud.

## *Illiquidity*

Illiquidity is a risk for all markets during moments of crisis. Even vanilla MBS securities may be affected to some extent by the sudden withdrawal of capital by leveraged players.[22] However, the more complex an MBS security is, the more vulnerable it is to becoming illiquid when markets are unsettled, partly because people are uncertain how to value them. Their bid–offer spreads are likely to widen further than those of simpler instruments. Therefore arbitrageurs must take care not to create illiquid long portfolios.

## *Changing patterns*

Human behaviour does exhibit clear patterns, and these are recognized in prepayment models. However patterns of human behaviour may change over time, with important consequences for MBS investors.[23]

## Reaction to markets

### *Liquidity crises*

Volatility events tend to cause OAS to widen, since uncertainty about economic prospects and the path of interest rates increases. MBS arbitrageurs cannot fully protect themselves from widening spreads, so losses are likely. However, the ensuing period should offer above-average returns because of the increased carry and the potential for capturing profits as OAS narrow once more.

---

22. Market makers tend to take their lead from the behaviour of investors, taking fright during moments of panic. They tend to be long of MBS securities but since they are so short-term they only delta hedge their positions (that is, instead of offsetting the negative convexity of their longs they just short US Treasuries and iteratively adjust their hedge to account for their current exposure). This makes them particularly keen to escape from markets that are misbehaving. In 1998 Salomon shut down its arbitrage group, while Goldman Sachs and Nomura both scaled back their activities.

23. For example, in 2003 interest rates have reached lows that have not been seen since before the MBS market was properly developed. Prepayment models are therefore in new territory, and it is possible they will fail to capture the implications accurately. (The econometric models are being required to extrapolate, rather than interpolate.)

## *Flight to simplicity*

During crises investors shy away from complexity. MBS arbitrageurs are long MBS and short other, simpler securities, such as US Treasuries. This combination invariably leaves them 'net long of complexity'. During crises they can therefore suffer from a 'flight to simplicity'.

## *Slowing economy*

In a slowing economy investors switch out of equities into fixed income, driving down the yield on government bonds. This causes investors to search elsewhere for yield and increases demand for MBS, which suffer from fewer credit concerns than corporate bonds. This may increase their price and reduce the OAS on offer. A slowing economy might undermine house prices and reduce the collateral that backs MBS. However, regular repayments mean that borrowers continuously top up the equity they hold against their loans, and households manage their finances more carefully than most people realize. Slower economic activity tends to be accompanied by falling interest rates, which eases the burden on borrowers (although it increases prepayment speeds). Generally it is only subprime loans that are considered a greater risk during a recession, but investors can access these loans through senior tranches of CMOs with limited risk.[24] For these reasons economic slowdown does not seem to undermine this strategy.

## *Rising or falling rates*

MBS arbitrageurs ought to be hedged against modest moves in interest rates. However, there are undercurrents at work. As rates rise, reduced prepayment expectations cause the effective duration of MBS to increase. This causes long-only MBS investors to sell some of their Treasury holdings in order to rebalance their portfolio duration. Simultaneously, hedged MBS investors short more Treasuries against their rising duration. Because the MBS market is so large, the effect of this selling of Treasuries can be considerable, forcing rates up even higher and so inducing a fresh round of Treasury selling by MBS investors. The reverse pressures may apply when rates fall.

---

24. Subprime loans are in fact highly valued because of their low prepayment speeds and insensitivity to interest rates. It is only those investors who chose to buy junior CMO securities tied to subprime loans who subject themselves to this credit risk. These investors generally make the decisions knowingly because they believe credit risks are being mispriced by the market.

### Interest rate volatility

Because they have sold prepayment options to homeowners, almost all MBS arbitrageurs are short interest rate volatility to some extent. Increasing interest rate volatility can therefore be to their disadvantage as it increases the value of the options of which they are short. Big moves in interest rates are also a problem because many MBS arbitrageurs have some negative convexity in their portfolios, even if this has been mitigated by hedging.

# APPENDIX 1: KEY CONSIDERATIONS: HEDGED MORTGAGE BACKED SECURITIES

- What range of MBS securities do the managers use? Are certain instruments avoided? What types of non-agency and structured products are used?

- Do the managers have a particular duration or maturity preference?

- What exposure do the managers have to MBS derivatives? What types of derivatives do they use and for what purposes? Are these derivatives liquid under adverse conditions?

- How are their positions marked, and by whom? What steps are taken to ensure their derivatives are properly valued?

- What sort of leverage do they employ? How much leverage is implied in the particular MBS instruments they have?

- What risks are specifically hedged in the portfolio and what risks are left in? How do the managers deal with the risk of spreads widening suddenly? How do the managers approach prepayment and negative convexity risks?

- Are MBS instruments ever shorted?

- What are the managers' current economic, interest rate and prepayment expectations and how are these reflected in the portfolio? To what extent do the managers like to take such views?

- What sorts of models are used? Are they proprietary or from an external provider? What are their perceived limitations?

- For risk control purposes, do the managers supplement their models with scenario analysis, stress testing and holding period analysis? (Note that VaR analysis is not considered to work well with MBS portfolios. It is difficult to adapt it to reflect the non-linearity of the securities.)

- What sort of return profile do the managers target, and what sort of drawdown might they consider tolerable?

- Have steps been taken to ensure funding lines are secure?

# APPENDIX 2: GLOSSARY

**Agencies:** The three main issuers of mortgages in the United States: Ginnie Mae, Fannie Mae and Freddie Mac.

**Alternative-A loans:** Mortgages issued by one of the commercial mortgage lenders, generally with fairly modest credit quality.

**At-the-money:** In the context of a mortgage pass through, refers to the point at which the loan pool's coupon rate is the same as prevailing mortgage rates. Borrowers become increasingly likely to exercise the option to refinance once prevailing mortgage rates fall below this level.

**Burnout:** Refers to a decline in the rate of prepayments coming from a mortgage pool owing to prior swathes of prepayments.

**CMBS:** Commercial mortgage backed securities. Non-agency securities, generally secured against commercial property or multi-family housing. Behave differently from residential MBS because they do not have the option to prepay without a penalty.

**CMO:** Collateralized mortgage obligation. A structured product whereby a series of fixed income securities are issued against a portfolio of MBS.

**CPR:** Constant prepayment rate. Refers to the annual rate at which prepayments are occurring in a mortgage pool.

**Curtailments:** Partial prepayments

**Dumbo effect:** The fact that certain borrowers fail to realize they have the ability to refinance their mortgages at a lower rate.

**Effective duration:** The duration of a mortgage pool as calculated on the basis of expected prepayments, rather than on the basis of the weighted average maturity of the loans within it.

**Floaters:** A floating rate bond issued by a CMO, providing protection against rising rates and facilitated by the concurrent issue of an 'inverse floater'.

**Homeowner mobility:** The rate at which the homeowners represented in a loan pool sell their properties and remortgage.

**Inverse floaters:** A bond issued by a CMO whose coupon varies in inverse relation to interest rates. Provides considerable leverage to falling interest rates. Issued in support of floating rate bonds.

**IOs:** Interest only security from a CMO, provides access to the interest payments from pass throughs.

**Jumbo loans:** MBS relating to pools of larger loans made to more affluent borrowers.

**MBS:** Mortgage backed securities. Covers a wide spectrum of securities related to mortgages, including pass throughs, structured securities and non-agency securities.

**Media effect:** The disproportionate increase in prepayment rates once interest rates reach new lows, attributed to media attention.

**OAS:** Option-adjusted spread. A means of expressing a mortgage backed security's spread over Treasuries that accounts for the value of the prepayment option.

**PAC bonds:** Planned amortization class. Securities that resemble conventional bonds as long as prepayment speeds in the underlying portfolio remain within predefined bounds.

**Pass through:** Pools of mortgage loans that have similar characteristics, bundled up and issued as a single security. The cash flows thrown off by the pool of mortgages are simply 'passed through' to the holder of the security.

**Pool factor:** The outstanding balance of repayments remaining within a mortgage pool, expressed as a percentage of the original amount.

**Pool factor tape:** The monthly publication of a mortgage pass through's key characteristics.

**POs:** Principal only security from a CMO, provides access to the principal repayments from pass throughs.

**Prepayment duration:** The measure of a security's price sensitivity to an instant 10 per cent change in the prepayment rate.

**Prepayment option:** The mortgage borrower's option to prepay a mortgage if interest rates fall.

**Prepayment speed (or rate):** The rate at which mortgage borrowers 'prepay' their loans.

**PSA:** Public Securities Association. Publishers of data describing prevailing rates of prepayment.

**REIT:** Real Estate Investment Trust.

**Sequential bonds:** Bonds with a range of maturities, issued by a CMO and paying investors in the order that cash flows are received from the underlying pass throughs.

**Single monthly mortality:** The speed at which mortgages are prepaid within a mortgage pool each month.

**Spread duration:** A security's price sensitivity to a 100 basis point widening in OAS.

**Subprime loans:** MBS relating to pools of smaller loans made to less creditworthy borrowers.

**TBA:** When a pass through trades on a 'to be announced' basis the buyer does not know exactly which pass through will be delivered, although parameters for its characteristics are set.

**WAC:** The weighted average coupon being paid by a pool of mortgage borrowers.

**WALA:** The weighted average loan age of the loans remaining within a mortgage pool.

**WAM:** The weighted maturity of the loans remaining within a mortgage pool.

**YCS:** The yield curve spread, indicating the yield spread over US Treasuries that a mortgage security offers.

# 12

# Global macro and CTAs

> Only one fellow in ten thousand understands the currency question, and we meet him every day.
>
> Kin Hubbard

CTAs and global macro funds share a number of common characteristics. They are speculative, directional trading strategies that use leverage to enhance their returns. They concentrate, for the most part, on capturing market trends. CTAs and global macro funds differ from other hedge fund strategies in that they are unhedged, they are volatile and they are not designed to preserve capital. Instead they are designed to make as much money as possible. Nevertheless, they are alternative investment vehicles and they have absolute rather than relative return objectives. Furthermore, they are indifferent between going long or short and they combine a series of directional long and short positions in their portfolios. As a result they exhibit a low correlation with mainstream asset classes and with other hedge fund strategies over most periods.

Global macro funds do as their name suggests. They have a global remit and they execute trades on the basis of fundamental, top-down macroeconomic and market views. They are 'big picture' investors who waste little time on bottom-up security selection. They express their macro views through any type of financial instrument they can find, so long as it serves their purpose, which generally means it ought to be quite liquid. Global macro managers have often hit the headlines because of the sheer scale and aggression of their activities. George Soros, Michael Steinhardt and Julian Robertson are almost household names. They are all global macro players.

CTAs differ from global macro managers because their views are rarely fundamental in nature. CTAs are the archetypal traders who implement trades principally on the basis of the technical analysis of price movements. CTAs develop trading rules and trade accordingly, sometimes executing the trades themselves and sometimes developing computer systems that trade by the rules they set. 'CTA' stands for commodity trading advisor, a term that reflects the origins of the strategy rather than its nature today. Most CTAs restrict their trading activities to futures markets, since these are liquid and provide easy access to leverage. Futures markets had their origins in the world of commodities, as did the CTAs, hence their name. Today, however, both the futures markets and the activities of CTAs are focused more on the financial markets than on the commodity markets. CTAs, also known as managed futures traders, first started to become popular in the 1970s.

# GLOBAL MACRO

Global macro managers scour the world in search of economic and market trends. The larger macro funds tend to have their own economic forecasting departments, building and running their own complex econometric models. Sushil Wadhwani, a well-known former member of the UK's Monetary Policy Committee, was previously an economist with one of the largest macro funds, Tudor. He now runs a fund of his own. Smaller macro funds are likely to employ a number of independent economic consultants. All are likely to draw on the investment banks for additional economic input. Global macro managers identify economic disequilibria that feed through to equity, bond and currency markets. These disequilibria do not correct immediately. However, once extremes are reached the chance of mean reversion increases. Ideally, trends gradually emerge and macro managers can observe them and profit from them.

A wide range of forces inspire trending movements in asset classes. For example:

- differences in growth rates between two countries cause capital to flow from one to the other, affecting the exchange rate;
- central banks signal and implement a series of interest rate moves in a slow, purposeful manner;
- governments announce significant changes in fiscal policy and subsequently implement them over time;

- large changes in current account surpluses and deficits develop gradually;

- market participants exhibit crowd behaviour that results in trends.

Global macro managers must anticipate the effects these forces will have. In order to generate good returns from an idea they must demonstrate superior foresight or have contrarian views. They must then identify the best manner in which to capture profits from their views, deciding upon long or short positions in liquid securities or derivatives. It is hard for macro managers to outsmart the markets, particularly so if they are trying to time a contrarian view. They must interpret market action and distinguish between short-term behaviour and a genuine sea-change. Since this is difficult they often find that the majority of their trades lose money, either because they are wrong or because they are too early. Thus excellent risk controls are imperative. They must be prepared to cut their losing trades in good time and to run with their winners. Even when they latch on to a winning trend they must be prepared to 'trade around it'.

With experience, global macro managers seem to be able to capture these trends in a profitable manner. Such profits may seem inconsistent with the notion of efficient markets. If global macro managers can anticipate developments in financial markets, other participants ought to be able to as well. Therefore the developments ought to be imputed into financial asset prices immediately, completing a trend instantaneously. It can be observed with the benefit of hindsight that some trends do complete over extended periods. Yet an advocate of efficient markets might suggest this reflects prolonged uncertainty over how events will unfold rather than the slowness of markets to incorporate information.

Although there may be an element of truth in this, markets do not always incorporate information properly. For example, in the run up to the creation of the euro, bond yields across Europe converged downwards to meet the lower yields offered by Bunds. This was a very clear trend that took a long time to complete. Admittedly, this delay reflected some uncertainty about whether the grand euro experiment would really get off the ground. However, a careful study of the situation led informed observers to conclude that the probability of success was very high indeed, and global macro managers were handsomely rewarded for assuming the risk of failure from other market participants. A very similar argument might have been advanced in favour of holding Polish and Hungarian bonds for a long period in the late 1990s and early 2000s. Investors could have a high degree of confidence in the convergence of these economies with Western Europe, regardless of whether or not they gained admission into the EU. Thus it can be observed that markets sometimes misprice probabilities of events occurring (perhaps because the majority of market participants focus primarily on security selection rather than asset allocation).

Moreover, great imbalances arise between *different* markets. Nobody suggests, even in theory, that the relationship between different markets is efficient. The efficient markets hypothesis relates only to the pricing relationship between securities within a single market, not between markets. This provides global macro managers with opportunities for cross-over investing, comparing risk premiums associated with different asset classes and different markets geographically.

Global macro funds rose to prominence during the late 1980s and early 1990s. A number of them posted a string of outstanding returns and grew so large that they would move the markets themselves. They were even blamed for forcing the pound out of the ERM in 1992. Investors threw money at George Soros and bought shares in his funds on the secondary market at a large premium. During this period global macro funds came to represent the majority of the hedge fund universe. However, global macro funds are vulnerable to sudden interruptions or reversals in trends, and given the amounts of leverage they use it is hardly surprising they experience upsets. Global macro funds are generally leveraged three or more times and sometimes have 100 per cent of their NAV invested in a single directional bet, such as a currency position. As a group, global macro funds suffered serious losses when the Fed suddenly raised rates in 1994. They received another blow in 1998, not only because they were heavily involved in emerging markets but also because the LTCM crisis hurt them elsewhere in their portfolios. These big losses took the shine off the track records of macro managers and alienated many of their investors. 'Global macro' came to be a dirty phrase. Investors gradually deserted them, and assets shrank to a small fraction of their earlier size. Many macro funds closed down or were repositioned to pursue other types of strategy. Today, global macro represents a relatively small portion of the hedge fund universe. (See Figure 12.1.)

Over the last few years a new breed of global macro manager has emerged. Conscious of how unpopular their strategy has become, they have branded their new approach under the title of 'smart macro'. They have cast themselves as more measured individuals than their swashbuckling forebears, and claim to take a more academic and subtle approach. Smart macro managers claim to implement their

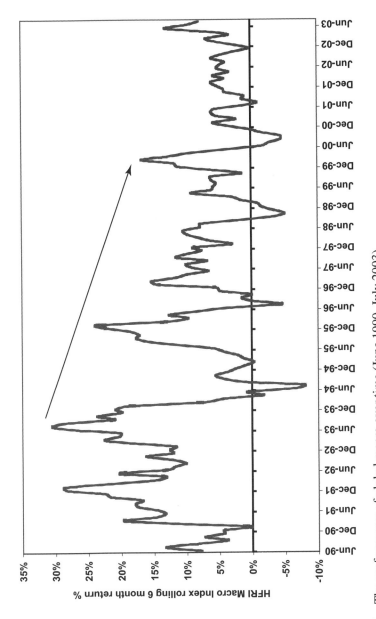

**Figure 12.1** The performance of global macro over time (June 1990–July 2003)
After some strong returns in the early 1990s, global macro began to post lower returns after 1994, together with more frequent losing periods.
Source: HFRI.

views with less leverage and more care, using derivatives, risk controls and other innovations in an attempt to construct asymmetric positions that inflict limited losses if they go wrong. Some managers have even started hedging parts of their portfolios, combining directional and relative value trades. As a result, smart macro funds claim to be less volatile and more palatable to today's buyers of hedge funds, most of whom prioritize capital preservation over capital appreciation. In keeping with the general spirit of renaissance, smart macro funds like to keep their funds small in size so as to prevent their activities being detected in the market and to ensure they remain flexible. In reality, 'smart macro' does not represent a significant departure from the old ways. It is 'macro lite' but the flavour remains the same.

Investors sometimes include macro funds in their portfolios of hedge funds for reasons of diversification. However global macro funds sit uneasily alongside other hedge funds, which are usually conservative in nature. Unlike other hedge funds, macro funds are directional and remarkably speculative investment vehicles. Some investors may have an appetite for their capital appreciation potential, but hedge fund investors should be under no illusions about the risks these funds take. About four or five years ago I went to visit Soros Fund Management and met their CEO regarding their emerging markets fund (I was managing a fund of emerging markets funds at the time). Two things surprised me. First, the exposures the fund took beggared belief. Their net assets amounted to billions of dollars, which already made them one of the largest investors in emerging markets. Using leverage, these billions were invested a couple of times over into directional positions in the emerging equity markets and several more times into the emerging bond markets. They had a footprint of many of billions of dollars in some of the world's smallest, least liquid and most volatile markets. Second, the CEO was a charming man but he was quite surprised to see me. Apparently, their potential and existing investors were not in the habit of asking questions. They just wired the money.

After some difficult years, several of the more famous global macro funds have started to allocate an increasing percentage of their portfolios to other types of strategy, in particular to forms of arbitrage. Some macro managers have built their own arbitrage expertise in-house while others have invested in other funds, leveraging into them to enhance their returns. When investors set out to invest in a global macro fund, few of them envisage buying a leveraged multi-strategy fund of funds. Before investing, it is worth establishing clearly how a global macro fund is allocated.

# GLOBAL MACRO: OPPORTUNITIES, DIFFICULTIES, REACTION TO MARKETS

## Opportunities

### *Risky, but not suicidal*

It is important to emphasize the riskiness of global macro funds within the context of hedge funds. In the broader context, however, macro funds may be no more volatile or risky than holding equities long-only. Most global macro managers are talented individuals. Although they are prepared to risk capital in pursuit of returns they nevertheless wish to preserve capital. They generally have significant investments in their own funds.

### *Considerable profit potential*

Many investors are happy to assume high levels of risk in an attempt to generate high levels of return. Depending on an investor's circumstances this may be a perfectly rational decision, and most investors want a little bit of fun somewhere in their portfolios. When they work, global macro funds have the potential to generate some very handsome profits.

## Difficulties

### *Beating the markets*

Global macro players try to beat the markets. To make money they must be right when everyone else is wrong. It is difficult to maintain an informational edge and to have routinely superior insights. It may be possible to do this for periods of time but the strategy does not seem to work with much consistency.

### *'Fooled by randomness'*

Global macro funds tend to take relatively few decisions but they take big ones. A select few macro funds get several leveraged macro bets correct in a row, sometimes backing trends that last for quite long periods of time. The resulting returns may be misleading to investors because they appear to demonstrate consistent skill over a period of years. Some funds become enormously popular as a result. Those that make mistakes go out of business. To some extent the success of macro managers reflects randomness. Survivorship bias is therefore an important consideration when assessing this strategy.

### The selection problem

For the reasons mentioned above it can be hard to assess and monitor a macro manager's skill. The returns may not be a reliable guide. The task is made harder because so many of these funds are secretive about their enormous positions. Perhaps the selection process for most types of hedge fund is hampered in the same way (all hedge funds are skill-based and secretive). Yet with many other types of hedge fund, a certain return can be extracted simply by executing a strategy competently.[1] Additional skill merely enhances these returns. Success or failure is a little more binary for global macro funds, and their decision making is the main determining factor.

### Asset allocation

These funds can wreak havoc with an investor's overall asset allocation. Consider an investor who has allocated 40 per cent to equities, 40 per cent to bonds and 20 per cent to hedge funds. Even if the investor places just 5 per cent of the 20 per cent with global macro managers it could upset the overall portfolio. It is conceivable that the investor's macro managers might be five times levered into bonds, taking the investor's effective bond allocation up from 40 per cent to 65 per cent. A few months later, the same investor might end up 50 per cent or 100 per cent exposed long of the euro, despite the fact that the portfolio is otherwise strictly dollar denominated. Perhaps global macro managers know best, but their activities can either countervail or compound important asset allocation decisions being taken by an investor.

### Diversification

Although the portfolios of global macro managers may differ from one another at turning points, there is usually considerable overlap in their positions. These are intelligent individuals who tend to come to similar conclusions. Such overlap may mitigate the benefits of diversifying amongst a number of macro managers.

## Reaction to markets

### Trends

Global macro funds enjoy strong, steady trends with limited volatility along the way. They tend to suffer from sharp reversals in these trends, temporary or otherwise (such as the reversals in the fixed income

---

1. Equity long–short and global macro and CTAs are perhaps the most obvious exceptions to this observation.

markets in 1994 and 2003). This means they classify as being 'short volatility', alongside a number of other hedge fund strategies.

### Instability

These funds need the imbalances and disequilibria that help to establish trends. Periods of economic stability or central bank discipline can reduce their opportunity set. Some observers consider the late 1990s to have been a dull period for this reason. Governments and central banks did not tolerate huge imbalances and the public developed greater confidence in their policy makers. Trends tended to complete over shorter periods, and most of the action appeared to be in the equity rather than in the fixed income or currency markets. Today, in late 2003, global macro managers are much more optimistic. Bush and Greenspan have taken their fiscal and monetary policies to extremes. Interest rates and inflation are near zero, and policy makers seem likely to make mistakes that result in new economic imbalances.[2]

# COMMODITY TRADING ADVISORS

CTAs are traders and they have a mentality to match. Unlike global macro managers, very few CTAs base their decisions upon top-down fundamental analysis. Instead they usually take a technical approach to trading, preferring charts and trading rules to economic theorizing. They restrict their activities almost exclusively to futures markets and currencies, rarely venturing directly into equities or bonds. Each CTA tends to specialize in trading a particular market. About 70 per cent concentrate on financial futures (generally interest rates and currencies),[3] with about 30 per cent focusing on commodity futures (especially energy and metals). In addition to these market specializations, CTAs often specialize by trading approach. Here comes the jargon:

- Trend followers: as their name suggests, trend followers seek to identify and ride trends. On the basis of observation they develop trading rules that capture basic market principles. Trend followers either focus on short-term opportunities or look for long-term

---

2. George Soros, who had retreated into relative value trading in the late 1990s, is once again beginning to show more interest in directional trades.
3. Some CTAs have tried trading equities, usually via the index futures. However, CTAs rarely seem to have an approach that suits the equity markets.

trends. Trend followers may also be broken down into the 'discretionary' and 'systematic' categories.

- 'Discretionary trend followers' are those traders that take their own trading decisions and implement the trades themselves. These are 'human traders' who rely on experience, intuition and their own technical trading rules to initiate and close trades. They use their discretion because a rigid rules-based approach can result in some obvious errors being made and can fail to adapt to a changing environment. Discretionary traders probably account for about 25 per cent of the CTA universe.

- 'Systematic trend followers' programme trading rules into computer systems, and implement trades strictly upon the basis of the trading signals the computers generate. A programmed rules-based system is unemotional, disciplined and prevents commonplace human errors such as running losses too long and taking profits too early.

● Systematic non-trend traders: these are comparable to systematic trend followers in that they too run off rules-based computer systems. However, they do not ride trends. Instead they exploit short-term directional trading opportunities in the futures markets, rather as some statistical arbitrageurs do in a hedged manner in the equity markets.

There is often little to separate one trend follower from another. Whether they are systematic or not they generally identify the same patterns, see the same charts breaking out and latch onto the same trends when they are in place. Once a substantial turn indicates a trend has turned, they are all likely to exit together. The key differentiating factor tends to be whether they are riding on long-term or short-term trends. Although they may seem relatively homogenous, this does not mean they are all as good as one another. They vary in their ability to identify newly emerging trends, to time their entry and exit points and to manage their risk when things go wrong. As with global macro managers, CTAs are supposed to be able to cut their many small losing trades early, allowing their few big winners to run.

Long-term and short-term trend followers can provide an effective combination in a portfolio. Long-term trend followers capture big moves and are generally more profitable. However they also tend to be more volatile because they lose money during short-term reversals. At these moments, short-term trend followers tend to make their profits, helping to offset the losses suffered by the long-term traders before the long-term trend is resumed. Combining the two helps investors to smooth the pattern of their returns.

Systematic non-trend trading programmes operate and behave quite differently. Rather than exploiting trends they operate high-frequency, high-turnover pattern recognition systems. For a better understanding of these programmes it is worth reading Chapter 7 on statistical arbitrage, as the two strategies share many underlying principles. It can be argued that both serve to provide liquidity to the markets, acting rather like automated market makers. They also face many of the same challenges, having to revisit their models to account for changes in market behaviour and needing to minimize their execution costs and 'slippage'.

Once that has been said, it is also worth noting how CTAs differ from statistical arbitrageurs. Statistical arbitrageurs claim to be tightly hedged, matching a long position in one equity with a short position in another equity that is statistically similar. CTAs tend to trade in futures. They would have no means of hedging them, even if they wanted to. Therefore they implement one-sided, unhedged positions. Furthermore, CTA trading programmes are likely to be driven by a statistical analysis of price behaviour rather than by any fundamental factor analysis, as is often used by statistical arbitrageurs.

Whereas long-term trend followers prefer modest volatility around a trend, systematic non-trend managers need volatility in order to throw up the anomalies that they trade off. They are often referred to as being 'long volatility' since they tend to profit most during volatile periods. They too combine well with long-term trend followers.

Many investors include CTAs in their portfolios because the best ones perform very well and they seem to be good diversifiers.[4] However a large proportion of them seem to run into serious trouble, and they are not for the faint-hearted. Because they are directional and they tend to be so volatile they do not necessarily fit very well into a portfolio of hedge funds. They are really a separate investment class that investors should consider as a component of their broader asset allocation. As with global macro funds, investors must consider the implications of the leverage involved, which is likely to be in the region of three to eight times net assets, depending on the CTA and the opportunities available. The assets being leveraged may not be particularly volatile but the risk of catastrophic loss is real.

---

4. See Schneeweis, Spurgin and Potter (1996), which found that combining CTAs and long-only equities in equal measure resembled an equity portfolio with low cost S&P puts. The combination exhibited positive skewness and low kurtosis.

# CTAS: OPPORTUNITIES, DIFFICULTIES, REACTION TO MARKETS

## Opportunities

### Market making
CTAs help to provide liquidity to the futures markets, which can be a very profitable activity if broker dealers are reluctant to commit capital.

### Diversification
CTAs seem to mix well with US equities. Different types of CTA also seem to mix well with each other. Although it can be difficult to predict which will perform best in an ensuing period, combining a range of trading frequencies can be fruitful. Mixing trend and non-trend managers also seems to work well.

### Applications in various markets
A robust trading system can be applied successfully to a variety of different futures markets. At least one of these markets is likely to be 'in trend' at any one time, increasing the likelihood that profits can be generated on an ongoing basis.

### Suits various risk appetites
Various levels of risk are available. A CTA occasionally suffering an 8–12 per cent drawdown might be classified as low risk, 12–15 per cent medium risk and 15–20 per cent high risk. However, many CTAs suffer much larger losses.

## Difficulties

### Difficult to identify ingredients of success
Both systematic and discretionary CTAs tend to be secretive about their methods. Even if they offer explanations it can be difficult to define exactly what results in success. Skill is particularly difficult to define, although investors can learn a great deal by considering how trades are implemented and how risk is controlled. Investing with CTAs may involve a leap of faith that many investors would be uncomfortable making. Investors may have to rely heavily on past performance figures, which some argue are a useful indicator in the CTA context.[5] Because CTAs are unlikely to disclose how their

---

5. See Schneeweis, Spurgin and McCarthy (1996).

models work, investors must focus their enquiries on the manner of their development, what issues have been addressed, whether the traders ever override their models and how problems are dealt with.

### Zero sum game
Unlike equity and bond markets, futures markets are a zero sum game. This raises the hurdle for CTAs, who are under pressure to generate positive returns. They may generate returns by outwitting other market participants, by behaving like a market maker or by acting as some form of insurance provider (acting as counterparties for hedgers).

### Managed accounts
Not all CTAs manage portfolios with limited liability. Traditionally CTAs run separate managed accounts for their clients rather than pooling them into investment funds.[6] Managed accounts are flexible vehicles for investors who want to define their own risk levels or who require liquidity. On the other hand, they do require a certain threshold sum to be invested or proper diversification cannot be achieved. More importantly, these accounts generally contain futures contracts that involve both leverage and theoretically unlimited liability. Stop losses can be left with futures exchanges in an effort to prevent disaster, but investors might conceivably lose more that 100 per cent of their invested capital and owe money to their account.

### Problems with quants
Systematic traders face the same challenges as other quantitative investors. They rely on backward-looking statistical tests that may not reflect future patterns of market activity. If a system runs into uncharted waters the CTA is faced with an awkward decision about how to react: should the model be redesigned or should it be left untouched?

## Reaction to markets

### Volatility
Many CTAs, notably systematic non-trend traders, flourish during periods of heightened volatility. These types of CTA can be particularly helpful during bad months for the S&P 500. Because so many hedge fund strategies tend to suffer during such periods this argument

---

6. Note that unlike most other hedge funds, CTAs do not use prime brokers because they do not borrow individual securities. Instead they use Futures Commission Merchants (FCMs).

is advanced for including CTAs within a portfolio of hedge funds. Note that long-term trend followers are more likely to suffer during such periods because their trends get disrupted.

### After strong performance
After periods of strong performance CTAs are more likely to experience corrections. This observation applies most of all to long-term trend followers. Unfortunately it is after periods of particularly strong performance that many investors choose to allocate capital.

### The liquidity cycle
Lean periods for CTAs seem to have coincided with tight economic conditions, which are often accompanied by financial market uncertainty. During these periods markets are denied liquidity and trend followers are squeezed. The reverse also holds. During periods of abundant liquidity CTAs seem to thrive.[7] This phenomenon helps to explain why several years of strong performance by CTAs seem to be interrupted by quieter periods. (See Figure 12.2.)

### Reliance on trends
As with global macro managers, most CTAs rely on there being trends to trade. There are periods when trends seem more abundant and enduring, which benefits CTAs. At other times trends fail to develop or they complete inconveniently quickly. Trends that reverse suddenly are likely to inflict losses on trend followers. For example, trend-following CTAs suffered when the US long bond yield suddenly backed up by nearly 1 per cent in July and early August 2003 after a long downtrend. This reversal induced many CTAs to reverse their stance and to adopt short bond positions. However, from mid-August onwards yields fell once again, inflicting further losses.

---

7.   Luek, Smith and Todd (2000) and also Howell (2000).

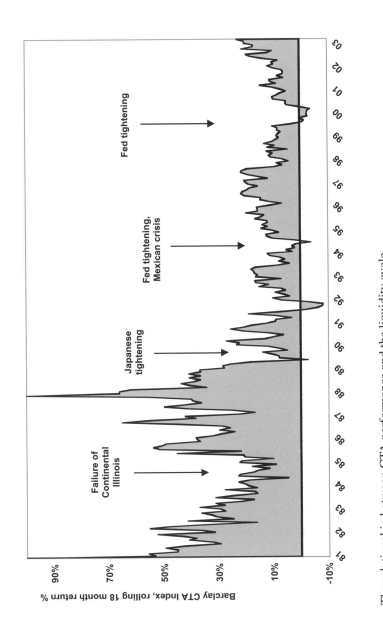

**Figure 12.2** The relationship between CTA performance and the liquidity cycle
Tight liquidity conditions tend to prove adverse for CTA returns, but CTAs thrive when liquidity is abundant.
Sources: Barclay Trading Group Ltd, Aspect Capital.

# 13

# Other hedge fund strategies

Financial professional: 'Professor Summers, if you are so smart, why aren't you rich?'
Professor Larry Summers: 'If you are so rich, why aren't you smart?'

There are a number of minor hedge fund strategies beyond the ones that have already been discussed in this book. Many of them are limited in the amounts of capital they can accommodate and therefore tend to be mentioned less often. This does not mean they are any less lucrative. All sorts of niche strategies can earn attractive returns. Here is a sample of hedge fund strategies that lie off the beaten track.

## COMMODITY ARBITRAGE

It might not be appropriate to discuss every strategy pursued by commodity arbitrageurs. There are very few arbitrageurs in this field and they consider the nature of their activities proprietary. For that reason let us focus on some of their more obvious trading methods.

Commodity arbitrage consists of relative value trades conducted between closely related commodity instruments, including physical commodities, futures and options on commodities and securities whose movements are fundamentally tied to a commodity price (such as royalty trusts or small producers).

## The opportunity

Given the huge array of commodities and their related derivatives, pricing anomalies between these instruments inevitably crop up.

- The heavy participation of both producers and commercial buyers in these markets gives rise to many of these aberrations. In pursuing their commercial priorities they often tolerate price discrepancies and may at times be altogether price insensitive, especially if a raw commodity represents a small proportion of their manufacturing costs.

- Other anomalies are caused by the reluctance of commercial organizations to hold much physical inventory, since it ties up their working capital.

- On occasions the activities of CTAs dominate particular commodity markets. They are generally motivated by technical analysis and price momentum, and the weight of their position taking can cause a commodity price to diverge from its fundamental level.

- The underlying assets are produced and consumed on a regular basis, so that demand and supply can easily get out of kilter, causing large and unexpected swings in price. Some of these imbalances are caused by weather, which is unpredictable.

- Many financial institutions that might otherwise participate in these markets are put off by their inability or unwillingness to hold a commodity in its physical form. Holding physical inventory requires a good deal of legal and administrative work. Furthermore, financial institutions are rarely prepared to shift goods around the globe, which may be the only way to eradicate a price discrepancy. The commodity markets are also tiny in comparison with the financial markets, so commodity arbitrage can accommodate relatively little capital.

## The strategy

Arbitrageurs apply a wide variety of techniques to capture price discrepancies. They might trade differences in prices of a single commodity in different locations, assuming the differences exceed the cost of transportation between the two. There may be subtler opportunities, such as abnormal price relationships between a processed and an unprocessed commodity that are inconsistent with the processing costs. In addition, most of the arbitrage techniques applied in financial derivatives markets may also be applied in the commodity markets. After all, the derivatives markets have their origins in the commodity world. Thus basis trades can be executed between commodity futures and their underlying commodities, very much as was described in the chapter on fixed income arbitrage.[1]

The inefficiency of commodity markets presents both opportunities and challenges. There is insufficient capital dedicated to making these markets efficient, which contributes to the number of profit-making opportunities. Unfortunately the absence of arbitrage capital also means that anomalies often linger or worsen, which generates uncertainty for arbitrageurs and increases their chances of suffering losses.

# DEPOSITARY RECEIPT ARBITRAGE

Depositary receipt (DR) arbitrage involves simple relative value trades between DRs (American Depositary Receipts and Global Depositary Receipts) and the locally listed equities they represent. The prices of DRs ought to move precisely in tandem with their underlying shares. If a DR price moves to a discount to its local shares, it can be purchased and the local shares sold short in anticipation of the discount closing. Conversely, if the DR moves to a premium it can be sold short against a long position in the local shares in anticipation of the premium eroding. Anomalies are most common in connection with emerging markets based companies. It is rarer to find significant discrepancies between the DRs and the local shares of large companies based in G7 countries, as there are usually enough cross-over investors to ensure parity is maintained.

## The opportunity

Locally listed shares and DRs have different investor bases and are therefore subject to different money flows. The different investor bases sometimes develop and express divergent views about a particular company. At other times the owners of DRs fail to pay proper attention to developments in the underlying share price. The different groups of investors are sometimes prevented by tax or regulatory barriers from crossing over between a DR and its locally listed

---

1. Of course, in commodity markets arbitrageurs are not concerned by which bond will be the cheapest to deliver. However, they have other subtleties to contend with, such as the costs of warehousing, checking, delivering and insuring the physical commodities.

share. For example, many US institutional investment mandates forbid the purchase of foreign shares, either for investment policy reasons or because custody arrangements are not considered secure. Likewise, many developing countries impose restrictions on investing capital overseas. These rigidities are often the reason that a company issues a DR in the first place. The issuing companies may contribute to anomalies by discounting new issues of either type of security. Once a divergence develops it is more likely to be sustained if it is difficult to establish short positions in either of the securities concerned.

These days it is usually straightforward to break open a DR and to release the underlying locally listed shares, making the two securities pretty fungible. In the past this was not as easy. This made DR arbitrage quite risky because a discount or premium might be sustained for prolonged periods without there being a mechanism to bring the two back into line. Arbitrageurs would play a mean reversion game in which they traded unusually large discounts or premiums in the hope that they would revert to more normal levels. These days DRs tend to involve clearer provisions, allowing them to be broken open. Because the securities are more demonstrably fungible, arbitrage opportunities tend to be smaller and more fleeting. However arbitrageurs can have greater confidence that discrepancies will be entirely eradicated.

## Difficulties

The strategy has its problems. If a DR is hard to break open, a discount or premium can act very strangely in a liquidity crisis. The very existence of a discount or premium is illogical, so it can be hard to know what prevents the situation from become less logical still. Emerging market DRs are sometimes dumped aggressively by overseas investors during moments of crisis. In addition, the strategy can accommodate little capital because volumes in many of the securities concerned are low, making it hard to get each leg of the trade on simultaneously. Furthermore, because these trades often involve emerging market securities, investors must also be prepared for the associated systematic risks. (See Figure 13.1.)

# CLOSED-END FUND ARBITRAGE

Closed-end fund arbitrage consists of trading a discount or premium between a closed-end fund's traded share price and its NAV per share. If arbitrageurs see a closed-end fund trading at an unusually wide

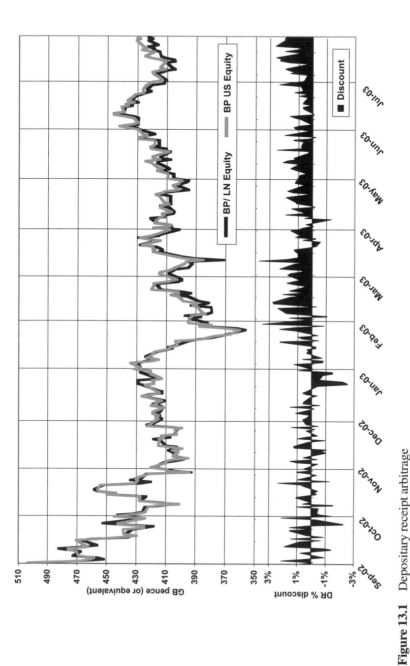

**Figure 13.1** Depositary receipt arbitrage

Specialist arbitrageurs with efficient execution can take advantage of oscillations in the premia or discounts at which depositary receipts trade.

Source: Bloomberg.

discount they buy its shares, hedging themselves by shorting an index or basket of shares that closely tracks the fund's NAV. This insulates them from movements in the NAV but leaves them exposed to changes in the discount. In theory arbitrageurs can short closed-end funds trading at unusually high premiums, hedging themselves with long positions in appropriate indices. In practice it is difficult to short these funds, so arbitrageurs usually concentrate on buying funds at wide discounts.

## Differences from DR arbitrage

The strategy bears some resemblance to DR arbitrage but there are important distinctions to be made. Closed-end funds are smallcap stocks and they are far less liquid than DRs. The funds also differ in that there is usually a mechanism for breaking a DR open to secure arbitrage profits, while there is no equivalent mechanism for cashing in the shares of a closed-end fund. The arbitrageur must rely on the market to recognize a gap and to close it up. It is unsafe for arbitrageurs to attempt to close a discount using the weight of their own money, since they will only widen it out again when they come to take their position off. They must 'ride' the closure of a discount rather than 'drive' it. The fund trades also involve greater hedging risks than the DR trades. Some closed-end funds can accurately and easily be hedged with an index future. Where this is the case, discounts are likely to be tight. The larger and more volatile discounts tend to crop up in less liquid funds where a hedge is more complicated to implement, such as an emerging market country fund.

## Obstacles

There are plenty of closed-end funds that trade at discounts, which should translate into plentiful arbitrage opportunities. Unfortunately there are structural reasons for these discounts to exist and for them to be stubborn. Closed-end funds are usually bought with enthusiasm at launch, often because they are invested into the latest hot concept. This enthusiasm often causes shares to go to a premium in the period after a fund's launch. The funds often have an imbalanced shareholder base, with several large institutional investors alongside numerous retail investors.[2] The result is a thinly traded market for the shares, punctuated by the occasional large, disruptive trade.

---

2.  This applies to UK and offshore closed-end funds. US listed funds are usually entirely retail affairs, with little institutional participation. Partly for this reason the share prices of US funds tend to lag movements in the NAV, causing discounts to widen in rising markets and to contract in falling markets. By contrast, the share prices of UK and offshore funds often reflect expectations for the NAV. Thus discounts widen in falling markets and contract in rising markets.

In time, enthusiasm for the underlying asset class usually starts to wane, too many copycat products are launched or a fund manager's performance goes into decline. Disenchantment almost always sets in, causing a discount to appear. Once it appears there is no fundamental mechanism for closing it other than arbitrage. The boards of directors are usually very friendly with the fund managers, and are unwilling to wind a fund up unless its discount is really very large indeed. Share buyback programmes tend to be half-hearted affairs and their effect is only temporary. A discount might inspire raiders to attempt to bust a fund open, but this threat does not seem to keep discounts tight: busting open a closed-end fund is difficult and risky. Purchasing sufficient shares to secure a wind-up vote tends to force a discount shut. Once a discount has closed it is harder to get other shareholders to vote in favour of busting a fund open. However, if raiders then retreat from their position by selling their shares they tend to widen the discount all over again.

All these hurdles seem very negative for closed-end fund arbitrage, yet this is an attractive area for a specialist. The closed-end fund markets are very inefficient, and small sums can be put to work effectively. The arbitrageur is handsomely paid for providing liquidity to the market, buying funds when they are least wanted and selling them once they are more popular. (See Figure 13.2.)

# REG D

Regulation D is a US securities regulation governing private issues of securities to less than 99 qualified investors. Companies issue securities under Regulation D when they wish to raise limited amounts of capital in a size too small to attract an investment bank's support for a public offering. The issues tend to be in the region of US $10 million to US $50 million in size, and they are placed directly with specialist 'Reg D' investors. The securities are issued at an attractive discount to the company's prevailing share price, anywhere between 15 per cent and 45 per cent depending upon the strength of the issuer. In time these securities can be converted into the common shares of the issuing firm and traded normally. However, Regulation D prevents the owners of these securities from trading them freely until two years after their issue, although they may be sold on to accredited investors after just one year.

## The strategy

Reg D investors subscribe to these discounted securities and sell short an equivalent number of the common shares as a hedge. They then

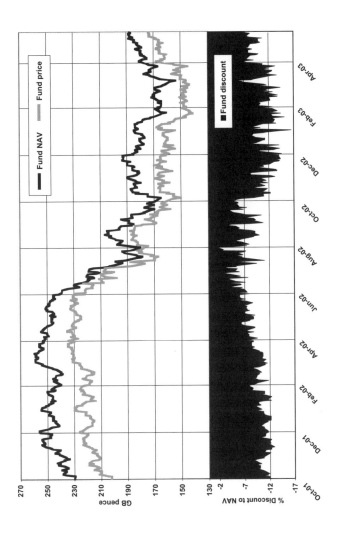

**Figure 13.2** Closed-end fund arbitrage

Although there are liquidity issues, arbitrageurs can trade variations in the discounts at which closed-end funds trade. Each closed-end fund discount is likely to behave in a different manner, so the arbitrageur must be familiar with the other holders of the fund and how they react, as well as remaining mindful of any corporate action the fund might be considering.

Source: Bloomberg.

await the end of their period of restriction until the two types of security become fungible and they can close their position out at a profit, having realized the discount. There are some added complexities. The Reg D securities are usually issued in the form of a convertible bond that pays a coupon. Reg D investors are therefore faced with a convertible arbitrage situation in which it may be desirable to adjust their hedge ratio (the number of common shares they have sold short) in reaction to movements in the underlying share price. The investment proposition is further complicated by the inclusion of warrants as an additional sweetener.

## Difficulties

Reg D investing has been plagued with difficulties over recent years and has developed a poor reputation. Many of the companies that raise this form of capital are small firms that are incapable of raising conventional forms of finance. They are too small for the high yield market, and bank debt provisions would prove too onerous. Many, but not all, are early stage ventures with precarious finances seeking emergency capital. During the technology boom of the late 1990s many small speculative ventures were attracted to this form of financing. This highlighted a number of weaknesses in the strategy.

- Some fairly solid companies issue Reg D securities. Yet because so many issuers of Reg D securities are weak credits with unstable businesses, the Reg D market tends to suffer from waves of corporate failure that affect all Reg D managers at once. It is hard for them to unload their securities to one another during periods of difficulty. Consequently this tends to be a risky and illiquid market in which to invest.

- If the underlying share prices rise and the warrants move into-the-money, their value rockets upwards. Most accounting regulations require Reg D funds to mark their warrants to market, or to theoretical value given that a market for them is unlikely to exist. If this causes a rapid rise in a Reg D fund's share price it can attract a wave of speculative investors into the fund. Unfortunately these warrants are volatile in both directions, and their value can collapse very easily. If this then triggers a wave of redemptions from the fund it can be almost impossible to liquidate the underlying holdings, particularly the warrants, as there are no active markets for them. The redemptions cannot be met. A number of Reg D funds imploded in this manner after the technology bubble burst in 2000, notably one managed by a firm called Brown Simpson. (See Figure 13.3)

- Some Reg D securities are issued with provisions that have come to be referred to as the 'death price spiral'. These provisions compensate a Reg D investor for a fall in the underlying share price below a certain level by increasing the number of common shares that the Reg D security converts into. The further the share price falls, the more shares the Reg D investor is allocated, so that the overall value of the equivalent shares holds steady. This arrangement has the potential to drive a company completely out of existence. As the share price falls the shareholders experience dilution, driving the share price lower still in a self-fulfilling spiral. If the Reg D investors are also shorting the common shares as a hedge, falls in the share price and the allocation of further shares will cause them to increase the number of common shares they sell short, driving the price down faster still. A firm called Sedona was one such death spiral victim.[3]

- Some Reg D funds run into trouble when an underlying share price falls rapidly in the wake of an issue of Reg D securities. This makes it difficult for them to short the shares quickly enough to establish an effective hedge. If they are too slow in getting their hedge on, the share price can fall to below the level of the discount at which the Reg D securities were issued. The Reg D investors are not permitted to prepare their short positions in the run-up to the Reg D issue, since by participating in the issue they have been made insiders.

- It is difficult to value these securities accurately. There are theoretical valuation problems, since they are debt–equity hybrids that can be constructed with various complexities in their terms. There are also practical issues because they are not actively traded. Certainty about a Reg D security's value is only established once it has been sold or converted into the underlying shares. In particular, the attached warrants may imply value that it is difficult to realize in practice. Provisions are therefore required to ensure that a Reg D fund prices applications and redemptions sensibly.

---

3. In the case of Sedona the SEC acted against Rhino Advisors, Inc, saying it had deliberately driven down the share price through short selling increasing numbers of shares – safe in the knowledge that it would be able to cover its shorts through the increased allocation of shares Sedona would apportion it.

- A number of Reg D funds are managed by broker dealers. They originate Reg D transactions and charge a placement fee for doing so. They then stuff the deals into the funds that they manage and take management and performance fees on top. This can result in conflicts of interest and excessive charging.

## Solutions

Although Reg D investing seems a little too nerve-racking for many investors, it is possible to execute the strategy profitably. While about 60 per cent of Reg D issues emanate from vulnerable corporations, about 20 per cent come from quality issuers. There are many small companies with strong and stable cash flows that rely on this type of financing. Reg D investors can stick with good companies and structure the issues so that they have some seniority or collateral. A cautious approach will lower the returns available but reduce the risk disproportionately.

Investors buying Reg D funds can reduce their risk by investing early in the business cycle and exiting well in advance of an expected downturn. Investors in these funds should also give careful consideration to how warrants are valued and how a fund handles applications and redemptions. Some Reg D managers have found ways to prevent mythical warrant 'profits' from being fully recognized until they have been safely locked in. There are potential stumbling blocks with this approach but it does seem sensible. Other managers address valuation problems by ensuring each of their investors has their own separate account.

# VOLATILITY ARBITRAGE

Volatility arbitrageurs take advantage of aberrations in all the options markets, including equities, fixed income, currencies and commodities. However, most specialist volatility arbitrageurs seem to concentrate on equity index options and individual stock options. Market practitioners value options in terms of implied volatility, and this tends to be the manner in which arbitrageurs assess whether options are appropriately priced. Volatility arbitrageurs generally avoid directional exposure to the assets underlying their options. They are unwilling to take fundamental views on asset prices so they maintain 'market neutrality' and construct positions that limit their

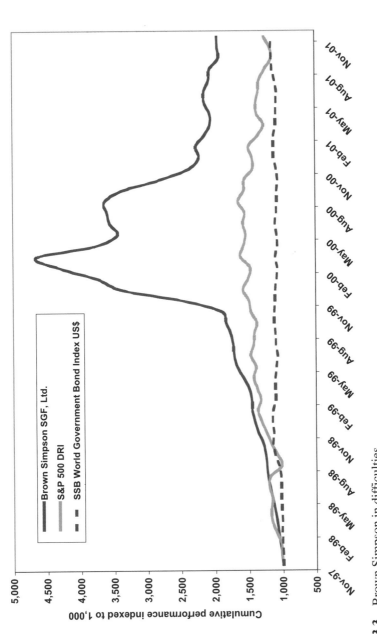

**Figure 13.3**  Brown Simpson in difficulties

The meteoric rise and fall of Brown Simpson's fund highlighted many of the difficulties of the Reg D strategy.

Sources: Brown Simpson Asset Management LLC, Altvest, PerTrac Indexes.

risks. They would rather focus their attention on the other factors that affect option values. Some arbitrageurs do express views on the direction of volatility, which can be just as aggressive as being outright long or short of an asset. Indeed, volatility is often referred to as another 'asset class'. (See Figure 13.4.)

## The opportunity

Option prices may imply volatilities that differ from observed levels of historical volatility, or from the future levels of volatility that arbitrageurs anticipate. The complexities of options pricing and the conflicting preferences of option users give rise to frequent price distortions in closely related options. A number of specific factors contribute to distorting option prices:

- Volatility exhibits patterns of behaviour that experienced arbitrageurs learn to anticipate. These patterns include the following:

  - volatility levels are themselves volatile but that seem to be mean-reverting;
  - volatility that has a habit of lingering: it tends to gap upwards but to trend downwards;
  - a negative correlation between index levels and the implied volatility of related options.

- Short-term volatility exhibits a tendency to be 'overvalued' relative to long-term volatility. Investors seem to want protection against events in the immediate future, but are less willing to fund the costs of owning options over long periods. It is also usual for implied volatility to exceed recently observed volatility: that is, the options markets tend to imply an expectation of rising levels of volatility.[4]

- The real world violates Black–Scholes option theory in a number of ways. The prices of securities sometimes jump, hedging has to be rebalanced in steps rather than continuously, and rebalancing involves transaction costs. Additionally, intraday moves in a security's price may exceed the movements of its closing prices. These factors cause the prices of options to differ from their theoretical values. For example, options traders can sometimes justify paying 'above the odds' for options because they can gamma trade

---

4. The difference in the implied volatilities of near-dated options and longer-dated options is known as the 'term structure of volatility' and can be likened to a yield curve for bonds. In addition to the various investor preferences for short- or long-dated options it reflects expectations for the future path of volatility. Changes in these expectations can cause the term structure to shift, usually in a parallel fashion right across the curve. These expectations may also be reflected in volatility swaps, which are forward contracts on realized volatility.

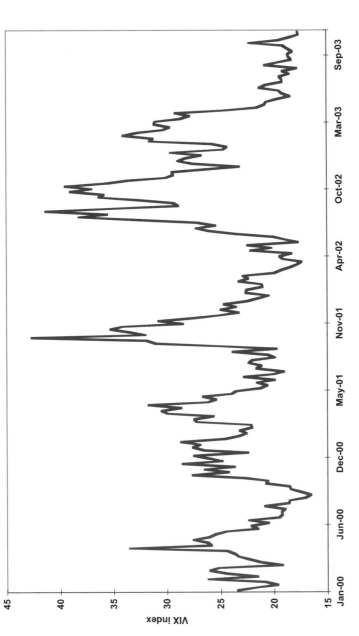

**Figure 13.4** The volatility of volatility

Volatility is itself volatile, as illustrated by the VIX index of implied option volatility (Dec 1999–Oct 2003). Options offer trading and arbitrage opportunities to the specialist investor.

Source: Bloomberg.

options on an intraday basis.[5] They can extract more profit from intraday gamma trading than would be implied by a 'fair valuation' of an option that was based off the volatility of closing prices alone.

- In the run up to August 1998 many prop desks were net short of volatility and they suffered greatly as a result. Since then, market makers and prop desks have been far less active in the area. They have concentrated their activities on earning bid–offer spreads instead of on the arbitrage activities that act to make markets more efficient.
- Most users of stock options buy them for their leveraged directional exposure or to hedge other positions. They tend to be less concerned about the precise pricing of option volatility.
- Many equity investors sell out-of-the-money call options against their long equity positions (covered calls) as a means of enhancing the returns on their portfolios. The popularity of this activity serves to suppress the pricing of stock options, meaning that volatility often becomes undervalued.
- While it is sometimes possible to find undervalued stock options, equity index options tend to be more expensive than mathematical models would suggest. Buying equity index options seems to be marginally more popular than buying stock options. Investors find it convenient to buy index puts to protect their entire portfolios, and speculators prefer to buy index calls when they take a view on the market.
- Theoretically, all puts and calls on the same asset should have similar implied volatilities. In practice they often do not. The demand for calls seems to be greatest at-the-money and the demand for puts seems to be greatest slightly out-of-the-money. This seems consistent with the bullish views being expressed by buyers of calls and the demand for insurance being expressed by the buyers of puts. (See Figure 13.5)
- Since the 1987 crash, the implied volatility of equity index options (both puts and calls) has remained slightly greater below-the-money than above-the-money, reflecting concern about the potential for markets to fall. Therefore the implied volatilities of out-of-the-money puts are slightly greater than those of out-of-the-money calls.[6] In principle there ought to be symmetry between the two.

5. For a discussion of how gamma trading works see Chapter 8 on convertible arbitrage.
6. As noted by Emmanuel Derman of Columbia University in his address to GAIM 2003 entitled 'Trading volatility as an asset class'.

There are various ways that volatility arbitrageurs can profit from these distortions. In doing so they must manage their net exposures to market direction, time decay and implied volatility. However, the thinking of options traders is guided by whether they feel implied volatilities reflect their expectations for the volatility that will actually be realized. Therefore many volatility arbitrageurs tend to be either long or short of volatility as a matter of policy.

## Short volatility

Given that equity index options tend to be expensive, arbitrageurs who specialize in them may chose to be structurally short of volatility, with some boundaries placed around their positions to ensure their losses during volatility events are limited. A simple way to do this would be to sell offsetting puts and calls and to protect them with purchases of puts and calls further out-of-the-money. The net effect would be to collect premium on most occasions, with occasional large losses at moments of crisis. The size of the returns and the potential losses depend upon where the short and long positions are struck.

## Long volatility

Arbitrageurs who specialize in individual stock options may be able to design portfolios that are structurally long of volatility. They can do this by opportunistically buying puts or calls on individual stocks when their implied volatilities seem uncharacteristically low. The arbitrageur can hedge long option positions with offsetting long or short positions in the underlying equities (in delta-adjusted proportions). Some of the cost of time decay can be recouped by gamma trading. Such positions give arbitrageurs positive exposure to event risk without being market directional. These arbitrageurs are likely to increase their exposures when market volatility is particularly low and to reduce exposures once implied volatility has risen. Unlike most arbitrage strategies, this one is likely to suffer small but steady losses during most periods but to enjoy occasional large gains.[7] Its advocates argue that unexpected events seem to occur more frequently than markets anticipate. On the other hand, the approach runs the risk of sharp losses if volatility dies away suddenly, either for market-wide or stock-specific reasons (such as when a company becomes subject to a cash takeover bid).[8]

---

7.  These funds can be compared with specialist equity short sellers. While they provide a hedge, or insurance, they can be expensive to carry in-between their winning periods.
8.  Arbitrageurs can reduce this risk by restricting their activities to options on larger companies that are less likely to be paid for with cash.

## Volatility neutral

Volatility arbitrageurs may pursue a variety of other strategies as well, some of which are more obviously 'volatility neutral'. Profits can be made from inconsistencies in the implied volatilities of different maturities or strikes in the same name, by going long of one option and short of another. Although these trades can be constructed in a manner that ought to minimize losses in almost all scenarios, they may be 'path dependent' (meaning that arbitrageurs are protected against a price moving in either direction but not against certain sequences of events). Another tactic is to trade the differences between the implied volatilities of index options and options on individual stocks represented in the index. This requires some expertise, since index options are different propositions from stock options. Indices represent diversified collections of stocks, some of which have low correlations with one another. It is therefore logical that the observed volatility of the index should be lower than the weighted average observed volatility of its components. For similar reasons the implied volatility of index options also behaves differently. It tends to be 'stickier' than that of stock options.

Investing in volatility arbitrage funds is not for the faint-hearted. They pursue complex strategies and it is difficult for investors to be confident that they fully understand the risks in a portfolio. It is complex for the arbitrageur as well. Relatively small oversights on their part can dramatically increase their risk profile. Funds that are short volatility are likely to suffer unpleasant losses during liquidity crises, so they may not be a very welcome addition to a portfolio of hedge funds. By contrast, investing in funds that are deliberately long volatility may be a good way to offset short volatility exposure elsewhere in a portfolio. However, it is very difficult to remain significantly long of volatility without paying dearly for it. Therefore a fund is only likely to be selectively long of volatility, and it cannot be depended upon to capture every volatility event.

# MUTUAL FUND TIMING

Mutual fund timing, now somewhat notorious, is a strategy that takes advantage of the features of mutual funds. There are two main ways in which mutual fund timers generate profits using mutual funds, but both are related to the same fundamental principle. This is the observation that throughout financial markets some assets are leaders and

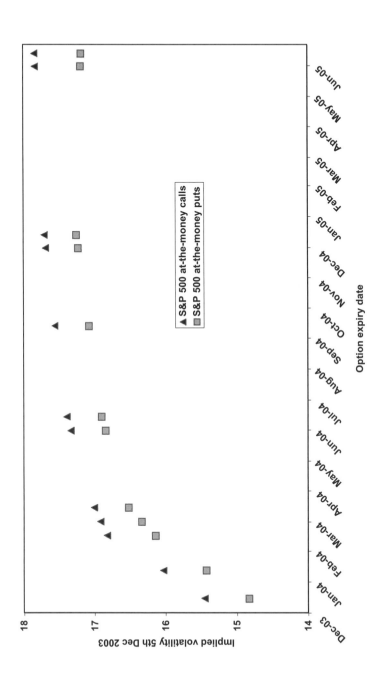

**Figure 13.5** The term structure of volatility

There is a term structure to implied volatility that reflects expectations for future volatility levels. This can be compared with an interest rate yield curve that reflect expectations for future short-term interest rates.

Source: Bloomberg.

some are laggards. Large moves in the leaders usually result in following moves in the laggards after a brief delay. For example, if the US equity market posts a particularly strong gain one afternoon it is likely to result in the Asian and European markets opening strongly the following day. The phenomenon is also detectable in other areas of the markets. Strong moves in largecap stocks tend to be reflected in smallcap stocks over subsequent days. Perhaps this is because busy investment managers attend to their largest and most liquid transactions first, only turning to their smaller holdings subsequently. Precisely why it happens does not matter, only that it does.

## Stale prices

The first means by which mutual fund timers make money is by taking advantage of stale prices. Even though mutual funds deal on the basis of forward pricing they may still have some stale prices in their portfolios. Imagine a US mutual fund that invests in global equities, including US, European and Asian stocks. Assume that it permits dealing at the end of every business day, based on a portfolio valuation struck at 4 pm, the close of the US market. At the valuation point the European markets have already been closed for 5 hours and the Asian markets even longer. However, for want of any better ideas the fund's administrators are likely to use prices for European and Asian equities as at the close of their respective markets a number of hours beforehand. This presents an opportunity to mutual fund timers on those occasions when the US market rallies strongly late in the trading day. The move in the US market will not have been reflected in the prices that the portfolio administrators use for the European and Asian stocks. The timer can place an order to buy the mutual fund at 3.45 pm, before the cut-off for dealing, with the expectation that the European and Asian stocks in the portfolio are likely to rise strongly the subsequent day. Although the method is far from foolproof, it is likely to work most of the time. The fund can be sold a couple of days later, once the overseas markets have properly incorporated the information from the United States.

## Liquidity

Not all mutual fund timers take advantage of stale prices. Some simply use mutual funds as a cost effective and efficient means of deploying capital to 'laggard' asset classes. Investing in smaller companies and certain overseas markets can be fiddly and involve a meaningful bid–offer spread. Mutual funds offer immediate and guaranteed execution, single pricing and zero price impact on the market. They are a trader's dream. Thus strong rallies in largecap stocks prompt managers to buy smaller companies' funds and to hold them for a few days while the followers catch up with the news. Although there is nothing very complicated about the principle, some fairly sophisticated statistical systems are likely to be used in order to establish how leader–laggard relationships work and how best to take advantage of them.

Mutual fund timers rarely hedge their investments in mutual funds, as hedging is not that compatible with their strategy. Instead they hold long-only exposure to the markets for limited periods of time. During most periods their portfolios remain in cash. The monthly returns generated by these occasional investments tend to show a very low correlation to the markets.

## Obstacles

The two main obstacles that mutual fund timers face are front end loads and capacity. They are unable to secure a profit unless they can negotiate sufficiently low front end loads on the funds they wish to purchase. Their expected profits from a trade must exceed this charge. Usually they consider the leader–laggard phenomenon to be sufficiently powerful to justify their paying some sort of a charge. They do not expect to get in for free. They usually aim to secure the blessing of the fund management group, as their activities might be considered to be disruptive to the funds they buy. The fund managers generally consent, but ration the capacity they allocate to mutual fund timers in order to limit their impact on a fund. If the timers fail to reach such an agreement, they may transact via an intermediary or broker that handles sufficiently large flows to be able to disguise the activities of the timers. These intermediaries may be able to net off quite a few of the investments being made by timers against redemptions being made by their other investors. Intermediaries will usually expect to be paid a small fee for cooperating with timers in this way.

## Controversy

Mutual fund timing has become a controversial strategy. At the time of writing the strategy is under investigation by the SEC and Eliot Spitzer, the New York State Attorney General. Their attentions were first attracted by some isolated instances of malpractice in which mutual fund groups permitted investments to be made after the dealing cut-off points for their funds (that is, on the basis of historic fund prices). Although very few mutual fund timers are guilty of such blatant misdemeanours the authorities have decided that their activities are generally abusive to other investors in mutual funds:

- Inflows and outflows cause mutual funds to hold higher levels of cash than they would otherwise choose to. This represents a drag on mutual fund performance.

- The higher level of turnover in the funds' portfolios contributes to increased transaction costs.

- Those funds that exploit stale prices deprive other mutual fund investors of returns by diluting their performance during certain periods.

Because the timers are considered a nuisance to other investors there seems no reason for the fund management groups to allow them in. Yet the fund management houses have a conflict of interest. They pocket a front end load on each occasion a timer buys their fund. For this reason they have sometimes encouraged such activities on a limited scale.

While mutual fund timing might be branded a nuisance, mutual fund timers are rarely overtly corrupt. On the other hand, the prosecuting authorities come out of this affair looking pretty poor. Mutual fund timing has never been a secret. It has been practised fairly openly for a number of years. If the authorities were not previously aware of the practice, they ought to have been. If they were aware of it they ought to have clamped down on it a long time ago, instead of condoning it by turning a blind eye. Now they have chosen to drive the strategy into extinction and to score political points for doing so.

## ASSET BACKED LENDING STRATEGIES

Asset backed lending strategies offer high rates of return for relatively low risk. This is because asset based lenders can charge disproportionately high rates of interest to capital hungry, uncreditworthy borrowers who have been turned away by credit based lenders. If the borrowers can offer good collateral and a loan is structured so that recovering the collateral is relatively easy, a loan becomes relatively secure. The source of the investment opportunity lies in this dichotomy. Asset backed lending strategies are diverse but can be broadly divided up between long-term lending in a securitized form, and short-term loans arranged directly with a hedge fund.

## Long-term, securitized lending

This universe includes a range of debt securities, such as secondary market bank loans, senior secured corporate bonds, commercial mortgages and structured securities tied to an underlying pool of secured assets.[9] The loans may be secured on all manner of assets including commercial real estate, manufacturing equipment, aircraft, aircraft landing slots, shipping vessels, or consumer receivables (such as portfolios of credit card receivables). When a hedge fund invests in these loans its primary analysis relates to these assets. It will still pay attention to the borrower's creditworthiness because, in the event of default, interest may be suspended and it may experience a delay in recovering capital. This can reduce its IRR. Yet if it has done the asset analysis it should achieve a very high recovery rate.

Most managers investing in these types of security choose to enhance returns by leveraging their portfolios. In doing so they may find themselves lending longer term but borrowing shorter term. They need to lock up their borrowing, particularly if the securities into which they invest have limited liquidity. The managers may attempt to moderate their duration risk with light hedges, such as short positions in government bonds. However, the pricing of these asset backed securities is not always as sensitive as US Treasuries, so it is usually inappropriate to hedge duration fully.

This is an interesting market niche, being leveraged junk on the one hand and senior secured cash flow on the other. There are some potential issues. Losses from defaults may not always be recovered, particularly if caused by fraud. Because of leverage, moderate losses in the underlying investment portfolio have a much larger impact on the hedge fund's shareholders. If a spate of problems hit the portfolio at once the results could be unpleasant. For the most part, however, the strategy provides consistent and attractive returns. Economic downturns can even be positive for the strategy. This is because higher quality borrowers are forced to turn to this form of financing, and desperation for capital keeps returns high even though the risk free rate may be falling.

## Short-term, direct lending

Funds that focus on short-term direct lending barely qualify as hedge funds. Because their activities are entirely insensitive to markets, they use no hedging whatsoever. On the other hand, it is this independence

---

9. Collateralized debt obligations (CDOs) or collateralized loan obligations (CLOs).

from the markets that makes them so attractive to hedge fund investors, and they act as a valuable addition to a portfolio of low risk hedge funds.

These funds tend to arrange loans directly with companies, or through specialist agents. Borrowers are typically small firms seeking small loans (US $0.5–7 million), which larger institutions are not willing to negotiate. The loans are generally issued in support of transactions, as a means of freeing up working capital. They usually involve trade claims, receivables financing or factoring, and can involve domestic or international trade. Although they come in a variety of shapes and sizes, common themes run through these transactions:

- They are usually heavily over-collateralized. The fund often has a lien over a shipment of commodities or finished goods that are subject to a haircut. More importantly, the purchase order for the goods is transferred into the fund's possession, meaning that after delivery, payment for the goods is owed to the fund (the lender) and not to the company that sold them (the borrower). The credit risk involved is therefore not that of the borrowing company but that of the purchasing company (usually a much more substantial entity).

- Loans are often cross-collateralized, so that if problems occur the fund has the right to seize other assets, which sometimes include the personal assets of the borrowing firm's owner.

- An additional deposit may be required from the borrower to guard against possible delays that might lower the fund's IRR.

- High rates of return are obtained because 'orphaned' borrowers fall outside the scope or understanding of mainstream lenders, because dealflow is hard to originate, and because the borrowers may be of questionable creditworthiness.

- The nature of collateral and the sources of credit risk tend to be highly diversified.

If a default does occur, delays in recovering capital may impinge on a fund's IRR, even though it is likely to recover 100 per cent. Poorly structured transactions can leave the fund exposed to a loophole, and fraud is also an issue. To prevent fraud, private investigators are often employed to perform background checks.[10] As appropriate,

10. Fraud is also a consideration for the investors into these funds. Because the underlying investments are direct loan agreements there are no securities to be held in custody by a third party, merely copies of documentation. Investors must therefore be very sure of the probity of the individuals concerned. A limited amount of reassurance on this front can be gained from the frequency with which these portfolios turn over and the short duration of the loans.

the fund may also improve its position using shipping insurance, credit insurance, credit analysis of purchasers and goods verification procedures.

Although there are risks with these investments, they are modest and of an entirely unsystematic nature. There is little or no reason why problems should necessarily coincide with difficulties in broader markets or with other hedge fund strategies. Economic deterioration and falling interest rates tend to cause no more than a marginal deterioration in dealflow, creditworthiness or the coupons charged. Sometimes they improve. There is no duration risk because the tenor is rarely more than 3–9 months and the funds employ no leverage. Liquidity issues are also minimal because the loans self-liquidate within short timeframes.[11]

---

11. Relevant information on these sorts of strategies can be found on the Commercial Finance Association's Web site: www.cfa.com.

# 14

# Selecting a fund of hedge funds

My boss carried only one brand of cigar. It sold for three cents. If a customer asked for a ten cent cigar, he was handed one which sold for three cents. 'The customer is always right,' my boss would say, 'so never let him be disappointed.'

W C Fields

## THE BENEFITS OF A FUND OF HEDGE FUNDS

Funds of hedge funds are diversified portfolios of hedge funds. Although they involve an additional layer of fees, these are useful vehicles for those investors who do not have the resources, time or inclination to invest in hedge funds directly. They fulfil a variety of functions:

- **Research:** ongoing research is time-consuming, since the hedge fund world is still 'translucent' as opposed to transparent. Investing in hedge funds is a relationship business, and gathering information is a full-time job for a team of experienced analysts.

- **Asset allocation:** managers of funds of hedge funds specialize in understanding the risks inherent within each strategy. They should be good at combining hedge funds and creating properly diversified portfolios. They should know how economic and market changes affect each strategy, equipping them to make sensible asset allocation shifts.

- **Critical mass:** in light of the ongoing research requirement and the minimum investments demanded by hedge funds, new investors are advised to commit at least US $100 million if they wish to invest into hedge funds directly.[1] For those with less, funds of hedge funds provide critical mass, together with the relationships that meaningful assets command. These longstanding relationships may allow funds of funds to secure access to successful hedge funds that are otherwise closed to new investors.

Managers of funds of hedge funds highlight these advantages when they pitch to their clients. There is an element of truth to all of them. However, the real way that these managers add value is far simpler. They fill the role of 'credit analysts'. The universe of hedge funds is diverse and complex. It is largely unregulated and is predominantly controlled by small, privately owned firms. It would be foolhardy to commit money to these funds without first exercising a degree of caution. Like credit analysts, managers of funds of hedge funds can prevent unqualified investors from making some really obvious mistakes.

# THE DRAWBACKS OF FUNDS OF HEDGE FUNDS

Funds of hedge funds have a mixed reputation. Investors often question whether they truly add any value, particularly when their (sometimes outrageous) fees are taken into consideration. Some people dismiss funds of funds as little more than marketing enterprises – conduits for funnelling smaller investors into hedge funds at an additional cost. Many hedge fund managers are also distrustful of them, finding them to be fickle and unstable investors. They have practical limitations too, as with any portfolio of hedge funds. Funds of hedge funds are likely to invest into a range of underlying hedge funds that contain some offsetting positions, as well as other positions that overlap, doubling up the investor's exposure.

Experienced fund of hedge fund managers do provide a valuable service. However, many newcomers to the industry masquerade as

---

1. In theory, most hedge funds have minimum investments of US $1 million, implying that just US $15 million would be enough to build a diversified portfolio. In practice, investors committing sums this small are unlikely to command the attention of hedge fund managers, and may be considered a nuisance. Sums below US $100 million are therefore incompatible with proper research.

experts. For this reason it is important to lay out the key issues investors should consider before buying a fund of hedge funds. There are six key areas to consider.

# PHILOSOPHY

It can be difficult to distinguish funds of hedge funds from one another. After beauty parades, investors would be forgiven for thinking that all funds of funds do the same things in the same ways. However, there are subtle differences in investment philosophy that investors should focus on.

- **How has the fund of funds been constructed?** Many funds of funds focus on particular types of hedge funds, such as low volatility absolute return funds, equity long–short funds, or directional strategies such as global macro and CTAs. Other funds of funds mix all these strategies together in a single portfolio. Neither approach is necessarily right or wrong. However, different hedge fund strategies behave in such different ways that it is important for investors to understand how a portfolio has been constructed.

- **Does the fund of funds manager rely heavily on the correlation argument?** Combining hedge funds that have low correlations with one another can help reduce a portfolio's volatility. Yet it is foolish to rely too heavily on these correlations, and they should not be used as an excuse to include individually volatile funds within a portfolio. The correlations between hedge funds are unstable, and are liable to rise when market volatility spikes (that is, at the worst possible moment). Instead, a portfolio of hedge funds should be assembled so that the weighted average expected maximum drawdown of its constituents lies within acceptable bounds. This is the drawdown that an investor can expect to suffer in a period of crisis, not the one that has been predicted on the basis of low correlations.

- **Is fund selection primarily quantitative or qualitative?** Some fund of funds managers emphasize quantitative analysis throughout their process. Beware. Quantitative analysis of track records is quick and easy. It is a prerequisite, not an alternative. 'Emphasizing' quantitative analysis is usually an excuse for shirking the hard work, which is qualitative analysis and due diligence.

- **How thorough is the research?** Unfortunately the research conducted by fund of funds managers is sometimes flaky, so it is worth asking to see an example of internal written research. Analysing hedge funds involves large amounts of information, and unless this is properly recorded and well ordered it is liable to be forgotten. With larger teams of analysts, written research becomes all the more important.

- **How fickle are the fund of funds managers?** Funds of funds that develop a reputation for being disloyal investors will soon find themselves being barred from the better hedge funds. This restricts their opportunity set.

# PEOPLE

People are a key ingredient with all actively managed investment products. Funds of hedge funds are no exception.

- **Who are the managers?** An enormous number of 'me too' characters have entered the fund of hedge funds industry. Although some have impressive credentials in other fields they do not always have a good knowledge of the hedge fund world or the requisite network of relationships.

- **How much experience do the fund of funds managers have?** As in any profession, experience is a valuable quality in the funds of funds world. Because so many hedge fund strategies are effectively 'short volatility' the ultimate success or failure of many hedge funds is determined by their ability to withstand occasional liquidity crises and not by their performance in the interim. Fund of funds managers with experience have a better feel for how occasional liquidity crises affect different hedge funds. This is because experienced fund of funds managers have witnessed more mistakes being made by hedge fund managers and have made more mistakes of their own. There is no short cut to this learning process.

- **What are their qualities?** Good fund of hedge funds managers know what research they should conduct and how to interpret information. They have the experience to ask hedge fund managers the right questions and how to assess the answers. They also have the ability to act decisively when required, as there are times when opportunities must be seized upon quickly.

- **How many are there?** The number of investment professionals required to manage funds of hedge funds depends upon their experience and the size of the asset base they are investing. Smaller

388    *How to invest in hedge funds*

sums can be managed very competently by relatively few individuals, as long as they are experienced. Additional analysts improve the research capability, but too many create a bureaucracy. Unfortunately, managing large sums results in capacity constraints with the underlying hedge fund managers. This necessitates an increase in the number of hedge funds that a fund of funds group invests in, which in turn necessitates a larger team to research into them.

- **Where are they?** In theory it should not matter where fund of funds managers are located as long as they are prepared to travel to see hedge fund managers. In practice there are great advantages to being located in New York, London, Geneva or Zurich. This is because most hedge fund managers pass through these investment centres as a matter of course, meeting existing and potential investors. Prime brokerage, third party marketing and funds of funds activities are centred on these locations. Funds of funds located elsewhere risk being left out of the information flow.

- **What are their motives?** Different fund of hedge funds managers are motivated by different things. Many apply greater effort to raising assets than to taking investment decisions.[2] Some attract large institutional clients by means of a meticulous investment process that throws up unnecessary barriers to investing. Others impose performance fees on their funds and then chase high returns by including risky hedge funds in their portfolios. A few are genuinely motivated by performance. They take delight in delivering high-risk-adjusted returns to their clients, maintaining a low correlation with other asset classes.

## SALES PITCH

You can tell a good deal about funds of funds from their sales pitch.

- **Do they show a pro forma record?** The real weasels of the funds of funds industry promote new funds of funds using pro forma track records. They show potential clients a back test that illustrates how a portfolio of their preferred managers would have performed had it been assembled a number of years ago. Inevitably these phantom performance figures are impressive. So they should be. By the same token I could assemble a portfolio of stocks that I

---

2. The team marketing a funds of funds is sometimes just as large as the team investing it. It is worth asking how large each team is, as this indicates where priorities lie.

observe have performed particularly well, run a back test on them and tout my pro forma track record as a talented stock-picker. If only life were that easy. This insidious practice is so common that investors must always question whether a fund of funds track record is real or imaginary.

- **Do they claim to use mean–variance optimization to construct their portfolios?** Although the practice is declining, many fund of hedge funds managers claim to employ mean–variance optimization to determine their portfolio weightings. While this appears sophisticated it is usually just a marketing gimmick. Sometimes optimizers are used with all sincerity, which is strange considering the theoretical and practical reasons that they should not be used for hedge funds. If a sales pitch claims a fund of funds uses mean–variance optimization to construct portfolios it signifies either a cynical attempt to bamboozle, or the ineptitude of the managers.

- **What sort of company manages the fund of funds?** Many large asset management firms now manage funds of hedge funds. Do not be beguiled by their size and their expertise in mainstream asset management. Until comparatively recently the fund of hedge funds world was dominated by boutiques, and these are still the 'blue chip' providers of this service. Large institutions that have entered the space late in the game have often done so because of the margins on offer, and they may lack the requisite knowledge.

## THE FUND AND ITS STABILITY

The size and contents of funds of funds are considerations, as is the nature of other investors in them.

- **How big is the fund of funds operation?** Fund of funds operations require a certain critical mass in order to operate successfully. Operations that are too small will not obtain proper access to hedge fund managers. Operations that are too large will face difficulty in getting their assets to work with the managers of their choice. Ways can be found to deal with size problems at either end of the scale, but assets under management between US $100 million and US $2 billion seem to allow for flexibility.[3]

- **What is the longevity of the fund of funds?** Older fund of funds portfolios enjoy certain advantages. They are more likely to

---

3.   This figure relates to conditions in late 2003.

contain a number of successful managers that are closed to new investors. They may also be more stable, as the fund of funds managers are likely to have settled upon those hedge funds that best meet the portfolios' objectives.

- **Who are the other investors in the fund of funds?** A number of funds of funds suffer from an unstable investor base. This can be very disruptive given that the portfolios' investments are relatively illiquid. Heavy redemptions from a fund of funds also damage the credibility of fund of funds managers. They are forced to pass these redemptions on to the underlying hedge fund managers, permanently damaging their relationship with them. These relationships are important in the hedge fund world because the best hedge funds often choose their investors, rather than the other way around.

# PRODUCT STRUCTURE

Potential investors should pay close attention to the structure of a fund of funds, since many contain aspects that are unacceptable.

- **What fees does the fund of funds charge?** Many participants in the fund of funds market earn fat fees for doing relatively little. The management fees charged by funds of funds vary considerably, and they can have a meaningful impact on an investor's end returns. Many funds of funds also charge a performance fee. Although these performance fees may provide additional motivation for the managers, many people consider them an unnecessary additional layer of charges. Few funds of hedge funds add sufficient value to justify them. A survey by Deutsche Bank of 50 funds of funds in 2000 found that all but 17 charged their own performance fee.[4] After reviewing the names of those 17 I suspect that some of them were supplementing their income by other means, such as kick-backs.

- **Do the fund of funds managers get kick-backs from the underlying hedge funds?** Some funds of funds attempt to secure fee reductions from the hedge funds that they invest in. Usually these fee rebates are credited to the fund of funds for the benefit of the investors. While these attempts are admirable in principle they may not be helpful in practice. Proven hedge fund managers rarely make such concessions, and if they do the recipients become less

---

4.  Coke and Fothergill (2000).

favoured investors. Hedge fund managers are more likely to provide additional investment capacity to those investors who pay full fees, and they may also be more cooperative in providing information. A minority of fund of hedge funds managers attempt to secure fee rebates for the benefit of their own firm rather than their investors. This is a dubious practice that is liable to distort a fund of funds manager's investment decisions.

- **How often can investors withdraw their capital?** Funds of funds that provide frequent redemption opportunities may appear more attractive. However, the underlying hedge funds rarely offer much flexibility. Funds of funds offering flexible redemption terms run the risks of a liquidity mismatch or of having their choice of hedge funds restricted to those that allow for easier dealing.

- **Is the fund a closed-end vehicle?** Some funds of hedge funds have been launched as closed-end companies in order to improve their tax treatment. This is a sensible structure for private arrangements between genuinely long-term investors. Unfortunately the investor base often consists of a handful of very large investors combined with numerous retail investors, some of whom require an active secondary market. Owing to the small size of these funds and their imbalanced shareholder registers the shares tend to be illiquid and to trade at a discount. The illiquidity and the discount inject additional volatility into the funds' shares. This defeats one of the main objects of the exercise, namely to generate low volatility returns.

## TRACK RECORD

All investors are likely to take an interest in a fund of fund's record. There are a couple of issues to bear in mind.

- **How long is the record?** The fund of funds managers should have a track record going back over a number of years. See how they performed during difficult periods, and ask what they have learnt from their experiences. Once again, be sure to identify whether or not a record relates to a live portfolio, and disregard any pro forma numbers.

- **How were the returns generated?** The fund of funds with the highest returns and the lowest volatility is not *necessarily* the best, especially if its record is fairly short. High returns and low volatility can be achieved by combining a series of higher risk hedge funds that have a low correlation with one another. In the short term this is likely to produce impressive results, but such a portfolio may be vulnerable to larger losses during moments of crisis, when the correlations between its components are likely to rise.

# CONCLUSION

The main issue facing the funds of hedge funds industry today is that the barriers to entry are so low. It does not take genius or a great deal of knowledge to appear to do a half-competent job in this area. This is a disadvantage for the more established players and an advantage for new entrants. However, the upshot is some fairly fierce competition, which up to this point has taken the form of 'showpiece' teams of hedge fund analysts that have been getting progressively larger, digging progressively deeper on the qualitative and due diligence side. This is to the disadvantage of new entrants, whose resources are smaller. It is not necessarily to the advantage of clients either. Beyond a certain point the additional returns derived from additional research are low, yet the costs increase in a unitary fashion. More recently, competition has started to spread to fees.[5] Some funds of funds providers are now offering their services on large mandates for very low fees. Although competitive pricing has yet to take hold of this market, there is the possibility of downward pressure on fees over the next few years. This is particularly likely if hedge fund returns continue to be muted.

---

5.  Funds of funds find it harder to compete on the basis of performance than the hedge funds themselves, because their performance is derived from an average of a pool of hedge funds. Different funds of funds often end up with broadly similar results. It is therefore natural that they should compete on other fronts.

# 15

# Concluding remarks

You didn't understand this at first, but my CONVINCING USE OF
CAPITAL LETTERS HAS MADE IT ALL CLEAR TO YOU.

J Nairn

Over the last few years the growth in the number of new hedge funds
has been exponential. It seems that everyone now wants to be a hedge
fund manager. We have reached a point where new managers are
struggling to concoct original names for their funds. Growth of this
kind cannot continue indefinitely. Hedge funds flourish as marginal
players in financial markets, and their activities are geared to quite
narrow specializations. This space cannot accommodate too many
assets or too many individuals. In time we will reach saturation point,
which will be marked by either a crisis or declining returns and disillusionment. When such difficulties materialize, only the strongest and
fittest hedge funds will survive.

Unlike most funds, hedge funds do not provide investors with
straightforward exposure to an asset class. Instead they provide
exposure to a range of other sources of risk and return, the most
important of which are the decision making abilities of talented individuals. This is an attractive alternative source of returns as long as the
individuals take good decisions. As increasing numbers of investment
professionals reinvent themselves as hedge fund managers, the average
hedge fund manager is likely to prove less and less successful. This is
why careful hedge fund selection will become increasingly difficult,
and important, over time. I hope that this book has helped in a small way
to further your understanding of how to invest in hedge funds.

# References

Amin, G and Kat, H (2002) *Stocks, Bonds and Hedge Funds: Not a free lunch!* Cass Business School, City University, London and University of Reading, ISMA Centre

Argarwal, V and Naik, N (2001) *Characterising Hedge Fund Risks with Buy-and-Hold Option-Based Strategies*, London Business School

Attari, M, Mello, A and Ruckes, M (2002) *Arbitraging Arbitrageurs*, University of Wisconsin – Madison School of Business and Department of Finance

Baquero, G, ter Horst, J and Verbeek, M (2003) *Survival, Look-Ahead Bias and the Persistence in Hedge Fund Performance*, Erasmus University Rotterdam Department of Financial Management and Tilburg University

Biggs, B (2002) The quest for Alpha, and endangering the Golden Goose, *Morgan Stanley US Investment Perspectives*, 6 Feb

Brooks, C and Kat, H (2001) *The Statistical Properties of Hedge Fund Index Returns and their Implications for Investors*, Cass Business School, City University, London and University of Reading, ISMA Centre

Burns, P (2003) Does my beta look big in this? *Burns Statistics*, 15 Jul

Capital Markets Company (2003) *Understanding and Mitigating Operational Risk in Hedge Fund Investments*, Capital Markets Company, New York

Coke, C and Fothergill, M (2000) Funds of hedge funds: an introduction to multi-manager funds, *Deutsche Bank European Research*, Aug

Credit Suisse First Boston (CSFB) (2003) *CSFB Leveraged Finance Outlook 2003*, CSFB, New York

Derman, E (2003) Trading volatility as an asset class, address to ICBI, GAIM 2003, 9–13 June 2003, Geneva

Economist (2003) Funds of hedge funds, an expensive touch of glamour, *Economist*, 20–26 Sep

Fung, W and Hsieh, D (2001) Asset-based style factors for hedge funds, *Financial Analysts Journal*, **58** (5), pp 16–27

Fung, W and Hsieh, D (2002) *Asset-Based Hedge Fund Styles and Portfolio Diversification*, PI Asset Management, LLC – General and Duke University, Fuqua School of Business, Durham, NC

Getmansy, M, Lo, A and Makarov, I (2003) *An Econometric Model of Serial Correlation and Illiquidity in Hedge Fund Returns*, Massachusetts Institute of Technology (MIT) Sloan School of Management, Cambridge, MA

Horwitz, R and Rodriguez, L (2002) *Merger Arbitrage Funds: Do they deliver what they promise?* Capital Market Risk Advisors, New York

Howell, M (2000) Tactical style selection, *AIMA Newsletter*, Sep

Hughes-Wilson, J (1999) *Military Intelligence Blunders*, Robinson, London

Kat, H (2002) *Taking the Sting out of Hedge Funds*, Cass Business School, City University, London

L'Habitant, F (2001) *Assessing Market Risk for Hedge Funds and Hedge Fund Portfolios*, Union Bancaire Privée, Geneva

Luek, M, Smith, A and Todd, A (2000) The return of managed futures, *AIMA Newsletter*, Dec

Mitchell, M and Pulvino, T (2001) *The Characteristics of Risk and Return in Risk Arbitrage*, CNH Partners and Northwestern University, Kellogg School of Management, Evanston, IL

Moore, K (1999) *Risk Arbitrage: An investor's guide*, Wiley, New York

Roy, A and Smith, J (2003) Managed funds: the perfect asset allocation package? *Investment Strategies*, May, p 12

Ruddick, S (2002) Can hedge funds time equity markets? *Hedge Funds International*, Apr, p 20

Salomon Smith Barney (SSB) (1999) *Guide to Mortgage Backed Securities*, SSB, New York

Schneeweis, T, Kazemi, H and Martin, G (2001) *Understanding Hedge Fund Performance: Research results and rules of thumb for the institutional investor*, Lehman Brothers, New York

Schneeweis, T, Spurgin, R and McCarthy, D (1996) *Informational Content in Historical CTA Performance*, Center for International Securities and Derivatives Markets, University of Massachusetts, Amherst, MA

Schneeweis, T, Spurgin, R and Potter, M (1996) *Managed Futures and Hedge Fund Investment for Downside Equity Risk Management*, Center for International Securities and Derivatives Markets, University of Massachusetts, Amherst, MA

Taylor, P (2003) How big is the risk of a 'blow up'? *Absolute Return*, Oct, pp 27–29

Weisman, A and Abernathy, J (no date) *The Dangers of Historical Hedge Fund Data*, Nikko Securities International (New York) and Stonebrook Structured Products LLC

Wong, A (1993) *Fixed-Income Arbitrage*, Wiley, New York

# FURTHER READING

Acito, C and Fisher, P (2001) *Fund of Hedge Funds: Rethinking resource requirements*, Barra Strategic Consulting Group, Sep, Berkeley, California

Alternative Investment Management Association (2002) *Guide to Sound Practices for European Hedge Fund Managers*, Alternative Investment Management Association, London, Aug

Altman, E and Fanjul, G (2003) *Default and Returns in the High Yield Bond Market: Third quarter 2003 and year to date analysis*, Salomon Center Stern School of Business, New York University, New York

Branch, B and Ray, H (1999) *Bankruptcy Investing*, Beard Books, New York

Brown, S, Goetzmann, W and Liang, B (2002) Fees on fees in funds of funds, Yale ICF Working Paper no 02–33, 21 Nov

Chandler, B (1994) *Managed Futures: An investor's guide*, Wiley, Chichester

CSFB (2002) *Hedging Convertible Bond Credit Risk: Asset swaps or CDS?* CSFB International Convertible Research, CSFB (Europe) Ltd, 8 Apr

Granville, C (2000) Prime brokers find themselves facing a new threat: the courts, *Global Custodian*, Spring, pp 154–55

Kender, M and Petrucci, G (2002) *Altman Report on Defaults and Returns on High Yield Bonds*, Salomon Smith Barney, United States Corporate Bond Research, 12 Aug, New York

Prince, B (2003) Independent research on hedge fund problems, ARC Conference papers, San Francisco, Nov

Reverre, S (2001) *The Complete Arbitrage Deskbook*, McGraw-Hill, New York

Woodson, H (2002) *Global Convertible Investing, The Gabelli Way*, Wiley, New York

# Index